The Origins of the Dual City

The Origins of the Dual City

Housing, Race, and Redevelopment in Twentieth-Century Chicago

JOEL RAST

THE UNIVERSITY OF CHICAGO PRESS   CHICAGO AND LONDON

The University of Chicago Press, Chicago 60637
The University of Chicago Press, Ltd., London
© 2019 by The University of Chicago
All rights reserved. No part of this book may be used or reproduced in any manner
whatsoever without written permission, except in the case of brief quotations in critical articles and reviews. For more information, contact the University of Chicago Press,
1427 E. 60th St., Chicago, IL 60637.
Published 2019
Printed in the United States of America

28 27 26 25 24 23 22 21 20 19   1 2 3 4 5

ISBN-13: 978-0-226-66144-5 (cloth)
ISBN-13: 978-0-226-66158-2 (paper)
ISBN-13: 978-0-226-66161-2 (e-book)
DOI: https://doi.org/10.7208/chicago/9780226661612.001.0001

Library of Congress Cataloging-in-Publication Data
Names: Rast, Joel, 1956— author.
Title: The origins of the dual city : housing, race, and redevelopment in twentieth-century
    Chicago / Joel Rast.
Description: Chicago ; London : The University of Chicago Press, 2019. |
    Includes bibliographical references and index.
Identifiers: LCCN 2019017192 | ISBN 9780226661445 (cloth : alk. paper) |
    ISBN 9780226661582 (pbk. : alk. paper) | ISBN 9780226661612 (e-book)
Subjects: LCSH: Housing policy—Illinois—Chicago. | Urban policy—Illinois—Chicago. |
    Chicago (Ill.)—Social policy. | Urban renewal—Illinois—Chicago—History—
    20th century. | Slums—Illinois—Chicago—History—20th century. | Blacks—
    Segregation—Illinois—Chicago. | Discrimination in housing—Illinois—Chicago. |
    Chicago (Ill.)—Politics and government—20th century.
Classification: LCC HD7304.C4 R37 2019 | DDC 307.1/4160977311—dc23
LC record available at https://lccn.loc.gov/2019017192

FOR CLIONA, NINA, AND YAN

Contents

Preface

L ike many historical studies that take a long time to complete, this book started out as something different from what it ultimately became. My original interest was to explore in some depth the antecedent conditions that gave rise to Chicago's much studied business-government alliance of the postwar era. While much is known about the efforts and activities of this alliance, less understood is the process through which the transition from the city's earlier governing arrangements to those of the postwar period was negotiated. After immersing myself for some time in various archival collections, I became increasingly consumed with one aspect of the new postwar power structure—the city's evolving approach to problems of slums and blight. With this new focus of attention, I found myself reaching further and further back in time to try to better understand why the city's postwar policy approach took the form it did.

As I began to piece together the threads of a narrative, two things in particular stood out. The first was the sweeping change in the goals of the city's anti-slum initiatives that took place over the course of the twentieth century. For decades, civic and political leaders took the view that slums were incompatible with the good city as they understood it. The aim was to eradicate slum conditions wherever they existed—an objective viewed as both possible and necessary for the city's survival. By the latter part of the century, however, this goal had been largely superseded by a radically different orientation that focused not on eliminating slums but on managing such areas and mitigating their most harmful effects while promoting development and gentrification of neighborhoods close to downtown and along the lakefront—what I (and others) call the dual city. A key question this book addresses is how and why this change in policy direction occurred.

The second insight was a theoretical one. Various groups, including those who saw the fate of blighted areas as tied to their own economic interests, mobilized around efforts to address slum conditions in twentieth-century Chicago. Yet as I worked through the archival materials—meeting minutes, correspondence, memos, reports, and the like—I became less and less convinced that conventional rationalist accounts that view behavior as a reflection of material self-interest were sufficient to explain the actions I was documenting. To be sure, actions and interests were closely intertwined, but a focus on interests and historical conditions alone would, it seemed to me, leave the specific form that behavior took significantly underdetermined in many instances. What became increasingly apparent was that motivations and behavior were shaped in key respects not simply by material interest but by the ideas actors held about how to best engage with slum and blighted areas. To understand why actors behaved as they did, I needed to understand what they were thinking and where those ideas came from. Over time, I came to see ideas as representing a big part of the causal story.

I am well aware that my efforts to assign ideas the causal importance I do will be met with a healthy dose of skepticism by many of my more materialist-oriented fellow social scientists. That is as it should be. Departures from conventional thinking should always be carefully probed and scrutinized, lest we become too easily distracted. Still, I am by no means alone in arguing that social scientists have too long neglected the role of ideas in political development. While still a somewhat small group, a growing number of scholars have argued that materialist perspectives must be accompanied by a theory of ideas in order to develop more complete explanations of political behavior. Significant steps in this direction have been taken by such scholars as Peter A. Hall, Mark Blyth, Colin Hay, Robert Lieberman, Alan Jacobs, Daniel Béland, Sheri Berman, Craig Parsons, and Vivien Schmidt. My hope is that with this book I have made a modest contribution to these efforts.

In researching and writing this book over a period of some years, I have accumulated many debts, and I would like to acknowledge and extend my appreciation to a number of people who helped me along the way. Various colleagues and friends read all or portions of the manuscript or otherwise helped inform this project. My thanks to Larry Bennett, Tim

Weaver, Clarence Stone, Richard Dilworth, Pierre Clavel, Heywood Sanders, Brad Hunt, Ivan Ascher, Werner Troesken, and Laura Evans. I am also deeply indebted to two anonymous reviewers for the University of Chicago Press, whose careful reading of the manuscript and insightful comments were invaluable to me as I brought the project to a conclusion. At UW-Milwaukee my friend, colleague, and partner-in-crime Marc Levine has been a steady source of inspiration for many years. Our frequent conversations about Milwaukee's dual city profoundly shaped my thinking about Chicago.

As I researched this project, a number of archivists and librarians were extremely helpful and generous with their time. I'm particularly grateful to Kevin O'Brien and Susan Glover at the University of Illinois at Chicago Library of the Health Sciences Special Collections and University Archives Department, and to Eileen Ielmini and Julia Gardner at the University of Chicago Special Collections Research Center. My thanks also to Michael Benami Doyle and Kelly O'Brien from the Chicago Central Area Committee, who very generously made the organization's archives available to me and provided me with office space to work through the collection—and to Lou Masotti for making the introduction.

I was fortunate to have the assistance of several exceptionally bright and hardworking graduate students from the Urban Studies Program at UW-Milwaukee at various points during this project. Katherine Kocisky, who developed the maps for the book along with Emily Pettit from the University of Wisconsin Cartography Lab, deserves special recognition. Peter Lund, Neal Johnson, and Rebecca Nole Wolfe spent many hours pulling together articles from the major Chicago newspapers dating back to the early twentieth century. In addition to graduate assistance, I received two Research Growth Initiative grants from UW-Milwaukee that gave me extra time to write and helped pay for my travel to and from Chicago and other destinations, for which I am very grateful.

At the University of Chicago Press, I would like to thank my editor Tim Mennel for his interest in this project and for his help, along with Rachel Unger, in shepherding me through the various stages of the publication process. Thanks also to the design and marketing teams, and to Ruth Goring for her meticulous copyediting of the manuscript.

Portions of chapters 4 and 5 have been published elsewhere. Chapter 4 is a reworked version of my article "Creating a Unified Business Elite: The Origins of the Chicago Central Area Committee," *Journal of Urban History* 37 (2011): 583–605. Portions of chapter 5 appear in

"Regime Building, Institution Building: Urban Renewal Policy in Chicago, 1946–1962," *Journal of Urban Affairs* 31 (2009): 173–94. I thank the editors of both these journals for allowing me to use this material.

Two chapters of this book were written in a small cottage in the Village of Dalkey in South County Dublin, just down the road from the town where my wife was born and raised. Some of the key theoretical ideas I develop in the book were worked out during long walks up Dalkey Hill, where my reward at the top was a spectacular view of the Irish Sea and the rolling hills of County Dublin. I would like to thank my Irish in-laws—Jaime and Daniella, Gene and Ger, Cynthia and Paul, John and Fiona, Ciara and John Mark, and their many wonderful children—for their friendship and hospitality during our six-month sabbatical. The cups of tea and conversation around the kitchen table, the walks in the countryside, the evenings in the pub, and the terrific storytelling are all moments I will treasure forever. For that trip, I'm especially grateful to my brother-in-law Hilary and his wife Joan in Chicago and to our friends Cathy and Eric in Milwaukee, who made it all possible by taking in our aging golden retriever while we were away.

As this book goes to press, my wife Cliona and I will celebrate thirty years of marriage. I could not ask for a better or more supportive life partner. She helped me through this project in endless ways, never once protesting as I returned home late yet again from another trip to the archives in Chicago. As this book was written we watched our older daughter Nina make the transition from a fun-loving and occasionally mischievous kid to a bright and engaging young woman, while her much younger sister Yan—equally clever and captivating—helped keep a pair of serious geezer parents from getting old too fast. I am so fortunate to have the three of them in my life, and I thank them for reminding me every day what really matters.

CHAPTER ONE

How Policy Paradigms Change

Not ideas, but material and ideal interests, directly govern men's conduct. Yet very frequently the "world images" that have been created by "ideas" have, like switchmen, determined the tracks along which action has been pushed by the dynamic of interest.—Max Weber[1]

It was getting on toward 2:00 p.m. and I was hungry. I got up from my desk at the nonprofit organization where I worked in the Wicker Park neighborhood of Chicago and walked outside, running through the options for a quick sandwich. It was early May and the weather was glorious, the sky a deep aqua blue and the temperature in the mid-seventies. As I stepped out the door, I felt the warmth of the sun on my face. Everybody seemed to be outside, as if determined to soak up the few short weeks of pleasant temperatures before spring gave way to the heat and humidity of Chicago summer. The sidewalk was teeming with passersby, and North Avenue was jammed with idling vehicles waiting for the red light ahead to change.

As I began to walk down the street I noticed something peculiar. The driver of an SUV sitting in traffic directly in front of me suddenly got out of his vehicle. Seconds later, one of his passengers also got out. Both were men in their early twenties, tough-looking guys with serious faces. One of them was holding a baseball bat. What happened next seemed to unfold in slow motion. The two men said nothing; they simply turned and walked straight to the car behind them. Suddenly the one with the baseball bat raised his arms and began smashing out the car's front windshield. The sound of glass shattering and hitting the street was jarring. In that car were four other young men. They began shouting threats and obscenities, but the guy with the bat moved wordlessly from one window to the next, methodically smashing all of them. When he was done, he and his companion returned to their SUV, got in, and drove off, the traffic light having changed to green by this point. The whole incident lasted perhaps thirty seconds.

As the scene played out in front of me, I was so shocked that all I could do was to stand there like a fool and watch. Only afterward did it dawn on me what a mistake that had been. Most likely this had been a gang altercation of some kind, one that could have turned into something far more consequential than the breaking of a few windows. Shots might have been fired. I could have become one of those stories Chicagoans see on the news too often—the passerby in the wrong place at the wrong time, hit by a stray bullet. As soon as I recognized what was happening I should have bolted. Instead I stood there transfixed, a sitting duck for someone's poorly aimed gunshot had the situation escalated to that point.

Of course altercations such as this one occur on a regular basis in Chicago and other major cities, often with tragic consequences. As everyone knows, violence is a part of big-city life. But violent encounters are not randomly distributed throughout the city. Geographic data on violent crime show that such activity is far more likely to occur in some neighborhoods than others, and that in certain neighborhoods the chances of being the victim of a violent crime are actually quite small. For example, Chicago had a total of 561 homicides during 2018, yet two-thirds of them were committed in just fifteen of Chicago's seventy-seven community areas. The largest number of murders, fifty, took place in the West Side neighborhood of Austin, while fourteen community areas experienced no homicides and another fourteen had only one. Data on other violent crime reveal similar patterns. City residents may not have the statistics at their fingertips, but most have a decent idea of which areas pose the fewest safety risks. As a result, many Chicagoans, residents of a city teeming with violent crime, can go about their business on a daily basis confident that the violence taking place in certain areas of the city—of which, thanks to relentless media coverage, they are well aware—is unlikely to personally affect them.[2]

Which brings me to my point. The incident I observed that afternoon in Wicker Park was jarring in part because it was not "supposed" to happen there. Located just northwest of downtown, Wicker Park has transitioned during the past several decades from a low- and moderate-income, mostly Latino community to a far whiter, far more affluent neighborhood bearing all the markings of a gentrified community in its maturity. As the demographics shifted in favor of middle- and upper-income whites, the gangs moved out and street crime decreased. To be sure, trouble was not far away; immediately west of Wicker Park is Humboldt Park, a neighborhood where gentrification—at least at that time—had made few inroads. Residents of Wicker Park were routinely reminded of this fact by the periodic sounds of gunfire coming from the west. But that was *over there*, and this was *over here*, and most of us who lived or worked in Wicker Park believed that Western Avenue, the street that divides the two neighborhoods, would somehow keep trouble out, as if it were a wall or a barbed-wire fence instead of a simple thoroughfare.

While my experience that afternoon momentarily disrupted this perception of safety and security, any anxiety I felt quickly dissipated. It was, after all, only one incident—the exception that proved the rule. Wicker Park, I understood deep down, was basically a safe community. Nothing bad had happened to me, and better still, I now had an entertaining story to tell. The *real* violence—the kind that sent people routinely to hospitals and morgues and made residents fearful to walk the streets after dark, or even during broad daylight—was still *over there*, across Western Avenue and beyond. Wicker Park was not Kansas, but neither was it Lawndale, or Austin, or one of any number of other Chicago neighborhoods where people had good reason to fear for their safety. If anything, what I saw that afternoon reinforced that understanding and the belief that any risks I was taking by living and working in this diverse urban community were minor ones.

Big cities like Chicago, as countless observers have pointed out, are in a sense two cities—one consisting of downtown and privileged, gentrified neighborhoods like Wicker Park, the other being the distressed and visibly decayed communities where low-income, predominantly minority residents live. There are, of course, areas that fall somewhere in between, but those areas are losing ground.[3] The trend, which is both pronounced and unmistakable, is toward increasingly stark divides between two distinct kinds of places with radically different prospects. That these two "cities" can exist alongside one another remains one of the major conundrums of urban America. The arrangement works because to a great extent, residents of these places occupy separate worlds. The account executive living in a Lincoln Park condominium knows about the stray bullets that have caused the senseless deaths of innocent children playing in parks, walking home from school, or even sitting in their living rooms on the city's South and West Sides. Yet she does not worry when she takes her own children to the park, or when she walks them to school, or when she sees them pass by the front window. Secure in the knowledge that such random violence is a fixture of certain neighborhoods and not others, she goes about her daily routine confident that the dangers lurking elsewhere in the city will not harm her or her family.

Somewhere along the line, political leaders in Chicago and other major cities discovered that chronic poverty, slums, and blight are not necessarily harbingers of a city in decline. After decades of white flight to the suburbs, Chicago's population, like that of many cities, has begun to stabilize, and certain areas—especially near-downtown neighborhoods such as the South Loop and the Near South Side—have undergone explosive population growth. Many of the new residents are former suburban dwellers whose parents and grandparents fled the city during the postwar years, frightened away by racial change and other perceived threats. Now cities have become desirable, even trendy locations—for members of the so-called creative class, new college graduates, retirees, and others who find the buzz of urban life a welcome change from the tedium of the suburbs.

Importantly, this demographic shift has been taking place even as poverty and joblessness in certain Chicago neighborhoods have reached epic proportions. The message for the city's political leaders is clear: urban decline in one city location is not incompatible with growth and affluence elsewhere. Increasingly city officials have come to terms with poverty and blight, treating it as a chronic condition of urban life that is best managed rather than attacked head on. This does not mean that Chicago and other cities have given up on their most economically distressed neighborhoods. There are programs in place to improve conditions in such areas, and in some cases they have had a tangible impact. But experience shows that poverty is stubborn; the high-poverty neighborhoods of fifty years ago remain, for the most part, high-poverty neighborhoods today, and few officials seem to believe their programs are likely to change that.[4] More than ever, Chicago is a dual city, where the rich and the poor traverse the city and move through their daily lives in spatial patterns that intersect, for the most part, in only the most superficial ways. The arrangement is not perfect—far from it. But on some level it works, and city officials seem resigned to it.

It was not always this way. For much of the twentieth century, slums (the common term for such areas until recent decades) were viewed as an urgent problem that demanded attention and resources, a problem that threatened the city's very survival. As early as 1911, business and civic leaders, fearful that Chicago's blighted areas would make the vision for the city laid out in Daniel Burnham's famous 1909 Plan of Chicago unrealizable, teamed with Progressive Era housing reformers to strengthen housing and building regulations in an all-out effort to eliminate slums.[5] The anti-slum crusade continued for decades, producing a series of policy initiatives and experiments that fell short of their goals but demonstrated the seriousness with which policymakers and civic leaders viewed the problem. By midcentury, slums had become a near obsession among the city's movers and shakers. Blight was often likened to a cancerous growth that would "infect more and more areas" unless it was completely removed.[6] This meant that the attack on the slums required a citywide strategy. Just as no cancerous tumor can be safely ignored, no blighted neighborhood could be neglected indefinitely, since inaction would allow the disease to spread to healthy areas of the city.

In addition to the threat they posed to healthy neighborhoods, slums were seen as a weighty financial burden, using far more in city services than they generated in tax revenues and forcing more prosperous areas to make up the difference. This condition, which sparked far more outrage during the 1940s and 1950s than it generally does today, also led to the conclusion that slums anywhere in the city could not long be tolerated.[7] It was no good to simply rearrange slum districts—to clean up one slum and have another one crop up somewhere else. Such places had to be eliminated altogether. The designers of anti-slum initiatives were passionate about abolishing slums, and any such program that fell short of this goal would have been judged a failure by their standards.

Of course, as we now know, the strategies pursued by the leaders of Chicago's anti-slum campaigns of the early and mid-twentieth century were flawed on multiple accounts. Eventually urban planners would come to realize that eliminating slums and blight was not a simple matter of providing new and better housing. Slums were a social as well as a physical condition, meaning that programs to combat poverty and racism were necessary as well. Moreover, history would not judge kindly the slash-and-burn tactics endorsed by Chicago's urban renewal pioneers of the 1950s and 1960s. As activist and social critic Jane Jacobs would argue convincingly, such practices undermined the vitality of city neighborhoods, replacing bustling, diverse city streets with dead zones and menacing "towers in the park."[8] And even if the outcome had been more favorable, few planners today would excuse the aggressive use of eminent-domain powers to clear entire neighborhoods, including homes in good repair, so that redevelopment could begin with a clean slate.

These sins were not minor ones, and there is no apologizing for them. Still, as misguided as their actions and ideas often were, the leaders of anti-slum initiatives held visions that were in at least some respects admirable. The city they imagined was one in which every citizen would have access to decent housing (although for African Americans and other minorities, not always in neighborhoods of their choosing). Slums would be abolished, replaced by attractive, healthy neighborhoods served by parks, transportation facilities, conveniently located shopping centers, and well-maintained schools with adequate playground space and facilities. Fears of rampant crime, disease, and other urban problems would be things of the past. Had this vision for Chicago's future remained embedded in the city's governing agenda, it is hard to imagine how contemporary civic and political leaders could perceive today's dual city as anything other than a catastrophic failure.

How did Chicago's approach to addressing the problems of the city's blighted areas change so dramatically—from a decades-long focus on eliminating slums altogether to a new orientation in which reaching an accommodation with such areas seems to be, for all intents and purposes, the long-term goal? It is this question, above all, which guides this book. Answering it convincingly will require us to move beyond the factors urban scholars have traditionally emphasized in explanations of urban policy outcomes—interests, coalition building, and structural economic change. While such factors are unquestionably important, taken together they can provide only a partial explanation for the policy shifts detailed in the chapters that follow. It is my contention that to understand how Chicago's engagement with its economically distressed areas changed so fundamentally over time, we need to move beyond material interests and the historical conditions they confronted to consider the *ideas* about the slums held by powerful actors in the city, how those ideas evolved, and how closely they were aligned with the city's institutional arrangements.

Why this emphasis on ideas—factors that urbanists and social scientists more generally have often dismissed as either epiphenomenal or impossible to observe and therefore measure—as opposed to more conventional variables? Put simply, ideas in the case described here are neither epiphenomenal—in the sense that they can be read off one or more sets of material interests—nor do they present insurmountable measurement problems. As I will argue in the chapters ahead, from the time that slums were identified as a pressing societal problem in early twentieth-century Chicago, powerful actors mobilizing around this issue had multiple options available to respond in ways seemingly consistent with their material interests. Actions were shaped not by simple calculations of interest but by the conventional wisdom of the time about how blighted areas should best be attacked or, short of that, managed. Solutions that were aligned with such beliefs and assumptions were more likely to win support than those that were not. To be sure, policy proposals were debated, oftentimes vigorously. But aside from exceptional periods when the conventional wisdom itself became the object of scrutiny, such debates generally took place within well-defined parameters.

What was this "conventional wisdom," and how did it shape perceptions and, ultimately, behavior? The dual city of today, with its tacit acknowledgment that blighted neighborhoods are here to stay and must therefore be managed in some way, is an example of what Peter A. Hall and others have termed a *policy paradigm*.[9] By Hall's definition, a policy paradigm is a kind of gestalt or interpretive framework through which actors understand societal problems and develop solutions. As John Campbell explains, such ideas may be "visible to actors yet taken for granted in the milder sense that they remain largely accepted and unquestioned, almost as principles of faith."[10] Paradigms both enable and circumscribe political activity. Ideas can be assembled and reassembled in different ways, but there are limits to what constitutes an acceptable course of action, and paradigms are powerful in part because such limits are rarely discussed or even acknowledged. Instead paradigms operate in the background, outside public debates over specific policy proposals. They are "common sense." As Campbell suggests, such ideas "constitute broad cognitive constraints on the range of solutions that actors perceive and deem useful for solving problems. . . . When [solutions] fit the dominant paradigm they appear natural and familiar and, as a result, are more likely to appeal to policy makers than alternatives that do not."[11]

Arguments that the behavior of political actors may be shaped by paradigmatic assumptions are supported most convincingly by examining multiple time periods in which a distinctive paradigm for a given policy area is a feature of each period. Consider, for example, the shift in recent years to better incorporate public transit, cycling infrastructure, and pedestrian amenities into urban and regional transportation planning. A set of ideas that once privileged auto mobility to the exclusion of nearly everything else has given way to new approaches emphasizing the need for greater balance among multimodal forms of transportation. To be sure, these changes came about in part because key interests demanded them. However, they are also the result of changes in the beliefs and attitudes of planners themselves as the conventional wisdom about the role of the automobile in urban and regional transportation evolved.

As the above example suggests, policy paradigms shape and constrain behavior, but they also change over time, yielding in some instances to new ideas that depart significantly from previous assumptions and beliefs. Opportunities for new policy agendas are opened up, while previous agendas—or portions of them—lose credibility and support. This change in policy paradigms will serve as the centerpiece of my explanation for how Chicago's engagement with its most economically distressed areas changed so dramatically over the course of the twentieth century. As I will demonstrate, three distinct paradigms for addressing the problem of slums and blighted areas surfaced at various points during the twentieth century, each one both enabling and circumscribing the efforts of actors mobilizing around this issue. Each of these three periods featured extensive policy experimentation. But what is especially noteworthy is how little most of these experiments deviated from the dominant policy paradigm of each period. Actors mobilizing around this issue sought to advance their interests, but with the exception of periods when paradigms fell into crisis, they did so almost invariably by working within the parameters established by the dominant set of ideas at the time. As those parameters shifted, so did the strategies actors pursued.

Do Ideas Matter?

For many social scientists, the notion that ideas represent significant determinants of political behavior is unconvincing. Conventionally, interests rather than ideas are seen as driving behavior. As one set of scholars has observed, "the view of the world that still informs much political economy scholarship is both materialist and rationalist."[12] What actors want is frequently unproblematized, viewed simply as a function of structurally given material interests that actors, behaving rationally, seek to maximize.[13] Because preferences are assumed to be determined exogenously by the material environment, there is no need to invoke ideas to explain political behavior. Interests alone are sufficient. For example, when downtown business leaders enter the policy arena to engage with issues such as poverty or urban blight, the presumption is that material concerns motivate them to do so, and that rational decision-making processes on their part will lead to the endorsement of policies that best meet their own material needs. If ideas enter into explanations at all, they are often portrayed instrumentally as weapons or "hooks" used by elites to legitimize their actions, rather than as sources of information to guide behavior.[14] When policies change, explanations are found in the changing distribution of power among interest groups or in the context in which political actors are situated, not in the ideas actors hold.

If policy preferences can indeed be read off material interests and political context in this way, then the concept of policy paradigms has little explanatory power. Instead of shaping behavior, such ideas are simple distractions, information that, along with other ideas, actors must sort through in the process of identifying their "true" interests in a given situation.[15] Yet this materialist view of political behavior has been the subject of criticism in recent years. As political scientist Mark Blyth and others have argued, interests must be recognized before they can be acted on, meaning that it is actors' *perceptions* of their interests, rather than interests themselves, that determine behavior.[16] To the extent that actors correctly perceive their "genuine" interests in a given situation, this condition does not in itself contradict materialist accounts. If, however, interests are not so clear to actors, and if they may be interpreted in multiple ways, then interests alone become insufficient predictors of behavior and it becomes necessary to investigate more directly how preferences are formed. Ideas, including policy paradigms, may be contributing factors.

In fact, there are reasons to suspect that interests may be less transparent to political actors than materialist accounts assume. To say that actors choose strategies that maximize their interests is to assume that individuals are well equipped to correctly anticipate the consequences of their actions. An actor's choice of strategy A over strategy B is explained not simply by what the individual *believes* to be in her best interest but by what *is* genuinely in her best interest. But choices are not always so clear cut. Suppose I am the owner of a hotel in a major city that is proposing to raise taxes on hotel rooms. My inclination is to oppose this tax, since it appears to be contrary to my business interests. However, suppose I learn that the proposed tax is going to be used to fund a new program to provide shelter for homeless people, a program I favor because homeless individuals often congregate in the vicinity of my hotel. My interests in this new tax are now less clear. There may be an optimal choice, but I have no way of knowing what it is. I could support the tax, but there is no guarantee that the new program will reduce the homeless population near my hotel. Because my interests in this case are not clear to me, I may be open to suggestions. I may discuss the issue with colleagues in the hotel industry to see what they think. I may read editorials about the issue in the local newspaper. What others say about this new tax may help determine how I perceive my own interests. In short, because there seems to be no way to determine objectively the optimal choice, ideas matter. What I *perceive* to be in my best interest, not what is objectively in my best interest, is what determines my behavior.[17]

If it is indeed *perceptions* of interests rather than "true" interests that determine behavior, and if perceptions can vary from what is materially given, it would seem to follow that the ideas actors hold about how to navigate the political terrain they occupy require careful scrutiny. Indeed some scholars have taken this insight to stand the conventional argument about ideas and interests on its head: ideas are said to be causally prior to interests—what Alexander Wendt calls "ideas all the way down."[18] Argues Elizabeth Anderson: "Political actors' interests are not naturally predetermined by their material circumstances; rather, interests are constructed ideationally in response to actors' cognitive interpretations and normative beliefs."[19] This is so, not simply because actors have insufficient information to determine their true material interests but because interests themselves may be defined and interpreted in various ways. As Abdelal, Blyth, and Parsons maintain, "While people are fairly rational and their views and actions indeed vary with their material surroundings, views and actions also vary a great deal in terms of the myths, identities, symbols, norms, and conventions that people construct to motivate and prioritize their actions. From this point of view, not even the least uncertain material environment is free of potential variation in meaning."[20] For such scholars interests are purely subjective, a product of whatever actors understand them to be. Their link to the material environment runs only as deep as a given actor's understanding of that environment and the constraints and opportunities it presents.

Such arguments may go too far. While interests may well be ambiguous and actors may interpret them in various ways, the suggestion that interests are in no sense structurally given is an ontologically tenuous position. To give one example, real estate developers may be open to various policy solutions for regulating development, even ones that do not seem particularly advantageous to them. However, some ideas are likely to be inherently objectionable because they are so clearly anti-development and will be perceived as such. To suggest that interests are purely social constructs, that it is genuinely ideas "all the way down," is to throw out the baby—the useful insight that structures do not fully determine perceptions and behavior—along with the bathwater of rump materialism. A more compelling approach is to recognize interests as structurally given, but only in part. Ideas are not determined by interests but are still tethered to interests in some fashion, meaning there are limits beyond which actors will not go. Within those limits, however, material constraints are indeterminate. As Blyth argues, "Structures do not come with an instruction sheet. There is still plenty of room for agents to make history apart from their structurally given interests."[21] Ideas—including the conventional wisdom about how problem solving should proceed in a given policy area—may help determine how interests are perceived.

Of course, even if actors are clear about their preferences, there is no guarantee they will get what they want. Regardless of whether ideas or interests are driving policy preferences in a given situation, actors are routinely required to build coalitions around their policy proposals in order to advance them.[22] Under such circumstances, compromises are often necessary. As Craig Parsons observes, "Whatever individuals debate, objective pressures in coalition building may ultimately impose one view on policy choices."[23] In such cases ideas may not matter, not because they are materially determined but because they are an insufficient basis for political action. As Clarence Stone has argued, the need for coalition building is especially pronounced in the urban arena, given the institutional weaknesses of city government and the need to rely heavily on nongovernmental actors—particularly business—to accomplish goals. In *Regime Politics*, his classic study of development policy in postwar Atlanta, Stone shows how goals were repeatedly modified in order to satisfy coalition partners. Actors, recognizing that they could not get precisely what they wanted, settled for what *could* be accomplished because the alternative—preserving the status quo—was considered to be even less desirable. According to Stone, it was the maintenance needs of the governing coalition that drove behavior in the Atlanta case, not the ideas held by powerful actors about what should be done.[24]

Stone's argument that preferences are fluid—that actors will compromise on goals if the alternative is to accomplish nothing—is persuasive. Yet fluid preferences do not in themselves imply that ideas are unimportant. While it is true that powerful actors in Atlanta did not get everything they wanted, they got much of what they wanted. As Stone himself describes it, business leaders, structurally advantaged by "investor prerogative," successfully engineered a massive program for downtown redevelopment and the rearranging of land use in Atlanta's central area. The need for support by the city's African American leadership pushed business elites to endorse racial moderation, affirmative action, and other benefits for blacks, positions they would have probably not otherwise taken. But such compromises were, in the bigger scheme of things, minor ones, concessions that business leaders were quite willing to make in order to protect the key components of their development agenda. Given this, a large part of the explanation for why Atlanta's postwar redevelopment program took the form it did resides in the preferences held by powerful actors who conceived and orchestrated the program. Whether ideas or material interests alone led them down this path, these views require an explanation.

Ideas as Policy Paradigms

Ideas come in various guises. In addition to policy paradigms, they include societal norms, cultural attitudes and beliefs, ideologies, frames, discourse, public philosophies, and programmatic ideas and beliefs. Some ideas are very general, others far more precise. They can operate in the foreground of public policy debates, as in ideas relating to specific policies and programs, or in the background, as in public philosophies or policy paradigms.[25] Ideas can be cognitive or normative. Cognitive ideas tell actors what kinds of policy solutions are likely to be effective or ineffective. Typically they specify or imply cause-and-effect relationships—if policy X is pursued, outcome Y will result. By contrast, normative ideas focus on what is legitimate or appropriate. They are justifications for rather than guides to action, aimed at "satisfying policy makers and citizens alike that [policy solutions] serve the underlying values or public philosophies of the polity, whether long-standing or newly emerging ones."[26]

This book will chiefly address two kinds of ideas that are closely related: policy paradigms and programmatic ideas. Programmatic ideas are causal ideas about specific policies or programs, often "technical and professional" in nature, that guide actors seeking solutions to policy problems.[27] Typically such ideas are framed in ways that align with established policy paradigms. As Campbell explains, "In contrast to cognitive paradigms, which provide an overarching understanding of how the world works and, in turn, how political institutions and policy instruments ought to be organized in order to achieve broad policy goals, programmatic ideas are more precise guidelines about how already-existing institutions and instruments should be used in specific situations according to the principles of well-established paradigms."[28] Policy paradigms thus set constraints on the kinds of programmatic ideas that are likely to be considered practicable and legitimate. Yet when paradigms falter, a subject to which we will turn shortly, it is programmatic ideas that often pave the way for new paradigmatic assumptions. As Jal Mehta argues, "The best policies literally remake the public philosophy in their wake."[29] Particularly during times of uncertainty when confidence in long-held beliefs is shaken, policy ideas that fall outside the parameters of existing paradigms not only may be politically viable but, if proved effective, may help bring about paradigm change.

As described earlier, policy paradigms are shared conceptual frameworks that guide political behavior by offering a vision of how society functions (or should function) and setting boundaries around "what is thinkable, possible, or acceptable."[30] For example, neoliberalism, a policy paradigm that has dominated thinking about state-society relations since the 1980s, is said to be directly implicated in the diminished presence of the state in many policy areas where it was once heavily engaged, including social welfare policy, regulation of banking and industry, public education, environmental protection, industrial relations, and urban policy.[31] Neoliberalism emphasizes privatization, deregulation, reduced government spending, and other efforts to minimize the role of government and reorient public sector activity more directly around the accumulation of capital and wealth. Neoliberal principles have become so ingrained that public officials are reluctant to veer from them even when outcomes have been shown to be suboptimal. To use Timothy Weaver's example, during the 1980s and 1990s political leaders in the United States and the United Kingdom championed enterprise zones, programs that targeted distressed areas of cities for tax relief and deregulation as a way of stimulating investment. According to Weaver, these politicians continued to favor the approach despite its seeming ineffectiveness because it was consistent with neoliberal principles they endorsed emphasizing market mechanisms for addressing urban poverty and joblessness.[32]

By most accounts, contemporary usage of the term *policy paradigm* dates back to a seminal 1993 article by Peter A. Hall.[33] While acknowledging that paradigms are in part empowering in that they present actors with a set of ideas that can be drawn upon to pursue an agenda, Hall focused chiefly on how paradigms constrain behavior. As he put it, "Policymakers customarily work within a framework of ideas and standards that specifies not only the goals of policy and the kind of instruments that can be used to attain them, but also the very nature of the problems they are meant to be addressing."[34] Paradigms thus serve as a kind of policy lens, allowing actors to "see" some types of potential policy solutions but not others. Not only do paradigms serve as screening devices in this fashion, selecting for policy ideas that are consistent with paradigmatic assumptions, but they do so in ways that are largely invisible to the general public and, in many cases, to policymakers themselves. Argues Hall: "Like a *Gestalt*, this framework is embedded in the very terminology through which policymakers communicate about their work, and it is influential precisely because so much of it is taken for granted and unamenable to scrutiny."[35] As the conventional wisdom, paradigms occupy a privileged position in policy discourse. Challengers—when they surface at all—are apt to be dismissed out of hand as unrealistic, outside the mainstream, or downright wacky.

Yet assuming paradigms do in fact shape preferences in this way, what are the mechanisms through which this occurs? Why, in concrete decision-making situations, do actors lean so heavily on the conventional wisdom in a given policy area? One explanation is that the alternative—to use data and otherwise reason analytically to develop solutions tailored individually to specific choice situations—is simply too cognitively burdensome. According to Alan Jacobs, political elites routinely face decision-making situations in which potential choices are too complex to fully evaluate.[36] Actors must therefore economize, focusing more attention on certain data and causal possibilities than on others. Drawing on literature from social and cognitive psychology, Jacobs suggests that policy paradigms and other conceptual frameworks serve as "mental models" that help simplify complex choices. Instead of working through all potential consequences of a policy choice, as standard rationalist accounts assume, decisionmakers use paradigms and other mental models to narrow choice sets. In so doing, argues Jacobs, actors "devote disproportionate attention to those lines of causal reasoning that happen to be captured by the mental model they are employing and those pieces of information that are relevant to and support those causal logics. They will, in turn, invest fewer cognitive resources in processing arguments and data that are inconsistent with or orthogonal to the model."[37] As a result, solutions that fall outside the model are disadvantaged, while those consistent with it are privileged. Suboptimal solutions consistent with the model may well be favored over optimal solutions that run counter to the model's expectations.

Jacobs's argument is attractive in part because it seems consistent with everyday decision-making processes. Consider one example. As the parent of a teenage girl who has not yet begun driving, I am frequently called upon to provide transportation to and from the homes of friends located in various parts of our suburban Milwaukee community. In planning my route for such trips I do not start from scratch. Instead my itinerary inevitably favors those streets that I routinely use to get from certain areas of the village to another. With this "mental model" of the village as my starting point, I make the necessary refinements to map out more precisely how I will get to my chosen destination. Importantly, because this mapping process biases certain streets (the ones I routinely use) over others, my route may not be the most efficient one. However, to identify the optimal route would often require an investment of significant computational resources on my part, since streets in our village are laid out not in a grid but in a pattern containing numerous twists and turns, zigs and zags. Every time I use a preferred street to get to a chosen destination, my mental map of the village is reinforced. Occasionally it becomes apparent to me that a segment of my map can be more efficiently constructed through a different route, and I make the necessary adjustment. Such discoveries are, however, rare and usually come only after repeated observations.

While the argument that paradigms perform the useful function of making complex decisions manageable—therefore causing decisionmakers to favor them—is certainly plausible, paradigms may also shape decision making in normative ways by instilling certain attitudes and beliefs about the kinds of policies that are considered to be legitimate or appropriate. In such cases it is normative considerations rather than cognitive limitations that prevent actors from seeing the full range of available solutions. For example, the conventional wisdom about the proper division of labor between state and market has changed significantly since the early twentieth century. Mid-twentieth-century innovations such as public-private economic development partnerships and government subsidies for real estate development would have been unimaginable to residents of cities during the early 1900s, because they violate what were then widely shared normative beliefs about how government should engage with the economy and society. Such views, inscribed in the policy paradigms of the time, excluded policy solutions that might have otherwise provided significant material benefits for certain kinds of actors. Contemporary neoliberalism performs a similar normative role through its favoring of market mechanisms in the formulation of policy solutions.

As Jacobs argues, the use of policy paradigms to simplify complex choice situations makes such ideas self-reinforcing, resulting in a kind of ideational path dependence.[38] Once entrenched, paradigms may thus have considerable staying power. At some point the ideas they embody are effectively institutionalized. According to Sheri Berman, this occurs when such ideas become "habitual, natural, or instinctive for a particular community. [Ideas] are institutionalized once they are no longer thought much about but are simply accepted or viewed as part of objective reality."[39] Policy paradigms, or components of them, that have become widely accepted as the conventional wisdom may be reproduced in this way, through the attitudes and belief structures of citizens and decisionmakers.

For others, the resilience of paradigms is explained not so much by cognitive mechanisms or normative commitments as through the embedding of such ideas in concrete policies and institutions. According to Kathryn Sikkink, "Ideas within an institution become embodied in its statement of purpose, its self-definition, and its research or training program, which in turn tends to perpetuate and extend the ideas. Once ideas become embedded in institutions, ideational change comes slowly and in an episodic manner."[40] Here again the path-dependent effects of ideas may be in evidence. As Judith Goldstein and Robert Keohane argue, while the institutionalization of an idea or set of ideas in this way may be traced to the efforts of powerful interests, once ideas are institutionalized they can continue to influence policy long after the interests that originally championed them are gone.[41] In such cases, ideas represent the "congealed preferences" of actors from some earlier period; they cannot be attributed to the desires or material interests of currently powerful actors alone, as in functionalist or power-distributional per-spectives.[42] Indeed, to the extent that the ideas embodied in policy par-adigms are institutionalized in this fashion, contemporary interests and power structures may reveal relatively little about where such ideas ac-tually come from.[43] To understand and explain why paradigms exist and have lasting impacts, we need to trace their movement through time and space, paying careful attention to those actors serving as "carriers" of new paradigmatic ideas and closely examining the ways in which such ideas shape behavior and outcomes beyond the time they are originally introduced.

Unfortunately, investigating policy paradigms and their effects pre-sents potentially troublesome epistemological challenges. According to Daniel Béland and Robert Henry Cox, "we know that ideas are essential when we can identify an idea and trace its influence on a particular po-litical outcome."[44] To do so requires, in part, "the utterance of an idea." To the extent that actors articulate the ideas that are said to be influenc-ing their behavior, more convincing causal claims can be made. Yet pol-icy paradigms, as the conventional wisdom, are by definition ideas that are rarely voiced. Indeed, decisionmakers themselves may not be con-scious of the effects of such ideas on their own policy preferences. Can ideas that take this form be observed and measured in some way? One possible approach is to use counterfactual analysis to construct a causal chain in which the policy paradigm does not exist. If the removal of ideas from the causal chain appears to change the outcome in some significant way, it can be argued that reference to material interests alone cannot account for the observed behavior and that ideas have in fact played the hypothesized role. Alternatively, scholars might try to determine what behavior would best satisfy the material interests of some actor or set of actors in a given context. If actions seem to be at odds with mate-rial interests, or if interests could be realized more fully through alter-native behavior, an argument might be made that ideas, not simply inter-ests, are driving behavior. Or as Craig Parsons has suggested, a group of actors holding similar material positions in a particular context might be observed to see whether they behave uniformly. To the extent that be-havior diverges, it could be argued that ideas explain at least some of the variation.[45]

None of the above approaches require that ideas be observed di-rectly—an advantage for perspectives focusing on policy paradigms and their effects. At certain times, however, it may be possible to directly examine the ideas embodied in policy paradigms. This is particularly the case during periods of paradigm change, when existing ideas are called into question and new ones proposed. At such times what was formerly the conventional wisdom becomes openly contested, and a debate ensues over which new ideas will serve as the replacement paradigm. Public intellectuals and policy entrepreneurs may figure prominently in contests of this nature, voicing ideas that are readily observable in records of public discourse. Consider, for example, the highly public roles played by economists Friedrich von Hayek and Milton Friedman—both harsh critics of Keynesian economics and activist government more generally—in the transition from Keynesianism to neoliberalism in the 1970s.[46] If at some point a new set of ideas becomes institutionalized, and if actors routinely behave in ways consistent with those ideas, an argument can potentially be made tracing the observed behavior back to those ideas even if they are no longer publicly voiced. Such arguments are strengthened to the extent that policy proposals inconsistent with or contradictory to such ideas are routinely rejected.

A Model of Paradigm Change

While policy paradigms may be resilient, they do not last forever. The movement from one policy paradigm to another is generally recognized as a sequential process beginning with a loss of confidence in an existing paradigm, followed by a period of experimentation and political contestation in which proponents of new approaches and defenders of the current paradigm vie for dominance, and ending with the adoption and institutionalization of a new paradigm.[47] While scholars can generally agree on this much, theoretically there is much about the process of paradigm change that remains underspecified. To begin, how do we know when paradigm change has in fact occurred? Conceivably, there could be a significant change in policy ideas in a given setting that still falls short of genuine paradigm change. In Hall's formulation, inspired by Thomas Kuhn's famous treatise on scientific paradigms, paradigm change is operationalized as what Hall describes as first-, second-, and third-order change. First- and second-order changes are defined as incremental adjustments to policy instruments and their settings—akin to Kuhn's notion of "normal science" in which practitioners limit their activities to the articulation and refinement of existing scientific paradigms. Third-order changes, by contrast, are changes to "the overarching goals that guide policy in a particular field."[48] According to Hall, only when first- and second-order change is accompanied by fundamental departures in policy goals can it be said that a change in policy paradigm has in fact occurred.

A key question in studies of paradigm change is how existing policy paradigms become unstable—and therefore susceptible to change—in the first place. Here Hall's observations are less illuminating. Studies of paradigm change, like studies of political development more generally, frequently adopt a "punctuated equilibrium" view of change.[49] From this perspective, political development most of the time conforms to a kind of "politics as usual" in which conflict is present but generally resolved in predictable, routine ways. Stability and incrementalism are the norm.[50] Only on rare occasions are such patterns disrupted—or "punctuated"—by moments of extraordinary change, and such episodes are typically followed by a return to stability around a new equilibrium. As Robert Lieberman observes, punctuated equilibrium theories typically identify two stable periods, "before and after some transformative change" that radically disrupts existing arrangements.[51] Yet if such periods are defined as equilibrium solutions or otherwise stable arrangements, then what explains the ruptures that usher in new arrangements? Punctuated equilibrium approaches must identify factors outside the model to explain such occurrences, since there is nothing in the model itself that can account for them.

A second feature of punctuated equilibrium theories is that change of a genuinely transformative nature is viewed as abrupt and discontinuous. Break points represent "episodic rupture[s] with the past," ushering in new arrangements that are incommensurable with what came before.[52] For example, Kuhn describes the "scientific revolutions" that produce new scientific paradigms as follows: "The transition from a paradigm in crisis to a new one from which a new tradition of normal science can emerge is far from a cumulative process, one achieved by an articulation or extension of the old paradigm. Rather it is a reconstruction of the field from new fundamentals, a reconstruction that changes some of the field's most elementary theoretical generalizations as well as many of its paradigm methods and applications."[53] Scientific revolutions, like social revolutions, are not a matter of negotiation and compromise between defenders and opponents of the intellectual status quo. Instead such episodes involve a wholesale rejection of what came before, closing with "total victory for one of the two opposing camps."[54]

Studies examining how policy paradigms change frequently adopt both of these features of punctuated equilibrium theories: new paradigms are characterized as fundamental breaks with past ideas, brought about through some exogenous factor or event that calls into question the effectiveness of existing policy ideas and assumptions. For example, in describing Britain's shift from the policy paradigm of Keynesianism to the radically different paradigm of monetarism during the early 1980s, Hall points to the twin pressures of inflation and economic stagnation— developments that according to Keynesian logic should not have occurred simultaneously. Economic crisis was the trigger that paved the way for paradigm change, undermining confidence in the conventional economic wisdom and emboldening challengers. Exogenous events of this kind are often viewed in the literature on policy ideas as key turning points, moments when extraordinary change is suddenly possible.[55] Argues Campbell: "When shocks, crises, and other disturbances create policy problems for which prevailing paradigms provide little guidance, policy makers search for new ones that help them envision new policy solutions, especially if they believe that there is evidence that the new one will work."[56] Figure 1.1 shows a simple model of paradigm change that exemplifies this pattern. A formerly stable policy paradigm is called into question through some exogenous disturbance, which paves the way for transition to a new paradigm and convergence around a new ideational equilibrium.

Case studies such as Hall's have provided convincing illustrations of this model of paradigm change. Still, critics of punctuated-equilibrium approaches have questioned whether paradigm change always conforms to this pattern, or even whether it routinely does. Berman, for example, has suggested that dissatisfaction with an existing paradigm may be the result not of some sudden unexpected external shock or event but of "gradual yet increasing disillusionment and the slow delegitimization of

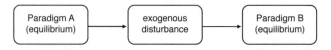

FIGURE 1.1   Punctuated equilibrium model of paradigm change.

existing beliefs."[57] Paradigm change, in other words, may have endogenous causes as well as exogenous ones, and may occur gradually rather than all at once. However, Berman fails to identify specific mechanisms through which endogenous change might occur, suggesting only that loss of confidence in an existing paradigm creates "political space" that may be filled by new ideas.

For considering the possibility of endogenous paradigm change, a useful starting point might be to examine what punctuated-equilibrium approaches frequently take for granted: the stability of a paradigm prior to any external disruption that might upset the status quo. Here scholarship from the field of American political development (APD) may provide helpful guidance. A key question that has animated APD scholarship is the alignment, or "fit," between policy ideas and goals on the one hand and institutional arrangements on the other.[58] In this perspective, institutions are sometimes seen as "selecting" for policy ideas, creating fertile environments for certain kinds of ideas and policy goals while throwing up barriers to others.[59] If the fit between a policy paradigm and institutional arrangements is a poor one, resulting in failure to advance policy goals, a search for new ideas may ensue. The paradigm, in other words, is unstable and susceptible to change.

In addition to the fit between ideas and institutions, scholars have examined the properties of paradigms themselves, focusing on whether paradigmatic ideas and goals are internally consistent. As Vivien Schmidt points out, "Any program is the result of conflicts as well as compromises among actors who bring different ideas to the table," meaning that policy goals and ideas may have competing impulses.[60] To the extent that paradigm goals clash with one another, actors will encounter obstructions and the paradigm itself may be vulnerable to change, particularly when the pursuit of one paradigm goal undermines the achievement of another.

Finally, we should also consider the impact of policy paradigms on organized interests, particularly when paradigms are newly emerging and not yet fully institutionalized. As scholars have long recognized, public policies generate "feedback effects" that influence interest group activity. Policies may cause certain groups to mobilize, or they may lead to the formation of new ones. As Theda Skocpol argues, "Public social or economic measures may have the effect of stimulating brand new social identities and political capacities, sometimes groups that have a stake in the policy's expansion, sometimes groups that seek to repeal or reorient the policy in question."[61] Newly emerging policy paradigms may also generate such feedback effects, particularly if they are accompanied by more concrete programmatic ideas. The key question is whether interest group activity works to reinforce or to impede the current trajectory of the paradigm. Paradigms may prove to be unstable to the extent they stimulate interest group activity that pushes in alternative directions.

In sum, scholars examining paradigm change should not simply assume that policy paradigms are for the most part stable configurations of policy ideas, disrupted on rare occasions by exogenous shocks of some kind. Instead the fit between ideas and institutions, the alignment among ideas and policy goals themselves, and the feedback effects generated by the paradigm should all be closely examined to determine whether paradigm instability and change may have endogenous causes. Figure 1.2 illustrates this model of paradigm stability. In cases where one or more of these three variables point in the direction of change, any instability that is observed may have endogenous causes. Conversely, where all three variables suggest stability but the paradigm nevertheless changes, the cause of change may be exogenous.

So far we have considered factors that might cause an existing policy paradigm to become unstable, increasing its susceptibility to change. As yet, however, nothing has been said about the process through which a replacement paradigm might be constructed. The political space that opens up when confidence in a paradigm weakens creates an opportunity, but it may reveal little about how actors take advantage of such openings to advance new policy ideas. Completing the model of paradigm change requires the identification of specific mechanisms through which new paradigms are introduced and, ultimately, institutionalized. Here a useful starting point is the work of historical institutionalist scholars, many of whom have paid careful attention to questions of institutional change, identifying mechanisms through which institutional arrangements are transformed over time. While this work is concerned chiefly with institutions, not ideas, it may be possible to apply certain of these mechanisms to the study of ideational change.

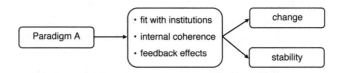

FIGURE 1.2. Model of paradigm change and stability.

Like studies of paradigm change, historical institutionalist scholarship was dominated for years by punctuated-equilibrium approaches. Institutions were seen as path dependent, reproduced through positive feedback mechanisms disrupted on rare occasions by exogenous shocks that made transformative change possible.[62] Others, however, challenged this perspective. Most prominently, Kathleen Thelen has argued that the emphasis on punctuated change in path dependence approaches has obscured important ways that institutions evolve incrementally, short of breakdown and replacement. In this view, feedback effects generated by institutions are a key cause of change. As Thelen argues, "When institutions are founded they are not universally embraced or straightforwardly 'adapted to,' but rather continue to be the object of ongoing conflict, as actors struggle over the form that these institutions should take and the functions they should perform."[63] Over time, incremental change driven by such contests may add up to major institutional transformation.

Thelen identifies several mechanisms through which such incremental change may occur, most importantly *layering* and *conversion*. Layering involves the "grafting of new elements onto an otherwise stable institutional framework."[64] Instead of replacing rules or institutions, actors seek "amendments, revisions, or additions to existing ones."[65] If such changes are substantial enough, they may alter the stable reproduction of an existing system and point it in a fundamentally different direction. Conversion is the redirection of institutions to new goals, functions, or purposes not envisioned by institutional designers. Such developments may result from "the incorporation of new supporters or the assumption of power by a new political coalition that, rather than dismantle old institutions, uses them in new ways."[66] Conversion is typically linked to feedback effects that activate new coalitions intent on steering institutions in directions they favor.

While Thelen's focus is on institutional change, the concepts of layering and conversion have sometimes been applied to the study of ideational change as well, including paradigm change.[67] For example, challenging the Kuhnian logic of paradigm change as an "episodic rupture" with past ideas, some scholars have suggested that replacement paradigms may be "hybrids" that include a mixture of older and newer ideas.[68] The layering of new ideas onto older ones may be sufficient to meet Hall's threshold for paradigm change, even if it occurs incrementally over substantial stretches of time. Likewise, paradigm change may occur incrementally through conversion, as actors disadvantaged by the

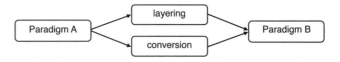

FIGURE 1.3. Model of incremental paradigm change.

ideational status quo appropriate paradigm ideas and reassemble them in new ways. Again, should changes of this sort add up to something more than the modification or extension of an existing paradigm, it may be argued that the transition to a succeeding paradigm has occurred. Figure 1.3 illustrates this model of incremental paradigm change, driven by endogenous rather than exogenous factors.

Importantly, whether change occurs through layering or conversion may have implications for the stability of a new paradigm. APD scholars have long recognized the destabilizing effects of layering on institutional arrangements. As Karen Orren and Stephen Skowronek have observed, the institutions of a given polity are not created simultaneously, with a common purpose in mind. To the contrary, institutions develop over time, driven by different interests and societal problems. This means that at any given time "several different sets of rules and norms are likely to be operating simultaneously."[69] As Lieberman argues, equilibrium under such conditions is possible at times, but at other times institutions "will collide and chafe."[70] The same might be said about policy paradigms constructed through layering processes. Stable outcomes cannot be ruled out, but the grafting of new ideas and agendas onto the remnants of older ones—a process certain to be driven by interests other than those responsible for the original paradigm—produces certain tendencies toward disequilibrium.

Conversion, on the other hand, may have the opposite effect, fostering stability rather than change. As Thelen observes in reference to institutions, conversion occurs when actors dissatisfied with an institution have an interest not in replacing it but rather in adapting it to serve new purposes.[71] In the long run, such efforts may contribute to institutional stability and survival by bringing the institution into sync with new political conditions, creating new vested interests that may prove to be powerful supporters of institutional arrangements reworked to better meet their needs. Policy paradigms retooled in this fashion may also prove to be resilient, supported by powerful interests and more closely aligned with organizational goals. Figure 1.4 illustrates how outcomes

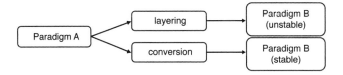

FIGURE 1.4. Incremental change with stable and unstable outcomes.

may differ depending on whether paradigm change occurs through the mechanism of layering or that of conversion.

We have now considered two models of paradigm change, one in which change is completely the result of factors exogenous to the policy subsystem, and one in which change is fully incorporated into the model, the result of factors endogenous to the policy process. Which is the more accurate? While considerable space has been devoted here to elaborating a model of endogenous paradigm change, there can be no doubt that in many and perhaps most cases exogenous factors play a role as well. In the urban arena specifically, a model that included no role for such external disruptions as deindustrialization, urban economic restructuring, or economic downturns would be no more convincing than a model of paradigm change that focused exclusively on such factors. Indeed it may well be that neither model by itself best captures the way that paradigm change normally occurs, and that what is needed is an approach that incorporates both exogenous and endogenous factors. Figure 1.5 illustrates such an approach, a hybrid that includes mechanisms of layering and conversion as well as exogenous factors.

This model brings together the earlier discussion of factors that may cause a paradigm to become unstable in the first place with a consideration of mechanisms through which replacement paradigms may be constructed. At the front end of the model, we see that the stability of

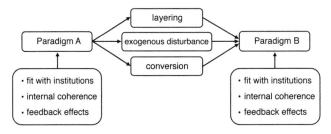

FIGURE 1.5. Model of paradigm change, endogenous and exogenous causes.

Paradigm A may be affected by any or all of the three factors previously identified: the paradigm's fit with institutions, its internal coherence, and the feedback effects it generates. Should the paradigm be unstable and susceptible to change, the transition to Paradigm B may occur through layering or conversion. Alternatively, or perhaps in conjunction with one of these mechanisms, exogenous factors may also play a role. At the back end of the model, factors that may affect the stability of the new paradigm are again considered. Significantly, the direction in which those factors point (stability or instability) may be influenced by the mechanisms through which change was effected. If Paradigm B was produced through the layering of new ideas onto older ones, its internal coherence may be negatively affected and it may prove to be unstable. Alternatively, if conversion was the principal mechanism of change, positive feedback effects generated through the mobilization of powerful interests around new paradigmatic goals and ideas may produce stabilizing tendencies.

The Argument of the Book

This book is, of course, by no means the first effort to trace the contemporary dual city back to key developments in the past. Historical perspectives on the dual city can be loosely grouped into two types of approaches that largely complement one another, one emphasizing politics and urban power structures, the other emphasizing economic factors, both paying careful attention to matters of race. Arguments in the former category generally focus on what Robert Salisbury called "the new convergence of power" following World War II.[72] In this view, powerful coalitions of downtown business leaders and city officials—alarmed by central business district decline, the spread of slums and blight in near-downtown areas, and white flight—came together in cities across the country to address what was perceived as a deepening urban crisis. With the rescue and revitalization of downtown business districts as the ultimate goal, plans were hatched to rearrange land use in the central areas of major cities, moving low-income minority populations away from downtown areas and replacing them with middle-class residents, mostly white—the preferred demographic for near-downtown residence. For this group of scholars the urban geography of today—featuring gentrified neighborhoods surrounding downtown and areas of concentrated poverty somewhat farther removed—can be traced to the decisions of these powerful coalitions and their pursuit of what some have called the "corporate-center strategy" for urban redevelopment.[73] Coming to grips with the slums meant creating "fortress downtowns" buffered from economically distressed areas by middle-class neighborhoods, sports stadiums, universities, hospitals, or other institutions.[74]

Other scholars, such as William Julius Wilson and Thomas Sugrue, have emphasized how economic changes have contributed to and reinforced urban inequalities, both social and spatial.[75] Such perspectives call attention to the devastating impacts of urban economic restructuring—especially deindustrialization—on blacks and other minority groups, creating a structurally disadvantaged population of impoverished residents largely excluded from urban labor markets. This is also the view taken by John Mollenkopf and Manuel Castells, whose edited volume *Dual City* inspired the title of this book.[76] The story of economic restructuring, however, is not simply one of concentrated poverty but of power and privilege as well, as those with the "right" backgrounds, education, and social standing have benefited immensely from opportunities in the burgeoning corporate and financial sectors of major cities. The dual city incorporates both of these trajectories, one leading to long-term poverty and a set of neighborhoods that seem permanently disadvantaged, the other leading to economic opportunity and neighborhood areas that those with options eagerly seek out.

Each of these perspectives has much to offer, and my analysis is substantially informed by both of them. But the argument here also departs from these approaches in important respects. Perspectives focusing on the contribution of economic restructuring to urban inequality often reveal more about how the dual city is reproduced than about how it came into being in the first place. The effects of deindustrialization were felt most strongly by cities during the 1970s and 1980s, when the vast majority of urban manufacturing jobs were lost. Yet as many have observed, the major postwar urban divides along racial, ethnic, class, and geographic lines were in evidence well before then. Economic change certainly reinforced these patterns, but it is less clear how big a role it played in initiating them.

The literature on postwar business-government redevelopment coalitions is perhaps more helpful in demonstrating how certain patterns of inequality—particularly spatial ones—were established, yet such perspectives have shortcomings of their own. Arguments about postwar urban power structures are, for the most part, very much materialist accounts in which downtown corporate leaders, clear about their interests, worked with city officials to rearrange land use in ways that optimized the downtown area for corporate and professional development. Such arguments generally take a punctuated-equilibrium approach to urban redevelopment in which the aftermath of World War II is seen as a watershed moment where organized action to address the problem of slums and begin the process of rebuilding cities was suddenly possible. In this view, the redevelopment agenda of the postwar years represented a distinct break from the previous governing agendas of cities, establishing a trajectory that remains—with certain modifications—in place to this day. The dual city is thus seen largely as a postwar creation, set in motion by powerful actors who recognized that saving downtown required a strategy for addressing slum conditions.

I argue, in contrast, that much of this literature is far too sanguine about the capabilities of actors to recognize and act on their interests. As I demonstrate in the chapters ahead, groups mobilizing around problems of slum housing and downtown decline in postwar Chicago did not simply assert power. Instead they struggled to identify solutions in a policy environment in which past experience was helpful chiefly in revealing what did *not* work. Uncertain where their interests lay, these actors looked to ideas for guidance, fully aware that whatever action they took would be experimental and that success was by no means assured. Indeed, as we shall see, today's dual city was not what these pioneers of urban redevelopment anticipated or desired.

Tracing these ideas back in time reveals the postwar period as a somewhat arbitrary break point. Against punctuated-equilibrium perspectives that portray the efforts of postwar business-government coalitions as a sharp departure from the past, I argue that developments prior to World War II weighed heavily on the actions these individuals took. Most important, their preferences and behavior were shaped by a legacy of anti-slum initiatives and experiments dating back to the turn of the century, initiatives that were informed by the ideas and policy paradigms of the time. These paradigms proved to be unstable for various reasons: because of poor fit with institutional arrangements, because paradigm goals clashed with one another, or because they were based on flawed assumptions. As a consequence, the policy experiments they gave rise to resulted, for the most part, in suboptimal outcomes, undermining confidence in existing paradigms and opening windows for the transition to new ones, of which the dual city is the most recent. Understanding the origins of the dual city in this way reveals an acute irony: that the dual city—with its tacit acceptance of slums and poverty as chronic and intractable manifestations of the urban condition—emerged out of years of hard-fought efforts to rid Chicago of its slum districts. A decades-long attack on the city's blighted areas evolved into a program for revitalizing downtown that sought an accommodation with the slums rather than their elimination.

*   *   *

Organized action to address slum conditions in Chicago began during the late nineteenth century, when Progressive Era housing reformers began mobilizing around policy solutions to promote slum rejuvenation. Actions were guided above all by widely shared beliefs that the government's involvement in housing markets should be highly circumscribed, limited to regulation and oversight of building construction and maintenance to ensure adequate safety and sanitation. Like Sam Bass Warner's Philadelphia, Chicago was a "private city," a place where solutions to public problems were to be found chiefly in the marketplace and where property owners were vigilant in their efforts to ward off activities they perceived as government overreach.[77] For housing reformers at the time, two goals were paramount: the elimination of slums wherever they existed and the provision of safe and sanitary housing for slum residents. These goals were to be achieved through the creation of stringent housing and building regulations accompanied by effective enforcement mechanisms. The relationship between the public and private sectors in housing markets was therefore adversarial: the job of government, using the full force of the law if necessary, was to require property owners to provide safe and sanitary housing. Privatism proved to be a largely ineffective set of ideas for eliminating slums—partly due to its poor fit with the city's machine-style institutional arrangements. But for decades it remained the conventional wisdom, with actors seeking to perfect this approach rather than pursue new directions in housing reform.

Commitment to privatism ultimately began to falter with the onset of the Great Depression. As housing markets collapsed, an openness to new ideas and policy solutions led to a period of experimentation in housing reform during the 1930s and 1940s. By the mid-1940s, the adversarial view of relations between government and property owners gave way to a new set of ideas for addressing slums built around the notion of public-private partnerships. In this new policy paradigm, government and private investors would work together to rebuild slum districts, the former clearing land and subsidizing land costs and the latter doing the redevelopment work. Like privatism, the new policy paradigm had two principal goals, one of which—the elimination of slums citywide— was carried forward from the privatist period. Privatism's other main goal—to provide safe and sanitary housing for slum residents—largely fell by the wayside. In its place was a very different objective: achieving the "highest and best use" of land. In this new approach, the real estate developer rather than the housing regulator occupied center stage; slums would be eliminated by creating favorable conditions for profit-seeking investors to initiate projects in blighted areas. As under privatism, slums were viewed as a physical problem, not a social one. From this it followed that eliminating slums was a simple matter of tearing down substandard structures and replacing them with new ones.

Largely through the urban renewal and public housing programs of the 1950s and 1960s, public-private partnerships successfully rebuilt portions of Chicago's slum districts. But slums proved to be a thorny problem, emerging in new areas of the city as fast as they were cleaned up in others. Enthusiasm for public housing eventually faded as such projects, filled increasingly with the city's most desperate and impoverished residents, became high-rise ghettos. By the 1970s, optimism that the attack on the slums would prove successful gave way to growing resignation that victory was still a long way off. As a set of ideas for addressing slum conditions, the public-private partnership revealed itself as a fundamentally flawed and inherently unstable policy paradigm. The layering of new goals (achieving the highest and best use of land) onto old ones (eliminating slums) produced contradictory imperatives that could not be reconciled. Moreover, the experience of public housing soon exposed fatal defects in the assumption that slums were a purely physical problem.

At the same time, powerful actors began to view the public-private partnership model in a new way. Mobilized by perceived opportunities in the urban renewal program, Chicago's business leaders sought to steer policy ideas in a direction that would more directly benefit them. Appropriating certain paradigmatic ideas (the rearranging of land use facilitated by government powers) while dropping others (the elimination of slums), business leaders used the mechanism of conversion to come to terms with what they now viewed as a deep-rooted and insoluble problem. Efforts now focused on mitigating the worst effects of the city's most economically distressed areas and creating a defensible corridor around the downtown area, to be occupied by middle- and upper-income residents. With the city's most powerful actors leading the way, the dual city was set in motion. In time it would become the conventional wisdom, an approach so ingrained in the minds of civic leaders, policymakers, and residents that it no longer needed to be voiced.

As we move now from theory to narrative, there are two points I wish to make. First, my emphasis on ideas and policy paradigms is not an argument that interests are somehow unimportant or less important than ideas. My intent is not to substitute an ideational approach for a materialist one but rather to place both ideas and interests—along with institutions—in a "single analytical frame," as Rogers Smith puts it.[78] My quarrel is not with materialist accounts per se but with accounts that endow actors with exaggerated powers to identify optimal solutions. To give but one example, during the course of Chicago's anti-slum campaigns, organized interests were very much in evidence as paradigms faltered and openings were created for new policy ideas. Yet even then, actors struggled to identify solutions they anticipated would be both effective and consistent with their interests. Policy ideas that did not have the support of powerful actors failed to gain traction, but the support of the powerful was no guarantee that ideas would actually work. At other times, when policy paradigms became entrenched as the conventional wisdom, such ideas seemed to exert an influence that transcended interests, defining the scope of policy actions that actors of any kind could conceivably take. Ushered in with the help of powerful interests, such ideas took on lives of their own.

A second point I wish to emphasize is that in focusing on the city's approach to slum and blighted areas, this book has a specifically geographic orientation. While poverty and economic distress are important to the analysis, this is much more a story about impoverished *places* than about impoverished people. Ask any Chicagoan, and he or she will have at least a general sense of where those places are. They are fixtures of the mental maps most residents have of the geography of wealth and poverty in the city, maps that help them navigate the city, telling them which areas are safe to walk through or desirable to live in. The dual city is reproduced in part in this way, through the internalization of a set of boundaries that signify danger and disorder in some locations and safety and reassurance in others. These boundaries are on occasion redrawn—

altered by gentrification in once-struggling areas of the city and by dis-investment and decline in formerly stable neighborhoods—but what is unchanged is the continued presence of vast areas of economic hardship and distress.

As recently as the 1960s, the existence of such areas was seen as a prescient threat to urban stability, the mark of a city in decline. The danger now, after decades of learning to live with the slums, is that we grow resigned to such areas, writing them off as an unfortunate but unavoidable cost of urban living. Such an attitude would have baffled the leaders of Chicago's anti-slum initiatives of the early and mid-twentieth century, whose views were shaped by a very different set of ideas about what should be done.

CHAPTER TWO

Housing Reform in the Private City

There is some, but perhaps not too much, exaggeration in saying that social policy has developed in the interstices allowed to it by "sound economic thinking."—Hugh Heclo, 1974[1]

O n a frigid January afternoon in 1897, a group of settlement workers and other interested citizens gathered at Northwestern University Settlement on the city's West Side for a conference on Chicago's housing problems. The purpose of the event was "to set forth the insanitary and demoralizing condition of Chicago tenements, the growth of the rear tenement system and its evils, and to devise a plan for reforms in the housing and immediate environment of the poorer citizens of Chicago."[2] The notion that Chicago had a housing problem was not widely shared at the time. Just eight years earlier, Jane Addams and Ellen Gates Starr had taken up residence at Hull House, the city's first settlement house, on the Near West Side. Since then additional settlements had sprung up in other slum neighborhoods. But outside of a handful of settlement workers and public health officials, few people of means had reason to familiarize themselves with the dwellings of the city's least prosperous residents.

At the conclusion of the conference, attendees agreed on a three-point action plan for housing reform. First, reformers and their allies needed exhaustive surveys to provide information about the housing situation in slum areas. Reforms could not be implemented without adequate data to mobilize public support and inform the activities of housing officials. Second, the city's housing regulations needed to be strengthened and better enforced. Finally, the construction of model tenements—well designed and constructed apartment buildings for the working poor—was necessary to demonstrate to private builders that it was possible to build decent, affordable housing at a reasonable profit.[3] Conference participants could not have known it at the time, but these three activities—data collection, restrictive government regulation, and model housing—would represent the basic agenda for housing reform in Chicago for the next thirty years. Efforts to improve housing conditions would evolve over the years, but these activities would remain at the core of housing reform through the 1920s.

It is worth considering for a moment what conferencegoers did *not* recommend. They did not, for example, call for a program of government-operated housing to complement privately built housing for the laboring classes. Nor did they recommend government subsidies to make the cost of decent, privately built housing more affordable to working people. They did not advocate rent controls to achieve the same goal. All these measures would eventually be widely implemented, in Chicago as well as other cities. But in 1897 they fell outside most people's understanding of the proper division of labor between state and market in the provision of housing. Government, it was assumed, should simply not be empowered to do such things. The few who suggested otherwise were widely dismissed as socialists or anarchists.[4]

Understanding why housing reformers in turn-of-the-century Chicago recommended certain strategies and not others for addressing the problem of substandard housing requires attention to the role of ideas in the policymaking process. Although reformers may not have recognized it, their attitudes were shaped by the paradigm that informed housing policy at the time, a set of ideas whose assumptions about how government and the private sector should properly engage one another limited sharply the actions that public officials could legitimately take. Sam Bass Warner has captured this set of beliefs well in his study of Philadelphia from the revolutionary period to the early twentieth century.[5] In what he calls the "private city," the highly circumscribed sphere of legitimate government activity discouraged public officials from addressing many municipal problems the private sector could not solve on its own, including water supply, sanitation, disease control, compatibility among land uses, and housing. Problems festered in many cases until crisis conditions finally prompted elites to endorse government intervention. As Warner argues, the tradition of privatism was so taken for granted that it needed no defense. Actors could debate policy directions within the framework of privatism, but except in times of crisis, the ideas behind privatism were themselves largely unscrutinized. Like institutions, they served as rules of the game. Those seeking solutions to pressing societal problems were in most cases forced to work within their confines.

Housing reformers in late nineteenth-century Chicago found themselves in a similar situation. At that time government intervention in housing markets extended no further than regulation and oversight, and regulation was limited to the physical structures of buildings to ensure adequate safety and sanitation. It was thus acceptable for government to place restrictions on the construction and maintenance of houses and apartment buildings, but not to set limits on rents charged. Government could enact policies to encourage the private sector to produce housing of a certain type and quality, but it could not erect housing itself. To do so would have violated the tradition of privatism that governed housing policy at the time, and no one seriously entertained this proposition in turn-of-the-century Chicago.

As conference participants gathered on that January afternoon to develop their plans for reform, they no doubt considered the obstacles that lay ahead of them. As members of the group fully understood, their chances for success were deeply affected by the city's institutional arrangements, dominated at the time by a machine-style government that made reform of any kind, including housing, a dubious proposition. Yet there were signs of impending change. Chicago's new housing reform movement was connected to a broader municipal reform movement— under way for several years by this time—whose origins can be traced to the Columbian Exposition, a world's fair that Chicago hosted to commemorate the four-hundredth anniversary of Columbus's discovery of the New World. During the fair's six-month run from May through October of 1893, twenty-seven million people passed through its gates, an attendance record unsurpassed by any tourist attraction since.[6] Planned and designed by architects Daniel Burnham and Frederick Law Olmsted, among others, the exposition was an architectural extravaganza built on 685 acres of sand dunes and marshland along Lake Michigan eight miles south of downtown. The centerpiece of the fair was a "court of honor" featuring a series of imposing beaux arts palaces surrounding a large T-shaped basin adorned with fountains, sculptures, and Venetian-style bridges. The White City, as it came to be known, was an illusion— the buildings were framed with wood or iron, covered with a mixture of plaster of Paris and hemp fiber, and spray-painted white. Within a year it would all be gone, destroyed by fire. But to the casual observer in the summer and autumn of 1893, the White City was an American Venice, invoking the same sense of permanence and grandeur as the great European monuments.[7]

But it was not simply the architecture of the Columbian Exposition that impressed visitors to the fair. The exposition was its own city, with infrastructure, services, and governance structures set up by fair organizers independent of the city of Chicago. There were sewage, water, and power plants, fire and police protection, garbage removal, and a futuristic transportation system featuring electric-powered boats and elevated trains. The streets were clean and orderly, patrolled by a well-disciplined privately operated police force. Visitors to the fair, including Chicago natives, could not help but notice the contrast with their own communities. Turn-of-the-century Chicago, like most large cities at the time, was a case study of urban disorder. Sewage and water systems were primitive and inadequate, causing occasional outbreaks of cholera and other illnesses. Piles of uncollected garbage accumulated in streets and alleys, attracting colonies of rats and other vermin. Crime—including gambling, theft, and prostitution—was rampant, tolerated by corrupt law-enforcement officials. The White City was the antithesis of all this, a model of a more livable and orderly urban American to which all cities, including Chicago, could aspire.[8]

Certainly many Chicagoans were eager for change. Civic leaders and middle-class residents in particular had grown weary of the city's notoriously corrupt system of government. Political power at the time was centered in city council, where behavior generally conformed to the quid pro quo arrangements of machine politics. Votes were delivered and elections won in large part through favors granted by aldermen and ward bosses to residents and business owners, many of them working-class immigrants thankful for help finding employment, negotiating the city bureaucracy, or dealing with law enforcement.[9] When it came to council business, most aldermen were interested only to the extent they could personally profit. Perhaps more than in any other large city at the time, government decisions in Chicago were for sale.[10] The offerings extended all the way from business licenses and minor city ordinances to lucrative franchise agreements for gas, electricity, and streetcar service. Instead of adding to the city's revenue streams, the substantial sums of money that changed hands through such transactions went exclusively into the pockets of "boodling" aldermen.[11]

Chicagoans were aware of such goings on. Stories of corruption in city council appeared routinely in the city's newspapers.[12] But in the aftermath of the Columbian Exposition such behavior grew less tolerable. Civic leaders who had backed the fair as a way of showcasing Chicago's assets and can-do spirit were embarrassed by reports of the city's seamier side, including government corruption, compiled by visiting journalists.[13] By some accounts, the fair and the civic-mindedness it inspired marked the beginning of Chicago's brief flirtation with Progressive Era reform.[14] Leading the way, at least initially, was an unlikely character. William T. Stead was a well-known British investigative journalist and reformer who arrived in Chicago from London the day after the official closing of the exposition on October 31, 1893. Appalled by the conditions he observed, Stead organized a mass meeting two weeks later "to consider whether, if Christ visited Chicago, he would find anything he would wish to have altered."[15] The meeting—part political rally, part religious revival—led directly to the formation of one of Chicago's most prominent municipal reform groups, the Civic Federation. Organized by a group of business leaders and social reformers, including settlement house pioneer Jane Addams, the Civic Federation focused its efforts on government corruption and reform of municipal taxation.[16]

Additional reform groups followed, most prominently the Municipal Voters League. Business leaders created the group in 1896 partly out of frustration with existing reform efforts that had failed to put a significant dent in the boodling operations in city council.[17] The organization's main objective was to elect honest candidates to public office. The strategy was simple: compile information on the activities of all existing aldermen and candidates for office, including corrupt or otherwise unseemly behavior. Prior to every election this information, along with the league's endorsements, was disseminated to voters through direct mailings, pamphlets, and newspaper advertisements. With strong support from nearly all the city newspapers, the group quickly became a major political force. In the 1896 aldermanic elections, twenty-five of the thirty candidates the league backed were elected.[18] By 1900 two-thirds of the seats in city council were held by candidates the group had endorsed.[19]

As the nineteenth century drew to a close, it was clear that reform was having an impact on governance in Chicago. Due largely to the efforts of the Municipal Voters League, corruption in city council grew less rampant.[20] Still, reform was highly uneven. The league's successes were mainly in the city's "silk stocking" wards populated by prosperous middle-class immigrants who had little need for the paternalism of

the ward boss. For people like this, the notion of good government resonated. The slum wards, located mainly along the branches of the Chicago River, were an entirely different matter. Here machine-style governing arrangements had staying power, and their poor fit with the
agenda of housing reform was a condition that reformers were forced
to negotiate. After four unsuccessful attempts to defeat the notoriously
corrupt Nineteenth Ward alderman Johnny Powers, Hull House cofounder Jane Addams withdrew from ward politics.[21] The mostly Italian working-class immigrants here needed help, and Powers was happy
to oblige. As Addams wrote in her autobiography, *Twenty Years at Hull
House*, "We soon discovered that approximately one out of every five
voters in the nineteenth ward at the time held a job dependent upon the
good will of the alderman."[22] This, along with the many other forms of
assistance Powers provided to vulnerable immigrant families, made him
virtually unbeatable.[23] For reformers like Addams seeking to improve
conditions in the city's slum wards, there was simply no getting around it.
They would have to conduct their work in an institutional environment
where machine politics ruled.

* * *

It was against this backdrop of machine and reform that conference participants gathered at Northwestern University Settlement to discuss the
future of housing reform in Chicago. In addition to producing an action
plan for housing improvement, the conference led to the formation of
the city's first organization dedicated exclusively to housing reform. The
Improved Housing Committee, led by several settlement workers, advocated for better housing conditions in the city's poorest neighborhoods.[24]
The group's activities were taken over in 1900 by the City Homes Association, a broader-based and better-funded organization inspired by a
second housing conference held at the Chicago Art Institute in March of
that year. Financed by Anita McCormick Blaine, inventor and businessman Cyrus McCormick's daughter, the City Homes Association produced the first major survey of Chicago tenements.[25] Directed by University of Chicago sociologist Robert Hunter, the study examined three
areas on the city's West Side that were said to be representative of tenement districts throughout the city.[26]

Hunter's key finding was that many of the forty-five thousand people
in the areas he examined were living in squalor, the result of weak and

largely unenforced housing regulations. Landlords seeking to maximize rents built multiple structures on single lots. With little space between buildings, rooms were often dark and poorly ventilated. Approximately half the rooms examined lacked adequate light, and three-fourths of these had less than 400 cubic feet of air per person. Worst of all were the cellar and basement dwellings, where nearly five thousand people were found to be living in damp, dark rooms, infested in many cases with rats and other vermin.[27] In addition to overcrowding, Hunter found large numbers of buildings in ill repair. Defective plumbing and use of out-lawed privy vaults were widespread, and many buildings had no bath-ing facilities. Hunter linked the crowded and insanitary conditions of the tenements to outbreaks of disease such as tuberculosis and scarlet fever along with social problems like crime and alcoholism.

The study came as a shock to civic leaders and other city residents, many of whom had assumed that such conditions, to the extent they ex-isted at all, were exceptional. Unlike New York or London, Chicago, it was believed, had no genuine slum districts. The evidence compiled by Hunter strongly suggested otherwise. As the *Chicago Tribune* edi-torialized, the report provided "ample and unavoidable proof" that the city had a serious housing problem.[28] The question now was what was to be done about it. This was the real purpose of the study—not simply to document conditions in the tenement districts but to lay a basis for re-form. As Hunter maintained, "This report will be of little value unless it proves an incentive, and perhaps a partial guide in the future, to per-sistent and organized preventive and reform efforts."[29] To that end, the report concluded with a set of recommendations for reform in housing policy, emphasizing the need for stronger and more precise building and sanitation laws.

The timing of the study was fortuitous. Municipal reform in Chicago was gathering momentum, driven largely by the successes of the Munic-ipal Voters League in city council elections. With a plurality of league-backed aldermen now occupying the council chambers, the City Homes Association wasted no time developing proposed legislation. In May 1902 a tenement house ordinance the organization drafted was intro-duced by reform alderman William Mavor. A campaign by the Builders Association to defeat the ordinance was unsuccessful, and the measure easily survived a full council vote later that year, with forty-seven in fa-vor and only seven opposed.[30]

The tenement house ordinance of 1902 embodied the view of housing reformers that slums could be abolished if a rigid set of standards was created for the construction and maintenance of buildings, accompanied by adequate enforcement mechanisms. It was a view largely consistent with the paradigm of privatism in housing policy, which the new ordinance served to institutionalize. Housing would continue to be the purview of the private sector, but building owners would be compelled to supply decent housing. Even this idea was potentially controversial. As Hunter put it, "It is possible that at first many people will object to a municipal policy of interference which will hold in check the individual."[31] However, the prevailing view by this time was that housing regulation was a legitimate government function. As the *Tribune* concluded, "It is admitted now that when it comes to the erection of buildings it is inexpedient to let men do as they please with their own."[32]

But would it work? Could housing regulations alone eliminate slums? The new ordinance was a major victory for the City Homes Association and their allies. Provisions of the law directly targeted many of the practices Hunter's study had uncovered, although most applied to new construction rather than existing buildings. Rear tenements could no longer be erected. Limitations were placed on basement occupancy, and apartments now had to include kitchen sinks and private toilets. The ordinance established guidelines for lot coverage, room dimensions, and window sizes to ensure adequate light and ventilation. Provisions also covered the maintenance and repair of buildings.[33] All in all, if the law was properly administered, it should produce a noticeable improvement in the housing stock of the city's tenement districts.

So housing advocates assumed, but they would soon be disappointed. As argued in chapter 1, the prospects of policy paradigms are determined in part by their alignment, or "fit," with institutional arrangements. Housing reform had ridden the coattails of Chicago's municipal reform movement, but despite the impact of reform on institutions such as the city council, machine politics was still very much alive and well in Chicago. This was particularly so in the city's lowest-income wards, the very places that housing reformers hoped to change. There machine aldermen continued the practice of accepting cash payments in return for favorable council action. Only four months after passage of the tenement house ordinance, the council had approved twenty-eight exemptions to the new law.[34] It was never proved, but reformers strongly suspected that money had changed hands.[35] And the problem was not limited to city council. The first line of defense for the new ordinance were the inspectors from the Building and Health Departments, which together shared responsibilities for policing the construction and maintenance of all housing. Inspectors were underpaid, worked alone, and had weak civil service protections—all conditions that encouraged unprofessional behavior.[36] A 1903 Hull House survey of two thousand West Side homes following a typhoid epidemic blamed inadequate enforcement of housing and sanitary regulations for the outbreak, concluding that health inspectors were either incompetent or corrupt.[37] The ensuing public outcry resulted in the dismissal of nearly half the inspection force of the Health Department's Sanitary Bureau, with five inspectors charged with bribery.[38]

But it was not always simply rogue inspectors who were to blame. City council controlled both the Building and Health Departments, and aldermen frequently pressured inspectors to overlook code violations at the request of politically connected building owners.[39] As one city newspaper complained, "It is known that in many cases where the inspectors appear to have done all that lay in their power, action has been staid by the order of their superiors or at the request of aldermen."[40] For housing reformers it was becoming clear that passing new tenement legislation was only half the battle, if that. Attention would also have to be paid to the problem of enforcing housing laws within a political and institutional context frequently hostile to reform.

The crux of the problem should by now be apparent. Progressive Era reform, including housing reform, was not a matter of sweeping away all vestiges of machine-style government so that new institutional arrangements could function as their designers intended. Reform was partial and imperfect, reshaping certain institutions and geographies of the city while bypassing others entirely. This was the unfriendly terrain the leaders of Chicago's housing reform movement were forced to navigate. Taking advantage of new opportunities in one institutional arena, they found their efforts obstructed by contradictory arrangements in another. Instead of stability and equilibrium, the result was frustration and a continuous drive for change. Yet as actors sought resolution to the contradictions in which they found themselves enmeshed, their ability to imagine alternative solutions was itself limited by the set of ideas available to them. As we shall see later in this chapter, housing reformers experimented with new solutions to the problem of slum housing, but during

the early twentieth century such initiatives fell well within the boundaries of the private city. For the time being at least, privatism was the
conventional wisdom, and the views and creativity of housing reformers
reflected widely shared beliefs about the limited powers of government
to address a pressing societal concern.

*   *   *

For a decade and a half following the passage of the tenement ordinance
of 1902, Chicago's housing reformers concerned themselves largely
with the enforcement of housing regulations. During this time the coalition of housing reform groups broadened. Early on, the city's housing movement was led chiefly by a mixture of settlement workers, academics, charitable organizations, and several women's groups. Business
leaders were noticeably absent. However, by 1911 both the City Club and
the Chicago Association of Commerce had begun to take an interest in
the housing question, both groups forming active housing-improvement
committees.[41] Predictably, the concerns of business were somewhat different than those of other reform groups. Social welfare groups emphasized problems of death, disease, and bad citizenship that slum housing
fostered. Business leaders were concerned about these things as well, but
they also emphasized issues of class. Turn-of-the-century Chicago was
a hotbed of radical labor agitation, with frequent strikes and other un-
rest.[42] Better housing, it was thought, would produce a more compliant
and productive labor force, less susceptible to radical influences.[43] After meeting with residents receiving assistance from Northwestern University Settlement in July 1899, college president Henry Wade observed,
"One thing that has struck me forcibly during my investigations . . . is
that I have heard not one word of anarchy."[44] Wade, like other business and civic leaders, was convinced that better housing for the working classes was one way to defuse class conflict and make leftist ideologies less attractive to workers.[45] As the *Tribune* argued, "The evils of
Chicago's congested districts . . . should not be left as ammunition for
the radical agitator. They should be faced by responsible and constructive citizenship and dealt with practically."[46]

An additional concern of business was the impact that slum districts
had on the city's appearance, particularly following the completion of
architects Daniel Burnham and Edward Bennett's 1909 Plan of Chicago.

By this time, the City Beautiful movement in urban planning was in full swing, led principally by Burnham himself, who had overseen plans for Washington, DC, Cleveland, and San Francisco before undertaking the Chicago plan.[47] Like the 1893 World's Columbian Exposition, which Burnham also directed, the City Beautiful tradition drew its inspiration from Europe, emphasizing neoclassical building styles, large boulevards, and extensive park spaces. The Plan of Chicago was praised for these features, but it drew criticism for ignoring the city's tenement districts.[48] Argued Lawrence Veiller, New York City housing reformer, "Chicago will be tested far more by its housing than by its lakefront. It won't do you any good to have that beautiful architectural scheme worked out for the lakeshore if at the same time you have your slums and your bad tenement houses and alleys, as they now exist on the West Side."[49]

Such criticisms struck a chord with Chicago's civic and business leaders. As the *Tribune* editorialized in December 1911, "We are working enthusiastically nowadays for a 'city beautiful.' We shall not achieve it unless we solve the housing problem, and weed out the breeding places of epidemic, of wasting disease, of inefficiency and delinquency. These are the slums."[50] The Association of Commerce agreed. Its new housing improvement committee was created in part to address what had been overlooked in the Plan of Chicago—the need for attractive and livable neighborhoods for working people "in keeping with the 'Chicago beautiful' theory."[51] It was a theme that would carry over to the post–World War II era—efforts to beautify and redevelop one portion of the city were threatened by lingering blight elsewhere. Civic leaders in 1911 were largely in agreement on the solution: eliminate slum conditions wherever they existed.

Both the City Club and the Association of Commerce worked actively alongside other housing reform groups in support of better enforcement of housing regulations, with some success. At the urging of housing reformers, former secretary of the City Homes Association Charles B. Ball was appointed head of the Health Department's Sanitary Bureau in 1907. With the assistance of several reform groups, including the City Club and the Association of Commerce, Ball increased the agency's ranks from eighteen to eighty-one well-trained and closely supervised inspectors.[52] Ball earned high praise from business leaders for his efforts to professionalize the Sanitary Bureau during a time when the Building Department—the other agency responsible for enforcement of housing laws—grew increasingly corrupt and inefficient.[53] Partly through Ball's efforts, the idea that restrictive housing regulations, aggressively enforced, were the most effective way to eliminate slum housing was increasingly institutionalized.

Yet there were limits to what reformers like Ball could accomplish, even from positions of power within the municipal housing bureaucracy. Despite the increased number of sanitary inspectors, the enforcement of housing laws was challenging in part because the duties of staff were split between housing inspection and other activities. Ball called for the establishment of a new tenement house department, headed by himself, that would centralize all housing administration in one agency.[54] But he found it difficult to line up support. Machine politicians opposed the idea because it threatened existing sources of patronage and graft.[55] The City Club, while sympathetic, decided not to make it a priority, concluding that "the difficulties surrounding its immediate establishment are such as to jeopardize other important interests if it were to be pressed now."[56] An even greater setback to Ball's efforts was dealt by the election of William "Big Bill" Thompson as mayor in 1915. A machine mayor, Thompson filled administrative positions with his own political appointees; at the Health Department, both the department head and Ball's own chief assistant lost their jobs to Thompson cronies. Thompson also cut the number of sanitary inspectors from eighty-one to thirty-one and reduced the Sanitation Bureau's budget by one-third.[57]

The limitations of restrictive regulation as a strategy for housing reform were becoming apparent. New building laws, no matter how stringent, could not improve the city's housing stock if adequate enforcement mechanisms were not in place; however, creating such mechanisms alongside up-and-running machine-style governing arrangements was problematic. Housing reformers understood the challenges, but they seemed to have few alternative ideas. In a 1915 assessment of its progress during the previous seven years, the City Club's Housing Improvement Committee reported that its "future work" would focus on "development of a broader regulation of sanitary conditions than now exist, in the hope of ultimately making the regulations so rigid" that better housing would necessarily follow.[58] The goal, in other words, was to perfect existing strategies rather than pursue new directions in housing reform. It was a goal that, while perhaps unimaginative, at least made some sense at the time. Within a few years, however, conditions would begin to change, and the strategies of housing reformers would evolve accordingly.

Race and Model Tenements

Despite the poor condition of the housing stock and the overcrowding of the population in Chicago's slum areas, there had generally always been enough housing to go around. This changed beginning in 1917, when Chicago entered a period of housing scarcity that lasted until 1921. The shortage was brought on by rising labor and materials costs, accompanied by wartime building restrictions, that dramatically reduced new construction.[59] Building permits fell from more than 14,500 annually in 1915 and 1916 to roughly 5,000 per year between 1917 and 1920 even as the city's population soared as the war came to a close and servicemen returned from Europe.[60] At the height of the shortage in 1919, officials estimated Chicago's housing deficit at 50,000 homes.[61]

The housing shortage dealt a severe blow to the efforts of housing reformers to improve conditions in the city's slum wards. Landlords now found that virtually any living space, no matter how squalid, could be rented. Apartment buildings that had been empty for years and ready for the wrecking ball were once again "pressed into service" in order to squeeze the last profits out of them before they were finally demolished.[62] With demand for housing outpacing supply as never before, building owners had little incentive to maintain rental properties. Adding insult to injury, tenement dwellers saw their rents skyrocket—as much as double what they had previously paid—for apartments that in many cases were unfit or barely fit for human habitation.[63]

No one experienced the housing shortage more acutely than the city's African American residents. Despite steady population growth since the mid-nineteenth century, blacks in 1910 still represented only 2 percent of Chicago residents. During the decade between 1910 and 1920, however, the percentage doubled as the black population rose from 44,103 to 109,458 (table 2.1).[64] Much of this increase came during the latter part of the decade, as wartime mobilization and a shortage of white workers drew large numbers of blacks from the South to work in northern factories. From a housing standpoint, the timing could not have been worse. Blacks were already crowded into the least desirable section of the city—a long, narrow strip on the South Side sandwiched between two rail corridors. A 1912 survey deemed the area's housing the most "conspicuously dilapidated" of any of the city's neighborhoods.[65] Many African American families had sufficient means to live elsewhere, but whites

TABLE 2.1. **Black population of Chicago, 1840–1930**

Year	Total population	Black population	Percent black
1840	4,470	53	1.2
1850	29,963	323	1.1
1860	109,260	955	0.9
1870	298,977	3,691	1.2
1880	503,185	6,480	1.3
1890	1,099,850	14,271	1.3
1900	1,698,575	30,150	1.8
1910	2,185,283	44,103	2.0
1920	2,701,705	109,458	4.1
1930	3,376,438	233,803	6.9

Source: Thomas Lee Philpott, *The Slum and the Ghetto: Immigrants, Blacks, and Reformers in Chicago, 1880–1930* (Belmont, CA: Wadsworth, 1991), 117.

resisted—often with violence—the movement of blacks into their neighborhoods. The housing shortage exacerbated the problem. White residents, recognizing they had nowhere to flee if their neighborhoods did "go black," grew increasingly hostile and defensive. Still, blacks had to live somewhere, and existing black neighborhoods could not accommodate the thousands of African American families moving into the city. So the boundaries of the Black Belt shifted, haltingly in some cases and with great speed in others.[66]

By 1919 Chicago had become a racial powder keg. With growing frequency, mobs of angry white residents surrounded the homes of African Americans who dared to violate the color line, chanting and breaking windows. Gangs of white thugs attacked blacks who entered public parks or swimming pools in white areas. The bombing of homes occupied by blacks became increasingly commonplace, resulting in several deaths. Fights broke out in workplaces, on streetcars, and other public places.[67] On a Sunday afternoon in late July it all came to a head. A black teenager named Eugene Williams, accompanied by several friends, placed a raft in Lake Michigan between the white and black sections of a South Side beach. The raft eventually drifted into the white section, drawing the attention of several white beachgoers, who began throwing stones. Williams, who could not swim, became separated from the raft and ultimately drowned. Blacks who observed the incident approached a police officer present at the scene and demanded that an arrest be made. The officer refused, and fighting broke out. The violence spread quickly, resulting in five days of rioting in which 23 blacks and 15 whites were killed, 537 persons injured, and 1,000 people left homeless.[68]

These two developments—the city's racial crisis and the housing shortage—pushed housing reformers in directions they had never before taken, at least not with seriousness and commitment of significant resources. A biracial commission that Illinois governor Frank Lowden appointed to investigate the riots determined that "insufficiency in amount and quality of housing" was an "all-important factor" in perpetuating the city's racial turmoil.[69] Blacks needed more and better housing. So, for that matter, did whites. The current focus of reformers on housing regulation now seemed out of step with governing demands. Even if successful, such an approach could not expand the stock of well-constructed and maintained dwellings. Yet as Chicago entered the 1920s, this was precisely what was needed most. Somehow builders had to be induced to construct new residential buildings affordable to working people, both black and white.

New housing for blacks and new housing for whites—these were two separate problems integrally bound up with one another. From this point forward, privatism in housing policy would be joined by an additional set of ideas about race, dominated above all by the principle of segregation in housing. It was a principle that many civic leaders—both African American and white—largely accepted, at least tacitly. Both blacks and whites needed better housing, but the races would not mix. And housing for African Americans was a distinct and pressing concern because black ghettos, apart from being unsightly and contributing to social pathologies, were directly implicated in efforts to breach the color line. As long as housing was scarce and substandard in the Black Belt, blacks would continue to seek housing in white areas. Better enforcement of housing regulations could be part of the solution, but a focus on regulation alone would not fix the problem. New housing would have to be built.[70]

For the next decade, the effort to eliminate slums in Chicago would extend beyond housing regulations and their enforcement to the construction of model tenements and homes. Model housing, as envisioned by housing reformers, consisted of well-built and -maintained houses and apartment buildings selling or leasing at prices that working families could afford. Intended as demonstration projects, they were meant to show that construction of decent, affordable housing could provide acceptable rates of return for investors. The hope was that successful model housing projects would be imitated by other housing developers, resulting in additional projects either nearby or elsewhere in the city.

Ideally, the process would result over time in the clearing of slums and their replacement with attractive yet affordable residential areas. It was an idea fully consistent with the privatism that informed housing policy at the time. Private developers—not government or philanthropists— would supply housing, and they would do so without subsidies or other public support.

Model housing was not a new idea. The pioneers of Chicago's housing movement had identified it as an important goal even before the turn of the century.[71] However, efforts along these lines had never gotten very far. Some housing reformers argued that resources were better directed elsewhere. Sociologist Robert Hunter, author of the City Homes Association study that documented tenement conditions in Chicago for the first time, argued that enforcement of housing regulations should receive priority. Model homes, he predicted, would be limited in number, unable to make a significant dent in the city's slum problem.[72] Others, including Charles Ball, also expressed skepticism.[73]

Hunter's predictions proved to be on the mark. However, efforts to build model housing would encounter an additional problem that was equally troublesome—the inability to produce decent housing at prices sufficiently low for the laboring classes to afford. This was a conundrum that had bedeviled housing reformers from the beginning.[74] The wages of most workers at the time were pitifully small, barely enough to pay rents for tenements that came nowhere near complying with housing regulations. A 1927 study of unskilled and semi-skilled workers in Chicago found that 95 percent of such individuals earned less than $1,800 per year.[75] Even at the highest end of this range, a worker spending 20 percent of his income on rent could afford to pay only $30 per month. There was housing available at this price, but it was not likely to be in conformance with requirements for safety and sanitation specified by the city's housing laws.[76] As University of Chicago economist Edith Abbott concluded, "Bad housing and slums . . . remain together as one of the consequences of low wages, and it is difficult to see how, even if slums are abolished, they can be kept from reappearing unless people have adequate earnings to pay adequate rents."[77]

Here again, reform efforts in one arena were hampered by their incompatibility with institutional arrangements in another. In this case, however, action was impeded not by the presence of machine-style governing arrangements but by the existing regime of labor regulation, which placed limits on the ability of workers to extract a living wage from employers. In the early twentieth-century United States, two principal options were available to raise the earnings of workers at the bottom end of the pay scale: collective bargaining and legislation regulating wages. The former was of only limited value to many unskilled and semi-skilled workers given the dominance of the American Federation of Labor and craft-based unionism at the time. Craft unions organized only skilled workers, which maximized their bargaining power with employers but left a large segment of the labor force without representation.[78] In addition, many unskilled workers toiled in small establishments or as pieceworkers in their own homes where there was no opportunity for union membership.

For many social reformers, legislation to ensure a living wage was the more promising option. By 1910, concerns about the "sweating" of labor in a wide range of industries led to a national campaign to establish a minimum wage in the US, as Britain had done in 1909 with the passage of the Trade Boards Act.[79] Sweating, a term that became increasingly commonplace by the turn of the century, involved intense price competition and appalling pay and working conditions to minimize labor costs and maximize output. Although a federal minimum-wage law would not be passed until the Fair Labor Standards Act became law in 1938, sixteen states, the District of Columbia, and Puerto Rico passed minimum-wage laws between 1912 and 1933. While these laws applied to women and children only, reformers viewed them as a first step toward gender-neutral laws that could be advanced when political conditions grew more favorable.[80]

Illinois was among several states that introduced legislation that failed to become law. The push for wage legislation in Illinois was initiated in 1912 by the Chicago Woman's Club, which called for a state commission to investigate the pay and working conditions of women and to make recommendations regarding a minimum wage.[81] The city council of Chicago passed a supporting resolution, recommending a minimum wage for women of $12 per week.[82] The state legislature was receptive to the idea, and a Senate committee headed by Lieutenant Governor Barratt O'Hara began taking testimony from employers and workers in March 1913. One of the first employers to appear before the committee was Julius Rosenwald, president of Sears, Roebuck and Company, whose extensive mail-order operations employed 4,732 women, making it the largest employer of women in the city. The hearing did not go well for the Sears executive. Rosenwald revealed that more than 1,400 com-

pany employees earned less than $8 per week. Although there was dis-
agreement about what the minimum wage for women should be, were
such a thing to be established, no one argued that less than $7.50 per
week was sufficient, and most suggested it be considerably higher. Not
only that, but female employees appearing before the committee testified that Sears employed "official scolders" whose job was to "speed up"
the workers. According to testimony, women and girls were routinely
driven to tears by the harsh treatment they received.[83]

By all appearances, Sears was sweating workers. It was an embarrassing moment for Rosenwald, a prominent civic leader and philanthropist.
It was also ironic because Rosenwald, as we shall see shortly, was himself one of the pioneers of model housing in Chicago. His own Michigan Boulevard Garden Apartments would be a disappointment chiefly
because building costs could not be lowered sufficiently to make the development affordable to the low-income workers he sought to house. As
Rosenwald sat before the Senate committee in 1913, however, this contradiction does not appear to have registered. Other employers called
to testify were conciliatory, some even agreeing to voluntarily increase
wages for their female employees.[84] Rosenwald, by contrast, became
angry and defensive, charging the committee with "insincerity and in-
competency" and insisting that the testimony of Sears employees was
"biased, incomplete, and untrue."[85]

On the question of the committee's sincerity, at least, Rosenwald may
not have been completely off the mark. Following several weeks of hearings on the matter, the committee introduced a bill establishing a state
wage commission and setting a temporary minimum wage of $7.50 per
week subject to change by the commission.[86] Unlike similar proposed
legislation in other states, however, the Illinois bill failed to pass, and the
actions of the committee may help explain why. Advocates of minimum-
wage laws in other states emphasized the role of women as mothers. Legislation guaranteeing female workers a wage sufficient to sustain their
health and welfare was needed to protect their childbearing capabilities
and ensure "the future well-being of the race."[87] Given the growing publicity and awareness about the evils of the sweating system and its impact
on women and children in particular, this was a defensible proposition.
Society's interest in a healthy future generation could trump the rights of
individual employers to "freedom of contract."[88]

In Illinois, however, the debate took a different turn. Influenced by
a recent Chicago city council investigation into the connection between

low wages and prostitution, the Illinois Senate committee quickly became fixated on this issue. Dubbed the "white slave" commission by the local newspapers, the committee called to the witness stand a series of young women who testified that low wages had forced them into the streets. The hearings captivated the public's attention, generating nearly two solid weeks of front-page newspaper articles with lurid headlines such as "Legislators Hear Pitiful Tales of Traffic in Girls."[89] The testimony was at times gripping, but not everyone was convinced. Sensing an opportunity, opponents of wage legislation argued that character flaws and poor judgment on the part of women and girls themselves were the real culprits.[90] Members of the committee were forced on the defensive. Were low wages the cause of the "downfall" of women, or was it something else? Who was to say? No serious research was introduced to support either position. In the end, the issue of whether women, as mothers, required state protection was drowned out in a process that descended at times into sensationalism and scandal. Additional efforts to pass minimum-wage legislation in Illinois during the 1910s and early 1920s also fell short, and the state was without a minimum wage until federal minimum-wage legislation was passed in 1938.

By and large, housing reformers understood the implications. Abysmally low wages was the reality for a large segment of the workforce. Most realized that reconciling this fact with improved (and therefore more costly) housing would be challenging, but it did not stop them from pressing ahead with plans for model housing. Between 1919 and 1929 three model housing developments were built in Chicago, two for white residents and one for African Americans. The first was built by Benjamin Rosenthal, a wealthy businessman and civic leader who had been active in an ambitious housing development initiative for the Black Belt that failed to move beyond the planning stage. Rosenthal had big plans for his new development—as many as 10,000 homes by the time the project was fully built out. But it would start much smaller. In July 1919, the same month that the race riots broke out, the corporation Rosenthal formed to raise capital for the project acquired forty acres of vacant land between Eighty-Seventh and Eighty-Ninth Streets on the South Side. Plans were announced for 250 single-family homes for "the more poorly paid working people of Chicago."[91] Costs would be reduced by paying cash for the land and materials, permitting home prices of between $3,500 and $4,000 while still paying a 6 percent return to investors.[92]

The Garden Homes project, as it was called, was intended for white residents. No housing developer at the time would seriously entertain an integrated project. But when the riots broke out in July, Rosenthal briefly reconsidered. Perhaps the project should be for blacks instead of whites? As a member of Governor Lowden's riot commission and advocate for better housing for African Americans, Rosenthal understood that the housing needs of African Americans were greater than those of any other group. The problem was that the site Rosenthal had purchased lay well outside the existing Black Belt. When he broached the idea with others active in the better housing movement, he received no support. Settlement leader Graham Taylor probably spoke for many when he advised that new housing for blacks should be located in areas where it would not "arouse race antagonism."[93] Although Garden Homes became a white project, Rosenthal continued to push the idea of model homes for both the black and white communities as a way "to solve the race problem."[94]

In May 1920, as the Garden Homes development was nearing completion, Rosenthal's corporation was sufficiently optimistic that plans were announced for the construction of 2,000 additional homes. But it was not to be. Just three months later, it was announced that rising costs for materials and labor would force the corporation to increase the sale price of the newly completed homes by $1,700, placing them well outside the reach of the low-income working families they had been intended to house.[95] In the end, the residents of Garden Homes were relatively well-paid workers who came not from the tenements but from more prosperous working-class neighborhoods outside the slum districts.[96] Garden Homes provided these families with better housing than they could have otherwise afforded, but that, after all, was not the point. Recognizing he could not serve his intended population, Rosenthal canceled plans for additional homes, and none were ever built.

From the standpoint of housing advocates, there was an additional shortcoming with Garden Homes. As a project built on vacant land, it did nothing to improve the housing stock in the city's slum districts. This was not a major concern for Rosenthal; his goal was simply to provide better housing opportunities for low-income workers. But by the 1920s leaders of the housing movement were beginning to recognize how model housing might serve the dual purpose of providing decent housing for working people *and* eliminating slums. This was possible if model housing developments were located not on vacant land but within existing tenement districts, where "aged tenements" would be torn down and replaced with "pleasant, sanitary dwellings."[97] A new term entered the lexicon of housing advocates: *slum clearance*. Housing regulations and efforts to better enforce them had failed to check the growth of slum housing. Maybe model housing could do the job.

In fact, Rosenthal could not have used his project to clear slums even if he had wanted to. Illinois law allowed real estate improvement corporations such as Rosenthal's to purchase only vacant land. However, in 1927 the law was changed to enable such corporations to purchase improved as well as vacant property. The amount of land they could hold was also increased from 40 to 640 acres. Not only could slum clearance projects now go forward, but they could be carried out on a potentially massive scale. The bill was largely uncontroversial and passed easily. As the *Tribune* editorialized, it "merely frees private capital from statutory limitations which now make it difficult to engage in extensive housing operations for the poor."[98] By comparison, experiments in New York allowing housing corporations to condemn land and limiting profits on investment were deemed "socialistic remedies which Illinois is not willing to try." New York, in other words, had violated the boundaries of privatism as actors understood it at the time. Chicago was not prepared to go there—at least not yet.

The housing bill was the brainchild of the new Chicago Housing Commission, which reform mayor William Dever had appointed in August 1926 at the urging of housing reformers and civic groups, including the Chicago Real Estate Board. Despite the shortcomings of the Garden Homes project, interest in model housing projects was still strong, and the new Housing Commission made them a priority.[99] The commission included forty-two members drawn from the ranks of business, academia, and social services, but it was dominated by a smaller group of real estate interests, including individuals with plans for new model housing developments in the works.[100] Unlike Garden Homes, these new projects would be apartment buildings instead of single-family homes. With lower unit costs, the developments would be affordable to lower-income families while still generating returns sufficiently high to attract investors and spur additional projects. At least that was the hope.

Two projects were ultimately built, one intended for blacks on the South Side and another for whites on the North Side. They were announced within eight months of one another, and apart from the differ-

ent racial groups they served, they were very similar. The South Side development was undertaken by Julius Rosenwald. The Sears executive, a
member of the riot commission and longtime benefactor of institutions
serving the city's African American population, announced plans for
the Michigan Boulevard Garden Apartments in July 1928. The project,
a five-story apartment building with 421 units, was planned for a six-acre
site along Michigan Avenue between Forty-Sixth and Forty-Seventh
Streets.[101] The North Side project was developed by Marshall Field III,
philanthropist and heir to the Marshall Field's department store fortune.
Field's project, the Marshall Field Garden Apartments, was a five-story,
627-unit walk-up located near the city's Gold Coast just north of downtown.[102] Both developments were, in the parlance of the time, slum clearance projects. Both were located in already built-up tenement districts
where existing buildings had to be torn down, although several lots on
Rosenwald's South Side property were vacant.[103]

Although both men were philanthropists, both Rosenwald and Field
took pains to emphasize that their projects were strictly business ven-
tures, not philanthropic undertakings.[104] Both reasoned that model
housing developments, including their own, stood a chance of significantly impacting the city's housing problem only if other developers
were persuaded to follow their lead. Wealthy philanthropists were few;
profit-seeking developers were many. If the latter could be convinced
that money could be made on construction of model housing, then private enterprise might take the lead in efforts to upgrade the tenement
districts. As Alfred K. Stern, director of the Rosenwald project, put it,
"Mr. Rosenwald objects to the project being considered a charitable
enterprise. The purpose is to provide improved living conditions at a
price which will yield a business return on the investment. This experiment, Mr. Rosenwald believes, will demonstrate that large scale projects can be profitably undertaken in various sections of Chicago for any
group."[105] By "any group," Stern meant African Americans in particular.
A key objective of Rosenwald's project was to demonstrate what no one
else had so far—that carefully planned model housing developments in
the Black Belt could be lucrative business opportunities.

Both the Michigan Boulevard and the Marshall Field Garden Apartments were heralded with great excitement. Describing the Field project, the *Tribune* enthused, "This may be the beginning of the campaign
against the slum districts in Chicago."[106] However, the forecast turned

FIGURE 2.1. Michigan Boulevard Garden Apartments, 1930. Chicago History Museum, Hedrich-Blessing collection, HB-00266-A.

out to be premature—both projects encountered problems that severely limited their impact. Like the earlier Garden Homes project, escalating costs forced the developers to reconsider the income groups their projects would serve. As the project manager for the Field development put it, "Both land and construction costs were so high that we had to about face and make our appeal to an entirely different class of people than originally intended."[107] Instead of "people of very modest incomes," residents would now be people "with more means."[108] Tenants in Rosenwald's project included physicians, lawyers, and engineers, along with moderate-income working-class blacks.[109] More troublesome

still, even with higher-than-expected rents, neither development produced anywhere near the returns that were originally forecast. Rosenwald had promised investors in the Michigan Boulevard Garden Apartments a 6 percent return, but average earnings for the first seven years of
operation were only 1.13 percent.[110] The Field development fared no better, with yearly earnings between 1 and 2 percent.[111]

Finally, in a development that foreshadowed the urban renewal period of the post–World War II era, problems with site control dogged
both projects. When individual property owners learned the developers
were trying to assemble land for large projects, some held out for prices
well above market value. As Rosenwald and Field would learn, privatism under such circumstances had its limits. Unlike the urban renewal
period, when the powers of government were aggressively deployed to
deal with recalcitrant landowners, both Rosenwald and Field were left
to their own devices. Rosenwald was forced to cut a half-acre out of the
northeast section of his development when he could not reach an agreement with property owners.[112] Field managed to gain control of his entire site, but at a significant price—land costs were ultimately triple what
he had originally expected to pay. Not surprisingly, escalating land costs
played a significant role in the lower-than-projected returns on investment for both developments and the need to charge higher rents than
planned.[113]

In the end, neither the Michigan Boulevard nor the Marshall Field
Garden Apartments was successful in sparking imitation projects. No
additional model housing developments were built. It could be argued
that the onset of the Great Depression and the lull in building that followed were contributing factors. Yet even without the economic down-
turn, it seems unlikely that Chicago's model housing projects would
have been much of an inspiration to other developers. All three projects were intended to show that there was money to be made in housing
for low-income groups—that private enterprise on its own could rebuild
aging tenement districts and solve the housing problem. But they demonstrated nothing of the kind. If anything, they suggested strongly that
the private sector was not up to the task—that government would have
to play a stronger role. No matter how civic minded, developers would
not undertake large-scale projects if they could not purchase land at fair
market values. And they would not build projects for low-income people
unless the gap between the incomes of the city's poorest residents and
the cost of decent housing could somehow be closed.

Rent Control and the Challenge to Privatism

One way of narrowing the gap between incomes and housing costs was, of course, to increase wages. But there was also another way—limiting by law the amount of rent that landlords could charge. For a brief period during the early 1920s Chicago flirted with this possibility, and the outcome is telling. It was the peak of the housing shortage in 1921, and rents were skyrocketing, sometimes doubling or more in a matter of months or even weeks as "rent-gouging" landlords took full advantage of the situation.[114] Tenants were furious. The country was in a deep recession and wages were falling, making the rent hikes especially difficult to swallow. Support grew quickly for government intervention of some kind. As one local politician put it, "Constituents will be hanging legislators to the nearest lamp post if something radically decisive is not done to choke these rent hogs."[115]

That winter lawmakers introduced two bills in the state legislature. The first, which tenants groups supported, sought to reduce upward pressure on rents by stimulating housing construction. It called for a joint legislative investigation of "alleged conspiracies in the building trades and allied interests" to maintain high labor and materials costs.[116] If such costs could be lowered, the bill's proponents argued, housing construction would resume and rents would come down as the supply of housing expanded. But it was the second bill that aroused the most interest and enthusiasm among tenants' groups and their allies. This bill would authorize cities to create rental commissions "with power to fix rents and terms upon which an owner or agent could let property."[117] It thus had the potential to provide immediate relief for renters. The bill was introduced on behalf of the Chicago Tenants Protective League by Senator Harold C. Kessinger, a reform-minded Republican legislator from Aurora.

The former bill was largely uncontroversial and received little attention. However, the Kessinger bill became the subject of intense political debate, particularly in Chicago. Real estate interests, not surprisingly, vociferously opposed it. But they were vastly outnumbered by thousands of mobilized angry renters who turned out in large numbers for rallies in support of the legislation. The city's aldermen, many undoubtedly seeking to score political points, endorsed the bill and authorized Mayor Thompson to appoint an aldermanic delegation to visit Springfield and lobby on its behalf.[118] The day before testimony on the bill began, 5,000 people gathered for a rally on Chicago's North Side. Later that morning 1,000 tenants boarded a train for Springfield to attend a demonstration and parade in favor of the proposed legislation.[119]

Despite this outpouring of support, the bill was defeated in the Senate when it failed to obtain the supermajority required by the Illinois constitution.[120] Nearly two-thirds of the Cook County delegation either voted against the measure or failed to go on record.[121] Existing sources do not allow a conclusive explanation for this outcome, but certain developments are noteworthy. Of the two bills introduced to address the rent crisis, only one was consistent with the existing division of labor between state and market in housing policy. The Kessinger bill violated that understanding, and it was on those grounds that it was most aggressively attacked. Until then, rent levels, like the prices of other commodities, had been assumed to be fully within the sphere of the marketplace, off limits to government controls. Kessinger's bill would change this, representing, according to critics, "an unprecedented invasion of the right of private contract."[122] The *Tribune* questioned "the wisdom of establishing a precedent for public control of private property," calling the bill "a long step toward state socialism, if not communism," and a threat to "our entire economic system."[123] The bill, in other words, violated accepted understandings of privatism in housing policy and could be rejected on those grounds alone.

Anticipating such criticisms and perhaps uncomfortable himself with certain implications of the bill, Kessinger devised what seemed a clever solution to this predicament. Housing, he argued in the bill, was not just any commodity. It was a public good—a utility just like electricity, water, or gas. All citizens required housing, just as they needed water and electricity. The prices of these utilities were regulated by government; housing should be no different. If the "light a man reads by and the gas his wife cooks by are public utilities," Kessinger reasoned, "so why not the rooms they read and cook in."[124] Unfortunately for Kessinger, this strategy turned out to be a double-edged sword. Critics argued that investing the state with such broad jurisdiction over housing would be the first step toward a state-run public housing program, an idea that had little support.[125] More damaging still, opponents were quick to recall the lucrative contracts that boodling aldermen had awarded to unscrupulous businessmen for streetcar service, gas, and other public franchises years earlier. Did citizens really want a rent commission subject to control by the same corrupt elements in city hall?[126]

Such arguments may have swayed certain legislators. Still, there was the small matter of thousands of angry voters back home demanding that action in the statehouse be taken. A last-minute amendment to the alternative housing bill—the one calling for an investigation into price-fixing in the building trades—provided a possible escape hatch. The amendment, introduced by Representative John Devine of Chicago, extended the investigation to include rents as well as materials and labor costs.[127] Legislators endorsing this bill could now claim to be on record in favor of lower rents without voting for the Kessinger bill. Put another way, they could support lower rents while remaining faithful to the existing tradition of privatism in housing policy.

*   *   *

As it was, rent control, even if it had become law, would have done relatively little to close the gap between the earnings of low-income residents and the cost of decent housing. It was a short-term fix for what was largely a short-term problem. Rents eventually leveled off, although not enough to make adequate housing affordable to most working families. Yet the fault, for the most part, lay not so much with "rent-gouging" landlords as with a wage structure that provided inadequate earnings for a large segment of the city's workers. Model housing would not have benefited from rent control. Its developers did all they could to keep rents down. In the end, it was not enough.

What this case does reveal is an unquestioning commitment to privatism in housing policy. Proposals to extend state controls to rental markets could be rejected not simply because they would not work (although opponents certainly made this argument) but because they violated widely shared beliefs about the proper division of labor between state and market in the provision of housing. Government had the right to require builders and landlords to furnish safe and sanitary dwellings. It could impose penalties, including demolition of unsafe buildings, on those who failed to comply with housing laws. This was necessary to protect the public's interest in decent housing. However, the price of housing was a different matter entirely. Here the market ruled, and any intrusion by government was an affront to the system of free enterprise, an overreach by an ever threatening state that had to be stamped out quickly before it spread like a brushfire.

So overpowering was this ideological tradition that despite the failure of housing regulation and model housing initiatives to improve the situation, housing advocates could scarcely imagine alternative solutions. And those few who did were able to muster little support for their proposals. Thirty years of experimentation with stronger housing regulations, better enforcement of regulations, and the construction of model homes as demonstration projects had produced few positive results. Economist Edith Abbott's assessment of Chicago's tenement districts in 1936 could have been drawn from the pages of Robert Hunter's study of the same areas more than thirty years earlier. She writes: "Great masses of people still live in very miserable homes and in conditions of almost unbelievable discomfort for this modern period—without the accepted conveniences of modern life, without bathrooms, without a single private toilet for family use, with broken and frozen plumbing, occasionally without a sink, sometimes sleeping in windowless rooms, in dark rooms, in cellars and basements, in attics, in rooms many times illegally crowded."[128] By 1930, the leaders of Chicago's housing movement had largely exhausted what privatism had to offer in the realm of housing policy. And the slums were not going away. Housing reform had reached an impasse.

CHAPTER THREE

A Formula for Urban Redevelopment

There is no agony equal to the birth-pangs of a new idea.—Harold L. Ickes, director, Public Works Administration, 1936[1]

On July 2, 1947, Illinois governor Dwight Green signed into law two housing and slum-clearance bills that would shape the direction of housing and development policy in Chicago for decades to come. The Blighted Areas Redevelopment Act included an appropriation of $10 million for slum clearance, to be carried out by public municipal corporations known as land clearance commissions vested with eminent domain powers. Property acquired and cleared of existing structures was to be sold to private housing developers at prices sufficiently low to attract private investors—hence the need for public subsidy. A companion bill provided an appropriation of $3.3 million for the construction of public housing intended for low-income persons displaced by projects carried out under the Redevelopment Act.[2] While the legislation applied to municipalities throughout the state, it was proposed by civic leaders in Chicago as a tool for addressing that city's housing crisis.

Together, these two bills represented a new formula for urban redevelopment, one that would bring public and private actors together for the first time in partnership around a program for redeveloping the city's blighted areas. Just fifteen years earlier such an arrangement would have been unthinkable. For the first three decades of the twentieth century, relations between the public and private sectors in housing policy had been decidedly adversarial, with government's role limited mainly to restrictive regulation. When that failed to curb the growth of slums, experiments with model housing proceeded largely independent of government, relying almost exclusively on the powers and initiative of private developers themselves.

How did Chicago make the leap from full-throttle privatism in housing policy to the public-private partnerships envisioned in the Illinois redevelopment and housing acts of 1947? Answering this question requires attention once again to the concept of policy paradigms. As we have seen, paradigms serve to constrain political behavior by placing limits on the range of policy solutions that actors perceive as legitimate and achievable. With privatism representing a point of departure rather than a subject of debate in housing policy, housing reformers whose efforts fell short of the mark found themselves with few options. They were, in a sense, boxed in by a set of ideas so taken for granted that even in the face of undisputed policy failure, few could imagine alternative solutions. Yet policy paradigms and the ideas behind them change over time, and in this chapter we shift our focus from the role of paradigms as constraints on behavior to examine how old policy ideas are exchanged for new ones.

Of course there are alternative approaches that could be used to explain Chicago's new formula for attacking the slums. For many social scientists, a more promising direction would be to focus less on ideas—which many view as largely epiphenomenal—and more directly on the material interests at work in this case. Indeed the most widely read and influential account of the 1947 redevelopment legislation, Arnold Hirsch's *Making the Second Ghetto*, takes exactly this sort of materialist approach. According to Hirsch, a small group of powerful "downtown interests," alarmed about the impact of Chicago's blighted areas on the city's business climate and downtown real estate holdings, prepared the bills and maneuvered them through the state legislature and the governor's office. As he explains it, "Locked in a desperate struggle for survival, the city's large institutions used their combined economic resources and political influence to produce a redevelopment and urban renewal program designed to guarantee their continued prosperity."[3] In Hirsch's account of this new policy direction, the mobilization of business leaders and the economic crisis they faced do much of the explanatory work. The ideas behind the new legislation largely follow from the particular constellation of interests that surfaced and the historical conditions they confronted. For Hirsch, the more interesting story is how these actors overcame collective action problems to build the base of support necessary to win the endorsement of the governor and move their proposal through the state legislature.

While Hirsch's argument that downtown interests were the principal force behind the new program is undoubtedly correct, as an explanation of the new legislation his account suffers from two key shortcomings. First, Hirsch does not explain why business leaders selected the policies they did, as opposed to some other approach they may have perceived as equally consistent with their interests. Economic crisis provides a motivation to act, but it tells us little about the concrete form action ultimately takes. Argues Judith Goldstein, "The translation of interests into behavior is not straightforward. The choice from a range of possible strategies to realize economic interests may be as important, perhaps more important, in explaining political behavior than are 'objective' material interests themselves."[4] As Mark Blyth emphasizes, particularly under conditions of uncertainty, ideas are important. They "diagnose 'what has gone wrong' and 'what is to be done.'"[5] As this chapter will show, the views of postwar business and civic leaders about how the problem of Chicago's blighted areas should be addressed evolved over time, and ideas played a key role in the decision of business interests to endorse the approach on which they ultimately settled.

Second, Hirsch's account of the 1947 legislation says little about why or how previous efforts to address the problem of slum housing in Chicago were abandoned in favor of this new approach. As this chapter will argue, the 1947 Redevelopment Act was not a sudden response to a newly perceived problem but rather an effort to break from existing strategies and move in a different policy direction. The new legislation was deeply conditioned by what came before, as well-established practices, power structures, and ways of thinking about housing policy all had to be disrupted before new arrangements could be put in place. In short, the 1947 Redevelopment Act was a case of paradigm change, and to understand how it took place, we need to examine the longer-term process through which one set of ideas and practices about housing policy was rejected in favor of a different approach.

As argued in chapter 1, the transition from one policy paradigm to another begins with growing awareness that existing policy ideas are not working—a condition that may result from endogenous factors such as poor fit with institutional arrangements or exogenous disturbances like economic crisis. Berman and others have argued that the weakened commitment to an existing paradigm under such conditions opens up a "political space" that new ideas can penetrate.[6] At such times, possibilities for policy innovation are greatly expanded. Previous assumptions about the goals of policy and the range of policy instruments appropriate for pursuing those goals are relaxed, as actors may no longer be clear exactly what the paradigm is or even whether or not a paradigm still exists.

Widespread recognition that previously unchallenged beliefs may no longer hold creates confusion and uncertainty about how to proceed.[7] Those for whom the status quo holds appeal may push for minor policy adjustments in the hope that new problems can be addressed without substantial policy revisions.[8] Others, disillusioned with existing approaches but lacking a clear path forward, may experiment with new initiatives on a trial-and-error basis. New, untested policy directions are likely to be accompanied by high failure rates and the need for periodic and substantial course corrections.[9] Actors, in short, are unsure about how to best realize their interests, pressing forward in the knowledge that the new initiatives they champion may fall well short of expectations. Hugh Heclo has criticized power-based models of political behavior, arguing that the policy process is also a form of social or political learning in which policymakers and leaders of interest groups, acting with imperfect information, routinely make mistakes. As he puts it, "Politics finds its sources not only in power but also in uncertainty—men collectively wondering what to do. Finding feasible courses of action includes, but is more than, locating which way the vectors of political pressure are pushing. Governments not only 'power' . . . they also puzzle. Policy-making is a form of collective puzzlement on society's behalf."[10] Such an argument may hold more generally, but it seems to capture particularly well the uncertainty and openness to experimentation that typically accompany a shift from one policy paradigm to another. As this chapter will show, the break with privatism that took place in Chicago's approach to housing policy during the early 1930s was followed by years of mostly unsuccessful policy innovation and experimentation before actors coalesced around the new set of policy ideas embodied in the 1947 Redevelopment Act.

Once a paradigm falls into crisis and the search for an alternative ensues, what factors are most important in determining which of the various new policy ideas being championed becomes hegemonic? Some have used the metaphor of ideas as "road maps" or "flashlights" that illuminate policy solutions during periods of confusion and uncertainty.[11] In this view, the ideas that offer the policy solutions most convincing to those actors powerful enough to advance them hold an advantage. Similarly, Campbell argues that ideas that are presented in a simple, parsimonious, and easily digestible fashion may be more appealing than ideas that are more complex and potentially difficult to comprehend.[12]

Others have cautioned against too great a focus on the properties of ideas themselves, arguing that the success of new ideas ultimately rests on the distribution of power in a given polity. As Hall observes, the decision to reject one set of policy ideas in favor of another is never made purely on the merits of the ideas themselves, since policies inevitably favor certain groups more than others.[13] While paradigms may be discarded because they are deemed ineffective tools for solving societal problems, it does not follow that new ideas achieve prominence simply because they are expected to outperform rival candidates. Instead the selection of new policy ideas is a deeply political and highly contested process. As Hall maintains, "[T]he outcome will depend, not only on the arguments of competing factions, but on their positional advantages within a broader institutional framework, on the ancillary resources they can command in the relevant conflicts, and on exogenous factors affecting the power of one set of actors to impose its paradigm over others."[14] Here Hirsch's account of the 1947 Redevelopment Act is instructive. The ideas behind the new legislation carried weight in large part because of the political influence of their proponents. While a focus on material interests may be insufficient to explain where new policy ideas come from, it can tell us much about whether or not such ideas, once they become the subject of public discussion, are likely to gain traction.

This chapter examines how actors in Chicago responded to a period of uncertainty in housing policy beginning in the early 1930s with the onset of the Great Depression. As I will demonstrate, the federal government's emergency housing program, created during the early New Deal years, called into question long-standing assumptions about how problems of substandard housing should be addressed. The entry of government into the housing market as a developer and operator of housing opened the door to a series of previously unimaginable policy ideas and experiments led by real estate interests, housing reformers, policy entrepreneurs, and other actors in Chicago and elsewhere. By the mid-1940s the question was no longer whether privatism in housing policy could be successfully defended, but rather what form the new division of labor between state and market in the production of housing would take. Both ideas and interests would be critical in determining the final outcome.

A New Deal for Housing

December 14, 1935, was a momentous day for housing policy in Chicago. That morning ground was broken for the Jane Addams Houses, a 1,027-unit public housing development built by the Public Works Administration (PWA) under the auspices of the Roosevelt Administration's New Deal. It was the first and largest of three housing developments the PWA built in Chicago between 1935 and 1937. Located two miles west of the Loop in what PWA officials characterized as a "slum area," the Jane Addams Houses was originally announced as a massive, 160-acre slum clearance project that would require the relocation of ten thousand current residents of the area.[15] These plans were scrapped when it became clear that achieving site control over such a large area would be impossible without lengthy condemnation proceedings.[16] However, the project did go forward as a less ambitious but still historic 24-acre development. The two additional PWA housing developments in Chicago—Julia C. Lathrop Homes on the North Side and Trumbell Park Homes on the South Side—were 35 and 21 acres in size, respectively.[17]

As a New Deal initiative, the PWA's public housing program was designed as a temporary economic stimulus measure that would generate employment and construction activity while responding to the widely recognized problem of substandard housing.[18] All together, the PWA built fifty-one projects in thirty-eight cities before the agency's Housing Division closed its doors in 1937, just four years after it began operations.[19] Although the program was defined from the start as a short-term initiative, plans were being laid for a permanent federal housing program even before ground was broken on the Jane Addams Houses. In the spring of 1935, a group of progressive housing reformers persuaded New York senator Robert F. Wagner to introduce a public housing bill in Congress.[20] After two failed attempts, a revised bill was passed and signed into law by President Roosevelt in 1937. The United States Housing Act created a permanent federal agency, the United States Housing Authority, empowered to work with local housing authorities to finance and build public housing projects. Despite intense opposition from real estate interests, there would be no turning back. The federal government was in the housing business to stay.

The short-lived PWA housing program and the permanent program that followed violated long-accepted understandings about the range of solutions to problems of slums and blight perceived as legitimate and practicable. For decades, housing reformers had labored under the assumption that better housing would be supplied through private initiative, either at the insistence of housing regulators or through more enlightened and socially minded developers of model housing. Now, suddenly, it began to appear that government rather than the private sector would take the lead in clearing slums and providing new and better housing for the residents of such areas. Yet the federal housing and slum-clearance projects of the 1930s and early 1940s did not produce a new consensus about how problems of substandard housing should be addressed. Rather, the entry of government into the housing market opened the door to a series of experiments in housing and redevelopment policy and a lengthy and extensive debate about what the formula for attacking and rebuilding the slums should be. This period of policy innovation took place both on the national stage and in cities around the country.

Given the extent to which privatism dominated thinking about housing reform at the time, the appearance of the PWA housing program and the Housing Act of 1937 require an explanation. How was it that existing ideas about the proper roles for government and the private sector in the pursuit of better housing were so thoroughly reworked? In fact, arguments in favor of public housing had been voiced for some time prior to the New Deal. They had just never found a constituency powerful enough to act on them. Certain public intellectuals had insisted for years that decent housing for the laboring classes could not be supplied through market mechanisms, even if stringent housing regulations were enacted and enforced. The most prominent of these thinkers was Edith Elmer Wood, a New York housing reformer with a doctorate in political economy from Columbia University. In her dissertation, published in 1919 under the title *The Housing of the Unskilled Wage Earner*, Wood meticulously documented the shortfalls of housing regulation and model housing projects in cities around the country, arguing that such initiatives would not in themselves provide adequate housing for low-wage workers.[21] Rather than limit housing reform to such efforts alone, Wood urged that European experiments with housing—including government-built housing—be replicated in the United States. A second book authored by Wood, published in 1931, amplified this argument, this time pointing to a structural gap between the wages of unskilled workers and the cost of building new standard homes. This gap, which was "universal and permanent," made the housing problem "insoluble" under the "ordinary laws of supply and demand."[22] By Wood's estimate, a full one-third of Americans were forced to live in substandard housing due to the failure of the market to adequately serve this income group.[23] Once again, she identified public housing initiatives in such countries as Great Britain and Germany as promising solutions.

Although evidence mounted during the 1920s vindicating Wood's arguments about the insufficiency of restrictive regulations and model housing, it was not until the Great Depression that political leaders became sufficiently disillusioned with privatist solutions that the idea of a public housing program could be seriously entertained. As Sheri Berman argues, policy paradigms can become vulnerable to challenge either through some kind of exogenous shock or crisis that calls existing beliefs into question, or through a more gradual process in which current ideas are increasingly viewed as ineffective for problem solving.[24] By the early 1930s, both of these processes combined to create a fertile climate for new ideas in housing policy. The Great Depression was the trigger. In 1933, Roosevelt's first year in office, weak demand for housing combined with a squeeze on financial institutions to bring housing construction to a virtual standstill. Housing starts that year were a mere ninety-three thousand nationwide, just one-tenth what they had been in 1925 during the height of the building boom. Half of all mortgage holders had by this time either lost their homes to foreclosure or fallen behind in their payments.[25] As the crisis deepened, even conservatives began to lose faith in market mechanisms. Warned President Hoover's secretary of the interior Ray Lyman Wilber in 1932, if private investors failed to step forward in sufficient numbers to provide adequate housing for American citizens, then "housing by public authority is inevitable."[26]

As Hall argues, new policy ideas do not displace old ones simply because they appear to represent more convincing policy solutions. Ideas, in addition to offering credible solutions to pressing societal problems, must also hold political appeal for the politicians responsible for moving them through the policymaking process.[27] The declining credibility of privatist solutions to the nation's housing problems took place in a political climate that had become highly favorable to policies benefiting urban working-class voters. The Great Depression set in motion a party realignment that dramatically improved the electoral position of the Democratic Party, which went from a regional party based in the rural South to a national party with new strongholds in northern industrial cities.[28] Urban voters overwhelmingly rejected the laissez-faire approach of the Republicans to the economic crisis and threw their support behind Roosevelt and Democratic congressional candidates in the 1932 elections. Together with a reapportionment based on the 1930 census that favored urbanized areas, the political mobilization of urban voters helped produce large Democratic majorities in both the House and the Senate. Roosevelt and the Democrats, anxious to tie these new urban voters permanently to the Democratic Party, pursued policies that benefited urban areas, including housing policy.[29] The PWA housing program and the 1937 Housing Act were thus partly the result of changing electoral conditions and the eagerness of Democratic politicians to capitalize on and cement the new Democratic majority.

In 1931, perhaps recognizing the favorable political conditions, several New York City settlement house workers and housing reformers banded together to form the National Public Housing Conference (NPHC), an organization dedicated to the promotion of government support for the housing of low-income people.[30] The group included a number of influential housing reformers, most prominently Edith Elmer Wood and Mary Simkhovitch, the latter a personal friend of Eleanor Roosevelt and New York senator Robert F. Wagner. An opportunity presented itself in the spring of 1933 as Democratic leaders drafted the provisions of what would become the National Industrial Recovery Act (NIRA). Aware that the proposed legislation was to include a major program of public works, Simkhovitch and another cofounder of the NPHC traveled to Washington and urged Senator Wagner, a key architect of the bill, to insert a provision on public housing.[31] Wagner, long an advocate for legislation benefiting low-income and working-class citizens, agreed, and Title II of the NIRA authorized the "construction, reconstruction, alteration, or repair under public regulation or control of low-cost housing and slum-clearance projects."[32] The bill made its way through Congress with few changes and was signed by President Roosevelt in June 1933 as part of the administration's first hundred days of emergency legislation.

Title II of the NIRA established the Public Works Administration, and Roosevelt appointed Secretary of the Interior Harold Ickes to head the new agency. Ickes, a Chicago native active in the city's municipal reform movement, immediately set up a housing division within the PWA to implement the agency's new housing program. Although empowered by law to initiate a program of direct housing construction, Ickes did not immediately do so, choosing instead to extend a program begun by the Hoover administration that provided loans to builders of limited-dividend model housing.[33] Hoover's program had been unsuccessful, due in part to its tight credit provisions. Under the PWA interest rates were lowered, loan periods extended, and equity requirements reduced to 15 percent of the total cost of a project.[34] The response by municipalities was largely enthusiastic. Expectations were high—in some cases wildly exaggerated. Business groups liked the program because of its reliance on private enterprise and the possibilities for profit it presented. In Chicago, civic leaders rapidly assembled a list of ten blighted areas identified as priority sites for PWA funding. Government-financed redevelopment projects for each of these areas would, it was hoped, solve "the city's entire slum problem" by demolishing the worst of the city's substandard housing and replacing it with well-constructed and sanitary buildings.[35]

In fact, the PWA's program turned out to be only marginally more successful than the Hoover administration's earlier limited-dividend program, producing a total of seven completed projects, none in Chicago.[36] Project sponsors had trouble meeting the 15 percent equity requirement and were likely discouraged by the cap of 6 percent on dividends, imposed to keep rents affordable to working-class families.[37] Just seven months after initiating the program Ickes reversed course, announcing its suspension and replacement with a program of direct housing construction.[38] Not surprisingly, the Housing Division's new focus generated opposition, particularly among real estate interests and conservative politicians. Argued one New York congressman, "The federal government has no more right to engage in the ownership, construction and operation of apartment houses than it has in any other private business. It might just as well become the butcher, baker, candlestick maker or undertaker."[39] Ickes was unapologetic, insisting that public housing and other New Deal public works programs were necessary due to "the timidity of private capital and its refusal to come out from under the bed."[40] Private enterprise, according to Ickes, had "left the slums of America's cities to stew in their own unhealthy juice."[41] Indeed the difficulty lining up qualified investors under the Housing Division's limited-dividend program seemed to substantiate this claim. By introducing this program prior to the program of direct housing construction, Ickes and other PWA officials could argue that they gave private investors the first chance to respond to the housing crisis.[42] Only when that failed did the PWA turn to a program of publicly built housing.

Hall argues that resistance to paradigm change by groups benefiting from existing arrangements may mean that a change in the "locus of authority" over policy is necessary for a paradigm shift to occur.[43] With the introduction of the PWA housing program, key decisions about how the problem of substandard housing should be addressed were suddenly being made not by locally based housing reformers or municipal government officials but by federal bureaucrats. This explains how housing reform efforts in cities like Chicago, for decades governed by the dictates of privatism, could be so rapidly and thoroughly refashioned. No new local institutions had to be established to implement the PWA housing program. No local coalition of housing reformers and political leaders had to be assembled on its behalf. Federal bureaucrats ran the program themselves, with minimal participation by local actors. Ickes, a Chicagoan and Progressive Era reformer with firsthand knowledge of machine politics, preferred to avoid local government altogether, fearing PWA housing would otherwise become entangled in patronage politics.[44] In announcing the PWA direct-build program, he indicated that the agency would build housing where it chose to do so, "without the request or aid of the city" if need be.[45]

But what exactly would public housing seek to accomplish? For Ickes the answer was obvious: public housing would clear slum dwellings and replace them with suitable accommodations, to be occupied by the existing residents of such areas.[46] These two goals—slum clearance and public housing construction—were inseparable, since the existence of slums was what gave rise to the need for a government-operated housing program in the first place. Arguments for slum clearance took multiple forms, one being that slums were morally objectionable. As Senator Wagner put it in 1936, wiping out slums had widespread appeal "in humanitarian terms because all of us are human beings, who shrink from the horrors of the slums and want the children of America to live and work and play in healthy surroundings, rather than in an atmosphere oppressively heavy with disease and crime."[47] But the more common argument was economic. Put simply, slums were an economic drain on cities because they used more in services than they generated in tax receipts. This meant that the residents of more prosperous neighborhoods provided an ongoing subsidy to residents of slum areas. In Chicago the gap between tax receipts and the cost of services for fire, police, courts, and public health in the three originally planned PWA housing locations was estimated at $1.5 million per year.[48] A study of Cleveland's slum districts found that such areas required an average annual subsidy of more than three hundred dollars per family. In Indianapolis the chamber of commerce determined that slum areas absorbed 26 percent of the city's funds for services while representing just 10 percent of the city's population.[49] Findings such as these were widely used to justify slum clearance efforts in cities around the country.

For both moral and economic reasons slums could no longer be tolerated, and public housing was needed because new buildings affordable to slum dwellers could not be furnished through private enterprise, as the experiences of model housing developments had already shown. Ickes and other PWA officials repeatedly referenced Edith Elmer Wood's market-failure argument—that one-third of the population was forced to accept substandard housing because that was all they could afford—in justifying the need for government subsidy.[50] It was not simply that private investors lacked motivation to serve this market. Rather, wages for this segment of the workforce were simply too low to pay the costs of decent housing. As Ickes himself maintained, "The record of American housing is proof positive of one thing. Private initiative cannot, unaided, properly house our low income families. It is simply not in the cards. It can make . . . profits by housing our people badly. It cannot make money by housing them well."[51] Public housing would do what private initiative would not and could not accomplish: rehabilitate slums and provide safe and sanitary housing for the people who lived there.

Ickes's views largely converged with those of progressive housing reformers such as Mary Simkhovitch and the NPHC, but not everyone who supported public housing was in agreement. The PWA housing program and subsequent push for a permanent government program revealed competing visions for the future of public housing in the United States, and a significant philosophical divide opened up within the leadership of the housing reform movement. Challenging Ickes and progressive slum reformers was a group of East Coast planners, architects, and intellectuals who had been meeting regularly since 1923 to discuss housing and community planning. The Regional Planning Association of America (RPAA) included, among others, social critic Lewis Mumford and his protégé Catherine Bauer, a recent graduate of Vassar College who would go on to become the leading voice of her generation in housing policy with the publication in 1934 of her widely influential book *Modern Housing.*[52]

Bauer's argument, shared by Mumford and her other RPAA colleagues, was that public housing in the US should follow the example of European countries, where housing built by government following World War I was part of an overall strategy to create new planned communities integrating housing, transportation, schools, and green space. As RPAA cofounder Henry Wright put it, "Real housing is not just a matter of housing: it is a matter of community building."[53] Importantly, this required building on vacant land, not in slum areas, where it would be too costly and time-consuming to acquire sufficient land and prepare it for new development. Slum clearance projects of the sort the PWA endorsed "simply create a small oasis in a surrounding wall of slum," as RPAA fellow-traveler Albert Mayer complained.[54] Bauer herself proposed letting the slums "rot" until land values decreased sufficiently to allow new productive uses.[55] She and others believed that the profitability of slum housing artificially inflated land values in slum districts. Shifting residents out of slum areas to new public housing projects on formerly vacant land would, by Bauer's reasoning, reduce demand for slum property and bring land prices more into line with their real use values.[56]

The PWA did in fact reduce its emphasis on slum clearance and begin to build on vacant land, although this was due more to a US district court ruling that curtailed the agency's use of eminent domain powers than to the arguments of Bauer and her contemporaries.[57] Still, the RPAA and its sympathizers were influential, particularly in the push for a permanent federal housing program. Bauer went on to become Senator Wagner's top housing adviser and coauthor of the Housing Act of 1937, and her ideas about modern housing are evident in the legislation.[58] Among the most significant of these ideas were the arguments Bauer and her RPAA colleagues made about land use. Progressive housing reformers had always assumed that the people living in slum districts would remain there, their situations improved through housing reform and redevelopment efforts that would rehabilitate such areas. Now, suddenly, the future of land use in slum neighborhoods was subject to debate. Should these areas continue to be occupied by low-income residents, or should such individuals be moved to lower-cost vacant land away from the city center, as Bauer and the RPAA urged? If the latter, then what would become of existing slum areas? Should future land use be determined by its potential for profit, or should other objectives be prioritized? Such questions would loom large as debates over housing policy inspired by the new federal housing programs grew more pronounced.

Privatism Revisited

From the start, public housing was controversial, producing cries of protest that were loudest among real estate groups. Yet even in such quarters criticism was at first somewhat sporadic and disorganized. The real
estate crisis, several years under way by the time the PWA Housing Division was established in 1933, had placed real estate interests in a weakened position. Protests were confined mainly to local actions, and even
these often represented more of a nuisance than a genuine threat to the
PWA's housing plans.[59] Opposition may have also been muted somewhat by PWA officials' assurances that public housing would not compete with private enterprise. This was Ickes's mantra, repeated over and
over by him and other PWA officials. Public housing would accept only
those tenants forced to live in squalid conditions because decent housing at prices they could afford was unavailable.[60] Public housing, in other
words, would compete only with slum landlords, and since such individuals were violating building and sanitary laws, they were legitimate targets. As one PWA administrator put it, public housing "will not harm the
owner of good modern housing. Rentals will be markedly below those in
other comfortable decent quarters. One of the chief rental policies of the
housing corporation will be to keep out of the new developments those
families who have paid or are well able to pay higher rents."[61]

As it turned out, however, the PWA was unable to deliver on these
promises. Building and operating costs proved too high and government
subsidies insufficiently deep to set rents low enough for most slum dwellers to afford. As a result, the PWA drew many of its tenants from the
middle rather than the bottom segment of income earners. In 1939, for
example, the poorest third of Chicago families earned $1,250 or less per
year, yet half the tenants in the city's three PWA housing projects had
family incomes greater than that amount, and families earning as much
as $2,332 were eligible to apply.[62] In Atlanta, monthly rents in the city's
whites-only Techwood PWA project ranged from $24 to $39 even though
a 1934 survey found that nearly 50 percent of the city's white tenants
could afford no more than $20.[63] Other cities reported similar findings.[64]
As the realization set in that despite PWA assurances to the contrary,
public housing was drawing a sizable portion of its tenants from middle-
income private housing markets, real estate interests and their allies became more vociferous opponents of public housing.[65]

But it was not simply that PWA housing was available to more than the lowest-income earners. Other aspects of public housing also proved controversial. As discussed earlier, a key justification for government-sponsored housing was that it would be used to rehabilitate slum districts. Slum housing would be replaced by modern, sanitary structures that would improve living conditions and make such areas less of an economic drain on cities. However, building in slum areas required the PWA to obtain titles to the scores of individual properties located within project boundaries, no simple task. Some owners inevitably refused to sell or demanded more compensation than the government was willing to offer, causing delays and in some cases termination of projects. During the PWA's first several months of operation, its bargaining position with individual landowners was strengthened by its eminent domain powers, authorized by Congress.[66] However, in January 1935 a US district court ruled in favor of a Louisville property owner who challenged the constitutionality of the use of condemnation for public housing. When an appeals court upheld the decision several months later, the PWA largely abandoned slum areas in favor of vacant land sites where condemnation proceedings were unnecessary. Twenty-four of the PWA's fifty-one housing projects were ultimately built on vacant land, including two of Chicago's three PWA projects.[67] This pleased the likes of Catherine Bauer and her RPAA colleagues, but others objected. After all, if public housing was neither clearing slums nor providing housing for the lowest income groups—both stated goals of the PWA Housing Division—then what was the justification for this form of government intervention? Ickes and PWA officials were increasingly forced on the defensive.[68]

Finally, public housing developments drew criticism because, as government-owned properties, they were exempt from local property taxes. This meant, in effect, that the owners of taxable property were paying the costs of schools, fire and police protection, sanitation, and other government services used by public housing residents. The PWA did pay a service charge to local governments in lieu of taxes, but the amounts were far less than the assessments that would have been levied had the properties been privately developed. In Chicago, for example, the PWA paid a fee of $39,731 annually on its three housing developments in the city. But according to an estimate by the Chicago Civic Federation, property taxes for the year 1937 would have come to roughly $340,000 if the developments had been under private ownership.[69] Landlords in particular also resented the tax exemption because it lowered the government's housing costs, creating what they viewed as unfair competition with private rental markets.[70]

Real estate interests and their allies criticized all these aspects of public housing, but for much of the 1930s such arguments were weakened by the failure of public housing's detractors to advance a positive program of their own for attacking the slums. Critics of public housing tended to fall back on ill-defined arguments about the need to preserve a role for private enterprise. However, years of experimentation with model housing and other privatist solutions to the problem of slum housing had produced little in the way of results. Public housing may have had its shortcomings, but it at least offered an alternative to the widely acknowledged failures of the past. If a government-sponsored housing program was not the most effective way to rehabilitate slum districts and provide decent housing for those forced to live in squalor, then what was?

In 1938 a group of Chicago civic leaders and real estate professionals claimed they had found the answer. Due in part to the effectiveness of New Deal institutions such as the Federal Housing Administration, whose federally guaranteed mortgage insurance program made homeownership affordable for broad segments of the population, housing markets rebounded significantly by the late 1930s.[71] The recovery energized real estate interests, restoring profits and giving real estate professionals renewed confidence in the ability of private enterprise to meet the nation's housing needs. Especially with the passage of the Housing Act of 1937—creating a permanent government-operated housing program to continue the work initiated by the PWA Housing Division—real estate interests were newly emboldened to defend their turf and head off what appeared to be a serious threat of long-term government intrusion into the housing market.[72]

In Chicago, this new sense of urgency on the part of real estate interests led to the creation of the Chicago Building Congress, an organization established in December 1938 to develop plans and advocate for legislation to facilitate the rebuilding of Chicago's blighted areas by private enterprise.[73] The group, the brainchild of several members of the Chicago Real Estate Board and National Association of Real Estate Boards (NAREB) executive vice president Herbert Nelson, singled out land assembly as the principal barrier to effective action.[74] Previous efforts to redevelop the slums through private initiative had foundered in part on this question. As we saw in chapter 2, philanthropists Julius Rosenwald and Marshall Field both made attempts to replace slum districts with model housing for working people; both projects were compromised by uncooperative landowners who either refused to sell or held out for prices well above market value. Housing reformers at the time were in agreement that projects to clear and redevelop slums should be substantial in scale, a minimum of four square blocks.[75] This would allow a new development to define the character of its project area, removing all vestiges of blight. But it also meant that a small number of holdouts could threaten entire projects. A way had to be found to prevent this from happening.

The solution the Chicago Building Congress devised was deceptively simple: create a vehicle to provide private developers with eminent domain powers they could use to achieve site control. The organization's proposal, which would require new state legislation, called for the creation of "public service building corporations" that would be chartered by the state and operate under state supervision in much the same way that public utilities were regulated.[76] Such entities could function only in areas which the Illinois Housing Board had certified as slum and blighted; project boundaries would also be subject to board approval. Developers would have to purchase at least 51 percent of the properties in their project areas by private contract, but with board approval they could use condemnation powers to assemble the remaining properties. Real estate interests and other business leaders praised the proposal, hopeful that a solution to one of Chicago's most vexing problems was on the horizon.[77] Armed with new tools to facilitate land assembly, private developers might be enticed to experiment with new slum clearance projects. Argued one officer of the Chicago Real Estate Board: "It is not inconceivable to suppose that within a few years from the passage of the act, the slum districts . . . enveloping and smothering the downtown retail areas may be transformed into healthy residential communities."[78]

Of course real estate interests and other members of the business community liked the idea, not simply because they thought it might work but because it represented an alternative to the redevelopment of slums through government action. The proposed legislation was in part an effort to ward off the ominous threat of a vastly expanded public housing program. Its backers sought to resurrect privatism in housing policy, providing new tools that would enable private developers to do the job this time around. Public service building corporations offered both a rationale for privatism's earlier failures and a recipe for future success. Defenders of the proposal repeatedly drew sharp contrasts between their plans to redevelop the slums through private enterprise and the federal government's public housing program, now permanently institutionalized and threatening to engulf even more of the private housing market.[79] Stark choices were presented between public housing, funded by tax dollars through ongoing subsidies, and public service building corporations, which required no subsidies whatsoever.[80]

In certain respects, the goals that public service building corporations were intended to achieve were similar to what developers of model housing like Julius Rosenwald and Marshall Field had envisioned a decade earlier. Both men sought to rehabilitate slum areas by gaining control of a substantial area of land, removing existing structures, and erecting in their place good modern housing. Moreover, both sought to demonstrate that such efforts were possible through private initiative. But the similarities largely ended there. Like the progressive housing reformers with whom they sympathized, Rosenwald and Field were concerned most about the living conditions of slum dwellers. The model homes they built were intended as residences for low-income families and individuals, even if they largely failed to realize these ambitions. By contrast, members of the Chicago Building Congress had other plans for the future population of the city's blighted areas. Seizing on an idea that Catherine Bauer and other members of the RPAA had endorsed several years earlier, organization leaders identified the rebuilding of the city's blighted districts as an opportunity to rearrange land use.

Bauer and her colleagues had called for the construction of public housing on vacant land, which would siphon low-income residents out of blighted areas and create opportunities for new types of land use there. While opposed to public housing, the Chicago Building Congress liked the idea of opening up the future of land use in such areas to discussion. As its supporters pointed out, many of the city's blighted areas were in otherwise desirable locations, close to downtown and the lakefront, the city's major parks, museums, universities, and train stations.[81] Features such as these suggested that there were other, potentially more profitable uses for such areas than housing for low-income residents. Slum clearance represented an opportunity to start anew. Why not base decisions about future development on the "highest and best use" of land instead of assuming that previous uses should set the pattern for the future? As one member of the Chicago Building Congress insisted, "It is fallacious thinking that the current use of a slum area should be its continuing use. Merely replacing unfit buildings with other buildings for [low-income residents] does not necessarily put the area to its highest and best use, nor does it assist orderly city development. The proposed public service building corporations would use their property so as to conform to its proper and best uses."[82]

In making such arguments, backers of the plan drew sharp distinctions between housing for low-income people and slum clearance. This was a new idea. All previous slum clearance initiatives in Chicago, including model housing and the PWA housing program, had been undertaken with the rehousing of low-income residents as the ultimate goal. Slum clearance and low-income housing went hand in hand, the former justified by the need to provide safe and sanitary dwellings for residents of the city's blighted areas. By contrast, the Chicago Building Congress and its allies based their arguments for slum clearance on a desire to maximize the profitability of land. The housing of low-income people was a separate question that did not much concern them. If anything, reclaiming blighted areas for their highest and best uses seemed to rule out prospects for much in the way of housing affordable to the city's lower-income residents.

Arguments about rearranging land use in the city's slum districts proved alarming to residents of such areas, particularly African Americans. Black leaders portrayed the new plan as a "land grab" whose purpose was "to reclaim the near south side from Negroes for white loop workers and large apartment buildings . . . from which Negroes would be [excluded] either because of color or inability to pay high rents."[83] Restrictive covenants still in force in white areas of the city would leave displaced blacks with few options other than to seek alternative housing within the Black Belt. The outcome would no doubt be further overcrowding and doubling up within the city's least desirable black neighborhoods, the best locations having been cleared of existing residents and rehabilitated for use by middle-class whites.[84]

For black Chicagoans, housing reform had been a decades-long string of disappointments, and this was just the latest injustice. Restrictive housing regulations enacted during the early twentieth century had done little to improve living conditions for African Americans, who occupied the worst of the city's slum districts. Experiments with model housing had not fared much better. Julius Rosenwald's Garden Homes project had cleared several blocks of substandard housing in the Black Belt and provided superior living conditions for the few who were fortunate enough to secure accommodations there. However, most black families could not afford the rents, and Rosenwald's project had failed to spark interest in the construction of additional model housing projects in the city's black neighborhoods.

More recently, the PWA housing program had been a particular source of frustration for African Americans. Shortly after the announcement of its first Chicago project for the West Side in September 1934, the PWA announced a second Chicago project, this one intended for blacks.[85] The thirty-five-acre project was located near Lake Michigan several blocks west of the white middle-class South Side communities of Kenwood and Hyde Park. Residents of these lakefront communities protested, arguing that the development would harm their property values and serve as a gateway for the movement of blacks into their communities.[86] Efforts to halt the project slowed progress, and by the spring of 1936 frustrated PWA officials announced its abandonment.[87] Although the PWA eventually reconsidered, the funds earmarked for construction had by this time been appropriated elsewhere, and it would be years before the project was finally complete.[88] As the debate raged over the public service building corporation plan in the spring of 1939, three PWA housing projects were already in operation, all in white or mostly white areas of the city.[89] Meanwhile the city's African American population, which everyone agreed was the group most in need of housing relief, was left with little more than the assurances of federal housing officials that public housing would eventually serve their communities.

When a bill creating enabling legislation for public service building corporations was introduced in the Illinois General Assembly in March 1939, blacks were determined to fight it. The bill, drafted by the Chicago Building Congress, was sponsored by Richard J. Daley, the future Chicago mayor who was then a newly elected state senator serving as an emissary for the Chicago Democratic organization in Springfield.[90] As written, the proposed law would apply to all municipalities with twenty-five thousand or more residents. This meant that a substantial number of communities throughout the state had a direct stake in the outcome. Any misgivings about the bill among downstate legislators would have to be offset by a strong show of support from the Chicago delegation. As the bill's sponsors prepared for its first reading in the Illinois Senate in June, however, support among Chicago lawmakers was not unanimous. Not surprisingly, the city's black state legislators registered strong opposition.[91] In addition, the city council's subcommittee on housing, under pressure from an influential black alderman representing the African

American Second Ward, voted to recommend against passage.[92] To the dismay of supporters, dissent from the Chicago delegation was accompanied by criticism from downstate legislators when the bill finally made it to the Senate floor. Some lawmakers argued that the eminent domain provision allowed private corporations too much discretion, while others expressed concerns about the absence of any provision to help families displaced by slum clearance projects obtain new housing.[93] Support in the Senate proved strong enough to weather the opposition, and the bill made it through on a vote of 35–3.[94] However, it died in the House when fierce opposition prevented it from coming up for a vote before the end of the legislative session.[95]

Two years later when the General Assembly convened for its sixty-second session, the Chicago Building Congress decided to try again. This time they were taking no chances. A major outreach effort designed to win over previously skeptical lawmakers had resulted in dozens of changes to the bill.[96] Most important, restrictions on eminent domain powers were tightened. Developers would now have to secure at least 60 percent of the property in their project areas by private contract before condemnation powers could be exercised, up from 51 percent under the previous bill. Black opponents found themselves far more isolated than before, and after strong votes of approval in both the House and the Senate, Governor Green signed the legislation on July 9, 1941.[97] African Americans were bitter. As the *Chicago Defender*, the city's most prominent African American newspaper, editorialized, "With the acute housing problem existing in Negro communities, the legal mechanism of restrictive covenants and the impossibility of Negroes to obtain available housing units in other areas, the measure will only serve to make more chronic an already untenable condition."[98] This assumed, of course, that the new legislation would be used by private developers to initiate slum clearance and redevelopment projects. But whether this would really happen was still an open question.

Old Adversaries, New Friends

The new redevelopment legislation sparked an initial flurry of activity in Chicago, mostly by public officials. Just nine days after Governor Green signed the bill, the Chicago Plan Commission designated the boundaries of three "blight districts" that would be suitable for redevelopment under the new law. The purpose was "to give private capital an idea of where neighborhood redevelopment most effectively might be started."[99] Two of the three areas were in mostly white neighborhoods on the North and West Sides; the third was in the South Side Black Belt. To help generate interest and enthusiasm, the Chicago Association of Commerce organized a tour of the three areas for developers and civic leaders.[100] Soon afterward, the city council passed an ordinance authorizing the mayor to appoint a five-member redevelopment commission, a requirement of the state enabling legislation.[101] However, just three weeks later Japan attacked Pearl Harbor and the country was suddenly at war. Dreams of massive redevelopment were replaced by the hope that "one or two demonstration projects" might be possible "to set the pace for the future."[102] Even that proved to be overly optimistic. Between the impact of World War II on construction and a court challenge to the constitutionality of the new law, not a single project had been initiated by the time the war began winding down in 1945.[103]

By this time skepticism had grown, both in Chicago and elsewhere, that eminent domain powers alone were sufficient to interest private developers in slum and blighted areas. During the early 1940s, ideas about how the attack on the slums should commence were circulated by a number of interest groups, public intellectuals, and government agencies, all seeking to influence the agenda for what was expected to be a significant federal government role in urban redevelopment when the war finally ended. As one observer noted at the time, "The air is full of schemes for the large-scale rebuilding of cities."[104] Although various ideas were proposed, most emphasized participation by the private sector, and most agreed that in addition to the problem of land assembly, a second key obstacle had become increasingly apparent: the prohibitively high cost of land in blighted areas. This seeming paradox was explained by the scarcity of land in urban centers and the proximity of many slum areas to such amenities as downtown business districts and transportation arterials, creating "exaggerated hopes for future use."[105] Excessive land costs meant that private developers had trouble making slum clearance projects work financially. Prospective investors realized that once they had purchased the properties in a project area and paid for demolition and clearance, costs would be too high to allow for adequate returns on investment. They would be better off building in the suburbs, where land was cheap and plentiful.

Among the various proposals for urban redevelopment being floated during the early 1940s, two stood out as particularly influential. One study was produced by NAREB's Committee on Housing and Blighted Areas, the other by two economists, Alvin H. Hansen and Guy Greer.[106] Both addressed the issue of high land costs in slum areas head on, and they came to similar conclusions. What was needed, according to both studies, were federal subsidies for the purchase and clearance of slum properties so that land could be offered to developers at prices in line with its actual redevelopment value. Government funds would be used to "write down" the cost of land by an amount necessary to make slum clearance projects financially attractive. As historian Mark Gelfand described the thinking at the time, the "difference between the price and reuse value determined the 'write-down' that would have to be absorbed by society if any new building on these sites were to occur."[107] Although NAREB and Hansen and Greer had different ideas about how this arrangement might be structured in practice, all were in agreement that federal subsidies in some form were needed to bring land costs down to a level that would spark developer interest and make blighted areas competitive with locations in the suburbs and outlying areas of central cities.

For real estate interests in particular, the idea of federal subsidies for private housing developers was a drastic departure. Ever since housing reformers began pushing for stronger building and sanitary regulations as a way of improving slum districts, the relationship between government and property owners had been an adversarial one. Government's role involved intervening in real estate markets in ways that real estate interests frequently perceived as interfering with their ability to extract the maximum value from property, whether it was restrictive regulations or the production of government-owned and -operated housing. Now, suddenly, government was no longer the enemy. The call for federal subsidies to stimulate private development involved a dramatic rethinking of the way in which the public and private sectors should properly engage one another in housing policy. It was a frank admission by real estate interests that privatism had failed and that the adversarial relationships of the past would have to give way to new forms of public-private cooperation. As NAREB's Arthur W. Binns put it in 1941, "Urban blight is destroying city values. Short of nationalizing real estate, government alone cannot solve the problem. Unaided private effort cannot solve it. We propose a partnership between private and public effort that can wipe out mistakes of the past, [and] tremendously strengthen our whole urban economic structure."[108]

From this point forward, the idea of public-private cooperation would be central to new slum clearance and redevelopment initiatives, whether they originated with the federal government or with individual states and cities. Both the NAREB and Hansen and Greer proposals formed the basis for new federal urban redevelopment bills introduced separately in the spring and summer of 1943 by Utah senator Elbert Thomas and New York senator Robert F. Wagner.[109] Although neither bill made it to the Senate floor, both were influential in the emerging national debate over urban redevelopment. During the next two years, as the prospects for new federal legislation remained uncertain, several states, including Illinois, passed urban redevelopment legislation of their own in which public subsidies to write down the cost of slum properties were identified as a key mechanism to induce private investment.

The Illinois legislation was drafted by the Metropolitan Housing and Planning Council (MHPC), a Chicago-based civic organization formed in 1934 that had become one of the city's most influential housing reform groups. Originally known as the Metropolitan Housing Council before changing its name to acknowledge the organization's growing involvement in planning, the MHPC was a diverse group whose board of governors included real estate professionals, business leaders, labor union officials, industrialists, city planners, academics, and better housing activists. Its president, Ferdinand "Ferd" Kramer, was a prominent real estate broker and developer with liberal political leanings who supported public housing and sympathized with the views of progressive housing reformers. Kramer had expressed strong misgivings about the Chicago Building Congress's proposal to provide private developers with eminent domain powers, questioning whether any new housing produced in this fashion would be affordable to the low-income and working-class families currently living in slum areas.[110] Arguments that redevelopment projects should adhere to the principle of "highest and best use" irrespective of concerns about how displaced slum residents would be rehoused were objectionable to Kramer and many of his MHPC colleagues. Still, MHPC's membership included real estate interests and other members of the business community, and many, including Kramer himself, were drawn to the idea of private developers playing a prominent role in slum clearance and redevelopment projects. New ideas about public-private partnerships and government subsidies for slum clearance were attractive to organization leaders as long as such plans did not rule out public housing "for those who cannot pay an economic rent."[111]

In the fall of 1942, MHPC established a committee on postwar planning, whose efforts included the development of a legislative agenda to foster the rebuilding of slum areas after the war came to a close.[112] By the winter of 1944, with federal urban redevelopment legislation stalled in Congress, the committee had begun work on two pieces of proposed state legislation. The first was a "modification" of the US Senate bill based on Hansen and Greer's proposal for a government write-down of land costs for slum clearance projects.[113] MHPC's proposed law placed the responsibility for land assembly and clearance with local public agencies—either housing authorities or land clearance commissions—authorized to receive grants from the state. Land clearance commissions could use state funds to assemble and clear land for private development, in keeping with the Hansen and Greer idea of public subsidies to reduce land prices. Local housing authorities could do likewise, but they could also use the money for public housing, a provision that MHPC viewed as essential but that would become the subject of considerable contention. A second bill authored by MHPC proposed amendments to the state's insurance statutes to liberalize restrictions on insurance companies' participation in housing developments. This was considered necessary because insurance companies were viewed as the most likely investors in new housing developments to be carried out under the provisions of the first bill.[114]

Getting the bills through the state legislature would be no simple task. However, MHPC was able to use its influence to recruit the state's two most powerful politicians—Governor Dwight Green and Chicago mayor Edward Kelly—as sponsors. Kelly agreed to sponsor the first bill and Green the second, and both men pledged support for the entire legislative package. It was an unlikely alliance. Green was a Republican elected in 1940 just one year after losing to Kelly in a bitter and hard-fought contest for mayor of Chicago. Kelly, boss of the Cook County Democratic organization and de facto leader of the statewide Democratic Party, competed with Green and downstate Republicans for votes and patronage.[115] Yet the two rivals had certain incentives to reach an accommodation. While the Republican Party had firm control of the State Senate, the House was almost evenly split between Republican and Democratic legislators.[116] Given this, neither Green nor Kelly could be confident about passing legislation that lacked bipartisan support. Moreover, Green had just narrowly defeated his Democratic challenger in the 1944 governor's race and was feeling the need to broaden his electoral base.[117] Being identified with initiatives that benefited Chicago might help boost his vote totals in the city and Cook County. In January 1945, at the invitation of the governor, Kelly visited the executive mansion in Springfield for a much-heralded meeting with Green at which the two former enemies promised to work together on a series of initiatives, including housing and slum clearance, Chicago's public transit system, and redistricting.[118]

Of the two urban redevelopment bills MHPC drafted, it was the one enabling local public agencies to receive state grants for demolition and clearance of slum properties that proved most controversial. The legislation had the support of labor and housing reform groups, including the National Public Housing Conference.[119] However, it was strongly opposed by members of the Chicago Real Estate Board, who disliked the provision allowing local housing authorities to receive state funds. They wanted all state funding to be used to subsidize private development, an outcome that would be certain only if land clearance commissions rather than housing authorities were the conduit for state grants. Such an arrangement was unacceptable to Mayor Kelly, the sponsor of the bill.[120] Kelly was a supporter of public housing who had taken a special interest in the Chicago Housing Authority (CHA) since its creation in 1938, protecting it from political interference and pointing to it with pride as a "clean" agency off limits to the spoils system of machine politics.[121] For Kelly, the new legislation was an opportunity to further enhance the capacity and prestige of one of his showcase public agencies. Moreover, blacks were key members of Kelly's electoral coalition, and new public housing for African Americans would no doubt enhance his standing within the black community.

MHPC was also agreeable to the designation of the CHA as recipient of state urban redevelopment funding. For the organization it was an arrangement well suited to help local government achieve a proper balance between private development and public housing, since local housing authorities could either clear and sell land to private developers at a discount or build public housing. In the end, however, ambiguities about which type of housing—public or private—would be emphasized made the legislation largely unworkable in practice. With the support of both Governor Green and Mayor Kelly, the bill easily passed both houses of the General Assembly and was signed by the governor in the summer of 1945.[122] However, the ink was barely dry on the new law before fighting erupted over how the money would be spent. As expected, Mayor Kelly refused to create a land clearance commission and designated the CHA as the recipient of Chicago's share of the new state funds.[123] In combination with a new municipal bond issue, this would give the CHA up to $9.3 million for slum clearance and redevelopment. Kelly wanted the money used exclusively for public housing, arguing that was the intent of the legislation. Green, whose main interest in the bill was its potential to support private development, made the opposite claim—that the law was meant to stimulate private investment, not build public housing.[124] Any hope of a compromise seemed to vanish when the chairman of the state housing board, the agency responsible for dispersing state funds, announced in November that all applications from the CHA for funds to support the construction of public housing would be denied.[125] MHPC could only look on helplessly as the bill it had painstakingly crafted and shepherded through the legislature did little more than reignite the debate over public housing versus private enterprise as the preferred vehicle for attacking the slums. Two years after the bill became law, ground had yet to be broken on any housing, public or private, built under the new legislation.[126]

A New Partnership

Despite years of policy innovation and experimentation, a workable method for urban redevelopment continued to elude proponents of slum clearance and better housing in Chicago. Public housing developments built by the PWA and the US Housing Authority had provided improved living conditions for some, but even most public housing supporters agreed that this was only a partial solution. In the ten years since ground had been broken on the city's first PWA project, public housing had cleared just 150 acres of an estimated 15,000 acres of blight.[127] Private sector involvement seemed crucial, but legislation authorizing eminent domain powers and public subsidies for private developers undertaking slum clearance projects had yet to produce any positive results. Slum clearance legislation passed in 1941 and again in 1945 to facilitate private sector participation had not been used to initiate a single project.

Still, as unsatisfactory as these experiments had ultimately been, something had been learned from each of them, and there was a sense on the part of slum clearance and better housing advocates that even though efforts up to this point had come up short, they were at least on the right track. Despite the disappointing aftermath of the 1945 slum clearance legislation, MHPC and other business and civic leaders remained convinced that the basic idea behind the law—using the powers of government to assemble slum land and offer it to private developers at a reduced cost—was sound.[128] The problem was that the legislation did not offer a direct and unambiguous path for achieving this objective. Broadly permissive, the new law could accommodate various approaches to urban redevelopment, including ones emphasizing public housing rather than private initiative, as Mayor Kelly's actions had shown. Kelly's preference for public housing not only violated MHPC's intent in framing the legislation but also revealed the uphill battle that any new state law appropriating funds for public housing construction would face.

At first MHPC tried to make the existing legislation work by better articulating the organization's slum clearance goals, reworking its ideas about the role of public housing, and seeking public support for its program. Continuing its role as slum clearance policy entrepreneur, MHPC formed a redevelopment committee in 1946 whose objective was to develop and "bring into use" a workable formula for urban redevelopment.[129] The committee developed a four-point "program of action" that included the following steps, to be taken by public officials: "acquire slum land" using eminent domain powers where necessary; provide a "one time subsidy" to bring the cost of land down to its "real use value"; market discounted land cleared of existing structures to private developers; and offer assistance "to displaced families in finding other housing."[130] With the exception of the final item, the formula was by now mostly familiar. As the committee itself noted, the idea was "in no sense original in concept or thinking," having found "some expression as public policy in laws of various states, in proposed federal legislation, etc."[131] It was also largely consistent with what organization leaders had had in mind when they framed the 1945 slum clearance legislation. Noteworthy this time around, however, was the absence of any direct reference to public housing. This was no accident. The public housing provisions of the 1945 bill had made it highly controversial, jeopardizing its passage, and MHPC was eager to downplay any role that public housing might assume in its current plans.

As it turned out, public housing would figure prominently in MHPC's four-point program but not in the way organization leaders had envisioned or advocated in the past. Until now MHPC had distinguished itself from real estate interests by insisting, along with liberal housing reformers, that government-operated housing was needed to address the failure of private initiative to provide suitable housing for low-income residents. However, recent experience had shown that there was an additional problem that public housing could potentially help solve: the need to find new homes for residents displaced by slum clearance projects. With residential occupancy rates in Chicago approaching 100 percent, it was inconceivable that all such individuals could find someplace else to go, and slums could not be cleared until they were completely vacated.[132] New public housing units could provide a refuge for these residents, allowing slum clearance projects to move beyond the planning phase.

Politically, there were good reasons to link public housing and slum clearance in this fashion. Real estate interests found arguments for public housing based on market failure unpersuasive, but they might accept a certain number of housing units as the price to pay for a potentially lucrative slum clearance and redevelopment program. It was worth a try. From this point forward, public housing in Chicago became identified more and more with relocation housing. Even the liberal Ferd Kramer made the adjustment, arguing in 1950 that public housing was no longer "merely a resource for raising the shelter standards of the low-income group" but instead "the critical key to freeing land for redevelopment by private enterprise. In the last analysis, the rate of relocation will determine the construction schedule."[133]

John Campbell argues that ideas that are presented in a simple, parsimonious, and easily digestible fashion may be more appealing than ideas that are more complex and potentially difficult to comprehend.[134] Certainly MHPC's four-point plan was direct and simple to grasp, far more so than the vaguely worded slum clearance program it had drafted and helped maneuver through the legislature the previous year. The plan was publicly unveiled in October 1946 at a carefully orchestrated luncheon to which some three hundred civic and political leaders, along with media representatives, were invited.[135] As MHPC's Ferd Kramer later recalled, "It was probably the first time in history that all of Chicago's five newspaper publishers attended the same civic luncheon."[136] The keynote speaker was Henry T. Heald, president of the Illinois Institute of Technology, a South Side institution whose efforts to purchase and redevelop neighboring slum properties had contributed to MHPC's thinking about slum clearance and redevelopment. In a passionate speech based in part on personal experience, Heald implored the audience to rally behind MHPC's program, carefully articulating why it was necessary and likely to succeed.[137] Grace Skogstad and Vivien Schmidt emphasize the importance of "discursively strategic political actors" to paradigm change, emphasizing their capacity "to exploit contextual developments, particularly contexts of uncertainty, to create a 'crisis narrative' that creates an opening for new understandings of public policy."[138] Heald's speech was designed to communicate a new sense of urgency about the problem of Chicago's slum neighborhoods—that inaction now would lead to irreversible decline in the future: "We really [have] only two choices—to run away from the blight or to stand and fight. I submit that this is everybody's choice—and that behind the principle of 'Stand and Fight' is where we must all be counted."[139]

Heald's speech did not call for new legislation, emphasizing instead the powers granted by existing state laws, said to be "clear and adequate" for the pursuit of the proposed action plan.[140] Within months, however, MHPC's legislative committee had drafted three new bills designed to remove ambiguities in the 1945 legislation and prevent a repeat of the standoff between Governor Green and Mayor Kelly. The first bill provided funds for the write-down of slum properties for sale or lease to private developers, the second extended funding for the 1945 slum clearance act, and the third appropriated funds for relocation housing for residents displaced by slum clearance projects.[141] By separating the funding streams that would support public housing and private development, MHPC believed the question of whether the program would be administered by both a local housing authority and a land clearance commission or by the former alone would be less of a stumbling block than before. After all, if the law specified how the money was to be allocated, it did not seem to matter so much which type of setup was used. Discussions among MHPC board members revealed some preference for the CHA as Chicago's sole implementing agency, due chiefly to concerns that multiple housing and redevelopment agencies would pose an obstacle to a well-coordinated rebuilding campaign.[142] But conversations with Governor Green appeared to rule out this prospect. Concerned that any such arrangement would favor public housing, Green insisted on a land clearance commission.[143]

Here there was a potential problem, given Mayor Kelly's past refusal to create such an authority. However, Kelly's days as mayor were numbered. For years the undisputed boss of Chicago's Democratic Party machine, Kelly was beginning to lose his grip on the party apparatus. Disturbed by the mayor's increasingly long absences from the city and a 1946 slate of candidates that many felt was "haphazardly" assembled, party leaders began to suspect that the seventy-year-old mayor's heart was no longer in the job.[144] On top of this, Kelly was facing heat from independents and reform groups for his tolerance of corruption in city government, and citizens were frustrated with the dismal state of basic city services under his administration.[145] In the November 1946 election confidence in Kelly's leadership reached a new low when five of ten Cook County congressional seats and a majority of contested county offices were won by Republicans. By this time Kelly had been stripped of his post as chair of the Cook County Democratic Party.[146] Fearful that the mayor's office would fall into Republican hands in the upcoming 1947 contest, the new party chief, Jacob Arvey, persuaded Kelly not to seek an additional term.[147]

Given the pressure for reform, Democratic Party leaders recognized that their best hope of fielding a successful candidate would be to select someone from outside the party organization, ideally someone without a political base of his own he could use to challenge the party's leadership. Arvey's choice was Martin H. Kennelly, a successful businessman and civic leader who had not previously held any political office and had no ties to the Democratic machine. Kennelly was well known in business circles, serving as vice president of the Chicago Association of Commerce and Industry, chairman of the Red Cross fund drive, a trustee of DePaul University, and a member of the Federal Reserve Bank's industrial advisory committee.[148] In a development whose irony was lost on no one, Kennelly instantly became the reform candidate, running against a little-known insider of the Republican Party organization. The gambit paid off for the Democrats. Kennelly had the support of business leaders, reformers, independents, and three of the city's four major newspapers. On election day, April 1, 1947, Kennelly received 59 percent of the votes for mayor compared with his challenger's total of 41 percent.[149]

After Kennelly's inauguration on April 15, things moved rapidly. During the election campaign, Kennelly had met privately with a delegation from MHPC and assured them of his support for their program.[150] Just three days after taking office, the new mayor created the Committee for Housing Action, whose purpose in part was to work with the mayor and the governor's office to develop a legislative program that would be acceptable to all.[151] The committee was chaired by Holman Pettibone, president of Chicago Title and Trust, a well-known title insurance company. Like MHPC, Pettibone had been actively seeking solutions to Chicago's housing problems, working on proposed state legislation and hiring a consultant to do a feasibility study for the redevelopment of two small areas south and west of downtown.[152] Also on the committee was Milton Mumford, an assistant vice president of Marshall Field and Company and MHPC board member who had chaired the committee that developed MHPC's four-point program for slum clearance and redevelopment. Two additional MHPC board members were also asked to serve.[153]

For several weeks, Pettibone and Mumford traveled back and forth between Springfield and Chicago in order to finalize the details of legislation both Governor Green and Mayor Kennelly would find agreeable.[154] With the General Assembly set to adjourn on July 1, there was little time to waste. Within weeks, all parties had agreed on the language for a set of bills largely consistent with what MHPC had drafted several months earlier. The first bill, S. 548, appropriated $10 million for the clearance of slum properties and resale at use value to private developers. Only land clearance commissions were eligible recipients for this funding, a provision that former Mayor Kelly would have no doubt found objectionable but Kennelly now deemed acceptable. A second bill, S. 549, appropriated $6.5 million, mainly to house veterans or "disaster victims," while the third bill, S. 550, allocated $3.3 million to rehouse displaced families and individuals.[155] When the bills were introduced in the General Assembly in late May, all parties were optimistic. With Kennelly pledging to lobby the Chicago delegation and Green working on downstate legislators, the bills passed easily and were signed by the governor in July.[156]

The Blighted Areas Redevelopment Act of 1947 (S. 548) and its two companion bills were now state law, yet there was little time to celebrate. Both the Redevelopment Act and the Relocation Act (S. 550) required local matching funds. Mayor Kennelly and the city council agreed on two municipal bond issues of $15 million each, well exceeding the required minimum local contribution, and an election to obtain voter approval was scheduled for early November.[157] Supporters of the bond issues were leaving nothing to chance. Since the bond tied to the Relocation Act was for public housing, there would no doubt be organized opposition. MHPC sought to win the support of the business community, recruiting "top flight business leaders" to speak before the Association of Commerce, the Civic Federation, and executive clubs about "the importance of slum clearance to the business men of the community."[158] A speaker's bureau was organized that gave presentations to twenty-seven civic groups from all parts of the city during the month of October.[159] In addition, the Chicago Art Institute hosted a slum clearance and planning exhibit with material directly related to the bond issues. Two large electric signs placed at both ends of Grant Park encouraged people to view the exhibit, and visitors were leafleted with pro-bond literature.[160] The efforts paid off. The bond issues had broad support from labor, business, religious, and educational groups.[161]

For certain of these organizations, the distasteful notion of additional public housing was undoubtedly made more palatable by its link to slum clearance. Reluctantly conceding that some public housing was necessary if redevelopment was to go forward, many traditional enemies of public housing either sat quietly or gave grudging support. As the *Chicago Tribune*, a longtime public housing opponent, editorialized: "We think the plan should be given a fair trial. We'll swallow the $15,000,000 of public housing that we don't like to get the $26,000,000 with which to assemble land for private development. If the experiment in wholesale reconstruction works, the city will be immensely benefited."[162] Most Chicagoans appeared to be in agreement. On November 4, 1947, voters approved both bond issues. With a land clearance commission appointed by Mayor Kennelly newly in place, Chicago was now eligible for funding under the Blighted Areas Redevelopment Act and its companion bills.

*   *   *

It had taken years, but a new policy paradigm for engaging with the city's slum districts was at last emerging. As we will see in subsequent chapters, the new legislation helped initiate a far-reaching slum clearance and redevelopment program that would dominate the attention of civic and political leaders for the next two decades. In the twelve years since ground was broken on the city's first PWA public housing project, housing reform in Chicago had come a very long way. A series of unsatisfactory experiments and otherwise disappointing outcomes had brought the city to this point. From PWA housing, itself a response to the failure of restrictive housing regulations and model housing to rehabilitate slum districts, to public service building corporations, to the public-private partnerships of the 1945 slum clearance act—all had fallen well short of the lofty ambitions of their supporters. Hugh Heclo's observations about political learning are worth repeating: "Politics finds its sources not only in power but also in uncertainty—men collectively wondering what to do. . . . Governments not only 'power' . . . they also puzzle. Policy-making is a form of collective puzzlement on society's behalf."[163] Because those leading the attack on the slums were unsure how to proceed, ideas mattered. They provided direction, however misguided, at a time when the way forward was unclear.

It might be argued that this emphasis on ideas is misdirected—that the real action in this case was being driven mostly by self-interested behavior, particularly on the part of business leaders and real estate interests. After all, prior to the 1930s, policy advocacy around the issue of substandard housing had been largely the domain of progressive housing reformers and their allies. Real estate interests had been relatively quiet. Not until the PWA housing program was launched and a permanent federal housing program was under discussion did real estate interests mobilize. Once they did so, their substantial political influence seemed to ensure that whatever form the new housing policy paradigm took, it would be favorable to them.

Clearly interests are important in this case. New policy ideas were not simply free floating. They were tethered to interests, and those ideas that achieved prominence owed their success in large part to the distribution of power in place at the time. This is evident in the shift that took place in housing policy goals during this period. As new, powerful actors—particularly real estate interests—entered the housing policy arena, widely shared beliefs about what housing reform should accomplish were increasingly called into question. The old idea that housing reform was about rebuilding blighted neighborhoods for the benefit of slum residents began to give way to a much different set of goals focused on the redevelopment of blighted areas to maximize financial benefit. In this new model residents were no longer viewed as the beneficiaries of housing reform. Rather, they were obstacles or inconveniences that had to be dealt with, hopefully at least in some humane way, so that profitability in real estate markets could be restored.

Material interests and shifting relations of power largely explain this new outlook. Still, to focus primarily on such factors is to miss much of the causal story in this case. The break with privatism ushered in by the PWA housing program led to a period of confusion and uncertainty in housing policy. As traditional methods for addressing problems of slums and blight lost favor, actors entered uncharted territory. Uncertain how to proceed, they looked to ideas for guidance. Interests mattered, but these were interests who were feeling their way, through trial and error, choosing solutions they hoped would benefit them but knowing full well they might be wrong. Only by navigating this period of policy uncertainty did actors finally arrive at a solution that appeared to be workable, at least for a time. And even then, civic leaders sounded a cautionary note. As the *Tribune* editorialized two days after the bond issues required by the 1947 Redevelopment Act were passed, "The plan is necessarily experimental. Nobody can be sure that it will work well or even that it will work at all."[164] Coming on the heels of decades of policy failures in housing reform, these words of caution are as revealing as they are well chosen.

CHAPTER FOUR

Creating a Unified Business Elite

In August 1958 the *Chicago Tribune* published a story on a new development plan for Chicago's downtown area. The plan—a twenty-two-year, $1.5 billion blueprint for "modernizing" Chicago's central area—was unveiled in Mayor Richard J. Daley's office before a large group of business and civic leaders.[1] The new plan included a number of improvements for Chicago's central business district, the Loop. However, its principal focus was the roughly ten-square-mile area surrounding downtown.[2] Land use in this area—dominated at the time by manufacturing, commercial development, rail freight operations, and low-income housing—was said to have produced an "unsound" relationship between the Loop and its immediate surroundings.[3] Under the plan, large portions of this area would be transformed into middle-income residential neighborhoods that would better complement the corporate and retail functions in the central business district, providing downtown businesses with both a nearby customer base and a pool of qualified workers.

More than a half century after its publication in 1958, the *Development Plan for the Central Area of Chicago* appears prophetic. In a pattern replicated in cities around the country, near-downtown loft buildings that once housed printing establishments, apparel manufacturers, and other light industries have been converted to residential dwellings for downtown office workers.[4] The construction of new high-rise condominiums and apartment buildings in areas surrounding the Loop continues at a brisk pace, fueling a downtown population boom that added nearly seventy thousand new residents to the central area from 1990 to 2010.[5] The new downtown residents are overwhelmingly middle class. Gentrification has pushed most low-income families outside the central area, creating a middle-class residential buffer between the Loop and impoverished neighborhoods to the south and west of downtown. Over time, the grinding poverty in these neighborhoods became a condition to be managed rather than eliminated. Increasingly public officials and civic leaders came to terms with the slums, focusing their efforts on upgrading portions of the city deemed salvageable and worthy of investment while other areas sank into a tailspin of decay and neglect.

To a great extent, the 1958 Development Plan was as an outgrowth of the Illinois Blighted Areas Redevelopment Act of 1947, which, as we saw in chapter 3, involved a dramatic reworking of long-cherished ideas about how the problem of slums and blighted areas should be addressed. The new law was intended to trigger an attack on Chicago's slum districts by private developers, supported by government subsidies and land assembly powers. The 1958 Development Plan incorporated this new thinking. The sweeping rearrangement of land use the plan envisioned was anticipated by the designers of the new legislation, many of whom would have no doubt found the displacement and gentrification that ultimately followed less than troublesome. Moreover, it was the Redevelopment Act and subsequent federal housing and redevelopment legislation that laid the groundwork for the public-private partnerships that would be used to develop and implement the new plan.

The passage of this new redevelopment legislation, both state and federal, was a major milestone in the attack on the slums. As projects making use of the new laws were announced during the late 1940s and early 1950s, actors grew cautiously optimistic that a successful formula for the rebuilding of Chicago's blighted areas had at last been devised. Old ways of thinking about slum conditions and how they could best be eliminated fell by the wayside as actors focused increasingly on the potential for urban redevelopment to revitalize the city's most economically distressed areas. Yet whether this new set of ideas would become the new conventional wisdom for addressing slums and blight was, at this stage, far from certain. As argued in chapter 1, the stability of a new policy paradigm and its prospects for institutionalization depend on several factors, including the paradigm's alignment with institutions and institutional arrangements, the internal coherence of paradigmatic ideas and goals, and the feedback effects generated by the paradigm and accompanying policy innovations. Should any or all of these factors point in the direction of instability and change, the institutionalization of a new paradigm is threatened.

This chapter focuses in particular on the feedback effects produced by the new redevelopment legislation, considering especially the effects of these new policy ideas on organized interests in Chicago. Feedback effects of public policies have not always been the subject of careful attention by social scientists, many of whom treat policies chiefly as dependent variables, brought into being through pressure by interest group activity or some other factor or set of factors. Others, however, have shown how causality may run in both directions, with policies representing not just effects but also causes of political mobilization.[6] Policies may shape political processes in part by influencing the goals and capabilities of citizens and interest groups, often providing incentives or resources that encourage particular patterns of mobilization. The effects on organizational forms may be profound. New interest groups may form, in some cases to take advantage of opportunities provided through a new policy, in others to oppose the policy or attempt to steer it in a different direction. When new policies represent paradigm shifts in a given policy area, as did the Illinois Blighted Areas Redevelopment Act, feedback effects may be important in determining whether or not the new paradigm is institutionalized in the way its creators intended. Should powerful actors mobilized by the emergence of a new set of policy ideas push in alternative directions, paradigmatic ideas may continue to evolve rather than converge around a new equilibrium.

In fact, the Blighted Areas Redevelopment Act and subsequent federal urban redevelopment legislation produced powerful and lasting feedback effects, and in this chapter we consider especially the impact of the new legislation on downtown business interests. The 1958 Development Plan was a collaboration between the Daley administration and a newly formed civic organization called the Chicago Central Area Committee. Created in 1956 to provide a unified voice for business leaders in redevelopment planning for the downtown area, the Central Area Committee played a key role in both financing and preparation of the plan. The new group was not a unique breed of organization in postwar urban America. Similar groups formed in cities across the country following World War II, providing the cohesive business leadership necessary for the formation of what Salisbury called "the new convergence of power"—formidable alliances between downtown business leaders and city officials directed toward the physical redevelopment of cities.[7] In partnership with city government, groups such as the Chicago Central Area Committee, Pittsburgh's Allegheny Conference on Community Development, the Greater Baltimore Committee, and the Boston

Coordinating Committee pioneered corporate-centered redevelopment strategies that transformed downtowns and their surrounding neighborhoods.[8] The end result was similar from city to city: revitalized downtowns geared toward tourism and the corporate and financial sectors, upgrading of certain city neighborhoods with the right kinds of attributes, and a grim realization in the worst neighborhoods that their problems were ones for which no one seemed to have answers.[9]

But we are getting ahead of ourselves. In the chapters to follow, attention will focus more directly on how the new convergence of power between business and government produced and institutionalized Chicago's version of the dual city. For this to happen, however, business leaders would first have to come together around a common purpose, and in Chicago and other postwar cities this development was not a foregone conclusion. In many cities, including Chicago, the challenges of the postwar era revealed important divisions that would have to be bridged before plans for redevelopment could move forward. Some business leaders favored urban renewal and redevelopment; others were more complacent, concerned that new downtown projects would benefit their competitors or bring in outside firms that would challenge their dominance.[10] Even among those who supported redevelopment, disagreements sometimes arose between those favoring aggressive public sector intervention, including the use of subsidies, and those advocating a more passive government role.[11] Ambitious redevelopment efforts such as Chicago's 1958 Development Plan could be advanced only if forward-looking, progrowth business elites could convince enough of their more conservative counterparts to play along. How such agreements were reached, in Chicago and other places, is a development that needs to be explained. The presence of a unified business elite in postwar cities cannot simply be assumed.

This chapter illustrates how feedback effects from Chicago's new redevelopment program brought downtown business leaders together around a shared concern with the future of the city's central area. As we saw in chapter 3, several prominent members of the city's downtown business community played key roles in the passage of the Blighted Areas Redevelopment Act. Such individuals no doubt viewed the new legislation as a powerful tool for the revitalization of downtown and its immediate surroundings. Yet the Redevelopment Act was designed not so much as a program for rehabilitating the downtown area as a vehicle for the clearing and rebuilding of slum districts, wherever they might be.[12] As various groups—intent on using the new legislation to initiate slum clearance and redevelopment projects of their own—became active in redevelopment policy, competing visions for how the redevelopment process should move forward began to surface. Business leaders grew alarmed as projects proposed for the city's central area were initiated in piecemeal fashion, uninformed by any comprehensive planning process that would connect them to an overall vision for downtown redevelopment. The Central Area Committee was a product of this contested and somewhat chaotic planning environment. Its formation was in part a defensive reaction by downtown business leaders designed to seize control of a redevelopment process in which nondowntown actors had come to play a significant role. Business unity was forged through political struggles over concrete planning initiatives in which business elites became increasingly cognizant of their collective interests in the city's redevelopment program.

Planning the Postwar City

Chicago entered the post–World War II era facing challenges similar to those of other older industrial cities at the time. Suburbanization of the city's white population was accompanied by a renewed influx of mostly lower-income blacks, boosting the city's African American population from 277,731 to 492,265 between 1940 and 1950.[13] Centrally located neighborhoods, particularly those within the city's Black Belt, grew increasingly distressed. A 1943 Chicago Plan Commission report designated a twenty-three-square-mile corridor surrounding the central business district—an area that included about one-fourth of Chicago's population at the time—as "blighted" or "near-blighted."[14] Downtown was suffering as well, with assessed valuations of property in the central business district falling 13 percent from 1939 to 1947 and no significant building activity since the 1920s.[15]

Despite these dire conditions, the city's political and civic leaders were, for the most part, slow to respond. Mayor Kelly, still in office as the war came to a close, was a public housing supporter but otherwise took a mostly caretaker approach to governance, emphasizing basic services and sound fiscal policies.[16] Business elites and other civic leaders were less complacent. However, their ability to act was hampered by institutional fragmentation and a lack of consensus about what should be done. Downtown interests were represented by several organizations, including the Chicago Association of Commerce, the Commercial Club, the Civic Federation, and the State Street Council. Each group had its own agenda, which it pursued independently, and none could claim to speak for the downtown area as a whole.[17] In a 1947 *Chicago Tribune* interview, State Street Council executive secretary Randall Cooper insisted that "blighted areas must be rebuilt" but identified work on the "all important parking problem" downtown as the organization's major focus of activity.[18] The Civic Federation was more skeptical of proposals for redevelopment, arguing against any plans that would increase tax assessments or include a public housing component.[19] The Chicago Association of Commerce established a Blighted Areas, Housing and Redevelopment Committee, but by 1947 the group had done little aside from recommending certain changes to the city's building code.[20]

As we saw in chapter 3, it was the Metropolitan Housing and Planning Council, working in collaboration with several downtown business leaders, that initiated the push for change through its sponsorship of the Blighted Areas Redevelopment Act and other legislation. Even before the Redevelopment Act was passed, MHPC had begun working with several members of the downtown business community on planning efforts that anticipated the new legislation.[21] Key participants included Holman Pettibone, Milton Mumford, and Hughston McBain, president of Marshall Field & Company.[22] While certain downtown business leaders were included in this group, it did not constitute a unified business elite. Many prominent business leaders were not participants, and MHPC represented a wider set of interests than downtown alone.

The Blighted Areas Redevelopment Act established a formula for urban redevelopment and provided some resources with which to initiate a program, but it was action by the federal government, beginning with the US Housing Act of 1949, that made redevelopment possible on a grand scale. The basic features of the 1949 law closely mirrored that of the Illinois legislation, giving the leaders of Chicago's program—who had been planning projects based on this formula for two years already—a head start in the race for federal redevelopment funds. The amount of money was substantial. Title I authorized $1.5 billion in grants and loans for the acquisition and clearance of blighted properties, providing municipalities with financing to purchase properties, demolish existing structures, and sell the land to developers at a substantial discount. Title III authorized federal grants and loans for the construction of 810,000 public housing units over the next six years.[23] Federal funds could be used to supplement funding already available through newly passed housing and redevelopment legislation in Illinois and other states, and cities around the country quickly mobilized to position themselves favorably in the competition for federal urban redevelopment dollars.[24]

While MHPC boasted that the program it had helped set in motion in Illinois was the inspiration for the new federal legislation, in reality the basic features of the 1949 Housing Act were already established with the first attempt to pass a new federal housing bill in 1945, years before the Illinois law was created.[25] With the United States facing a severe housing shortage as GIs began returning home from the war, President Truman made federal support for housing and slum clearance part of his Fair Deal agenda, outlined in his "Message on Reconversion" delivered to Congress in September 1945. That November a bipartisan group of senators—Robert F. Wagner of New York, Allen J. Ellender of Louisiana, and Robert A. Taft of Ohio—introduced the first version of what would ultimately become the Housing Act of 1949. The bill took four years to get through Congress, chiefly because of opposition to public housing by such influential organizations as NAREB, the National Association of Home Builders, the United States Chamber of Commerce, and the Home Building Industry Committee.[26] The breakthrough came in the 1948 presidential election campaign, when Truman successfully blamed the Republican-controlled Congress for the ongoing housing crisis and the absence of a federal government response. With Truman's victory over his Republican challenger Thomas Dewey and the return of Congress to Democratic control, the Taft-Ellender-Wagner bill passed by comfortable margins in both the Senate and the House, and it was signed by the president on July 15, 1949.[27]

In Chicago, the near certainty by the spring of 1949 that new federal housing and redevelopment legislation was forthcoming sparked intense speculation about the level of support the city could expect to receive. Local officials hoped to gain at least thirty thousand federally financed public housing units and an additional $50 million for slum clearance and private redevelopment.[28] Just six days after Truman signed the new bill, Chicago housing and redevelopment officials traveled to Washington, DC, to meet with Housing and Home Finance Agency (HHFA) administrator Raymond M. Foley, the top federal official overseeing the new program.[29] By this time Chicago had several redevelopment projects in the planning stages, and officials were anxious to learn how these projects might qualify for federal funding. Within months, the HHFA informed the Chicago Land Clearance Commission it had been designated as recipient of a $14.4 million grant for slum clearance, the second largest grant awarded by the agency so far.[30] By 1954 Chicago had received just over $20 million for the clearance and redevelopment of slum properties, nearly doubling the amount already secured through state and local redevelopment funds.[31]

The combination of federal, state, and local funds put Chicago in a strong financial position to embark on a redevelopment program. However, in addition to adequate financing, redevelopment of the magnitude that leaders of the program envisioned would require careful and sophisticated planning. The Chicago Plan Commission, a weak, underfunded agency controlled by city council, was not up to the task.[32] Instead planning for redevelopment was initiated by civic groups such as MHPC working in collaboration with business leaders and institutions located in areas of the city that the Plan Commission had identified as "blighted" in its 1943 survey. Such groups shared certain assumptions about central city decline and how it should be addressed, including the belief that slums and blight must be eradicated in all city neighborhoods, not just those in the most desirable locations. Yet there was more than one way to pursue this goal, and early planning efforts hinted at two distinct approaches. One approach—backed by downtown business leaders such as Pettibone and McBain—took an explicitly downtown orientation, with some arguing that redevelopment "should begin as near as feasible to the central business district of the city, working outward from that point."[33] This approach, which anticipated the corporate-center strategy of the 1958 Development Plan, viewed centrally located neighborhoods as appendages to downtown. Such areas were envisioned not as functionally integrated economic entities including both housing and places of work, but as residential areas for downtown office workers. The preference for individuals and families "of moderately high income" as future residents of such areas would require some displacement of the existing population.[34]

A second approach recognized near-downtown neighborhoods as places of both residence and employment, independent of downtown. This approach, pursued by neighborhood planning organizations, industries, and other institutional actors in the city's central area, emphasized the economic development potential of centrally located neighborhoods. Instead of an extension of the central business district, the neighborhood was viewed more as a self-contained economic unit. Efforts to promote and revitalize industrial development and other business activity in such areas would expand employment opportunities for local residents, most of whom would work in the neighborhood, not downtown.[35] Some proponents of this approach argued against neighborhood upgrading along class or income lines, insisting that redevelopment be carried out with no displacement of existing residents. Like the corporate-center strategy summarized above, this approach had the potential to attract investment dollars to portions of the city's central area. But its vision for redevelopment, centered on neighborhood areas more than downtown, threatened to clash with the views of those whose principal interest in a redevelopment program was to revitalize the downtown business district.

To some extent these divergent perspectives reflected unresolved tensions dating back to the 1930s about what redevelopment should accomplish and whose interests it should serve. For some, especially real estate interests, redevelopment was a means of rearranging land use to facilitate the "highest and best use" of land and make blighted areas attractive places for new investment. Such individuals insisted that housing affordable to low- and moderate-income residents be constructed only in locations where other more profitable uses were not considered viable. Others, concerned less with land values than with the well-being of the residents of slum districts, saw redevelopment as a way of upgrading blighted neighborhoods and providing better housing opportunities for the residents of such areas. The designers of both the Illinois Blighted Areas Redevelopment Act and the federal Housing Act of 1949 tried to reconcile this tension by including public housing for low-income families in the legislation, but the questions of who would live where and how redeveloped land would be used were never settled.[36] Instead, groups with different interests and perspectives about how redevelopment should proceed were left to battle over the details of the new programs.

Despite the potential for conflict, these two strategies—one centered on downtown, the other on individual neighborhoods—were pursued simultaneously and, for a time at least, were not seen as incompatible with one another. During the mid-1940s, redevelopment planning efforts focused on two experimental project areas, one on the Near West Side and the other on the Near South Side. Planning for the Near West Side, initiated by MHPC shortly before the close of World War II, assumed a downtown orientation. In 1945 MHPC produced a preliminary redevelopment plan for a 640-acre area between the Loop and a large medical complex west of downtown.[37] The area—a mostly white working-class community which included the Jane Addams Hull House—contained a large number of homes and buildings found to be substandard. According to MHPC, efforts to rebuild "blighted" areas such as this bordering downtown were particularly important because failure to do so would result in the "strangulation" of the Loop.[38]

MHPC developed a partnership with Pettibone and McBain, both of whom viewed redevelopment chiefly as a vehicle for rescuing downtown. As Arnold Hirsch has described, the two business executives collaborated in bringing the well-known Washington, DC, planner/architect Miles Colean to Chicago to do an exhaustive study of the area.[39] They also financed a survey of downtown workers to gauge their interest in living in a Near West Side residential development or elsewhere in the near downtown area. Colean's assessment of the area was largely positive, concluding that "the selected West Side location offers greater potential for redevelopment than any other location that might be considered at the present time."[40] Synergies between the Loop and a revitalized Near West Side were likely to be high, with the "principal demand for living quarters in the area [coming] from small families deriving their support mainly from clerical and executive work in the central business district."[41]

Despite these perceived advantages, postwar redevelopment in Chicago began not on the Near West Side but at a Near South Side location miles from the central business district. With a nonwhite population of 85 percent by 1947, Chicago's Near South Side was a very different area demographically from the mostly white Near West Side.[42] Much of the city's African American population lived in this area, and a renewed influx of black migrants from the South during the 1940s had led to extreme overcrowding.[43] Already grim housing conditions worsened considerably, and by 1947 planners judged one of every three housing units to be in need of major repairs or unfit for occupancy.[44]

Unlike on the Near West Side, redevelopment planning for the Near South Side was initiated by institutions located in the area rather than downtown business leaders. The principal actors were Michael Reese Hospital and the Illinois Institute of Technology (IIT), whose directors had grown increasingly alarmed about what they perceived as an encroaching black ghetto.[45] In 1945 Michael Reese Hospital hired a planning staff to develop a program for expanding the hospital's land holdings with the goal of rejuvenating the area immediately surrounding the hospital.[46] Motivated by the same concerns, IIT had initiated a similar program several years earlier.[47] Aware of the limitations of acting individually, the two institutions eventually joined forces in an effort to mobilize other actors and institutions on the Near South Side around a redevelopment agenda for the entire area. This effort led to the formation in 1946 of the South Side Planning Board, a diverse group that included local industries, labor and religious officials, academic institutions, and other South Side corporate and institutional interests, along with several downtown business leaders.[48]

Planners recognized that both the location and the demographics of the Near South Side would constrain redevelopment options for this area of the city. A 1947 study of the area surrounding IIT and Michael Reese, also prepared by Miles Colean, concluded that the "heavy concentration of Negro families in this section renders an investment in anything but a predominantly Negro project a dubious venture."[49] Moreover, unlike the Near West Side, few synergies between this portion of the Near South Side and the central business district were expected. The neighborhood in which IIT and Michael Reese Hospital were located was three miles from downtown. According to Colean, future residents of new housing developments here would not be downtown office workers but rather "Negro families of moderately high income whose employment base is in the large South Side Negro community and the adjoining industrial and commercial areas."[50] In short, a Near South Side project would help improve living conditions for certain residents of the area, a desirable goal from the standpoint of institutions like IIT and Michael Reese Hospital but not one that overlapped directly with efforts to revitalize downtown.

A second study of the Near South Side, led in this case by Near South Side institutions, seemed to reach similar conclusions. In 1947 Michael Reese Hospital, IIT, the South Side Planning Board, and several other organizations published *An Opportunity for Private and Public Investment in Rebuilding Chicago*, a sixty-two-page redevelopment plan for a three-square-mile area of the Near South Side including the site analyzed by Colean.[51] Like the Colean study, this plan did not link the redevelopment of the Near South Side to the central business district. Instead planners focused almost exclusively on the study area itself, identifying locations for housing, industry, commercial development, and parks.

An Opportunity was as much a marketing document as a redevelopment plan. Its chief purpose was to highlight the lucrative opportunities for private investment that existed on the Near South Side. To that end, emphasis was placed on institutional commitment to the area, including recent and planned construction activity by Michael Reese Hospital and IIT. Methods of land assembly and public incentives for redevelopment were spelled out in detail. The argument was persuasive. After touring potential development sites on the Near West Side and the Near South Side, representatives from the New York Life Insurance Company announced plans in 1948 for a 1,400-unit housing development on sixty acres of land on the Near South Side.[52] Following several lengthy delays, ground was finally broken for the Lake Meadows development in February 1952. Chicago's first urban renewal project was under way.

Contested Terrain

Downtown business leaders such as Holman Pettibone and Milton Mumford supported and even participated in efforts to plan and redevelop the Near South Side. Representatives from MHPC, Chicago Title and Trust, and Marshall Field & Company were members of the South Side Planning Board, and the boards of both IIT and Michael Reese Hospital included downtown corporate leaders. Yet despite the involvement of downtown interests, the leadership of these institutions maintained a strong South Side orientation. As the actions described above suggest, the redevelopment efforts they spearheaded were intended principally to revitalize the Near South Side, not to integrate the South Side into plans for downtown redevelopment. Whether this was a source of concern for Pettibone, Mumford, and other proponents of downtown revitalization is unknown. However, this much is clear: the South Side Planning Board claimed as its area of influence a vast, seven-square-mile swath of the Near South Side extending from Twelfth Street south to Forty-Seventh Street (see fig. 4.1). The northern boundary of this area was barely a fifteen-minute walk from the Loop. The possibility was strong that at some point plans developed by South Side interests for the near-Loop portions of this area would conflict with the planning preferences of those for whom downtown revitalization was of foremost importance.

It did not take long for such a conflict to surface. In 1948 the South Side Planning Board initiated plans for a follow-up study of the Near South Side. Unlike the earlier *Opportunity* report, which focused primarily on residential redevelopment, the new study would address industrial

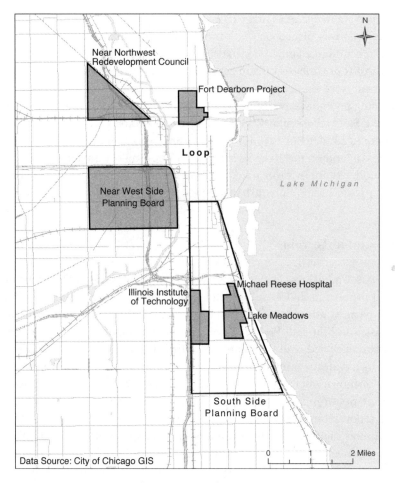

FIGURE 4.1. Central area planning groups and project areas, 1950.

development. Large sections of the Near South Side—particularly those areas closest to downtown—were devoted to manufacturing, with printing, warehousing and distribution, and related activities representing the largest sectors.[53] While Near South Side industries benefited from the area's proximity to downtown and its excellent transportation infrastructure, the viability of the Near South Side for manufacturing was threatened by poor planning.[54] Haphazard zoning had produced incompatible land uses in many areas. Industrial firms were often located too close to nearby residences or commercial establishments, and there was little space available for expansion. The South Side Planning Board included among its membership several of the major industrial firms in the area. The new report was intended both to "maintain the interest of . . . present industrial members" and to serve as a recruiting tool with which to expand the organization's industrial membership.[55]

In 1953 the South Side Planning Board released *An Opportunity to Rebuild Chicago through Industrial Development on the Central South Side*, a study which the organization hoped would "do for industry" what the previous *Opportunity* report had done for housing on the Near South Side.[56] Identifying the space needs of Near South Side manufacturers as a major concern, the report proposed the creation of a massive "Planned Industrial District" extending from the southern boundary of the Loop two miles south to Cermak Road, with State Street and the Chicago River serving as its eastern and western boundaries, respectively (fig. 4.2). Proposed features of the new district included centralized management to oversee building construction and tenant selection, shared services such as warehousing and freight consolidation, financial assistance for companies, and the grouping of complementary industries in proximity to one another. Tenant selection criteria would include the "ability and willingness to employ Negro workers, especially men."[57] Planners anticipated that the district would represent a major source of employment for South Side workers—including the "almost untapped and potentially valuable labor force of the Negro community"—and provide a superior operating environment for companies in the area.[58] The process of land assembly and clearance of existing structures would be identical to that of residential urban redevelopment projects, using powers and financial tools provided through the Blighted Areas Redevelopment Act and the Housing Act of 1949.

The study was well received by labor, industries, and other South Side groups. For downtown interests, however, the new plan was problematic. Redevelopment of the area immediately south of the Loop as an industrial district would perpetuate what many business leaders perceived as a dysfunctional relationship that currently existed between the Loop and adjoining areas.[59] Instead of more industrial development, they wanted middle-class residential development that would provide workers and customers for downtown business establishments.[60] Not surprisingly, when the 1958 Development Plan was released several years later, this

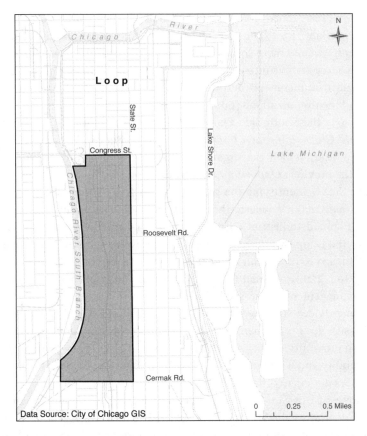

FIGURE 4.2. Planned industrial district, South Side Planning Board, 1953.

area was designated largely for residential redevelopment. The South Side Planning Board immediately protested, calling for a compromise that would permit some residential development but preserve other portions of the area for industrial use.[61] A meeting with Planning Commissioner Ira Bach was quickly scheduled, and the Department of Planning agreed to reconsider its proposal for a solidly residential corridor south of the Loop.[62]

In 1955 the South Side Planning Board once again took steps that set up a potential conflict with downtown interests. In this case, the organization announced plans to extend its area of influence north from Twelfth Street all the way to the Loop.[63] After conferring with institutions in the area, the organization released a land-use plan in 1957 covering portions of the central business district and areas directly south of downtown.[64] The idea was to link planning for these areas to existing planning and redevelopment efforts under way on the Near South Side. This move effectively stood the logic of the 1958 Development Plan on its head: planning for the central business district would serve the Near South Side instead of the other way around. It was a bold maneuver, invited in part by the failure of the city's corporate leaders to develop a plan of their own for the central area. For downtown business elites such as Pettibone and Mumford, the message was clear: either pull together downtown interests around a plan for the Loop and its immediate surroundings or someone else would fill the void.

The Near South Side was not the only area of Chicago where the postwar planning preferences of downtown business leaders began to conflict with those of nondowntown actors and institutions. Similar problems were surfacing on the city's Near West Side. Following the New York Life Insurance Company's choice of the Near South Side for Chicago's first urban renewal project, MHPC and its partners continued to explore options for a renewal project on the Near West Side. In July 1949, developer and MHPC board member Philip Klutznick arranged a meeting with the Chicago Land Clearance Commission to discuss the boundaries of a possible project area.[65] Meanwhile Pettibone continued to market the area to prospective investors.[66] The vision of MHPC and its allies for the Near West Side remained unchanged: redevelopment here should complement and support downtown revitalization by creating new housing opportunities for downtown office workers and their families. Slum clearance accompanied by substantial displacement of the existing low- and moderate-income population would be necessary to achieve this goal.

By this time, however, an alternative vision for the future of the Near West Side was taking shape. In June 1949 a group of community actors came together to form the Near West Side Planning Board. Like the South Side Planning Board, the Near West Side group was established to create a vehicle for neighborhood mobilization around redevelopment planning.[67] Its membership consisted primarily of actors and institutions located on the Near West Side, including industrial firms. Early planning efforts called for a large industrial district west of downtown that would reduce land-use conflicts among industries, residences, and commercial establishments and help retain industrial employment in the area, much as the South Side Planning Board proposed for the Near South Side.[68]

Despite these similarities to the South Side Planning Board, the Near

West Side group differed from its counterpart in two key respects. First, downtown business leaders had no role in the organization. Second, the organization was considerably more diverse than the South Side Planning Board, including on its seventy-six-member governing council an eclectic mix of neighborhood residents, community organizations, and small business owners, along with larger institutional actors.[69] This diversity of membership led the organization to take a strong position against displacement and demographic "upgrading" on the Near West Side, pitting the group against MHPC and its partners. Plans for the Lake Meadows housing development on the Near South Side called for the relocation of some two thousand families, mostly African American. By contrast, the Near West Side Planning Board insisted that redevelopment plans "must include all income groups" and criticized proposals to "rebuild the neighborhood . . . with luxury housing" for Loop employees.[70] Instead of slum clearance, the organization called for policies and programs that would facilitate the rehabilitation of the area's existing housing stock, allowing local residents to keep their homes. Neighborhood planning, organization leaders argued,

> must seek provision for some of all types of housing to meet the economic needs and the individual desires of the families who now live in the area and whose incomes are from low through medium and middle to high and even very high. Good individual homes that are here now must be preserved and more must be built. Existing good flats and apartment buildings must be kept and more at varying rentals must be added.[71]

In January 1950, disagreements between downtown and neighborhood actors over the future of the Near West Side came to a head when the Chicago Plan Commission recommended that a portion of the area be removed from the Land Clearance Commission's inventory of slum clearance sites, limiting revitalization efforts there to the rehabilitation of existing structures.[72] The action came as a result of pressure from the ward alderman, who had worked with the Near West Side Planning Board and other area stakeholders to develop plans for a "program of improvement" emphasizing housing rehabilitation rather than slum clearance and new construction.[73] The decision represented a major setback for MHPC and its allies. Holman Pettibone tried to reason with neighborhood leaders, extolling the virtues of the Lake Meadows slum clearance project at a meeting between downtown business leaders and representatives of the Near West Side Planning Board later that year.[74] While board members conceded that some buildings in the area were beyond repair and should be demolished, the two sides could not agree on the issue of displacement. For the Near West Side Planning Board, any development leading to the forced relocation of existing residents was unacceptable. For downtown business leaders, development that left the West Side population largely intact was unlikely to provide the boost to downtown revitalization they sought to achieve. Given the recent action by the Plan Commission, the Near West Side group appeared to have the upper hand.

A final example of conflict between downtown and neighborhood actors involved a development partnership initiated in 1950 between a Northwest Side planning group and several downtown business leaders. The Near Northwest Side Redevelopment Council, one of the city's first postwar neighborhood planning organizations, was created in 1945 to pursue the planning and redevelopment of a 290-acre area roughly one mile northwest of the Loop (see fig. 4.1).[75] Like the Near West Side Planning Board, the organization's membership consisted of residents, businesses, civic groups, and other institutions located in the immediate area. No downtown business leaders were represented. The organization came to the attention of Holman Pettibone in May 1947 when the group's chair, Walter La Buy, requested Pettibone's assistance with redevelopment planning for the area.[76] Convinced that much of the area's housing stock was too dilapidated to preserve, organization leaders were more receptive to a program of slum clearance and new construction than were their Near West Side counterparts.[77]

Soon after meeting with Pettibone, La Buy began a series of discussions with developer Philip Klutznick, who had worked with Pettibone on redevelopment planning for the Near West Side, and Evert Kincaid, former director of the Chicago Plan Commission and currently president of a downtown planning consulting firm.[78] The three parties agreed to form a partnership to pursue the redevelopment of the area, and a contract was signed in November 1950 identifying the Near Northwest Side Redevelopment Council as the sponsor of the project. Kincaid & Associates was designated as planning and architectural consultant and Klutznick's firm as developer.[79] This time downtown and neighborhood actors appeared to be largely in agreement about redevelopment plans for a portion of the city's central area. At La Buy's request, the Chicago Land Clearance Commission initiated a survey of the project area in October 1950.[80] The area was certified as blighted and added to the commission's inventory of slum clearance sites as Project Number Five, clearing the way for use of federal urban redevelopment funds.

Despite what was most likely perceived as a promising start, problems soon began to surface. In late 1950 the Near Northwest Side Redevelopment Council was taken over by Oran Mensik, president of a local savings and loan association, and Joseph Baran, the ward committeeman. According to La Buy, both were interested in the project "only from the standpoint of personal profit."[81] In 1953 Mensik lobbied successfully for state authorization to allow savings and loan institutions to finance private development in the project area.[82] With the financial institution he directed now positioned to play a key role in the project, Mensik proposed to increase the building density specified in the redevelopment plan. Klutznick disapproved of the idea, arguing that such a move would violate "modern standards of land use."[83] The two sides could not come to an agreement, and Klutznick withdrew from the project in frustration.

Soon afterward the project was dealt a fatal blow when two neighborhood organizations brought local stakeholders together around a conservation plan focused on rehabilitating existing building structures rather than slum clearance and redevelopment.[84] Arguing that many area homes were in salvageable condition, the group appealed to the Land Clearance Commission to drop its plans for slum clearance. Not wishing to be drawn into a neighborhood dispute over development and concerned that a viable redevelopment plan with solid community support had not yet surfaced, the commission agreed to remove the site from its list of active redevelopment projects.[85] By fall of 1953 the project was considered "dead as can be."[86] Once again, action by neighborhood actors had left the planning and development goals of downtown business leaders unrealized.

Forging an Elite Consensus

By the early 1950s, redevelopment planning for large sections of the central area south and west of downtown was dominated by groups that represented those individual areas. No single overarching vision informed planning for the central area. Instead planning consisted largely of the uncoordinated efforts of neighborhood planning organizations with few ties to one another and whose main objective was the revitalization of the areas they served. Even on the South Side, where downtown business leaders at least had a presence in the principal planning organization for the area, planning efforts focused inward on the neighborhood area itself, failing to link developments there to initiatives elsewhere in the city, including downtown. Through partnerships or simple persuasion, business leaders sought to reconcile neighborhood planning efforts with the downtown-oriented vision of redevelopment they embraced, but such efforts had been frustrated on multiple occasions.

Downtown business leaders might have attempted to assume control over central area planning through development and advocacy of their own plan, but at this stage there was no consensus among downtown interests around planning for the downtown area. The degree of fragmentation among business leaders at the time was highlighted in 1952 when the Chicago Plan Commission released its plan for a ten-year $1.5 billion program of public improvements for the central area.[87] The commission proposed a series of projects intended to stimulate private investment in the central area, including street improvements and highway building, new transit facilities, a new downtown railroad terminal consolidating existing passenger and freight facilities, a new civic center to be located on the Near West Side, and several other major public works projects. To finance the improvements, a new public service authority authorized to issue revenue bonds would be established.

In an effort to mobilize support for the proposal, Plan Commission chairman William Spencer made a series of presentations to the city's most influential business organizations.[88] Following a speech to the Commercial Club in December 1951, a special committee appointed by club president Robert Wood recommended that members form a group "which would encourage the accomplishment of such a public works program in every way possible."[89] Soon afterward, a group of downtown business leaders calling itself the Committee for a New Chicago began meeting to discuss a possible action plan. Holman Pettibone was named committee chair. Earl Kribben, vice president for civic affairs at Marshall Field, was appointed secretary. Although the group's immediate task was to mobilize support for the Plan Commission's public works program, early discussions suggested movement toward a broader agenda focused more generally on the city's redevelopment program.[90]

Despite the Commercial Club's endorsement, enthusiasm for the new group among the city's business leaders was not universal, and the committee disbanded following several meetings. In a letter to Petti-bone following the group's first meeting, Milton Mumford expressed fears that such an organization, particularly if it assumed a high pro-file, would "alienate other organizations" such as MHPC, the Civic Fed-eration, the City Club, the Chicago Association of Commerce, and the South Side Planning Board.[91] According to Mumford, such organiza-tions "consider[ed] themselves also qualified and interested in" many of the problems the Committee for a New Chicago would address. In addition, Chicago Association of Commerce president Leverett Lyon warned Pettibone that certain of the Plan Commission's recommenda-tions, including the proposed civic center and downtown rail terminal, would likely provoke "strong disagreement" among business leaders and other groups.[92] Partly for this reason, Lyon concluded that the "forma-tion of a . . . committee or other formal and announced entity at this time would not be the wisest next step."[93]

Although this attempt to unify the city's business leadership around an improvement program for the downtown area ended in failure, de-velopments during the next several years created more favorable con-ditions for such an effort. In 1954 plans were announced for a 151-acre, $400 million slum clearance project to be located on the north bank of the Chicago River directly across from the Loop (see fig. 4.1). The Fort Dearborn project would include five thousand units of middle-income housing in privately built apartment buildings and a $165 million civic center providing office space for federal, state, and local governments.[94] The project was conceived by Arthur Rubloff, a prominent real estate developer whose previous projects included the development of Chi-cago's "Magnificent Mile" along upper Michigan Avenue.

Although several major redevelopment projects were under way in Chicago by this time, Fort Dearborn was the first of these developments explicitly linked to downtown revitalization. In explaining the rationale for the project, proponents emphasized its positive impact on the Loop. As one supporter put it, the project would "give a north anchor for the Loop which would strengthen the position of the Loop as the commer-cial and business center of the city."[95] It would do so in part by elimi-nating what project sponsors described as "a badly blighted section ad-jacent to and adversely affecting the central business district."[96] Not surprisingly, the Fort Dearborn proposal attracted significant support within the downtown business community. By the time the project was officially launched in March 1954, a team of seven top business executives had been assembled to serve as project sponsors.[97] Both Hughston McBain of Marshall Field and Holman Pettibone were members. Marshall Field vice president Earl Kribben was named project director.

Despite this core of powerful supporters, the Fort Dearborn project quickly became a lightning rod for controversy. The project would require the displacement of nearly ten thousand residents and many commercial establishments north of the Chicago River.[98] As in other portions of the central area targeted for redevelopment, groups representing neighborhood interests opposed plans for slum clearance and displacement. Two planning organizations from the area, the Near North Side Planning Board and the Near Northside Land Use Committee, argued that the announcement of the project had destabilized real estate markets in the area by creating uncertainty about the future of the Near North Side.[99] These groups challenged the assertion that the Near North Side was blighted, insisting that profitable conditions for investment could be restored by removing the prospect of slum clearance in the area.

More problematic still, downtown interests could not agree among themselves on the Fort Dearborn project. Retailers and other real estate interests in the South Loop were "less than enthusiastic" about the proposal, fearing that the project would principally benefit the North Loop and the Near North Side.[100] With key members divided over the proposal, downtown business groups such as the Chicago Association of Commerce, the Real Estate Board, the Civic Federation, and the State Street Council avoided taking a position altogether.[101] Eventually organized opposition to the project took shape when a group of twenty-eight downtown business leaders dominated by South Loop interests formed the Committee for Government Buildings Downtown.[102] This group opposed the project primarily because of the proposed civic center component. Concerned about the impact on Loop property values of government offices locating or relocating outside the central business district, the committee proposed several downtown locations for new government buildings as alternatives to the Fort Dearborn site.[103] Opposition to the proposed government center threatened to kill the project, since without a new civic center as a project anchor, it seemed unlikely that significant new private development activity in the area would materialize.[104]

From the standpoint of the city's business leaders, opposition to the Fort Dearborn project within the ranks of the downtown business community did not bode well for the future of downtown redevelopment in

Chicago. If downtown interests could not agree on this project, what guarantees were there that future projects would not provoke similar dissent? Within this context, McBain, Pettibone, and several other business leaders resurrected discussions about the formation of a downtown business group.[105] Participants were carefully chosen to incorporate a range of downtown interests. Both South Loop and North Loop interests were represented, including one member of the Committee for Government Buildings Downtown as well as several sponsors of the Fort Dearborn project.[106] These discussions took place over a period of several months and were sufficiently productive that a decision was made to move forward. The Chicago Central Area Committee, formally launched in January 1956, would provide a collective voice for downtown business leaders in the planning and redevelopment of the Loop and its immediate surroundings.[107] Pettibone agreed to serve as chairman of the new organization, and a twelve-member executive committee including McBain and other top business executives was appointed.[108]

With the lessons of the failed Committee for a New Chicago still fresh in his mind, Pettibone took a number of steps to build support for the new organization. First, the Central Area Committee acknowledged the important contributions of the "many fine existing organizations in the Central Area" and the "valuable service" they provided.[109] The Central Area Committee would complement the activities of these groups, not replace them. In addition, the new organization would work largely behind the scenes, brokering agreements among Loop interests and announcing its support for a new project or initiative only after a consensus had been reached.[110] Given this, the group took no official position on the Fort Dearborn project until a compromise acceptable to all major downtown interests had been arranged.

The Central Area Committee formed during a time when Chicago's governing arrangements were in transition. In April 1955, just months before the organization's official launch date, voters elected Richard J. Daley as mayor. Daley's predecessor, Martin H. Kennelly, had been a politically weak mayor who allowed power to gravitate toward city council.[111] This arrangement had favored neighborhood development groups like the Near West Side Planning Board and the Near Northwest Redevelopment Council, which, as we saw earlier, formed alliances with aldermen and ward bosses around neighborhood revitalization plans that conflicted with the preferences of downtown interests. Given Ken-

nelly's weakness vis-à-vis city council, business leaders could not generally look to the mayor for support in conflicts with neighborhood groups.
Daley's election, however, upset this political balance. Daley was chairman of the Cook County Democratic Party organization, a post he continued to hold after assuming the office of mayor. By serving simultaneously as mayor and party boss, Daley quickly consolidated power over
an undisciplined city council.[112] For downtown business leaders, an alliance with Daley might allow them to prevail in contests with nondowntown actors over the future of the central area, since the mayor rather
than ward bosses and aldermen was likely to have the last word in decisions about how or whether redevelopment would go forward.

Daley was in fact sympathetic to the development goals of the Central
Area Committee, recognizing the economic benefits and prestige that
an ambitious, carefully coordinated downtown revitalization program
would likely produce.[113] He also recognized the need for a broad business consensus around plans for downtown redevelopment. For these
reasons he refused to take an active role in resolving the controversy surrounding Fort Dearborn and the proposed civic center. Instead he instructed his Department of City Planning to work with the Central Area
Committee on a new plan that would treat "all of the major problems
of the central [area] together."[114] With Pettibone's group playing an active role in the planning process, prospects were good that the new plan
would enjoy widespread business support.[115]

The 1958 *Development Plan for the Central Area of Chicago* marked
the triumph of the corporate-centered downtown approach to central
area development over the fragmented and piecemeal neighborhood approach advanced by such groups as the South Side Planning Board and
the Near West Side Planning Board. The new plan was informed by a vision of development that emerged from downtown in which surrounding
neighborhoods were integrated into a comprehensive strategy for downtown revitalization. This vision was explicitly postindustrial. In what the
authors referred to as "probably the most important objective" of the
plan, fifty thousand new housing units were recommended for areas surrounding the Loop.[116] New housing developments would replace substandard working-class housing and "blighted industrial and commercial areas" close to downtown.[117] "Special emphasis" would be placed
"on the needs of middle-income groups who wish to live in areas close
to the heart of the city."[118] In short, land use would be rearranged to

accommodate growth of the corporate center at the expense of the commercial and industrial establishments and low-income and working-class
residents currently occupying the area.[119]

*   *   *

It would take decades, but the vision articulated in the 1958 Development Plan would ultimately be realized. As the twentieth century drew
to a close, the manufacturing operations, freight yards, and low-income
housing that once surrounded the central business district were largely
gone, replaced by development that created more synergies with the
Loop. The slum housing and other signs of blight that so concerned postwar planners and civic leaders mostly disappeared from the central area,
although farther away from downtown such problems remained stub-
bornly in full view. In time, ridding Chicago of its slum districts, an objective central to the Blighted Areas Redevelopment Act, would largely
give way to the maximization of land values as the principal goal of urban redevelopment. As we shall see in later chapters, the policy paradigm ushered in by the 1947 redevelopment legislation proved to be temporary and unstable, creating openings for new ideas about how the
city's approach to slum and blighted areas should proceed. As a powerful organization representing the city's leading downtown business interests, the Central Area Committee was well positioned to play a key role
in setting the terms of that debate. An organization that did not yet exist when the Redevelopment Act was passed would figure prominently
in determining how the ideas set in motion by the new law evolved over
time, steering them in a direction very different from what the designers
of the new law originally intended.

While many have argued that Chicago's postwar redevelopment program was the product of powerful downtown interests, few have recognized that the opposite is equally true: the redevelopment program re-
constituted downtown interests as a powerful collective force. Through
feedback effects generated by the newly evolving program and the
neighborhood-level planning initiatives it inspired, downtown business
elites increasingly perceived the fragmentation of the business community as an impediment to the realization of their vision for downtown revitalization. Created partly in response to the proliferation of neighborhood planning organizations in the downtown area, the Central Area

Committee made such groups redundant. Over time, organizations such as the South Side Planning Board and its counterparts on the city's Near North and Near West Sides lost influence, while redevelopment planning for the central area increasingly assumed a downtown orientation. New organizations would eventually surface, but they would struggle to articulate and defend a neighborhood vision on turf that downtown actors had claimed for themselves.

CHAPTER FIVE

New Institutions for a New Governing Agenda

M etropolitan Housing and Planning Council president Ferd Kramer was alarmed. It was Friday, January 20, 1950, and he had just received word that the evening before, the Chicago Plan Commission had preempted the efforts of the Land Clearance Commission by passing a resolution reclassifying a one-half-square-mile portion of the Near West Side from a "blighted" area to a "rehabilitation" area. The change had potentially far-reaching consequences. If approved by the city council, it would mean that renewal efforts there would have to take place through the rehabilitation of existing structures rather than through slum clearance and rebuilding, an outcome MHPC viewed as not only undesirable in this case but also setting a dangerous precedent for urban redevelopment in Chicago. Residents of other areas designated by the city as blighted and hence eligible for slum clearance would no doubt agitate for similar treatment. Kramer immediately called Mayor Kennelly, warning of the "devastating effects of [the Plan Commission's] action on the entire redevelopment program."[1] Land Clearance Commission chairman John McKinlay urged the mayor to delay action on the matter until his agency completed a survey of the area, currently under way.[2] However, Kennelly declined to intervene, and one week later the city council planning committee approved the Plan Commission's decision by a 25–2 vote. In June the full council passed an ordinance making the decision final.[3]

Kramer's frustration with this turn of events was no doubt exacerbated by MHPC's long-standing interest in this area of the Near West Side. The boundaries of the area largely coincided with those of a demonstration redevelopment planning area MHPC had piloted in 1945. As noted in

chapter 4, a study of the area by the planner/architect Miles Colean concluded that no other portion of the city had stronger redevelopment potential. Proximity to the Loop was a key asset, because it would make new
housing developments here potentially attractive to downtown workers.
Years before the 1958 *Development Plan for the Central Area of Chicago*
made it the city's official policy, MHPC's plan anticipated a rearranging
of land use on the Near West Side. Slums would be cleared, low-income
residents would be moved out, and middle-class families would take their
places, helping to spark a revitalization of the downtown area.[4] But none
of this could happen if the Near West Side lost its blighted designation,
since such an outcome would place the area off limits to the Land Clearance Commission. Reclassification as a rehabilitation area would pose
a significant obstacle to the demographic upgrading MHPC envisioned.
Instead of eviction notices, residents would receive bank loans allowing them to make long-needed repairs to their homes, sealing the status of the Near West Side as a low-income area.[5] From the perspective of
MHPC and downtown business leaders, years of planning for downtown
redevelopment were suddenly jeopardized by the seemingly arbitrary decision of the Plan Commission. How could this happen?

Simply put, the reclassification of the Near West Side's blighted status
was possible because those with an interest in blocking slum clearance
were able to use the institutional arrangements governing urban redevelopment in Chicago to their advantage. Months before the Plan Commission's move and unbeknownst to MHPC, the Chicago Commissioner
of Buildings began meeting with a group of Near West Side stakeholders, including the alderman and ward boss, to discuss the possibility of
a rehabilitation program for the area.[6] All had an interest in such a program. Rehabilitation would provide new opportunities for the Department of Buildings, whose services would be needed to inspect buildings
and determine the need for repairs. It was less threatening to local politicians than slum clearance and displacement, which disrupted the personal relationships on which ward political organizations were built and
maintained. Residents, for obvious reasons, also preferred rehabilitation
to slum clearance. Persuaded that rehabilitation was the most advantageous approach to take, Twentieth Ward alderman Anthony Pistilli pressured Plan Commission officials to make the change.[7] Not surprisingly,
the agency quickly caved. City council controlled the purse strings of the
Commission, and planning officials generally went out of their way to
avoid conflict with aldermen.[8] Once city council approved the decision—

also not surprising, since it was common practice to defer to the wishes of aldermen in matters affecting their individual wards—the Land Clearance Commission's hands were tied. Slum clearance could be carried out only in areas the Plan Commission designated as blighted. Mayor Kennelly, himself an ally of MHPC and supporter of slum clearance, might have intervened, but his position was weak, both politically and institutionally. In sum, this case reveals what backers of the city's redevelopment program knew only too well: the set of institutions through which redevelopment policy was carried out in Chicago was exceptionally fragmented and disordered, making it inevitable that agencies and other governmental bodies would at times work at cross-purposes. Those seeking to influence or obstruct the program had multiple points of access, producing plentiful opportunities to derail projects or planning efforts.

For the most part, scholars of urban political development have paid little attention to the institutional arrangements through which postwar cities were governed. Instead of formal institutions, scholars have focused largely on the *informal* power structures that surfaced during this period, examining in particular how new alliances between city officials and business organizations such as the Chicago Central Area Committee shaped decision making in the postwar era.[9] There are seemingly valid reasons why urban scholars have taken this approach, which Clarence Stone spells out in the opening pages of his study of governance in postwar Atlanta, *Regime Politics*: "What makes governance in Atlanta effective is not the formal machinery of government, but rather the informal partnership between city hall and the downtown business elite. This informal partnership and the way it operates constitute the city's regime; it is the means through which major policy decisions are made."[10] Urban regimes—defined by Stone and others as long-term, multi-issue partnerships between government and nongovernmental actors—are useful, Stone explains, because resources needed for governing are partially controlled by nongovernmental groups. Particularly important are the economic resources that business possesses. The institutionally weak position of city government means that the governance of cities presents a different set of challenges than it does for states or the federal government. Formal institutions matter less than informal arrangements.

This is a reasonable argument, but the insight that informal arrangements are especially important has in practice too often been taken to imply the opposite about formal institutions: that they matter very little. In what amounts to a kind of crude functionalism, institutions are sometimes treated as largely derivative of urban power structures, carrying little explanatory weight. Such characterizations are misguided. As the incident recounted above illustrates, policy outcomes are determined in part by the fit between the goals of politically active groups and existing political institutions, the latter of which are in many cases far more resilient and difficult to change than functionalist perspectives acknowledge. Governing institutions serve as "staging grounds" or "rules of the game" for political action, favoring certain political actors and courses of action over others.[11] As political scientist Theda Skocpol has argued, "The overall structure of political institutions provides access and leverage to some groups and alliances, thus encouraging and rewarding their efforts to shape government policies, while simultaneously denying access and leverage to other groups and alliances. . . . This means that the degree of success that any politically active group or movement achieves is influenced not just by the self-consciousness and 'resource mobilization' of that social force itself."[12]

While the alignment between institutions and governing agendas may always be less than perfect, such incongruencies are likely to be especially pronounced when agendas change abruptly, as happened in Chicago and other cities with the passage of state and federal urban redevelopment legislation. The new policy paradigm ushered in by the Illinois Blighted Areas Redevelopment Act and similar legislation elsewhere suddenly placed vastly different demands on urban political institutions. Slum clearance and redevelopment required strong executive leadership and centralized planning and development authority. In many cases, however, the powers of city government were highly fragmented. Political machines, while typically in decline, were still a significant presence in many cities, dispersing power among aldermen and ward bosses.[13] Even in nonmachine cities, the predominance of weak-mayor, strong-council city charters left many mayors with little executive authority.[14] In machine and nonmachine cities alike, planning and development functions were often carried out by numerous agencies with little coordination among them.[15] Problems with fit between governing demands and institutional structures were exaggerated, as new agencies—often created in ad hoc fashion to administer different aspects of rapidly evolving redevelopment programs—struggled to find their way in increasingly dense institutional matrices.

Urban scholars have paid scant attention to such institutional shortcomings. However, the architects of postwar urban redevelopment were acutely aware of them. In cities around the country, governmental structures "designed for a different day and a different set of problems" created obstacles for those seeking change, stimulating a wave of fiercely contested administrative reform efforts that helped determine the prospects for urban redevelopment.[16] Such reforms, frequently initiated or championed by business leaders and other proponents of redevelopment, were opposed by machine politicians, certain city bureaucrats, and other political actors for whom the status quo held greater appeal. In Philadelphia, for example, business leaders mobilizing around urban renewal policy led a successful push for a new city charter that reorganized the municipal bureaucracy and created a strong-mayor form of government. The 1951 charter, staunchly opposed by the city's Republican machine, paved the way for a "vast campaign" of slum clearance and urban redevelopment during the 1950s.[17] In St. Louis a new coalition of business leaders championing slum clearance and redevelopment led a similar charter reform effort in 1957. In this case, however, government reorganization was blocked by a coalition of ward politicians, neighborhood groups, and labor leaders who argued that reform would undermine neighborhood representation in city government and favor "money interests."[18] In Boston a coalition of business elites and reformers overcame the opposition of machine politicians and neighborhood groups to push through a new strong-mayor city charter in 1949. Meanwhile, newly elected reform mayor John B. Hynes presided over a far-reaching municipal reorganization effort that reduced the number of city departments from thirty-eight to twenty-six.[19]

The political contests that surfaced over the institutional structures of postwar cities are consistent with Stephen Skowronek's observation that new or reformed governing institutions do not materialize simply because new governing demands produce a need for them.[20] In Chicago and other cities, redevelopment efforts were mediated through institutional arrangements that became objects of struggle in their own right. The success of groups pressing for slum clearance and redevelopment was determined in part by their ability to craft and successfully advance new institutional arrangements that favored their objectives over those of their political rivals. New policy ideas about how cities should address problems of slums and blight would likely prove fleeting should these efforts fall short.

In Chicago the fit between the city's governing institutions and the goals of politically active groups in urban redevelopment policy initially favored neighborhood organizations, civil rights groups, ward politicians, and other opponents of redevelopment, allowing such groups to successfully play an obstructionist role. However, changing political conditions created opportunities for institution building, and actors sought new arrangements designed to help them best achieve the type of rebuilding program they envisioned. As we saw in earlier chapters, for some this meant rearranging land use to rid the near-downtown area of low-income housing, industrial "nuisances," and other uses and activities that posed a barrier to downtown revitalization. Proponents of this approach were concerned above all with safeguarding the powers of the Land Clearance Commission—the agency responsible for clearing slums and paving the way for new uses of land—in proposals for government reorganization.

Other groups, while supportive of downtown redevelopment and slum clearance, grew more sensitized to the need for multiple approaches to problems of slums and blight. Recognizing that certain of the city's community areas would be better served by rehabilitation efforts—or "conservation," as it was eventually called—than slum clearance, these groups pushed to combine all of the city's redevelopment agencies, including those responsible for slum clearance and conservation, in one department. This arrangement, supporters argued, would promote better coordination of slum clearance and neighborhood rehabilitation activities. Importantly, it would also eliminate an agency—the Chicago Land Clearance Commission—whose sole purpose was to displace the existing population in designated areas of the city and create new opportunities to achieve the "highest and best use" of land.

In the end, neither faction got exactly what it wanted, but for those concerned above all with the revitalization of downtown, the outcome was satisfactory. As we shall see in this chapter, the election of Richard J. Daley as mayor provided an opportunity to coordinate informally a set of institutions that government reorganization efforts only partially—and, from the perspective of certain business and civic leaders, imperfectly—refashioned. Under Daley, reworked governing institutions were combined with Daley's informal powers as machine "boss" to produce a new set of governing arrangements highly conducive to downtown redevelopment. The combination of institution building and concentration of political authority in the mayor's office was a powerful one, and Daley's strong interest in a downtown rebuilding program ensured that such an agenda would assume a prominent position in the city's redevelopment program.

A Rocky Start for Urban Redevelopment

As the 1940s drew to a close, decades of disappointment with programs to eliminate slums and rebuild the city's blighted areas gave way to a new sense of optimism that Chicago was finally poised to achieve greater success. With the passage of the Blighted Areas Redevelopment Act, new financial resources were already flowing from state and municipal coffers, and the federal government's Housing Act of 1949 promised even greater sums. Politically there was also cause for optimism. Chicago had a new mayor. Martin Kennelly, elected in 1947, replaced previous mayor Edward Kelly and his scandal-ridden administration. Kelly had been viewed with suspicion and mistrust by backers of housing and urban redevelopment legislation, not least because of his support for public housing and the Chicago Housing Authority. Kennelly, by contrast, a business leader enthusiastic about the concept of public-private cooperation in housing and redevelopment policy, quickly cast his lot with backers of slum clearance and redevelopment through private enterprise.

All of this was no doubt heartening to proponents of the redevelopment program, yet as redevelopment went from an idea to the planning and implementation of actual projects, problems began to surface. Land assembly, slum clearance, and the building of new public housing units for displaced residents were all taking much longer and encountering more obstacles than originally expected, in some cases placing the completion of projects in jeopardy. The crux of the problem, most agreed, was the fragmentation of the city's administrative powers, which posed a barrier to quick, decisive action. Housing and redevelopment policy was administered by several different agencies—including the CHA, the Land Clearance Commission, the Chicago Dwellings Association, and the Office of the Housing and Redevelopment Coordinator—with responsibilities for slum clearance, redevelopment, public housing, and other activities divided among them. Other agencies, such as the Chicago Plan Commission and the Department of Buildings, were engaged in activities directly relevant to the housing and redevelopment program. By the early 1950s this structure had become unwieldy. Coordination was increasingly difficult to achieve, creating "many points at which success [could] be blocked; but none at which it [could] be assured."[21]

Given the far-reaching changes in the city's approach to problems of slums and blight that had taken place over the past several decades, it is not surprising that fit between the city's institutional arrangements and the goals of housing and redevelopment stakeholders became a source of concern. As the chairman of MHPC's newly formed Committee on Administrative Reorganization put it in 1953, "The present unwieldy administrative structure has been almost inevitable in the gradual expansion of the city's work from its original functions of enforcing health and safety ordinances to include planning construction of low-rent housing and middle-income housing, demolition, and redevelopment."[22] Not only were there more agencies, but those that had been in existence for some time already were being asked to take on new and in some cases very different responsibilities. For example, passage of the Blighted Areas Redevelopment Act forced a dramatic change in the CHA's role in the attack on the slums—from provider of low-cost housing for those unable to pay an economic rent, to builder of relocation housing for residents displaced by slum clearance. The CHA's new responsibilities were critical to the Land Clearance Commission, which could not clear slums until existing residents had been relocated. Yet there was never a close working relationship between the two agencies.[23] While the CHA took seriously its new charge of providing relocation housing, it also sought to make its own contributions to the attack on the slums, including the siting of public housing developments in locations the agency deemed most suitable. As we shall see shortly, controversy over the CHA's proposed sites delayed the building of new public housing units, causing ripple effects that constrained the slum clearance activities of the Land Clearance Commission.

Similar coordination problems surfaced between the Land Clearance Commission and other agencies. The Department of Buildings resisted suggestions that it step up enforcement activities as a way of persuading property owners in redevelopment areas to sell, claiming the practice would be discriminatory. The agency eventually became a "continual source of embarrassment" to the Land Clearance Commission by repeatedly citing buildings owned but not yet razed by the commission for code violations.[24] It had been hoped that conflicts such as these could be avoided through the creation in 1947, shortly after the passage of the Blighted Areas Redevelopment Act, of the position of housing and redevelopment coordinator. However, the powers delegated to the office were unclear, meaning that the holder of the position had to rely chiefly on the mayor's backing and his own personal prestige to exercise leadership and inspire cooperation. With a weak mayor currently in office, this was a serious handicap.[25]

Finally, as if things were not already complicated enough, housing and redevelopment policy did not stand still. Problems with the program created a need for periodic policy adjustments, which led in some cases to the creation of still more agencies. The most significant of these changes was the incorporation of conservation into the redevelopment program during the early 1950s. Existing state and federal legislation provided tools to address the problems of areas that were already blighted, but it did nothing for the city's "conservation areas"—neighborhoods that were for the most part sound but experiencing "gradual deterioration" and in danger of becoming blighted unless action were taken to halt further decline.[26] The hope had originally been that slum clearance projects, by rebuilding the city's blighted areas, would act as a stabilizing force for conservation areas, preventing the "cancerous" spread of blight into such communities. In the short term, however, slum clearance had the opposite effect: many people displaced by redevelopment projects resettled in nearby conservation areas, causing overcrowding and contributing to the onset of slum conditions there.[27] By one estimate, the city's blighted areas expanded their boundaries by approximately one mile in all directions during the 1940s.[28] Alarmed by such findings, city officials eventually signaled that conservation would become a key policy priority. As the city's housing and redevelopment coordinator explained in 1952, "The No. 1 housing problem we now have is this: How can we stop the many so-called conservation areas from becoming slums. It doesn't make sense for us to undertake the big job of clearing present slums and then at the same time to allow other areas to become slums."[29]

The expansion of the city's housing policy agenda to include conservation as well as slum clearance and redevelopment led to the creation of two additional agencies, both of which played significant roles in the urban redevelopment program but further complicated the administration of housing and redevelopment policy. The most important of these new agencies was the Community Conservation Board, established by city council in September 1953 following the passage of state enabling legislation several months earlier.[30] The Community Conservation Act was largely the brainchild of MHPC and a committee of experts it had assembled in 1952 to prepare what became an extensive, three-volume study of conservation released in 1953.[31] The study included language for a proposed conservation bill that would allow municipalities to set up conservation boards with the power to designate areas that met certain conditions as officially recognized conservation areas. Within such areas, municipalities would have broad powers to halt the spread of blight, including the authority to seize and condemn properties that were beyond repair and to forcibly make improvements to salvageable buildings, using tax liens on the property to recover costs.[32] Legislation was introduced in the General Assembly in May 1953. With strong backing from Chicago business organizations and qualified support from real estate and building interests, the measure easily passed both houses of the Assembly, and the Community Conservation Act was signed by Governor William Stratton that summer.[33] Passage of the federal Housing Act of 1954 the following year further reinforced the new emphasis on conservation and rehabilitation—a policy turn captured by the new term "urban renewal," used as a substitute for "urban redevelopment" in the 1954 federal housing legislation.[34]

While the need for conservation programs was widely acknowledged, both in Chicago and elsewhere, less appreciated were the coordination problems that the addition of still more agencies to already fragmented administrative arrangements would inevitably present. Officials from Chicago's new Conservation Board frequently butted heads with their counterparts from the Land Clearance Commission, with whom they shared responsibilities for the preservation and renewal of the city's community areas. In some instances this involved turf battles over whether an area should be designated for conservation or redevelopment.[35] In other cases the two agencies found themselves working on projects in the same areas, leading to confusion about which one of them—the Conservation Board or the Land Clearance Commission—was the most suitable for completing certain tasks. In addition, due to the similarities in their missions and activities, the two agencies often competed for staff, for federal and local funds, and for local public works projects to support renewal efforts, resulting in "costly waste and delay." The result, as one study described it, was "inevitable overlapping of effort, duplication of functions, and lack of effective coordination."[36]

*   *   *

In addition to the fragmentation of urban renewal agencies, a second and related obstacle to the speedy and efficient execution of projects was posed by the weakness of the executive branch of city government. Formally speaking, Chicago was a council-governed city. City council held the power of approval over mayoral appointments, it prescribed the duties and powers of most city officers, and it could create new city departments and agencies at will. It also exercised various administrative powers, including preparation of the city budget, awarding of city contracts, and approval of zoning variances. For urban renewal projects, council approval was required for designation of project areas, site plans, the terms of sale of city-owned land to developers, rezonings, and street closings. A council majority could block virtually any action by the mayor.[37]

As a comprehensive program for urban revitalization, urban renewal policy required a citywide perspective on the part of local government officials. However, aldermen were frequently indifferent to planning and development issues that did not directly concern their own wards.[38] In situations where their wards were affected, the needs and preferences of ward constituents typically came first. If a redevelopment or public housing project was opposed by a substantial number of ward residents, the alderman representing that district was likely to oppose it as well.[39] Without strong executive leadership, an uncooperative alderman or bloc of aldermen could derail plans for new development. In the past, the office of the mayor had been strengthened informally through the fusion of political and administrative power.[40] Previous mayors such as Edward Kelly had dominated city council by forming alliances with party leaders or by serving jointly as mayor and machine boss. Mayor Kennelly, however, distanced himself from machine leaders and made no effort to bring city council under his control. As he put it early in his term, "Chicago is a council-governed city. . . . I don't think it's a function of the mayor to boss the aldermen."[41] With control over urban renewal policy lodged, by default, in city council, coordinated action was extremely difficult to achieve.

Under these conditions, questions of fit between the city's governing institutions and the goals of urban renewal stakeholders became paramount, as illustrated by the experience of Chicago's first redevelopment project carried out under the Blighted Areas Redevelopment Act. Lake Meadows, announced by Governor Green in July 1948, was a proposed one-hundred-acre housing development in an African American neighborhood on the city's South Side.[42] The architect for the project was the Chicago firm of Skidmore, Owings & Merrill, admirers and practitioners of the then-influential tower-in-the-park approach to housing popularized by the Swiss-born architect Le Corbusier and other modernist thinkers.[43] Skidmore's plan called for the construction of 1,400 new housing units, all but 116 to be located in two large twenty-three-story

FIGURE 5.1. A building in the Lake Meadows apartment complex, 1959. Chicago History Museum, Mildred Mead photograph collection, ICHi-176171.

buildings surrounded by ample green space.[44] While the project received the endorsement of Mayor Kennelly and strong backing from the city's business leadership, it was controversial. More than two thousand families currently living in the area would have to be relocated. In addition, the developer, New York Life Insurance, insisted on the closure of a two-block stretch of Cottage Grove Avenue, a major South Side arterial that bisected the project footprint. This was also part of Skidmore's plan, necessary to achieve the "superblock" scale of development—another Corbusian innovation—that would protect the area from intrusions by traffic and allow the project to better define its environment.[45]

While celebrated in the media, the project quickly encountered organized opposition. Residents of the area perceived the new development as an effort to remove blacks from the South Side.[46] A group of twenty-three property owners filed suit to prevent the Land Clearance Commission from seizing their homes, challenging the constitutionality of the Blighted Areas Redevelopment Act and claiming that the designation of the area as blighted prevented them from obtaining bank loans to properly maintain their property.[47] When that effort failed, representatives from the Property Conservation and Human Rights Committee of Chicago—a group of South Side homeowners opposed to slum clearance—traveled to Washington, DC, to meet with federal urban renewal officials and deliver a petition requesting the federal government to withhold funding for the project.[48] Residents of nearby white neighborhoods, fearing an influx of displaced blacks, also mobilized against the project.[49] Finally, the Chicago Motor Club organized a campaign against the closing of Cottage Grove Avenue, arguing that the street was essential to maintaining an adequate flow of traffic on the South Side.[50]

To the dismay of New York Life officials, the various city agencies and governing bodies with a stake in the project could not come to an agreement on how to proceed. The Land Clearance Commission initiated efforts to gain control over the hundred-acre site. However, the Chicago Plan Commission was "unceasingly difficult," debating the closure of Cottage Grove Avenue for more than a year before finally making a weak recommendation that the street be vacated.[51] Several other city agencies—including the Chicago Transit Authority, the Department of Streets and Electricity, and the Park District—registered their opposition to the street closure.[52] Meanwhile, a group of South Side aldermen opposed the project altogether, arguing it would create unacceptable hardships for current residents of the area.[53] In a 1950 speech to members of the American Society of Planning Officials, an exasperated Ferd Kramer described the situation as follows:

> The vested interest of each department and bureau is something that you can only appreciate after having bumped head-on into it. The fact that a particular street has been in existence since the days of the Indians, whether or not that street performs an important function today, may be so potent that it will almost require an act of God, the Mayor, and the City Council to remove it. The investing corporation as one party to the agreement must be able to make instantaneous and definitive decisions, and it has one officer who is empowered to make those decisions. But the other party to the con-

tract, by the very nature of government make-up, is a superstructure of com-missions, committees, authorities, boards, and officials. There is no indi-vidual with complete and undisputed authority to make quick and binding decisions. When the plan gets to the mayor and the city council it may be ex-peditiously accepted in the matter of a month, or it may be made into a politi-cal football and languish for months if not years.[54]

By spring 1950, New York Life had begun to lose patience. In a let-ter to Mayor Kennelly, company vice president Otto Nelson warned that "fatal delay and eventual failure will result if the various agencies of the city who are involved yield to the temptation to compromise and pla-cate at every point where some individual or small group is affected ad-versely."[55] With the fate of the city's first urban renewal project hanging in the balance, Kennelly made a rare appearance before city council to express his support for the development, warning of dire consequences should the project go down to defeat. "I don't ever tell the council how to vote," insisted Kennelly, "but this is one of the most important things ever to come before the council. It is a question of whether we will be able to get the vital job of cleaning up the slums under way."[56] Not wish-ing to be blamed for the failure of a project of this magnitude, the coun-cil gave its approval the following month by a vote of 31–12.[57] In Febru-ary 1952, nearly four years after the development was first announced, ground was finally broken on the city's first redevelopment project. Al-though urban renewal proponents celebrated this milestone, the lengthy delays experienced by New York Life sent a strong message to private in-vestors that urban renewal in Chicago under the present political and in-stitutional conditions would require tremendous patience.

*   *   *

Progress with New York Life's Lake Meadows development and subse-quent slum clearance redevelopment projects was also impeded by diffi-culties lining up suitable replacement housing for residents needing relo-cation assistance. Slums could not be cleared until new housing had been found for the existing residents of project areas, and in postwar Chi-cago this was no simple task. The city's blighted areas were already se-verely overcrowded, yet because many of the residents being forced from their homes were African American, these were the only areas of the city where they did not face intense housing discrimination. The reloca-

FIGURE 5.2. Slum clearance area, Kenwood, 1951. Chicago History Museum, Mildred Mead photograph collection, ICHi-086656.

tion problem eventually became one of the "chief obstacles" to the start of construction for the Lake Meadows development, and this was just the tip of the iceberg.[58] By 1952 it was estimated that some five thousand families would have to be relocated each year for the next ten years to make way for new slum clearance and highway building projects.[59] Yet as crucial as the matter of relocation was to the city's redevelopment program, relocation efforts were badly administered. The CHA, the Land Clearance Commission, and the Housing and Redevelopment Coordinator all employed their own relocation staffs. An interagency committee on relocation was supposed to coordinate the efforts of the three

groups, but the pressure for individual agencies to satisfy the housing demands of their own programs was intense, and competition among agencies for scarce housing units meant that vacancies were not always allocated in the most judicious fashion.[60]

Of course not all displaced residents would need to find replacement
housing through the private housing market. New public housing developments were expected to absorb a substantial number of these families and individuals. A companion measure of the Blighted Areas Redevelopment Act had allocated $3.3 million for the construction of
public housing units for residents displaced by slum clearance projects,
and a bond issue approved by Chicago voters later that year added another $15 million to the total. With the passage of the federal Housing
Act of 1949 two years later, additional resources for the construction of
relocation housing became available. Yet despite this infusion of funding, Chicago lagged other cities in the production of public housing. By
1952, Chicago had just 3.2 public housing units per 1,000 residents. By
contrast, San Francisco had 12.2 units, Boston 12.1 units, Baltimore 10
units, Cleveland 7.2 units, Detroit 6.1 units, and New York 5.6 units.[61]
Here again the administration of the program was seemingly culpable.
Not surprisingly, the selection of sites for relocation housing proved to
be a thorny issue, with white residents strongly opposed to the building of public housing developments—which they feared would be populated by African Americans—in their neighborhoods. Under state law
the CHA had the authority to select housing sites. However, the law also
stated that all sites the CHA proposed were subject to approval by city
council, giving the council immense power over site selection.

A key problem with this power-sharing arrangement was that CHA
officials and the majority of the city's aldermen had very different views
about where and how public housing should be built. CHA director
Elizabeth Wood—influenced by Catherine Bauer's conception of public housing as community building and the ideas of Corbusier, Walter
Gropius, and their modernist contemporaries—favored large projects
with a thousand or more units that would create defensible space, in-
sulating new developments from encroaching blight.[62] The planning of
new public housing projects, Wood insisted, "must be bold and comprehensive—or it is useless and wasted. If it is not bold, the result will be
a series of small projects, islands in a wilderness of slums beaten down
by smoke, noise and fumes. . . . We know that if blighted areas are not

rebuilt in these protected superblocks, all expenditures will be wasted; the project will decay. Little plans will require a redoing of the total job within three generations."[63]

By Wood's reasoning—difficult to argue with—the preferred location for new public housing developments was on vacant land so that additional relocation of residents would not be required to make way for the new projects. Since there were few vacant sites large enough to accommodate projects of the scale the CHA envisioned within already developed sections of the city, this would mean building chiefly in outlying areas that were less densely populated. This presented a problem, however, because the residents of such areas were mostly white, while those eligible for space in the new relocation units were predominantly African American. Anticipating—no doubt correctly—the views of their constituents regarding this potential breach of the city's racial boundaries, aldermen representing the city's white working-class wards called for the building of smaller projects within the city's blighted areas.[64]

In the end, the leverage exerted by city council in decisions about relocation housing sites resulted in outcomes that few considered satisfactory, least of all the CHA and supporters of the slum clearance and redevelopment program. The CHA initiated site selection efforts in 1947 and again in 1949, the first round supported by the combined state/municipal housing program of 1947 and the second by the federal government's Housing Act of 1949. Negotiations between the CHA and the city council over the proposed sites dragged on for nineteen months in the two rounds combined, delaying the start of relocation housing and angering supporters of the redevelopment program, who feared that continued inaction would significantly impede slum clearance efforts.[65] Facing extreme public pressure to come to a resolution, CHA officials agreed to a final slate of sites that met few of the agency's criteria for relocation housing. For the state/municipal housing program, nine project areas were selected containing between 100 and 275 units each, a far cry from the 1,000-unit structures CHA officials envisioned themselves building.[66] With one exception, all sites were relatively small, and two-thirds were located in slum areas near railroads, factories, or other developments that raised questions about the suitability of the sites for residential development.[67] For the much larger federal program, the outcome was even more disappointing. The CHA had proposed 4,000 units in slum areas and 8,000 units on vacant land; what it got instead were 10,250 units in slum locations and just 2,100 units on vacant land.[68] Worst of all, the program would require the displacement of 12,465 families, resulting in a net addition to the city's housing supply of just 47 units.[69] To call this relocation housing seemed for many observers to be the height of absurdity.

Government Reorganization: Part I

By the early 1950s, supporters of Chicago's slum clearance and redevelopment program had identified the fragmentation of the city's urban renewal powers as a principal cause of Chicago's sluggish redevelopment efforts. As one civic group put it, "It is obvious that Chicago has too many agencies working on different segments of its housing problem, and that this creates pointless rivalries, overall administrative inefficiency, excessive costs and public confusion."[70] In 1951 the city council Committee on Housing commissioned a study of the organization and administration of the city's urban redevelopment program. The study was initiated by committee chairman Robert Merriam, a reform alderman from Hyde Park who had served as MHPC's director from 1946 to 1947. Released in July 1952, the study reaffirmed what MHPC and other urban renewal proponents had been arguing for several years: Chicago's "bewildering" administrative organizational structure had created a situation in which "all agencies locally involved in redevelopment and housing occupy compromised positions."[71] The study's principal recommendation was the creation of a new city Department of Redevelopment and Housing which would assume the duties of the CHA, the Land Clearance Commission, and several other existing urban renewal agencies, all of which would be abolished.[72]

While the report received considerable attention, the response was for the most part less than enthusiastic. During the housing committee's first day of hearings on the report, representatives from the CHA and other affected agencies repeatedly criticized the study findings, prompting one of Merriam's aides to suggest that nongovernmental groups be invited to testify at subsequent hearings.[73] As another observer concluded, "As long as the recommendation of the report involves the doing away with existing agencies and the transfer of power from others, we can anticipate that there will be considerable opposition."[74] Yet civic groups responded cautiously to the report as well. In a letter to the housing committee, the chair of MHPC's newly formed committee on administrative reorganization recommended a gradual approach to administrative change.[75] The proposal was "a fine plan in theory, but utterly dangerous to attempt at this time" because of the control city council would exercise over the proposed new department.[76] To be successful, administrative reorganization would have to be accompanied by a parallel reform effort to strengthen the executive branch of city government.[77]

Such an effort was, in fact, under way and gaining momentum at the time. In 1952 a reform group calling itself the Citizens of Greater Chicago launched an initiative to produce a new city charter for Chicago. Under the organization's proposed charter reform bill, administrative functions exercised by city council, such as preparation of the city budget, would be transferred to the mayor's office. In addition, the size of city council would be reduced from fifty to fifteen members, including five members elected at large.[78] Aldermen were largely dismissive of the initiative. As one council member put it, "This is just a reform group. They don't know what an alderman's job is all about. They all come from rich wards where they never have to go to an alderman to get anything done."[79] Confident that the machine could withstand this challenge to the ward system, most aldermen did not appear to take the proposal seriously.

Business leaders and civic groups were for the most part supportive of the Citizens of Greater Chicago. MHPC, which viewed charter reform as a necessary prerequisite for consolidation of the city's urban renewal agencies, quickly developed a partnership with the organization, and the MHPC board of governors voted in June 1953 to endorse the organization's charter reform bill.[80] Despite the backing of the city's business and civic leadership, however, charter reform faced an uphill battle in the state legislature. Opposition to the bill from Chicago Democratic legislators would have to be offset by strong support from downstate Republicans.[81] Republican support failed to materialize, however, and the bill was defeated in the state senate by a vote of 18–12. Chicago Democrats reportedly voted for a number of downstate bills in exchange for promises from Republican legislators to oppose charter reform. By one account roughly half the downstate Republican delegation "either sat silent or walked out of the senate chamber just before the roll call."[82]

While charter reform was being debated, Mayor Kennelly took steps of his own to reorganize city government. Concerned that the Citizens of Greater Chicago was "moving too rapidly" in its efforts to obtain a new charter for the city, Kennelly appointed a fifteen-member Home Rule Commission to study the organization of city government and provide recommendations for reform.[83] The commission, chaired by Chicago

Association of Commerce and Industry director Leverett Lyon, issued its findings in a 415-page report released in September 1954.[84] The report's recommendations were similar to those of the Citizens of Greater Chicago charter reform bill, advocating a "strong mayor" system of government and a downsized city council.[85] Moreover, as a body with official standing, the Home Rule Commission commanded a degree of legitimacy and respect that the Citizens of Greater Chicago did not enjoy.

The recommendations of the Home Rule Commission were enthusiastically endorsed by the city's major newspapers and top business organizations.[86] However, as the city's experience with charter reform a year earlier had shown, assembling legislative majorities around government reorganization in Chicago would be difficult without the cooperation of the city's Democratic Party regulars, and under the political conditions of the day the latter seemed highly improbable. As long as the mayor's office was occupied by someone who could not be trusted to further the interests of the Democratic Party organization, machine politicians had few incentives to support reform. Implementing a strong mayor system would simply increase Kennelly's ability to act independently of the city's political bosses.

By 1954 urban renewal in Chicago stood at a crossroads. At this juncture, the fit between the city's administrative structures and the goals of urban renewal stakeholders favored defenders of the status quo, providing multiple points of leverage for neighborhood residents, ward politicians, and other urban renewal opponents to delay and obstruct renewal efforts. For redevelopment to occur at the speed and scale envisioned by the backers of the program, institution building was necessary. The powers of the mayor would have to be strengthened, and the urban renewal bureaucracy would need to be reorganized. Government reorganization, however, could not proceed under the city's existing political arrangements. Either the machine had to be beaten, or the mayor's office had to fall into the hands of someone closely allied with or occupying a leadership position in the Democratic Party organization. With the election of Richard J. Daley as mayor in 1955, Chicago chose the latter option.

Government Reorganization: Part II

By the end of Martin Kennelly's second term as mayor of Chicago, the city's Democratic Party was once again on solid footing. Kennelly had served his purpose by restoring the machine's credibility with voters and was now viewed by the party's inner circle more as a liability than as an asset.[87] Given his political weakness, party leaders never expected the mayor to seriously pursue reform, and Kennelly had largely obliged. However, in certain areas, such as civil service appointments, he asserted his independence from the machine. Party leaders were incensed with his efforts to undercut the patronage system, which temporarily removed twelve thousand jobs from the control of ward bosses.[88]

When the Democratic Party's slate-making committee met in December 1954 to select its candidate for mayor, the committee bypassed Kennelly in favor of Richard J. Daley. Daley had risen through the ranks of the Democratic Party organization to become chairman of the Cook County Democratic Central Committee, the party's top post, in 1953. With Daley's election victory over independent alderman Robert Merriam in April 1955, the city's political and administrative powers were joined. As party boss, Daley commanded a vast army of patronage workers, which he used to bring an undisciplined city council under his control. Council members who faithfully supported his governing agenda were rewarded with patronage and other perquisites to distribute among precinct workers, while noncompliant aldermen saw the patronage positions at their disposal cut. Few aldermen were willing to risk the consequences of challenging the mayor. Informally, Chicago had once again become a "strong mayor" city.[89]

However, Daley was not content with exercising power informally. In his inaugural address he endorsed the findings of Kennelly's Home Rule Commission, calling for measures that would strengthen the administrative powers of the mayor.[90] During the Kennelly years, machine politicians had been reluctant to support legislation that would enhance the powers of an independent mayor, and Kennelly could not force them to act. Daley, on the other hand, had considerable influence in the state legislature and, as the Democratic Party boss, did not pose a threat to the machine. Ultimately the commission's report provided the framework for a rapid succession of administrative reforms carried out during Daley's first year in office. During the months before he was elected, Daley helped engineer state legislation to transfer city budget-making powers from city council to the mayor's office. A bill giving Chicago an executive-style budget was passed unanimously by the General Assembly and signed by Governor Stratton shortly after Daley was elected.[91] During the following months, new laws were passed shifting control over city purchasing and zoning variances from city council to the executive branch of city government. In addition, city council approved an ordinance to relinquish its control over the issuing of driveway permits, a long-standing aldermanic perquisite.[92]

During his first year in office, Daley also took steps to consolidate the city's planning powers in the mayor's office. Since 1909 the city's principal planning body had been the Chicago Plan Commission, an advisory body whose thirty-five members served without pay. Dependent on city council for its budget and for approval of its plans, the commission had no obligation to serve the city's executive branch. Business and civic leaders had long complained that the Plan Commission's subservient relationship to city council made it a "creature of the aldermen," compromising the professionalism of the agency.[93] As MHPC described the situation, "In its step-child relationship to the City Council, planning tends to become a political football, and the Plan Commission goes to extremes to please the City Council, individually and collectively."[94] With a limited budget, the commission was forced to spend much of its time responding to service requests from individual aldermen, which limited its ability to carry out constructive planning.[95]

In February 1956, Daley's housing and redevelopment coordinator, James Downs, presented the mayor with a proposal to create a new Department of City Planning.[96] Under the proposal, most of the Plan Commission's functions would be transferred to the new department, to be overseen by a commissioner appointed by and responsible to the mayor. The departmental status of the new agency would significantly diminish the authority of city council over city planning, a change applauded by MHPC and other business and civic groups.[97] A city ordinance was quickly prepared. With Daley's backing, the city council approved the ordinance, and the Department of City Planning was established in January 1957. Once again Daley had used his informal powers as leader of the Democratic Party organization to produce new legislation that expanded the formal powers of the mayor's office.[98]

With enhanced executive powers and a new planning department under his direction, Daley was in a considerably stronger position than his predecessor to pursue a program of urban redevelopment. He quickly signaled that redevelopment—including the rebuilding of the downtown area—would be a priority of his administration. In 1958 Daley's new Department of City Planning released the *Development Plan for the Central Area of Chicago*, laying out the city's plans to anchor the downtown

corporate and retail sectors with a series of public and private improvements in the downtown and near-downtown area.[99] As described in
chapter 4, the plan was a collaborative effort between the Department
of City Planning and the recently formed Chicago Central Area Committee. Like MHPC, the Central Area Committee served as a vehicle
for business input into the redevelopment process. In contrast to MHPC,
the focus of the Central Area Committee was limited to the redevelopment of downtown and its immediate surroundings.

While the Central Area Committee worked with city officials to finalize the 1958 Development Plan, MHPC renewed its efforts to promote administrative reorganization of the city's urban renewal bureaucracy. This initiative had stalled while Kennelly was mayor due to fears
that city council influence over a reorganized bureaucracy would undermine its effectiveness.[100] With the formal and informal powers of the
mayor vis-à-vis city council now strengthened, MHPC no longer viewed
this as a major concern. By this time six local agencies had come into existence to administer different aspects of urban renewal policy. Coordination of renewal efforts had become increasingly difficult, creating
"unnecessary costs and delays."[101] In addition, overlapping agency juris-
dictions were complicating relationships with the Housing and Home Finance Agency, the principal conduit for federal urban renewal funds.[102]
In 1957 Mayor Daley established an urban renewal coordinating committee which brought agency directors together with the mayor for biweekly meetings. However, the committee served as a vehicle more for
obtaining input from the mayor than for coordinating policy. In addition, since most urban renewal agencies had been set up as independent
authorities, the mayor could not always control them. MHPC was convinced that further progress with urban renewal would require a substantial reorganization of the city's urban renewal bureaucracy.[103]

The Daley administration appeared to share MHPC's interest in administrative reorganization. In June 1955, housing and redevelopment
coordinator James Downs asked MHPC to conduct a review of the city's
existing administrative structure for urban renewal and to make recommendations for reorganization.[104] In response, MHPC established
a committee on unification, which issued its findings in a draft report
completed in December 1956. The committee recommended that the
city's six existing urban renewal agencies be consolidated into two new
city departments—a department of housing and a department of urban
renewal—under the mayor's control. Housing was to be kept separate

because public housing was the most controversial program associated with urban renewal. MHPC feared that combining housing with other renewal operations would jeopardize support for the entire urban renewal program.[105]

Mayor Daley indicated to MHPC that he was "anxious to push unification."[106] At the city's request, MHPC drafted state enabling legislation to expand Chicago's home rule powers in urban renewal policy. The proposed statute, an amendment to the Illinois Cities and Villages Act, was broadly permissive, allowing Chicago and any other Illinois municipality to determine "the number, or kind, or powers" of urban renewal agencies they chose to create.[107] Although MHPC did not recommend such a structure for Chicago, the bill would permit communities to combine all urban renewal operations, including housing, in one agency. The specific form that any reorganization of agencies took in a given community would be determined locally by city ordinance.[108]

Efforts to reorganize the city's urban renewal bureaucracy sparked a heated debate between two parties that had until this time been close allies in the planning and implementation of the city's redevelopment program: MHPC and Central Area Committee chairman Holman Pettibone. While both agreed on the need for administrative reorganization, they disagreed about the form reorganization should take. In a January 1957 letter to Daley, Pettibone cautioned the mayor against legislation that would permit the consolidation of either the CHA or the Land Clearance Commission with any other agency.[109] Arguing that both housing and slum clearance were "unique fields," Pettibone recommended that all renewal operations with the exception of housing and slum clearance be combined in one agency. The resulting three-agency structure would be overseen by an urban renewal coordinator reporting directly to the mayor. MHPC, by contrast, preferred a two-agency structure maintaining the present status of the CHA but combining all other units, including the Land Clearance Commission, into one agency. The chief disagreement between the two thus centered on the status of the Land Clearance Commission and whether it should remain independent, as Pettibone argued, or combined with other agencies, as MHPC recommended.

What explains this difference of opinion within the ranks of the city's business and civic leadership about the reorganization of urban renewal agencies? The answer lies in the increasingly prominent role that conservation had begun to play in the city's urban renewal program by the mid-1950s, and the view by some that conservation should not be mingled with large-scale slum clearance. Pettibone fell into this camp. While supportive of conservation for certain areas of the city, Pettibone, as chairman of the Central Area Committee, was concerned chiefly with the central area, and he and others believed that extensive slum clearance—not conservation—was needed here. Large-scale slum clearance would facilitate the rearranging of land use the Central Area Committee deemed essential in reclaiming the downtown area, including removal of the area's low-income population.[110] No agency was more important to achieving this goal than the Land Clearance Commission, since slum clearance and redevelopment was its sole purpose. Combining its activities with those of agencies pursuing conservation posed a threat to downtown redevelopment, Pettibone feared, because it would dissolve the one agency dedicated exclusively to the clearance and redevelopment of land. In opposing such an arrangement, Pettibone sought to preserve an administrative structure that provided the best fit with his agenda of rearranging land use in the downtown area.

In contrast to the downtown focus of Pettibone and the Central Area Committee, MHPC had a more citywide view of urban renewal and redevelopment. Through such activities as its conservation study of 1953 and involvement with projects in Hyde Park and other conservation areas, MHPC grew increasingly preoccupied with the need to protect areas of the city not yet blighted but in danger of becoming so. While supportive of redevelopment and the rearranging of land use in blighted areas, MHPC came to view large-scale slum clearance as more the exception than the rule in urban renewal policy. Conservation, the organization argued in a 1956 report, "must eventually be the heart of the renewal program," in part because the city's conservation areas were "many times the size of the slum area."[111] For much of the city, blight could be controlled through a more surgical approach that combined "spot clearance" with the rehabilitation of existing structures. Slum clearance and conservation were thus "part of the same activity, like the two sides of a coin."[112] There was nothing to be feared in combining the two activities in one agency. To the contrary, such an arrangement was well suited to the prevention and elimination of blight wherever it existed.

The disagreement between MHPC and Pettibone over the position of the Land Clearance Commission in a reorganized urban renewal bureaucracy placed Mayor Daley in an awkward position. He had asked MHPC to prepare legislation enabling the city to proceed with administrative reform, but the bill was being opposed by a prominent business leader whom he most likely did not wish to offend. In the end Daley chose the status quo. In 1957 he agreed to introduce MHPC's bill in the General Assembly as city-sponsored legislation. Assuming that the mayor's endorsement of the bill would be accompanied by efforts on the part of the Chicago delegation to mobilize support in the General Assembly, MHPC did not organize a significant lobbying campaign of its own in the legislature. The bill received little support from the administration, however, and failed to pass.[113]

In the fall of 1960, MHPC began developing plans for a new legislative push. This time, however, the organization would not rely exclusively on Mayor Daley to guide its bill through the legislature. Instead it would present the bill to the mayor as legislation "which the Housing Council intends to advocate."[114] During the next several months, MHPC held meetings with business leaders, state legislators, and representatives from urban renewal agencies and the mayor's office to build support for new legislation. Previously the strongest opposition had come from Pettibone and Land Clearance Commission chairman Philip Doyle.[115] Both now signaled a willingness to compromise. Doyle in particular had become increasingly concerned about the Land Clearance Commission's status as an independent authority, which he believed compromised the agency's ability to withstand political opposition. At a November meeting with MHPC's Committee on Administrative Organization, Doyle observed that a department head could "speak for the mayor," giving him greater "prestige" than the head of an independent authority. "With the huge [urban renewal] program now contemplated, urban renewal [would] require 100 percent political backing." To deal more effectively with opposition to the expanding program, Doyle indicated he was "prepared to support consolidation" of renewal agencies in a new department of urban renewal under the mayor's direction.[116]

By the spring of 1961, Pettibone's objections had softened as well. While the reason for this change of heart is unclear, it may be that Pettibone did not want to stand in the way of a reorganization effort that by now enjoyed substantial support among business leaders, and that even the chairman of the Land Clearance Commission now endorsed.[117] It is also likely that some of his concerns about the effectiveness of the redevelopment program under a reorganized administrative structure were allayed by Daley's commitment to downtown redevelopment and the power he held over the city's governance structures. By this time it was clear that Daley's endorsement of a redevelopment or conservation project was generally sufficient to mobilize the necessary governing bodies on its behalf, making it unlikely that the absence of an agency devoted exclusively to slum clearance would significantly impede progress. Under these circumstances, the efficiencies gained through consolidation of agencies might, in Pettibone's mind, have begun to outweigh the potential risk to the downtown redevelopment program. In April, Pettibone presented his own reorganization plan to the mayor, which proposed that the same five individuals be appointed to oversee the activities of three existing urban renewal agencies—the Land Clearance Commission, the Community Conservation Board, and the Neighborhood Redevelopment Commission.[118] Significantly, this would be "a first step toward ultimate consolidation of Chicago's urban renewal activity into one entity operating under a single statute."[119] The long-term, if not the short-term, administrative reorganization goals of MHPC and Holman Pettibone now appeared to be substantially the same.

These developments meant that when MHPC's reorganization bill was introduced in the General Assembly the following month, the political hurdles it faced were substantially lower than they had been during the previous attempt at passage. Predicting success, one legislator described the current bill as "not controversial."[120] The Land Clearance Commission, no longer convinced that its status as an independent authority would provide it with the political protection it needed, dropped its opposition to the legislation. Support from other political and institutional stakeholders had been secured through MHPC's lobbying and organizing efforts. With differences fading among key administration allies around the issue of administrative reorganization, Mayor Daley held a press conference to endorse the legislation.[121] As expected, the General Assembly acted favorably on the bill, which was signed by newly elected Democratic governor Otto Kerner in the summer of 1961. A city ordinance creating a new Department of Urban Renewal was passed in September 1961, and the department began operations the following January.[122]

*   *   *

The creation of the Department of Urban Renewal marked the culmination of an institution-building process that had begun ten years earlier with the city council's 1952 study on the consolidation of redevelopment and housing agencies. The new department, together with the formal and informal strengthening of the mayor's powers under the Daley administration, significantly altered the balance of power among actors with a stake in urban renewal policy. Institutions that had once provided access points for neighborhood groups and other organizations to successfully oppose slum clearance and other disruptive urban renewal initiatives had now been reworked to minimize such opportunities. By 1962 the "rules of the game" increasingly favored proponents of urban renewal and redevelopment. Opportunities for neighborhood organizations, preservationists, and other political actors to interfere with redevelopment efforts were constrained, while renewal operations were streamlined through a new administrative structure that minimized turf battles and duplication of effort among renewal agencies.

Given the opposition to administrative reorganization that reformers encountered and the hesitancy even by reformers to back reorganization plans during the early 1950s, what explains the eventual success of these institution-building efforts? The turning point was the election of Richard J. Daley as mayor in 1955. To be successful, the pursuit of institutional change would have to be constructed on solid political footing, and political conditions during the Kennelly years were highly unfavorable for such an attempt. Proponents of bureaucratic reorganization were reluctant to press for new administrative structures when it was clear they would be controlled by ward bosses, yet efforts to strengthen the mayor's formal powers and assuage such concerns faced an uphill battle, blocked by the reluctance of machine politicians to grant a reform mayor increased independence. The election of a new mayor—who in addition to holding the most powerful position in city government also controlled the Democratic Party organization—changed this political calculus. Machine politicians now grew less hostile to proposals to strengthen the executive branch of city government. With a stronger executive branch, bureaucratic reorganization could in turn proceed with fewer concerns about meddlesome ward bosses. Ironically, it was Daley the machine boss rather than Kennelly the reformer who set the stage for change, easing the fears of both civic leaders and machine politicians that administrative reform would somehow work to their disadvantage.

It might be argued that the creation of the new Department of Urban Renewal was a victory for MHPC and its citywide approach to urban renewal, and a defeat for Holman Pettibone and others concerned chiefly with the rearranging of land use in the downtown area. The folding of the Land Clearance Commission's activities into an agency concerned at least as much, if not more, with conservation as with slum clearance was certainly not the arrangement Pettibone would have preferred, at least in the short term. Scholars of American political development have suggested that the winners in contests over institutional change hold an advantage in shaping the governing agenda in accordance with their preferences. Benefiting from new institutional arrangements that provide a closer fit with their governing demands, such groups are better positioned than others in struggles to shape the direction of public policy.[123] Yet while institutional reform may indeed confer important advantages on certain groups, it is important to bear in mind that institution-building efforts take place within an overall set of governing arrangements where formal institutions combine with other factors to determine how policy outcomes are shaped. The dissolving of the Land Clearance Commission looks like a defeat for those groups interested chiefly in the redevelopment of the downtown area until one considers the importance of Mayor Daley's backing of the downtown redevelopment program. Once Daley determined that downtown would be a priority, there was little chance that Pettibone and his allies would be fundamentally disadvantaged by the specific form administrative reorganization ultimately took. One structure might be superior to another, but both would get the job done. Conversely, MHPC's push for conservation on a citywide basis, seemingly advantaged by the new Department of Urban Renewal, would be severely handicapped if it failed to attract the interest and support of the mayor.

Given the vast power Mayor Daley exercised over the city's urban renewal program and city governance more generally, it might be argued, alternatively, that institutions do not matter very much in this case. Perhaps the prospects for urban renewal policy were determined largely by Daley's control over city government, not by the institutional arrangements through which policy was administered. Indeed much has been made of the way in which Daley's personal backing of Chicago's postwar redevelopment program contributed to its success, with many pointing to the mayor's immense power as the principal explanation for the city's ability to mobilize the public sector on behalf of the redevelopment campaign. By many accounts, the presence of a machine boss as mayor during the redevelopment period—a time when boss rule elsewhere had been largely vanquished—made Chicago distinctive, allowing much to be coordinated informally that in other cities had to be accomplished through formal governance structures.[124]

There is much truth to such arguments, yet to focus on Daley's informal powers to the exclusion of other factors risks oversimplification. As this chapter has shown, Daley himself recognized that there were limits to what could be accomplished through informal powers. This explains the strong push early in his administration for implementation of the Home Rule Commission's institutional reform proposals and his move to enhance the mayor's planning powers vis-à-vis city council by creating a new Department of City Planning. Although Daley acted more cautiously when it came to consolidating the city's urban renewal agencies, he supported this move as well once business leaders and key institutional stakeholders reached an accommodation over proposals for administrative reorganization. Chicago was distinctive, but not because of the absence of institution building or because such efforts were not important to the success of the redevelopment program. Rather, Chicago was distinctive because of the unusual way the institution-building problem was solved, relying in part on the crafting of new institutional arrangements and in part on the enhanced informal powers held by the city's mayor.

While this arrangement may have brought governing institutions more closely into sync with the new policy paradigm of urban redevelopment and public-private partnerships, the stability of new paradigms and their prospects for institutionalization depend on more than the fit between policy ideas and institutional arrangements. As argued in chapter 1, the extent to which newly emerging paradigms continue in the direction their creators intend is also determined by feedback effects generated by new policy ideas and accompanying policy initiatives, and by the internal coherence of paradigm goals and objectives themselves. As we will see in the following chapter, the latter of these two conditions became a particularly vexing problem for Chicago's urban renewal program. Layering new policy goals (the maximization of land values) on top of old ones (the elimination of slums citywide), leaders of the new program found it impossible to do both. Having reworked institutional arrangements to better align with their governing agenda, actors found themselves face to face with the contradictions embodied in that agenda.

CHAPTER SIX

The Attack on the Slums

We all recognize that slums are the spawning ground not only of disease and delinquency, but also of insecurity and frustration. They are the most strident examples of Democracy's failure, and they are here, spreading for miles, to be seen, photographed, and used against us by our enemies.—Ferd Kramer, president, Metropolitan Housing and Planning Council, 1952[1]

In December 1961 the *Chicago Tribune* ran a five-part series celebrating Chicago's downtown development program. Describing the three-year period from 1958 to 1961 as "one of the greatest building booms in the city's history," the *Tribune* identified forty-four "major construction projects in downtown Chicago" that had been completed during this time or were under construction or in the planning stages.[2] These projects—which included new office towers, hotels, apartment buildings, public buildings, and a new convention center on the lakefront—represented at least $1 billion in new investment. Upon completion, the new office buildings alone would add an additional ten million square feet to the inventory of downtown office space. For the most part the new building boom was the work of private enterprise, providing strong evidence "of the renewed faith in Chicago's downtown and its prospects for further growth."[3] It was all the more remarkable since virtually no new construction had taken place downtown for twenty years prior to the completion of the Prudential Life Insurance Company's forty-one-story Midwest headquarters building in 1955.

Chicago's postwar downtown development program was both envisioned and set in motion by the city's 1958 *Development Plan for the Central Area of Chicago*, produced in consultation with the Chicago Central Area Committee. A key objective of the plan, strongly endorsed by the Central Area Committee, was the rearranging of land use in "peripheral" areas adjacent to the central business district to provide better synergies with downtown. Organization leaders advocated use of the city's urban renewal powers to enable these "valuable but deteriorating areas" to be "rebuilt by private enterprise from slums to pleasant residential sections for more people close to the heart of the city."[4] As Central Area Committee chairman Holman Pettibone opined in 1957, "The central area is not a slum but it has some disgraceful areas. The only thing to do is to tear them down."[5]

The Central Area Committee's push for urban renewal as a vehicle for upgrading near-downtown areas is not surprising. As recounted in earlier chapters, Pettibone himself played a key role in the passage of the Illinois Blighted Areas Redevelopment Act and its companion bills, legislation that set the city's slum clearance and redevelopment program in motion. As chair of Mayor Kennelly's Committee for Housing Action, Pettibone and fellow business executive Milton Mumford had negotiated the final details of the legislation with downstate Republicans and Chicago Democrats to find a compromise acceptable to all. Following passage of the new legislation, Pettibone was instrumental in persuading the New York Life Insurance Company to sign on as developer of the city's first urban renewal project, the Lake Meadows housing development. As much as anyone, Pettibone understood intimately the mechanics of the new legislation and its potential to serve as a tool for upgrading and rearranging land use in blighted areas. In his new role as chair of the Central Area Committee, he quite naturally viewed the legislation he had helped pioneer as a promising mechanism for attracting new private development to the central area and achieving the highest and best use of land.

Given Mayor Daley's endorsement of the downtown development program and the seemingly close collaboration between city officials and the Central Area Committee in the preparation of the 1958 Development Plan, it might be expected that urban renewal policy would have featured a growing emphasis on projects in the downtown area, particularly those aimed at increasing the area's middle-class residential population. Curiously, however, downtown and near-downtown projects remained far more the exception than the rule in the city's urban renewal program. By 1961, fourteen years after the passage of the Blighted Areas Redevelopment Act, only one-third of the city's total acreage devoted to urban renewal projects was located within the boundaries of the central area. Of a total of twenty-six redevelopment projects completed or

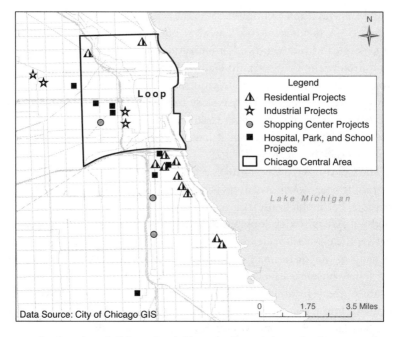

FIGURE 6.1. Location of Chicago Land Clearance Commission redevelopment projects, 1961. Source: Chicago Land Clearance Commission, Location of Commission's 26 Redevelopment Projects Comprising 895 Acres (Chicago, 1961).

under way, eight were located in the central area, and of these only two were residential projects (fig. 6.1).[6] This pattern is consistent with Mayor Daley's public pronouncements about the urban renewal program, which repeatedly emphasized the elimination of slums citywide as the program's long-term goal. For Daley, downtown development and the attack on the slums were for the most part discrete and separate policy goals. Urban renewal powers were used to clear and redevelop blighted areas located in most cases some distance from downtown. To be sure, downtown development received strong support from the Daley administration. However, with a few key exceptions, the city did not use what was by far the most powerful tool in its development arsenal to support the downtown redevelopment program.

Why would Mayor Daley concentrate resources on an overwhelming and seemingly unrealizable quest to eradicate slums wherever they existed rather than use those powers to support a newly emerging downtown redevelopment program that, by all indications, seemed to have great potential for success? Daley's actions are less puzzling if we return once again to the role of ideas in the policymaking process. Daley and others involved in the city's redevelopment program viewed slums as a key impediment to the achievement of a stable and economically prosperous urban community. Slums were costly, imposing "unusually heavy expenses for fire and police protection, for hospital care and for relief."[7] Not infrequently slum properties were tax delinquent, further magnifying the gap between tax receipts and the cost of services in slum areas. More ominously, the slums were growing, expanding at an alarming pace to engulf stable areas and induce white flight to the suburbs. The "cancerous" spread of slums led the designers of the Redevelopment Act to the conclusion that the attack on the slums required total victory. Even those concerned chiefly with the welfare of downtown agreed that slum conditions, wherever they existed, must be stamped out altogether. As Mayor Kennelly's Committee for Housing Action, chaired by Holman Pettibone, wrote in a 1947 report, "The rotting cells which we know as the slums are threatening to infect more and more areas unless immediate and heroic steps are taken to cut off their gangrenous growth. The situation dictates the radical surgery of amputation if we are to avert complete collapse. The new and healthy tissue of clean, decent and well-planned housing must be grafted onto our conservation areas by whatever processes are available."[8]

This view of slums as incompatible with the achievement of the good city was shared by key members of Mayor Daley's planning staff and most likely by the mayor himself.[9] Daley had a long history with the city's slum clearance and redevelopment program, dating back to his days as an Illinois state senator in the late 1930s. As noted in chapter 3, it was Daley who sponsored the unsuccessful bill to create public service building corporations as a way to stimulate private sector involvement in slum clearance projects. Proponents of the bill cited the excessive costs of slums and the inability to contain them as justifications for the new legislation, much the same as backers of the Redevelopment Act did in 1947.[10] By the time Daley became mayor in 1955, he had heard such arguments repeated for many years, and there is no evidence that his views departed from what by this time had become widely shared beliefs about the need for a comprehensive program to eliminate slums. Given the prevalence of such beliefs, Daley's approach to slum clearance and redevelopment is understandable. To focus the urban renewal program on the downtown area, while neglecting other parts of the city where blight was even more advanced, would have seemed foolhardy at best.

The goal of eradicating slums wherever they existed thus remained firmly embedded in the new policy paradigm for attacking the slums ushered in by the Redevelopment Act of 1947 and reinforced by the passage of federal housing and urban redevelopment legislation two years later. This had been the objective of better-housing activists since the days of the Progressive Era slum reformers, and it did not change even as public-private partnerships replaced restrictive regulations as the preferred policy instrument for renewing the city's blighted areas. Yet with private sector participation came an additional goal near and dear to the hearts of real estate interests: achieving the highest and best use of land. This new goal did not replace the previous objective of eliminating slums. Rather it was layered on and combined with existing policy objectives for attacking the slums. As we will see in this chapter, the new and the old were not easily reconciled. Efforts to achieve the highest and best use of land had the perverse effect of extending and reproducing slums rather than eliminating them. As fast as slums were cleared and rebuilt by private enterprise, they reappeared somewhere else, leaving policymakers and housing advocates at a loss to identify a practicable course of action. Housing and redevelopment policy during the 1950s and 1960s was a matter of working through these contradictions.

Downtown Redevelopment, Neighborhood Renewal

By the early 1960s Chicago's downtown construction boom was attracting national and international attention, winning accolades from architecture critics around the world and serving as a major source of economic development and job creation. With the completion of the Prudential Insurance headquarters building in 1955, additional projects soon followed. The first was the Inland Steel building at the corner of Monroe and Dearborn Streets, finished in 1957. Designed by Skidmore, Owings & Merrill, the nineteen-story structure was built with no interior columns, an innovative feature that created 10,200 square feet of open space on each floor. Soon afterward came the twenty-one-story Borg-Warner building, built during 1957 and 1958 at the corner of Michigan Avenue and Adams Street. Additional office towers included the Hartford Fire Insurance Company building at the intersection of Monroe Street and Wacker Drive, the Home Federal Savings and Loan Association building at the corner of State and Adams Streets, and the Mercantile National Bank of Chicago building at Jackson Boulevard and Clinton Street, among many others.[11]

These buildings and others of this period were of modest size. By the mid-1960s, however, genuine skyscrapers began to appear, punctuating the skyline in the Loop and further north along Michigan Avenue's Magnificent Mile. The first was the 60-story First National Bank building constructed over a four-year period from 1965 to 1969 on a full city block at the center of the Loop. Extensive demolition was required to make way for the new structure, with casualties including the bank's existing building, a hotel, and "a host of lesser office areas, shops, bookstores, restaurants, and bars."[12] The new building drew attention for its sloping design, expanding from 29,000 square feet of floor space at the top stories to 59,000 square feet at grade level. Built at roughly the same time was the 100-story John Hancock building on North Michigan Avenue, completed in 1970. Designed by Skidmore, Owings & Merrill, the building was distinctive not only for its height—at 1,449 feet it was the world's second tallest building when finished—but also for its X-braced exterior, a widely heralded innovation that allowed for a more open floor plan and near-record height. Following soon afterward were the 108-story Sears Tower, completed in 1973 and for decades holding the distinction as the world's tallest building, and the 83-story marble-clad Standard Oil building on East Randolph Street, which opened for business the following year.[13]

Mayor Daley, whose oversight of the downtown redevelopment program and other major construction activity earned him the nickname "Dick the Builder," was happy to accept his share of the credit for Chicago's downtown building boom. Indeed actions taken by Daley and other public officials contributed mightily to the downtown renaissance. For starters, the 1958 Development Plan sent a strong message to private investors that the city intended to make downtown redevelopment a priority. Public projects completed under the plan—including a new University of Illinois campus southwest of downtown and new government buildings in the Loop—helped anchor the central business district and encourage new private building activity. Downtown infrastructure projects, such as the extension of Wacker Drive south to Congress Parkway from its former terminus at Lake Street, opened up additional real estate for development.[14]

Builders of new high-rise projects benefited as well from a rewrite of the Chicago Zoning Ordinance in 1957. The new ordinance raised building density limits for the central business district by 33 percent, permitting the construction of taller buildings. More important, it introduced a new Planned Development process through which developers of property that met certain size requirements could negotiate directly with planning officials over building heights and densities. In exchange for such amenities as public plazas or building setbacks, designed to reduce the canyon effect of high-rise construction and allow more light and fresh air to reach the street, developers received zoning bonuses that allowed them to exceed height and density limits. Absent this provision of the new zoning ordinance, new skyscrapers such as the First National Bank building and the Sears Tower could not have been legally constructed.[15]

When all else failed, there was always Daley himself. With his vast control over city council and the city's development bureaucracy, Daley could personally smooth the way for projects he favored. Much has been made of Daley's legendary meeting with Sears chairman Gordon Metcalf, who received the mayor's personal assurances that city council would agree to vacate a one-block section of Quincy Street to make way for the footprint of the world's tallest building. Aldermen looking to shake Sears down in return for their cooperation would not hold up construction of the Sears Tower under Daley's watch.[16] Even when Daley did not become personally involved, his presence was a comfort to developers. Unbelievably, the developers of the sixty-story First National Bank building began construction in 1965 without a building permit. As the bank's CEO Gaylord Freeman later recalled, "We tried time and again to get the permits but they [the building department] were so goddamn fussy about this and that so I said, 'Let's go without them.' If we had had less of a man as mayor, we wouldn't have had the courage to do that."[17] When it came to downtown development, Daley had little tolerance for what he perceived as red tape, a view he communicated unambiguously to his staff. As the city's building commissioner explained, "[Daley] told me to enforce the code, but he also expected the least interference possible with all that new construction. If I went to his office and told him I had stopped construction of a major office building like the First National because it didn't have a permit, he would have sent me to a psychiatrist—or fired me."[18]

In these ways—through planning, new public buildings, infrastructure improvements, zoning, and his own political clout—Mayor Daley supported the downtown development program. Some observers have pointed to such activities as evidence that public policy during this time was focused overwhelmingly on the downtown area.[19] Certainly downtown redevelopment was a key preoccupation of Daley and his planning and development staff, but arguments that development resources were concentrated largely on the downtown area are exaggerated. While the downtown building boom was taking place, Daley was mounting a spirited attack on the slums in the city's outlying neighborhoods, an effort that consumed the vast majority of the city's federal housing and redevelopment funds. Despite claims to the contrary, the millions of federal dollars that began flowing into the city each year following passage of the Housing Act of 1949 were, with a few exceptions, not used to support downtown redevelopment. Indeed business leaders bristled at the suggestion that the reality was otherwise. When opponents of a 1966 bond issue to provide local matching funds for a new round of federally funded urban renewal projects claimed that "loop business interests" would be the key beneficiaries, the Central Area Committee issued a terse press release. Claiming that "nothing could be further from the truth," the statement read as follows: "During the past ten years we have seen a virtual rebuilding of the central area, with a commitment of more than $871 million in private investment capital. This has been going on while public development funds have been used solely to improve outlying neighborhoods. We will expect the city to continue improving the neighborhoods while the central area maintains its policy of relying on private investment."[20]

In his campaign against the slums Daley made use of two main policy tools, urban renewal and public housing, and during the early years of his administration it was not clear that either program would be ineffective. Although rumblings, particularly about the design and location of public housing projects, were already being heard by the mid-1950s, there was still much optimism that the combination of slum clearance, public housing, and new private investment would prove successful in rehabilitating the city's slum districts. What would become Chicago's most notorious high-rise public housing projects—including Stateway Gardens and the Robert Taylor Homes on the South Side, the Henry Horner Homes on the West Side, and much of the Cabrini-Green Homes development north of downtown—were all built during Daley's tenure as mayor. That these projects were abysmal failures was, by the mid-1960s, beyond dispute. However, during the 1950s the question of whether housing for low-income persons should take the form of high-rise construction was

far from settled. Among architects involved in the design of public housing, Corbusian ideas about the advantages of high-rise developments remained influential. Even liberals such as Monsignor John Egan, director of the Chicago archdiocesan office of urban affairs during the 1950s,
did not immediately recognize the warning signs. As Egan later recalled, "When [the extension of Cabrini Homes] was being planned in
the 1950s, it seemed like a good idea. The people who planned it were
high-minded people who wanted to put up decent housing, and, for a
number of reasons, high-rises seemed to be the way to go."[21]

Among those who did begin to have serious misgivings, many held out
hope that the new high-rise structures would at least be superior to what
they replaced. By the mid-1950s the Metropolitan Housing and Planning Council had grown concerned about the concentration of new public housing projects on the South Side, which organization leaders viewed
as threatening the viability of urban renewal projects there, including the
new Lake Meadows development. However, the organization was reluctant to take a public position on the issue due to fears that doing so would
rally "all the traditional opponents to public housing which might kill for
all time to come a program acutely needed in Chicago."[22] Besides, as one
board member argued, new public housing units "would, at any rate be
an improvement on existing slums, even if they created other social and
racial problems."[23] As D. Bradford Hunt points out in his study of public
housing in Chicago, Mayor Daley was himself less than enamored of the
use of high-rise construction for public housing projects. In 1959, testifying before a Senate committee, he pleaded with senators for more flex-
ibility on per-unit cost limitations to enable the CHA to build walkup
and row houses in addition to high-rise developments.[24] When his efforts came up short, however, he offered no apologies. "Public housing
is a wonderful thing for our city," he told the *Chicago Tribune* in 1966.
"Look at 35th and State. I lived there and went to school there. It was one
of the worst areas of the city, but what do you see now? The concept is to
put the people in good homes and give them opportunity."[25]

But if slum dwellers were to be rehoused in what Daley and others
viewed as better conditions, it would not be in white areas of the city.
Under Daley the pattern of locating new public housing developments in
existing slum areas was institutionalized. Virtually all new CHA units
constructed after Daley became mayor in 1955 were placed in all-black
neighborhoods.[26] Daley's views on race and housing had been substantially shaped by the renewed influx of African Americans into the city

following World War II and the pressure that placed on housing markets, both in the Black Belt and in transitional areas. Between 1950 and 1960, Chicago's black population grew by 320,372 residents, while the city's white population shrank by nearly 400,000 residents.[27] The trajectory was unmistakable. If the trend were not reversed, Chicago would lose much of its white middle-class population to the suburbs, leaving behind a city with a substantially weakened tax base and a population that placed growing demands on city services. The culprit, many believed, was the state of housing in the Black Belt. There was not enough to accommodate the influx of blacks, and what did exist was for the most part in abysmal shape, forcing blacks into transitional areas that soon became extensions of the ghetto. White residents fleeing such areas typically headed for the suburbs, fearful that other city neighborhoods would eventually experience the same conditions they had just escaped.

In Daley's mind, public housing and urban renewal, by providing better housing and eliminating slums in the Black Belt, could stabilize this situation. With improved housing and more livable neighborhoods, blacks might be content to stay where they were, in the city's existing African American areas. Residents of white neighborhoods, no longer experiencing the threat of invasion by blacks, might be less inclined to relocate to the suburbs.[28] The idea that improved housing in black neighborhoods could reduce pressure on the city's racial boundaries was not a new one. As we saw in chapter 2, the block-by-block expansion of the Black Belt was a key cause of the city's 1919 race riot, and Governor Lowden's riot commission called for more and better housing for blacks to better fix the boundaries of the city's African American neighborhoods. Daley's approach, while never publicly acknowledged as such, was based on similar reasoning. Of course, as we now know, there are multiple reasons why this strategy, based as it was on a tacit endorsement of segregation, would never work. Even with better housing, a population of low-income minorities cut off from job opportunities, good schools, and social networks that include middle-class residents cannot thrive. Back then, however, the belief that good housing could on its own go a long way toward producing stable communities was a widely held principle, and Daley was not alone in thinking that new public housing developments in the Black Belt were a key antidote to the problems these areas were undergoing.

*   *   *

Like public housing, the urban renewal projects of the 1950s drew some criticism, but there was also substantial support and considerable optimism about the program's potential to rehabilitate slums. By 1957 the partially completed Lake Meadows housing development was being trumpeted in the media as a "showpiece" for urban renewal, attracting visiting planning and development experts from around the globe.[29] By the time the last building was completed in 1960, the project's developer had invested $35 million in a location the *Chicago Tribune* described as "a vast, rotted, and seemingly irreparable slum."[30] Annual tax yields on the 101-acre site went from $222,525 prior to redevelopment to $565,712 by 1962, two years after the final building was completed.[31] City officials were quick to claim victory. As Chicago Land Clearance Commission director Philip Doyle enthused, "The success of the project has fully proved the soundness of our formula for enabling private industry to play the major role in redeveloping the slums."[32] Indeed Mayor Daley was so proud of the new development that he had it added to the itinerary of then-presidential candidate John F. Kennedy during an October 1960 campaign stop in Chicago.[33]

Lake Meadows was just part of a much larger rebuilding effort that by 1959 encompassed 732 acres on Chicago's South Side (fig. 6.2).[34] In 1958 the first of five nineteen-story buildings opened in the new 1,710-unit Prairie Shores urban renewal project, directly north of Lake Meadows. The $20 million project, built mainly to house doctors, students, nurses, and other staff at nearby Michael Reese Hospital, filled quickly, further generating confidence in the viability of former slum property for middle-class residential development.[35] Meanwhile both Michael Reese Hospital and nearby Illinois Institute of Technology (IIT) aggressively pursued expansion plans, aided by federal and state urban renewal funds. By 1959 IIT had completed thirty-four of fifty new buildings planned since the end of World War II, growing the size of its campus from 7 to 110 acres at a cost of $26 million.[36] Michael Reese initiated a smaller but still significant building program in an 80-acre expansion area, spending $13 million for new patient and research facilities, a blood center building, a psychiatric institute, and physical plant structures.[37]

By the 1960s Chicago's urban renewal projects were making substantial contributions to the city's tax base as well as boosting property values and private investment activity in nearby areas. A 1962 study by the Chicago Land Clearance Commission found that the twenty-seven projects undertaken by the agency since its creation in 1947 had increased

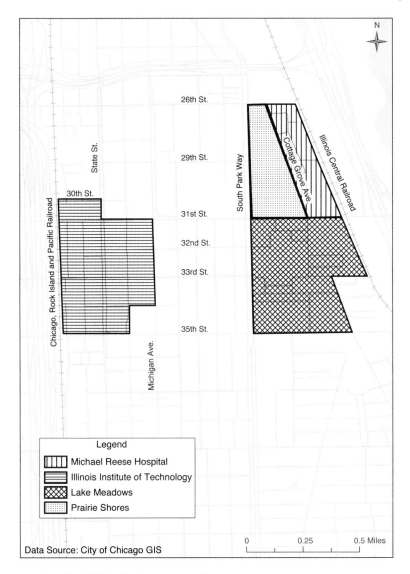

FIGURE 6.2. South Side redevelopment area, late 1950s.

annual tax yields by a combined total of $2.5 million.[38] Along with Lake
Meadows and Prairie Shores, other renewal projects also attracted national and international attention. Although castigated in the black press
as "Negro removal," a redevelopment and conservation program the
University of Chicago spearheaded in the city's mostly white Hyde Park

neighborhood also won praise for its efforts to preserve racial diversity, despite a growing black population.[39] Just north of the central business district, the twenty-two-acre, $46 million Carl Sandburg Village provided evidence of a strong market for near-downtown middle-class residential development in one of only a few residential slum clearance projects to be built in the central area.[40]

Pointing to these projects and others like them, Mayor Daley made the first of what would become a series of promises to eliminate slums in Chicago. Testifying before a House subcommittee in January 1959, Daley called for a federal commitment of $500 to $600 million per year in housing and redevelopment funds, claiming such an amount would be sufficient to "remove slums from the cities of America in the next decade or two."[41] By 1962 Daley had grown more optimistic. Insisting that "renewing Chicago's neighborhoods and communities" was his administration's highest priority and emboldened by new US Census data showing that substandard housing in Chicago had declined from 65,447 units to 30,926 units between 1950 and 1960, Daley pledged that the city's slums would be eliminated within five to six years.[42] By 1966 he was poised to declare victory. Campaigning for passage of a bond issue to provide the local contribution for the next round of federal urban renewal funds, Daley claimed the program would allow the city to "revitalize every neighborhood in Chicago, removing every slum and blighted building by the end of 1967."[43]

Yet even as Daley repeated such promises to end slums in Chicago, there were signs already by the early 1960s that the city's housing and redevelopment program might not be up to the task. New developments such as Lake Meadows and Prairie Shores were celebrated by many as key milestones in Chicago's campaign against the slums, yet for the most part they did not provide shelter for displaced residents of these areas. Average rents paid by nonwhite families for substandard units in Chicago were $67 monthly at the time Lake Meadows began renting. Of a total of 55,078 families living in substandard housing units at the time, only 1,794 paid $120 or more in rent. Yet rentals at Lake Meadows for two-bedroom apartments began at $137 per month. At Prairie Shores two-bedroom units started at $148 monthly, and at Carl Sandburg Village north of the Loop, apartments of this size rented for a whopping $240 per month and higher.[44] Although displaced residents received priority in the application process for apartments in the new developments, few could afford the rents. Most of the new occupants were in "professional or managerial occupations," with incomes in the "middle-to upper-income brackets."[45] As the project manager for Lake Meadows joked, "We have enough physicists in Lake Meadows to build our own H-bomb."[46] Priced out of the market for the new high-rise apartments built on the ruins of their former homes, existing residents of these areas would for the most part have to find somewhere else to go.

By the early 1960s complaints that urban renewal was producing "luxury housing" unaffordable to present slum dwellers had become widespread.[47] Yet the fact that projects took this form is far from surprising given the content of urban renewal legislation and the actors spearheading Chicago's new redevelopment projects. From the time that real estate interests became involved in the debate over slum clearance during the late 1930s, arguments that the redevelopment of blighted areas should proceed according to the principle of highest and best use had become increasingly pronounced. By this logic, areas that could support high-end residential construction should be developed accordingly, while housing affordable to low- and moderate-income residents and other modestly profitable kinds of development would be confined to less desirable locations. The market, in other words, would drive the redevelopment process. Despite some dissenting voices, urban renewal policy largely incorporated this maxim. Through the creation of public-private partnerships and the privileged position of developers in the renewal process, the principle of highest and best use was institutionalized. For developers and city officials, it was a mutually beneficial arrangement. Developers would maximize profits; city officials would maximize property tax receipts.

Of course the principle of highest and best use did not in itself imply that housing produced through the urban renewal program would be limited to high-rent developments. It simply meant that where such projects were viable, this was the form redevelopment should take. Yet the set of actors who set Chicago's early residential redevelopment projects in motion made it extremely likely that high-rent developments would be the outcome. South Side institutional actors—including the University of Chicago, Michael Reese Hospital, and IIT—were the drivers behind the majority of Chicago's residential slum clearance projects during the 1950s and early 1960s. Fearful of being boxed in by an expanding black ghetto, these institutions pursued planning and rebuilding efforts designed in part to create a stable middle-class presence in their immediate surroundings. Strong institutional commitments to the area and attractive, well-located sites for new housing developments drew inter-

FIGURE 6.3. Prairie Shores apartments, 1961. Chicago History Museum, Hedrich-Blessing collection, Skidmore, Owings & Merrill series, HB-21917-A.

est from developers, who understood the potential for profit. Clearly there were opportunities here to do more than simply rehouse existing slum residents in dwellings they could afford. With key South Side institutions leading the way, city officials worked with developers to finalize the details of redevelopment plans that would upgrade the area's demographics.[48]

Still, it was never intended that residential redevelopment would both begin and end with high-end housing. For MHPC's Ferd Kramer and other pioneers of the city's urban renewal program, developments like Lake Meadows and Prairie Shores were initial steps in what was envisioned as a far-reaching attack on the slums, extending ultimately to the farthest corners of the city's slum districts. As Kramer put it in describing the Michael Reese Hospital and IIT rebuilding area, "This project will combine and fill out much of a larger scheme. It carries out the now recognized principle that the advantageous starting point for an attack on blight is adjacent to some key structure, such as an educational institution, a hospital, a manufacturing plant of a non-nuisance type, or other substantial improvement."[49] With key institutions serving as "anchors

for redevelopment," renewal efforts could gain a foothold and move outward from there. As redevelopment made its way into areas the market
deemed less attractive, the highest and best use of land would include
housing for moderate-income families.

It seemed like a reasonable plan, but events proved otherwise. Prior to
redevelopment, nearly ten thousand families, mostly African American,
lived on the sites of the Lake Meadows and Hyde Park urban renewal projects alone.[50] Those families would have to find somewhere else to live, and
housing options were few. The city's African American neighborhoods
were already severely overcrowded. A 1966 study of the city's renewal areas found that over half of residential structures had been converted, illegally in most cases, to provide additional dwelling units. Families were
squeezed into tiny apartments in buildings originally constructed to contain half or fewer as many units.[51] Unable to find housing within the city's
Black Belt, many displaced residents moved to transitional areas on the
edges of the ghetto, where the combination of white flight and building
owners seeking to profit from racial succession soon created new slum
conditions. As one observer at the time characterized the process,

> One can make a nice profit out of people who have no bargaining power by
> becoming a slumlord. You buy an old building—one with six five-room apart-
> ments, say; drive the [white] tenants out by reducing maintenance and ser-
> vices; and then replace them with a Negro family in each of the five rooms
> of the six apartments. Rent from 30 families instead of the six that the build-
> ing was intended to house is a pretty good take, especially if you put nothing
> back into maintenance. Thirty families using the plumbing intended for six
> spells certain trouble; multiply those clogged drains by similar overburden-
> ing of all other facilities and you can see why that building will become a ruin
> within a few years. But you will have gotten back your original investment
> many times over, and you can afford to abandon it.[52]

Had race not been a factor in the rehousing of persons displaced by
such projects as Lake Meadows and Prairie Shores, the outcome might
have been very different. Displaced persons would have had access to the
full Chicago housing market, where vacancies in white areas of the city
could have accommodated them.[53] As it was, however, the highest and
best use of land, paired with a dual housing market—one for whites and
the other for blacks and other nonwhites—proved to be a toxic combination. Displaced residents found themselves caught up in a game of musi-

FIGURE 6.4. Subdivided building, Kenwood, 1954. Chicago History Museum, Mildred Mead photograph collection, ICHi-176170.

cal chairs where the ability to find a seat was determined by race and income, both of which worked against them. Instead of eliminating slums, urban renewal produced what one report called a "rolling ghetto," where the revitalization of one area generated conditions that were directly implicated in the decline of another.[54] Short of the creation of a genuinely open housing market, this phenomenon seemed unstoppable unless new urban renewal projects could themselves house a greater proportion of displaced residents, particularly those families with incomes too high to meet eligibility requirements for public housing.

*   *   *

By the time John F. Kennedy became president in 1961, the scarcity of moderate-income housing produced through urban renewal policy— including housing for families displaced by slum clearance projects— had become a widely recognized shortcoming of the program.[55] Public housing could take care of low-income families, while those with modest incomes and higher could find adequate housing through the private market. It was the families in between—too well off to qualify for public housing but not prosperous enough to afford decent privately built housing—whose needs were not being met. Kennedy, eager both "to project an image of creativity and progress" and to reward urban voters who had helped elect him president, was motivated to take action.[56] With new federal housing legislation working its way through Congress during the spring of 1961, there was an opportunity to address the situation.

One solution might have been to expand income limits for public housing residents to accommodate moderate-income families in addition to the low-income families the program presently served, but any such effort would have faced immense political hurdles. Instead Kennedy and his advisers sought ways to build on the already established principle of public-private partnerships in housing policy. What became Section 221(d)(3) of the Housing Act of 1961 was intended to expand the provision of new privately furnished, moderate-income housing by offering below-market mortgage rates to developers targeting this segment of the housing market. The FHA-insured mortgages, featuring rates of only 3 percent when the program was initially established, made it possible to charge modest rents while still achieving acceptable returns on investment. Eligible mortgagors included public agencies, cooperatives, nonprofit corporations or organizations, and limited dividend corporations.[57] To ensure that the program provided housing for those groups it was intended to serve, the FHA placed ceilings on both rents and tenant incomes. For Chicago, the income limit was $8,400 per year for a family of four. Monthly rents for a family this size could not exceed $140.[58]

Section 221(d)(3) housing was not limited to urban renewal projects, but by the mid-1960s the new tool was being used extensively in such areas. Mayor Daley, stung by criticism of the high rents in developments such as Carl Sandburg Village and Prairie Shores, became a strong enthusiast of the program. Yet the effort to shift the emphasis of housing produced by urban renewal from middle- and upper-income to more modestly priced developments clashed at times with the principle of highest and best use and introduced contradictions of its own. One of the early experiments with the new program involved a redevelopment site on the South Side in the same area where both Michael Reese Hospital and IIT were undergoing expansion, and where the new Prairie Shores and Lake Meadows housing developments were located. Redevelopment of the thirty-one-acre P-shaped parcel would "bridge the last gap" in the South Side redevelopment area, linking the various projects together to create a large swath of slum-free, defensible space.[59] After spending six years and $7.2 million acquiring properties and clearing land, the Department of Urban Renewal was finally prepared to market the site. In the spring of 1964 the agency issued a request for proposals calling for a large residential project.[60]

In drafting language for the department's request for proposals, urban renewal officials faced a number of pressures. Institutional interests and other major landowners in the area were eager to see the pattern of high-end residential development set by Prairie Shores and Lake Meadows extended by redevelopment of the new site for middle- and upper-income housing. This was particularly important because of the concentration of high-rise public housing in the near vicinity, the development of which they had strongly opposed (see fig. 6.5). Prairie Shores and Lake Meadows were both integrated projects, drawing middle-class whites back to an area of the South Side that whites had all but abandoned. Residents of public housing, on the other hand, were mostly low-income blacks, and their growing presence made it increasingly difficult to market Prairie Shores and Lake Meadows to middle-class whites. New upper-income housing would tend to attract significant numbers of white tenants, boosting the white population in the area and increasing the area's appeal to white renters. Moderate-income housing would likely have the opposite effect, drawing larger numbers of African American tenants and possibly threatening the racial balance at Lake Meadows and Prairie Shores. As an IIT spokesperson explained in voicing his institution's opposition to moderate-income housing, "We do not want a poor economic ghetto. We are concerned about housing for our staff."[61] City officials were sympathetic to such fears, yet they also knew that development of additional high-rent housing in this area would expose them to criticism. Unable to reconcile these competing pressures, offi-

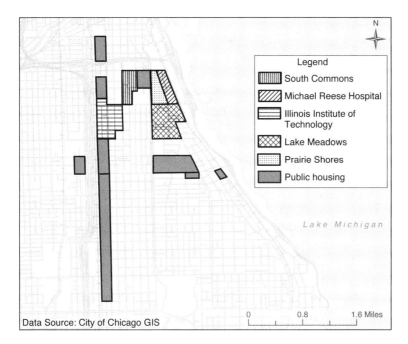

FIGURE 6.5. South Side redevelopment area, mid-1960s.

cials provided little guidance to developers on the matter of housing affordability, stating simply that "at least a portion of the dwelling units must be available to families whose incomes are within the limitations established for Chicago, Illinois by the Federal Housing Administration under section 221(d)(3) of the National Housing Act."[62]

The four proposals the department received included varying amounts of Section 221(d)(3) moderate-income housing. One proposed that nearly all housing units be of this variety, another limited moderate-income units to only 2 percent of the development, while the remaining bids fell somewhere in between.[63] The proposal calling for the least number of moderate-income units was submitted by the real estate firm of Draper and Kramer, of which Ferd Kramer was chair. Not incidentally, Draper and Kramer was also the developer and manager of Prairie Shores, and through his work with MHPC, Kramer himself had been intimately involved with many aspects of the redevelopment of Chicago's South Side, working closely with various South Side institutions on renewal plans. Kramer thus had a personal as well as a professional stake in the project under consideration, and his proposal to seek the highest and best use for the property was consistent with the preferences of the area's key institutional interests.

In December 1964 Kramer read a prepared statement to the commissioners of the Department of Urban Renewal in support of his firm's proposal, and his comments reveal the extent to which redevelopment on the South Side was bound up with issues of race and class. Kramer began on a self-congratulatory note, proclaiming that his firm's nearby Prairie Shores development had "set a national standard for racially integrated housing." This racial balance was threatened, however, by the growing concentration of public housing developments in the area, making it "almost miraculous that private developments have been successful." On the matter of public housing Kramer was uncharacteristically blunt. "Let's face it," he stated, "these projects are racial and economic ghettos. They perpetuate and extend rather than diminish the pattern of racial segregation in Chicago." This was why the selection of his firm's proposal emphasizing middle- and upper-income housing was so important. "We are not at all sure," he continued, "that Section 221(d)(3) housing can be racially integrated in an area overwhelmingly occupied by Negroes. . . . Unless the pattern of racial integration is extended beyond Lake Meadows and Prairie Shores, the long term stability of integration in these projects will be threatened," with potentially dire consequences. Warned Kramer, "The demographers and sociologists tell us that unless a super-human effort is made, this city will be made up almost entirely of people with low incomes, plus a few with very high incomes. This trend must be reversed, and we believe that here is one of the areas where a real start can be made."[64]

There are several reasons why the bid submitted by Draper and Kramer would most certainly have drawn careful consideration by urban renewal officials, not least because it proposed a "higher and better" use of the land than the other three proposals. Apart from that, however, Ferd Kramer was a well-respected, politically connected real estate professional with a track record of successful development projects on the South Side and elsewhere in the city. And it was his proposal that South Side institutions endorsed. Nevertheless, when urban renewal department staff made their recommendation to the board, the proposal they endorsed was a competing bid in which 55 percent of housing units were to be financed through the FHA's Section 221(d)(3) program.[65] When South Side institutions protested, the amount of moderate-income housing was negotiated down to 40 percent, but that was as far as the department would go. In the end, reactions among area stakeholders were mixed. While IIT proclaimed itself "very pleased" with the final decision, others were not so sure. As a representative from nearby Lake Meadows protested, "Only a minimum amount of moderate income housing should have been included in the project. . . . The south side already has a large amount of low income housing."[66] In December 1966, construction began on what would become the South Commons residential development, a $20 million project consisting of four high-rise apartment buildings, eight mid-sized buildings, and seventy-two townhouses (see fig. 6.5).[67]

Why urban renewal commissioners made the decision they did is unknown. However, the reality was that city officials found themselves caught up in a set of contradictions that made any decision on the redevelopment of this parcel a fraught one. If they supported the highest and best use of the land, they would fan the flames of opposition to urban renewal, providing further evidence that the real objective of the program was to move poor people out of the way so that middle-class whites could reclaim the city's most desirable locations.[68] Moreover, upper-income housing would do nothing to address the housing needs of existing slum residents, whose inability to find suitable homes in black neighborhoods contributed to the block-by-block transition of formerly white working-class neighborhoods into new all-black slums. Yet moderate-income housing came with its own set of baggage. As Kramer argued, it might jeopardize the tenuous racial balance at Lake Meadows and Prairie Shores, particularly with the large amount of nearby public housing. Considerable energy and resources had been expended to redevelop a substantial area of the South Side for its highest and best use. Did the city really want to risk undermining these efforts by introducing new development that clashed with rather than extended the pattern established by these new projects?

Given this set of trade-offs, it is not surprising that the commissioners chose to compromise. While perhaps favorably disposed toward Draper and Kramer's proposal and sympathetic to Kramer's concerns about the potential impact of moderate-income housing on the South Side redevelopment area as a whole, the commissioners also knew that the political costs of endorsing the highest and best use for the site would have been substantial. Compromise was a safer bet. Yet no matter what form compromise took, the trade-off would be a potentially costly one. Urban redevelopment was becoming an increasingly difficult needle to thread. As criticisms of the program continued to mount, efforts to reconcile the desires of developers for profits, the requirements of institutions for stable surroundings, and the needs of slum residents for better housing became a growing challenge.

Reselling Urban Renewal

In January 1964 Fred Bosselman, an attorney with the Chicago law firm of Ross, Hardies and O'Keefe, wrote a memo to MHPC's legislative committee outlining a set of suggestions for improving the administration of Chicago's urban renewal program. Bosselman, a member of the committee himself, began by listing what he viewed as the key political challenges the program currently faced. First, he argued, the city's African American population was by now "thoroughly convinced" that urban renewal was being used for "Negro removal" rather than to provide better living conditions for black residents. White residents, meanwhile, feared the program was being used to promote racial integration, an objective many whites did not share. Certain ethnic groups, Bosselman continued, were upset about "the breakup of old neighborhoods to which they [had] become accustomed." Finally, a "sizeable group of intellectuals" were persuaded by the arguments of writer and activist Jane Jacobs that "large-scale urban renewal [was] bad per se" because the hardships imposed on displaced residents were unacceptable.[69]

To these political challenges Bosselman might have added some others, such as the anger and resentment caused by the extended periods that renewal sites typically lay vacant before new development was initiated, two years or longer in many cases.[70] Sometimes properties were never redeveloped at all. As one former resident of the area cleared to make way for Lake Meadows complained twelve years after being relocated, her former block still nothing but a weed patch, "I don't know what they plan to do with it, if anything. They never did tell us what they wanted the land for. They didn't have to. They just wanted us to clear out."[71] Others objected to the ham-handed approach to redevelopment used by urban renewal authorities intent on clearing large, multiblock areas of land regardless of whether all buildings were in disrepair. And for many, the development of middle- and upper-income apartment buildings to house tenants for whom plenty of good housing options were readily available was a misuse of public funds.

As Bosselman and many others increasingly recognized, urban renewal was in trouble. "These changes in political climate," Bosselman wrote, "have brought urban renewal in Chicago to a virtual halt. The dynamic spirit that built Lake Meadows, Sandburg Center and the University of Illinois, and that planned so optimistically for rehabilitation in Hyde Park, is gone. Urban renewal has degenerated into a holding action, an attempt to bring to fruition the dynamic plans made when urban renewal was popular." Despite these problems, however, there was still hope. "Even if you agree in part with some of the criticisms of Chicago's past urban renewal program, as I do, the one conclusion that you must not draw is that urban renewal should be abandoned. This is to cure the disease by executing the patient. Urban renewal is Chicago's life—propose any treatment you wish, but do not kill it!"[72]

Although supporters of urban renewal seemed to be caught off guard by growing criticisms of the program, it was inevitable that a program this disruptive would eventually face stiff political headwinds. The first major sign of trouble came in 1962 when a proposed $22.5 million urban renewal bond issue came before the voters in April of that year. Under the legislative formula in which the federal government paid for up to two-thirds of project costs, the bond issue would be combined with an additional $37.5 million in local public works projects to support a $180 million program, nearly equaling the $200 million that had been spent or allocated since the redevelopment program began fifteen years earlier.[73] All the city's newspapers urged a vote of yes on the bond issue, and even the fiscally tightfisted Civic Federation gave its endorsement.[74] Two previous bond issues for urban renewal had been approved by the voters, in 1947 and 1957. This time, however, voters signaled their disenchantment with the program, rejecting the bond issue soundly with a vote of 351,019 against and 268,325 in favor.[75] Five additional bond issues also on the ballot went down to defeat as well. A subdued Mayor Daley tried to put an optimistic spin on things. "I still feel we have a great city," he reflected, "and I think the public will see fit to support many of these issues in the future."[76] In truth, the vote was a major setback for Daley's campaign against the slums. Without local matching funds no new projects could be initiated. The federal urban-renewal spigot quickly dried up, and the program limped along for the next several years using funds that had been allocated but not yet spent under previous rounds of funding. In 1963 only one project of 42 acres was proposed for clearance, compared with five projects totaling 214 acres the previous year.[77]

In a speech to the National Association of Housing and Redevelopment Officials in October 1963, Commissioner of Urban Renewal John Duba identified a number of factors that in his estimation contributed to the defeat of the bond issue, including inadequate public promotion of the renewal program, public dissatisfaction with rising taxes, failure of the program to provide tangible benefits to many neighborhoods, and racial concerns raised by the program.[78] Privately, however, Duba "seemed to give much more weight to [a] single factor—the race issue."[79] As one study observed, many blacks perceived urban renewal as a racially targeted initiative aimed at removing African Americans from the city's choicest locations, while whites blamed the program for the city's shifting racial boundaries, much as Bosselman had argued.[80] Results of the 1962 referendum suggested the latter group was a particular concern. One analysis of the vote returns showed that opposition was strongest in the city's "bungalow belt"—outlying majority-white wards that were not yet experiencing racial transition but whose residents likely perceived it as a major threat.[81]

Whatever the cause of the voters' crankiness, Mayor Daley was unwilling to risk another defeat. Through a senior aide, he indicated to urban renewal supporters that he would not propose additional bond issues unless organizations like the Association of Commerce and MHPC promised to "carry the brunt of the educational work."[82] In response, civic leaders embarked on a major campaign designed to "resell" urban renewal to the public. A new civic organization called the Committee on Urban Progress (COUP), designed to bring together civic and community leaders around solutions to Chicago's growth problems, formed a subcommittee on urban renewal in early 1964. The new group quickly tasked itself with the mission of getting the redevelopment program back on track. Committee members were largely in agreement on several matters: that resistance to urban renewal threatened the future of the program, that much of the opposition "center[ed] on race," and that "the public must be re-sold on the need to renew."[83] On the question of what should be done, however, there was less consensus, and differing views about the proper goals of urban renewal led to divisions about how opposition to the program could best be overcome. Satisfaction by some with the existing direction of the program seemed to cloud judgment on this question, and the committee struggled with its mission of reselling the program to the public.

For certain members of the committee, the chief purpose of urban renewal was to make the central city attractive for residence once again to middle- and upper-income families. Such individuals viewed projects like Lake Meadows, Prairie Shores, and Carl Sandburg Village as "dramatically visible achievements" that if reproduced elsewhere could help convince the public that the program was working and that the sacrifices of some, while unfortunate, were justified. For these individuals the question was how more projects like these could be set in motion.[84] For others, however, it was precisely these kinds of developments that represented all that was wrong with urban renewal. As Monsignor John Egan, a member of the committee, wrote in a letter to COUP's research director Morris Hirsh,

> The appropriate objective of an urban renewal program is to make every neighborhood in the city a desirable place to live, regardless of the age of its structures, regardless of the income level of its residents. This objective cannot be obtained by clearance projects like Lake Meadows and Carl Sandburg Village, which displace lower-income families with residents from higher-income brackets. . . . It should now be obvious that upper-income families, through the normal operation of the real estate market, can take care of their own housing needs; they can *buy* a good neighborhood. . . . The proper target of urban renewal is the improvement of living conditions in the parts of the city where the traditional institutions of private property ownership have been insufficient to create and maintain a good neighborhood environment.[85]

For Egan and certain other members of the committee, urban renewal was to be judged not by how well it housed middle-class families but by how it addressed the housing needs of the less fortunate. Widespread public support for the program could not be anticipated if the latter goal were ignored. Although Egan's views about how urban renewal should proceed were in the minority, it is hard to imagine that his argument failed to strike a chord among committee members. By this time it was obvious that the program had done very little so far to provide improved housing for the city's mostly African American slum residents. For many blacks, "Negro removal" was a phenomenon they had experienced firsthand. Shouldered with a disproportionate share of the costs of the program, such individuals had little reason to support it, particularly when costs were unaccompanied by discernible benefits.

Still, to follow Egan's advice and refocus the program around the rehousing of slum residents presented difficulties of its own. Such an approach seemed to violate the accepted wisdom that the proper place to begin renewal of the city was near some key institutional anchor, where the prospects for rebuilding a slum area would seem less daunting to developers. Such areas, with good potential to support middle-class residential development, were, in the minds of many supporters of the program, not appropriate places to rehouse former slum residents. Redevelopment would eventually make its way into neighborhoods where moderate-income housing was the highest and best use of the land. However, this would take time. For now, backers of urban renewal could point with pride to new racially integrated residential developments such as Lake Meadows and Prairie Shores which, even if they failed to house many former slum residents, did at least replace large numbers of ramshackle homes with buildings that were structurally sound and, for many, aesthetically pleasing.

Unable to reconcile the preferences of its membership for the highest and best use of land with the fears of the public about displacement and racial transition, COUP never did articulate a clear political strategy for getting urban renewal back on track. That task fell principally to MHPC, which commissioned a new study of Chicago's urban renewal program in 1964 whose release was to be timed to support an anticipated urban renewal bond issue referendum the following year. Members of MHPC's urban renewal committee, where plans for the project were initially hatched, at first debated what the study should try to accomplish. One committee member suggested that "it would be helpful to know why there is so much opposition to urban renewal." Another "felt it would be more desirable to change this attitude than to spend time diagnosing the reasons for it."[86] The latter perspective carried the day. In the end, there was agreement that the study "should not be blind to the deficiencies of urban renewal, but that it should be concerned with urban renewal's margin of benefit. It should give the uninformed public a reasonable basis for supporting renewal bond issues."[87]

The study, prepared by the University of Chicago's Center for Urban Studies, was "cleared" with Mayor Daley, who promised the city's full cooperation.[88] With the bond issue referendum now delayed until June

1966, the seventy-three-page report was released in March of that year. Not surprisingly, the authors found little about the renewal program to criticize. Key performance indicators examined—such as property values in renewal areas, tax receipts, improved housing units, private investment activity, and economic impact—all suggested the program was performing as intended. The report even managed to put a positive spin on relocation, finding that 94 percent of displacees moved into standard housing. Of course the figure, undoubtedly exaggerated, did not capture those families whose new "standard" homes became new slums as remaining whites soon fled the area.[89]

The report received extensive press coverage, mostly positive. The *Tribune* quoted MHPC president Thomas Nicholson, who described the study as "eloquent proof of what can be achieved thru a large-scale expansion of urban renewal activities."[90] Just days after the report was released, Daley held a press conference to announce the placement of a new set of bond issues on the ballot that June, including one to support the urban renewal program. This time Daley was taking no chances. Business and labor leaders appeared with him to endorse the $200 million package. Other endorsements followed, including that of state treasurer William Scott, a Republican. Appearing before the City Council Finance Committee, Daley promised the bonds would not raise taxes, addressing an issue viewed by some as significant in the defeat of the last bond referendum.[91] In the end the voters were persuaded to give urban renewal a second chance: they approved the bond issues by a comfortable margin.[92] Later that summer Daley announced plans for a major injection of public funds into the program, using $25 million from the bond issues to leverage another $70 million in federal urban renewal funds. By one estimate, the combined local and federal expenditures would produce up to $500 million in new private investment.[93]

Still, as welcome as this injection of public funds was to backers of the renewal program, the attack on the slums was entering a new phase. Earlier that year, Martin Luther King Jr. had arrived in Chicago to start his own campaign against slums. Linking slum conditions to the civil rights issues he had been championing in the South, King introduced new complications into efforts to eliminate substandard housing in the city. Not surprisingly, in his focus on housing conditions in the city's black neighborhoods, he found an issue that resonated deeply with the city's African American population. With King's arrival on the scene, race and renewal would be joined as never before.

Martin Luther King Jr. and the Racial Challenge

The decision by Martin Luther King Jr. and his political organization, the Southern Christian Leadership Conference (SCLC), to bring the civil rights movement north to Chicago was the result of several developments. First, the movement had by this time achieved key victories, including passage of the Civil Rights Act of 1964 and the Voting Rights Act of 1965, which overturned Jim Crow laws in southern states. Public sympathy had swung solidly behind civil rights, thanks in part to the brutal responses of southern law-enforcement officials to nonviolent protesters. For some members of the SCLC, including King himself, the timing seemed right to expand the movement to northern cities, where blacks also faced intense discrimination, even if it was not always legally sanctioned. As a place to begin the northern campaign Chicago had certain advantages. A solid organizational infrastructure around civil rights was already in place, led by the Coordinating Council of Community Organizations (CCCO), which had been staging a campaign in favor of school desegregation for several years. Moreover, civil rights leaders in Chicago actively courted King and the SCLC. Unlike other cities such as New York and Philadelphia, where influential black leaders had warned King to stay away, Chicago seemed to be a place where alliances with local groups would be possible.[94]

Organization leaders made a decision to focus the northern campaign around the issue of slums, which, more than anything else, seemed to embody the oppressive conditions under which urban blacks were living. In early January 1966, what became known as the Chicago Freedom Movement was formally launched following a two-day series of meetings between the SCLC and local black leaders. The objective of the campaign, King announced, would be "to bring about the unconditional surrender of forces dedicated to the creation and maintenance of slums."[95] The "Chicago Plan," drafted by organization leaders during the previous several months, identified a three-part strategy. Phase one would involve a campaign of education and organizing to gain a better understanding of slum conditions and the reasons for their existence. In phase two, beginning in March, a detailed strategy for addressing the problem would be developed, while phase three would consist of "massive action" of an unspecified form.[96] To draw attention to the plight of Chicago's mostly African American slum dwellers, King and his wife

Coretta rented a four-room third-floor apartment in Lawndale, in the heart of the West Side ghetto. "I have to be right here with the people," said King upon moving in. "I can learn more about the situation by being here with those who live and suffer here."[97]

At first King and the SCLC behaved almost as if they did not know that Chicago already had programs designed to eliminate slums and provide better housing for poor people. By this time, hundreds of millions of dollars in public funds had been plowed into the city's urban renewal and public housing programs. King might have directly targeted these programs, calling for changes intended to make them more responsive to the needs of slum residents. But in the early months of the Chicago campaign organization leaders largely ignored the city's own anti-slum initiatives. Instead King and movement leaders focused on the problem of slum landlords, organizing tenants unions and encouraging the use of rent strikes to pressure building owners to comply with housing regulations. In one well-publicized incident in late February, leaders of the Freedom Movement took control of a West Side tenement building several blocks from the apartment King had rented, claiming they had established a "receivership" over the building. Rents would be withheld, paid instead into a fund that would be used to finance needed repairs to the building. Asked whether his actions were legal, King responded evasively: "We are not dealing with the legality but with the morality of the situation."[98]

King's efforts to draw attention to poor housing conditions in the city's black neighborhoods were embarrassing to Mayor Daley, who at one point went so far as to deny that Chicago had slums.[99] However, King's tactics were ones that Daley could easily enough manage, at least initially. While King emphasized the problem of slum landlords, he made it clear that he also viewed city government as culpable. After all, if the city's building regulations were properly enforced, buildings in disrepair would have to be rehabilitated or demolished. Daley was eager to avoid the sort of confrontation that had worked so well for King in the South. Rather than criticize King and set himself up as a convenient target, Daley went to great lengths to demonstrate that he shared the Freedom Movement's objective of improving housing for slum residents. "All of us, like Dr. King, are trying to eliminate slums," insisted Daley.[100] On March 1, the mayor announced a "massive" new code enforcement program targeting fifteen thousand residential structures on the city's West Side, including the Lawndale neighborhood where King

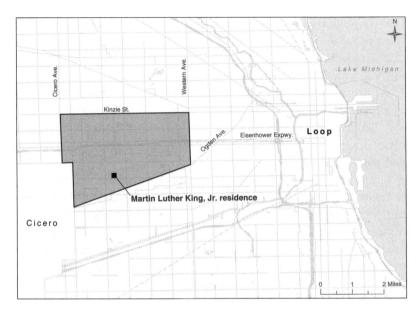

FIGURE 6.6. Housing code enforcement inspection area, 1966.

had taken up residence (fig. 6.6). Extra personnel would be assigned to conduct door-to-door inspections of all residential buildings with three or more apartments. Warned Daley, "Those who will not cooperate in eliminating code violations will be taken directly to court by the city."[101] Several weeks later Daley announced the appointment of two additional full-time judges to the city's housing court to handle the extra workload the inspection program created. Then on March 28 the mayor announced the city was ramping up its rodent control program, addressing a persistent complaint of slum residents. An additional $250,000 would be allocated to treat all of the city's alleys during the next two months.[102]

In its efforts to highlight the contribution of building code violations and slum landlords to the creation and reproduction of slums, the Chicago Freedom Movement had, perhaps unwittingly, brought the city back around to an approach that had been central to slum rehabilitation efforts during the early twentieth century. As we saw in chapter 2, Progressive Era housing reformers sought to eliminate slums principally through the creation of stronger building regulations accompanied by aggressive enforcement of building and sanitary laws. It was not a particularly effective approach then, and for similar reasons it failed to have much of an impact this time around. Both the Building Department and the municipal housing court were political operations, and slum landlords could often avoid compliance through bribery or through their political connections. Several months after Daley announced his new building inspection program, the city's deputy building commissioner admitted that of 5,400 code violation notices issued since the program was announced in March, only 300 had actually gone to court.[103]

As historian Beryl Satter has argued, Daley's new anti-slum initiatives were "mostly smoke and mirrors."[104] The truth was that Daley had long been trying to rehabilitate slums, and even if he sensed by this time that his programs were not performing as intended, he did not have alternative solutions. Stepped-up building inspections and better rodent control might do little to end slums, but they would at least help take the wind out of King's sails. As a social movement, King's Chicago campaign would require the mass mobilization of blacks and white sympathizers, including demonstrations and other protest activities. This could be accomplished most easily if there were a clear target on which protesters could focus their anger, someone like Birmingham's Bull Connor in the South. But Daley refused to be cast in that role. By holding repeated press conferences to champion his own slum elimination efforts, Daley made King's efforts appear redundant. Even King's "receivership" of the West Side tenement failed to produce the desired confrontation. Questioned about the legality of King's tactics, Daley responded, "The situation . . . is a matter between the lawful owner and those who attempt to assume ownership. We all recognize that what is being done is good for our city—the improvement of housing and living conditions."[105] Daley, it seemed, was doing everything King asked and more. The Chicago Freedom Movement was faltering, and King knew it.

That June, King and movement leaders made a decision to refocus the Chicago campaign around an issue to which they had heretofore paid little attention: housing discrimination. The new goal was to make Chicago a "racially open city," where blacks would be free to live wherever they chose. Strategically, such an approach made sense. As one member of the Freedom Movement argued, discriminatory behavior by real estate agents—who routinely refused to serve black customers—was not unlike that of department store owners who turned blacks away from their lunch counters in the South.[106] For most Americans this kind of blatant prejudice did not sit well. Highlighting the racist practices of the real estate industry would produce clear villains and victims, just as the lunch

counter protests had. Open housing thus represented the kind of polar-
izing issue around which mass mobilization might be achieved.[107]

More to the point, in focusing on housing discrimination, King and
movement leaders finally seemed to be zeroing in on a problem that was
central to the creation and reproduction of slums. It was, after all, the
dual housing market that led to the overcrowding of black neighborhoods and the illegal conversions of apartment buildings to house many
more tenants than they were built to accommodate, even with healthy va-
cancy rates in white neighborhoods. Without the dual housing market,
the "rolling ghetto" produced by urban renewal—where displaced residents were steered into transitional areas that soon became new all-black
slums—might have been much less in evidence. Open housing seemed to
be a vehicle through which the mechanisms that created and perpetuated
poor, all-black neighborhoods and their attendant hardships could be
disrupted. Free to select housing in any neighborhood they could afford,
blacks would have access not only to better housing but to better schools,
more diverse social networks, and a wider range of job opportunities.

The open housing campaign was publicly announced by King at a
rally held at Soldier Field on Sunday, July 10. It was billed as a major
event, and organizers hoped to turn out one hundred thousand people.
Less than half that many showed up, perhaps due to the exceptionally
hot and humid weather that day, but the event still received widespread
media attention. After the rally King led a march to city hall, where he
taped a list of demands to the front door. Topping the list were two key
items directed at the real estate industry. The first called for public statements by real estate boards and brokers that "all listings will be available on a non-discriminatory basis."[108] This was to put an end to the
common practice of racial steering, in which real estate agents failed to
make information about properties in white areas available to black applicants. The second item, also aimed at real estate boards and brokers,
demanded that these groups declare their "endorsement of, and support
for, open occupancy."[109]

Publicly, Mayor Daley had long expressed support for the principle of
open occupancy. "I think the Negro should be permitted to move anywhere he wants to," said Daley several months earlier. "I'm for freedom of residence, and I voted for it when I was in the legislature."[110] Yet
Daley hardly embraced the Chicago Freedom Movement's new housing
agenda. The truth was that open occupancy was far more problematic for
Daley than the campaign's previous focus on slum landlords and build-

ing regulations had been. It was one thing to take steps to try to improve housing conditions in neighborhoods where blacks presently lived; it was quite another to call into question the city's racial boundaries themselves. Daley wanted to end slums, but he also saw himself as nurturing a precarious racial balance in which the mass exodus of whites from the city was an ever-looming threat. In calling for open housing, King had crossed a line. Unless whites were willing to accept African Americans as neighbors, rigorously enforced open housing policies would lead not to integration and better housing for blacks but to further white flight and urban decline. At least that was what Daley feared.

In fact, Daley was not alone in his reservations about open occupancy. Even liberal groups that were strong supporters of integration wrestled with the issue. MHPC shared Daley's fears about the potential impact of open occupancy on neighborhood stability and white flight. The best way to attack segregation, MHPC argued, was not through unqualified open housing policies but through "managed integration," where racial quotas would be used to "insure that housing projects and neighborhoods begin and remain substantially interracial and do not become either all white or all Negro." Racial balances at both Lake Meadows and Prairie Shores had been achieved through such quota systems, which, in addition to capping the percentage of units to be occupied by blacks, involved careful screening of black applicants. For MHPC, such examples of integrated housing developments and neighborhoods had an important "educational effect," preparing the public for a time when "complete freedom of residence" would be possible. "As more and more neighborhoods in the metropolitan community become inter-racial," MHPC argued in a draft policy statement on open occupancy, "the need for managed integration will diminish. At some appropriate future time it [will] no longer need to be sanctioned and open occupancy [will] then become the one and only standard governing the transfer of housing."[111]

Whether King and other members of the Chicago Freedom Movement genuinely believed that unqualified open housing policies were the best way to achieve racial integration is impossible to say. However, even if movement leaders had felt that attaching certain conditions to open occupancy would have done more to advance the cause of integration than unrestricted open housing, any effort to do so would have diluted their message and potentially compromised the movement's impact. Managed integration—or something similar—was not the sort of clear-cut agenda people could be mobilized around. With King taking an all-or-nothing position, Daley was predictably noncommittal. Following a three-hour meeting with the civil rights leader the day after the Soldier Field rally, the mayor tried to turn the tables: "We asked them," he complained to the press, "'What would you do that we haven't done?' They had no answers. I asked for their help and suggestions, and they frankly said the answers were difficult."[112] As was the pattern, however, Daley refused to be branded as uncooperative. "We have need for massive action," he conceded. "We will continue it. I am not proud of the slums. No one is. We will expand our programs."[113] It was not enough for King. Arguing that Daley was proposing only "surface changes," King warned that the time had come for "direct confrontation with the forces of power in Chicago."[114]

The long-awaited direct action phase of the Chicago campaign began less than a week later when a group of about 120 demonstrators marched from the black neighborhood of Englewood into the nearby white community of Marquette Park on the city's Southwest Side. Marquette Park, along with the adjacent communities of Gage Park and Chicago Lawn, had been identified by movement leaders as strongholds of the kind of white resistance that black Chicagoans seeking housing outside established African American neighborhoods faced. Although all three neighborhoods had housing affordable to middle-class blacks, the entire area was virtually all white. Realtors made sure of that. By the time marchers first headed into Marquette Park on July 16, the Freedom Movement had documented 121 cases of housing discrimination. During the next several weeks marches took place in all three communities.[115] Residents, relatively quiet at first, became increasingly confrontational and abusive, shouting racist epithets and pelting marchers with rocks and bottles. On a march into Marquette Park on August 5, King was hit above the right ear by a large rock and knocked to the ground. Residents screamed, "Kill those niggers," shouting "Kill him, kill him" as King walked past.[116] King later said, "I've been in many demonstrations all across the south, but I can say that I have never seen—even in Mississippi and Alabama—mobs as hostile and hate-filled as I've seen in Chicago. I think the people from Mississippi ought to come to Chicago to learn how to hate."[117]

Leaders of the Chicago Freedom Movement were finally getting the kind of response they had been hoping for, and Mayor Daley was growing more distraught by the hour. When SCLC organizer Jesse Jackson announced plans for a march into the all-white suburb of Cicero—a move expected to produce the most violent reaction from white residents yet—

Daley had had enough. Determined to prevent Chicago from becoming the Selma of the North, Daley announced plans for a summit meeting at which city officials, real estate interests, and movement leaders could reach an agreement on open housing that would end the marches. After debating whether or not to participate, leaders of the Freedom Movement finally decided to attend.[118]

The summit took place on August 17 in the meeting hall of a Catholic church just north of the Loop. In attendance were nearly seventy representatives of various segments of the community, including religious leaders, business leaders, city officials, the Chicago Real Estate Board, and leaders of the Chicago Freedom Movement. Daley, by this time eager to compromise, quickly agreed to the movement's demands, which included better enforcement of existing fair housing laws, the building of new CHA units in white areas of the city, and the relocation of residents displaced by urban renewal projects on a nonsegregated basis.[119] The Real Estate Board was less conciliatory, but under pressure from Daley the organization agreed to alter its stance on open occupancy, affirming freedom of choice in housing as "the right of every citizen" and promising to withdraw its opposition to open occupancy legislation in Springfield.[120] When the language of the agreement was finalized just over a week later, both Daley and King claimed victory. In truth, the victory was much more Daley's than King's. While both the city and the Real Estate Board had made concessions, the language of the agreement was vague, and enforcement mechanisms were weak and ill defined. By November, Daley's city council floor leader Thomas Keane was denying that a genuine agreement existed. "There were only certain suggestions put down and goals to be sought," said Keane.[121] Daley did not deny it. King, long gone from Chicago by this time, called Keane's statement "distressing," but there was little he could do about it.[122]

In the end, the Chicago Freedom Movement's campaign against the slums had a somewhat limited impact. The city temporarily stepped up its building inspection and rodent control programs in response to King's efforts to highlight slum conditions. But such steps were more cosmetic than substantive, carried out mostly to deflect King's criticisms and direct attention away from the real problem—that Daley's own anti-slum initiatives were failing badly. The open housing campaign went more to the heart of the issue. Although King and movement leaders failed to achieve all they had hoped for, they did convincingly link the problem of slum housing with the issue of segregation in a way that few had done before. Henceforth it would be difficult to talk seriously about ending slums without considering the role played by the city's racial geography. The days of focusing slum rehabilitation efforts on providing better housing for blacks in black neighborhoods—while ignoring the dual housing market and other harmful effects of residential segregation—seemed to be over.

Still, movement leaders were better at identifying the problem than offering a workable solution. For open occupancy to perform successfully as a strategy to break down slums and foster integration, residents of white communities would have to stay put even as the racial composition of their neighborhoods began to change. Even with a stronger, more enforceable open housing agreement than the one that was ultimately reached, there was no way to force whites to remain in neighborhoods into which blacks were moving. And just as Daley feared, if whites fled such areas, they would most likely become new slums. Without a change in the attitudes and behavior of white residents, actions by the city and the Real Estate Board to desegregate housing markets—even if they were genuine—could not achieve the desired outcome. In that respect, the open housing campaign differed sharply from King's experiences in the South. There legal victories alone counted for much. Blacks in Alabama and Mississippi could now vote, where they previously could not. They could eat in restaurants that formerly turned them away. In Chicago, however, public policy changes were only half the battle. How to fight the other half—the battle for the hearts and minds of the city's white working-class residents—was a far thornier question, one that the Freedom Movement never seriously addressed.

*   *   *

As the 1960s drew to a close, the attack on the slums was winding down. With an expensive war in Southeast Asia to fight and inflationary pressures at home, President Nixon sought to reduce spending on domestic programs. Funding for urban renewal was cut by 20 percent in the administration's first budget and an additional 50 percent the following year. Allocations for public housing construction were also reduced.[123] Both programs were by this time politically unpopular. Neither one had achieved its intended results or showed promise of doing so in the near future. Far from it; the high-rise public housing projects of the 1950s and early 1960s were now widely viewed as unmitigated social disasters.

Within a few years, the infamous Pruitt-Igoe public housing development in St. Louis would be dynamited, only sixteen years after its completion in 1956. And despite hundreds of millions of federal dollars spent for slum clearance and redevelopment, slums had not been eliminated in Chicago or any other major city. By the early 1970s Mayor Daley's promises to end slums within a few years had ceased. Instead Daley now counseled patience, conceding that the problem was more complex than previously thought. "Eliminating slums involves people," the mayor explained in a 1973 speech at the University of Chicago. "And it's obvious that working out problems of individuals is more taxing and time-consuming than working with the physical environment. . . . In the human situation we have very little control and the problem changes constantly."[124]

For well over a decade Mayor Daley had waged a vigorous campaign to rebuild and rehabilitate Chicago's blighted areas. If the attack on the slums ended in failure, it was not for lack of effort or initiative. Like others at the time, Daley viewed the presence of slums as incompatible with his vision of the good city. Such areas were expensive eyesores, places where the city was forced to spend heavily for fire and police protection and other public services. With a disproportionate share of the city's tax-delinquent land and stagnating property values, blighted areas failed to generate anywhere near the tax receipts needed to cover the costs of city services in such places. It would be one thing if the boundaries of the slums were fixed, so that even if such areas did impose certain burdens on the rest of the city, blight would not threaten or otherwise interfere with more prosperous neighborhoods. But the slums could seemingly not be contained. Instead, despite efforts at conservation, they pressed further each year into stable working-class neighborhoods whose residents became prime targets for developers of new suburban communities.

Daley knew all this, and it was in part this knowledge that drove the attack on the slums. To be sure, there were powerful interests involved as well. Institutions such as the University of Chicago, IIT, and Michael Reese Hospital pushed hard for slum clearance and redevelopment; it was the planning efforts of these institutions, more than anything else, that had set the attack on the slums in motion. But Daley was receptive to their arguments in part because the initiatives they proposed fit well with his own understanding of how best to respond to an urgent problem, one that threatened the city's survival. The slums had to be eliminated because the alternative was a dying city. Powerful interests or not, something would have to be done.

When, in the end, the attack on the slums proved unsuccessful, it was not because Daley had chosen to concentrate development funds on other areas of the city, or because he had grown preoccupied with downtown redevelopment, or because he simply did not care very much about poor people. Rather, the attack on the slums failed because the formula embodied in state and federal urban renewal and public housing legislation was itself flawed as a vehicle for ending slums, and because public officials used the new tools at their disposal in ways inconsistent with the elimination of slums. Public housing could only reproduce slums—not eliminate them—as long as it concentrated low-income residents in existing blighted areas, isolated from services and opportunities in more stable areas of the city. And the redevelopment of land for its highest and best use—a condition attached to urban renewal by the central role of real estate developers in the renewal process—meant that high-rent housing, not housing for moderate-income families, would be the default scenario for many slum clearance projects. By uprooting existing slum residents and pushing them into transitional areas, such projects were instrumental in the creation of new slums and the extension of the ghetto into formerly stable areas. Like public housing, they reproduced slums rather than eliminated them. And as long as housing markets remained segregated, there seemed to be no way to disrupt this pattern. Mired in contradictions, urban renewal collapsed partly of its own weight, setting the stage for the emergence of new ideas about how the city should be rebuilt and the problem of slums and blight addressed.

Ever since Progressive Era housing reformers declared war on the slums at the turn of the twentieth century, the primary goal of anti-slum campaigns had been the same: eliminate substandard housing and other signs of blight wherever they existed. Yet as Chicago entered the 1970s, nearly seventy years after the tenement house ordinance of 1902—the first major effort to rid the city of slums through government action—was passed, the slums appeared more intractable than ever. Decades of experimentation with anti-slum initiatives had failed to produce a workable formula for attacking the problem. It was time, perhaps, for a rethinking of the situation. Could a city that contained large sections of blight and disrepair—together with an increasingly impoverished minority population—be viable? Could the city learn to live with the slums?

CHAPTER SEVEN

The New Convergence of Power

In 1972 word began leaking to the Chicago media about a new plan for the city's central area. It would be the city's official plan for the downtown area, but it would be produced not by city planning officials but by the Chicago Central Area Committee. The downtown business group had organized a fundraising drive to cover the entire cost of the $375,000 plan, at the time an unprecedented sum of money for a city plan. Just weeks before it was publicly unveiled in June 1973, one journalist described it gushingly as "the biggest, most elaborate, costliest plan for central area revitalization in the history of the United States."[1] Titled *Chicago 21: A Plan for the Central Area Communities*, the plan presented a $15 billion thirty-year program to transform the city's downtown and its surroundings in accordance with "a vision of the Central Community of the 21st Century."[2] Major new developments were proposed for the downtown and near-downtown areas. Meigs Airport on the lakefront would be demolished to create new park space and improved access to the lake. A new pedestrian mall was planned for State Street; sidewalks would be widened, with vehicular traffic limited to city buses. Just north of downtown, Navy Pier—a little-used docking structure for lake freighters and passenger boats completed in 1916—was to be transformed into a lively entertainment area with restaurants, exhibits, and an auditorium. Capping it all off would be a "miniature supercity" for 120,000 residents built on 650 acres of underutilized land, mostly defunct railroad yards, just south of the Loop. Residents of the new development would be connected to the central business district by a futuristic rapid transit system in which a passenger "would enter a small car, push a button on a map showing his destination, and zip away automatically."[3]

Chicago 21 was the first new plan for the central area produced since the publication of the *Development Plan for the Central Area of Chicago* in 1958, and it is worth considering for a moment what had changed during the fifteen-year period since the earlier plan was released. The 1958 Development Plan had been prepared during a time when the attack on the slums was still in its infancy. New urban renewal projects such as Lake Meadows and Prairie Shores—at the time still under construction on the city's South Side—inspired hope on the part of business leaders that areas bordering downtown would soon be targeted for a similar upgrading. Through a combination of new public housing developments and private construction under the urban renewal program, the city's political leaders promised to eliminate slums and blight wherever they existed, and downtown business elites looked forward to a time when the city's central business district would be the economic center of a city of stable, well-kept neighborhoods. Some areas would, of course, be more prosperous than others, and those would ideally be located close to the central business district. However, even families of little means would at least live in neighborhoods where the amount of housing available was sufficient to meet the demand and where homes and apartment buildings were well constructed and properly maintained.

Downtown business leaders watched with great interest as the attack on the slums unfolded during the 1950s and 1960s, and what they saw was both disappointing and alarming. Contrary to their wishes, very little new housing was built in the near-downtown area through the urban renewal program. As we saw in chapter 6, institutions that were being rapidly engulfed by the South Side ghetto—the University of Chicago, Michael Reese Hospital, and the Illinois Institute of Technology, in particular—made pressing claims on the city's urban renewal funds, matched by ambitious planning efforts and commitments of institutional resources. From the city's standpoint it made more sense to concentrate the attack on the slums here, in the heart of the ghetto, rather than in areas bordering the central business district where blight was less pronounced and area stakeholders not as well organized. While there were exceptions to this pattern—most notably the Carl Sandburg Village north of the Loop—little progress was being made on the fifty thousand new units of centrally located middle-income housing called for by the 1958 Development Plan.

Equally troublesome, the city's efforts notwithstanding, the slums were proving to be a particularly knotty problem. For every new Lake Meadows or Prairie Shores–type housing development, there were acres

upon acres of blighted areas that by now seemed to be more or less permanent features of the urban landscape. The hopes of the 1950s and early
1960s that the attack on the slums would ultimately prove successful—
that blight would be abolished wherever it existed—were giving way to
a sinking realization that the slums were not going away. As leaders of
the Central Area Committee prepared for the first update of the central
area plan in fifteen years, they perceived a twofold challenge: first, a way
had to be found to populate the near-downtown area with the types of
residents most valued as office workers and patrons of downtown restaurants, cultural attractions, and retail establishments; second, the new revitalized central area would need protection from impoverished areas of
the city extending for miles south and west of the downtown area, a condition now recognized as intractable.

The situation, while dire, was not altogether hopeless. The attack on
the slums was winding down, but certain ideas that came out of that initiative would continue to be useful going forward, even if eliminating
slums was no longer always the principal objective. Thanks to the urban
renewal program, the use of public-private partnerships to rearrange
land use and bolster land values was now viewed favorably by members of the development community as well as civic and political leaders. Through redevelopment or rehabilitation, neighborhoods and other
areas that were not realizing their full potential for profit could be upgraded. Such areas might or might not be slums. The more important
question, as the urban renewal program came to a close, was whether
or not land was being used as productively as it could be. If not, perhaps
some combination of public and private effort could effect a change in
land use or, short of that, at least make existing uses more profitable.
Such was the thinking of leaders of the Central Area Committee as they
pondered how to move forward with central area planning in the post
urban renewal period. The policy paradigm for engaging with the city's
blighted areas was once again in flux. Old ideas had been found wanting;
convergence around a new set of ideas had not yet occurred. But whatever form the new conventional wisdom ultimately took, downtown business leaders—acting through the Central Area Committee—were well
positioned to ensure that it would bear their imprint.

One thing was certain: further progress would require a partnership
of some kind between city officials and downtown business leaders. Yet
the matter of public-private collaboration, and the form it might take
going forward, raised potentially thorny questions. Despite what seems

to have been close cooperation between the city and the Central Area Committee in the preparation of the 1958 Development Plan, the relationship—at least initially—failed to progress. In his study of urban redevelopment in postwar Atlanta, Clarence Stone emphasizes the close working relationship that developed between the city's leading downtown business group, Central Atlanta Progress, and top city officials.[4] Through projects and planning efforts, city officials and business leaders came to know and understand one another, eventually sharing many of the same goals and objectives regarding the redevelopment of the city. The regime—the term used by Stone to define urban power structures featuring this type of sustained, multi-issue public-private cooperation— was constituted over time, as mutually beneficial undertakings encouraged further collaboration.

As urban scholars have shown, regimes were a feature of many postwar cities—perhaps the most common form of urban governance at the time.[5] Robert Salisbury, one of the first to identify the new phenomenon, called it "the new convergence of power."[6] Chicago, too, would witness the emergence of a regimelike power structure, but it would take time. Regimes do not form simply because they are useful. They emerge through cooperative undertakings perceived as advantageous by the parties involved. If cooperation does not produce the desired results, regime building will falter. Such was the case in Chicago for much of the 1960s, as several initiatives backed by the Central Area Committee and key allies failed to advance. With the publication of the *Chicago 21* plan in 1973 and its proposals for specific redevelopment projects—backed, in at least one case, with the promise of private investment dollars— conditions for regime building became more favorable. By this time, however, neighborhood actors had become hypersensitive to issues of displacement and renewal. As business leaders and city officials undertook preparations to make the near-downtown area an attractive location for the middle class, they would have to contend with vocal neighborhood groups that already called this area home.

One Step Forward, Two Steps Back

One can imagine that August 22, 1958, was a very good day for Holman Pettibone. That morning the chairman of the Central Area Committee stood alongside Mayor Daley and watched while the mayor and his planning staff unveiled the new *Development Plan for the Central Area of Chicago*, a plan the organization Pettibone chaired had had a significant hand in producing.[7] The precise nature of the CCAC's involvement in the drafting of the 1958 Development Plan is unclear. Pettibone himself downplayed the organization's role.[8] However, such claims were in keeping with the committee's modus operandi of staying below the radar screen and "letting all credit go to public officials and agencies and others involved in a downtown improvement project," as one observer put it.[9] Concerned that a more visible public profile would ruffle feathers among the city's political leaders and raise questions about the appropriateness of business involvement in public decision making, the CCAC was generally happy to avoid the limelight as long as the results obtained were consistent with its preferences. Pettibone's statements about the extent of the CCAC's involvement in the 1958 Development Plan should be considered in this light.

This much about the organization's activities is known. In 1957 the CCAC's planning and research committee had begun working with the city's own planning staff "in the development of basic concepts from which the Planning Department of the City [could] develop a basic plan for the Central Area."[10] As part of this effort, the CCAC developed a set of principles for downtown planning emphasizing the area's compactness, accessibility, and relationship with peripheral areas; these principles were incorporated into the city's own planning process for the central area. In addition, CCAC staff and consultants began work on several economic studies focusing on the central area, all financed by the organization. The studies, authorized by the CCAC's executive committee, were to be used by the Department of Planning in the preparation of what ultimately became the 1958 Development Plan. Also approved by the executive committee was a request for $3,600 "for the rental of a special office to be used in connection with the development of the Central Area plan."[11]

All this certainly suggests a partnership of some kind was in the making. Still, it is somewhat unclear how close the relationship was or how high up in the city's political hierarchy it went. A February 1959 memorandum from Marshall Field chairman Hughston McBain to the CCAC board of directors is intriguing in that respect. McBain, himself a CCAC board member, was describing a lunch meeting he had had several weeks earlier with Mayor Daley. The purpose of the meeting was "to give the Mayor a succinct and comprehensive report on at least the major projects in which the Committee is interested and on which it has done a good deal of work, or has taken a position." McBain began with a surprising statement: "It is important to keep in mind that communications between the Committee and the Mayor have been most infrequent and impersonal." In fact, according to McBain, today's lunch was "the first full dress meeting" Daley had ever had with "any director of the Committee." As a result, the mayor's understanding of "the actual program, accomplishments and objectives of the Committee" was in some cases "distorted."[12]

Coming just six months after the release of the 1958 Development Plan, McBain's comments about the CCAC's relationship with the mayor seem puzzling—unless Daley himself was not very involved in the day-to-day details of the preparation of the plan. Or perhaps the plan was developed primarily by the city's own planning staff, using information provided by the CCAC while failing to engage organization leaders very much in the actual planning process. Either scenario might explain the absence of close contact between the mayor and the CCAC. But there was more. The mayor listened attentively while McBain reported on the CCAC's activities, displaying what McBain perceived as "unusual interest, absorption and respect for the Committee." Yet Daley's reaction was not altogether positive. "The Mayor," wrote McBain, "indicated his belief that the Committee was concerning itself too much with projects and plans properly in the province of government and too little with projects and plans properly in the province of private organizations." What Daley wanted from business leaders was "the investment of more private capital." Daley, it seemed, viewed the CCAC's involvement in city planning as somewhat meddlesome. The city would plan. The job of private enterprise was to initiate projects that would facilitate the redevelopment of the downtown area in accordance with such plans. McBain concluded by noting the recommendation of CCAC staff that "additional and fairly frequent meetings" between the mayor and CCAC board members be scheduled, "particularly where, in the normal course of business, it would be a natural thing to do."

McBain's comments seem to suggest a somewhat arm's-length relationship between the mayor and the CCAC at this stage. To be sure, Daley understood that this group would be an invaluable asset in his efforts to redevelop the downtown area. But if there was to be a partnership it would be on his terms, and this meant respecting what the mayor viewed as the proper division of labor between the public and private sectors in city planning. Daley's unease about the CCAC's activities and seemingly chilly response to McBain's report can be explained at least in part by the fact that very little collaboration between the two parties had occurred around the execution of actual projects. Until now the CCAC had concentrated its efforts on two principal activities: studies and research related to the planning of the central area, and the securing of public support for the programs it endorsed.[13] Neither activity required the sort of close, day-to-day working relationship between public and private sectors that the development of bricks-and-mortar projects did. Equally important, neither activity produced the kinds of visible payoffs that make partnerships of this kind especially rewarding. In short, the relationship between the city and the CCAC was not progressing as fast as it might have because the nature of the work being undertaken did not require or actively foster close partnerships.

By 1959 the CCAC began to recognize its failure to move beyond planning, research, and advocacy to program execution and the completion of tangible projects as a shortcoming that needed to be addressed. In September of that year, a report by the CCAC's program committee praised the organization's many accomplishments to date, while conceding that "progress made toward . . . execution of CCAC projects has been slow."[14] This omission was a concern, the report stated, because "any movement must realize visible accomplishment to justify its continuing existence." Both the general public and the organization's supporters "must, in due time, be able to view tangible things if enthusiastic endorsement and support [are] to continue." Accordingly, the committee recommended that the CCAC reduce its research and study activities in order to place greater emphasis on "physical accomplishment." More specifically, it was suggested that the organization "select a few projects from its inventory that can be brought to fruition in a reasonable length of time and bulldoggedly see that they get done."[15]

In pondering where and on what sorts of projects such an action-oriented program might be focused, members of the CCAC no doubt considered the portion of the central area situated directly south of downtown. The area was presently a jumbled mass of railroad yards and rail lines, used by more than twenty railroad companies that owned the rail infrastructure and had long-term lease agreements with the city to disembark passengers at three railroad terminals in the South Loop area

FIGURE 7.1. Rail terminal area, Near South Side, 1970. View looking south from down-town. Photograph by Robert M. Lightfoot III. Chicago History Museum, Chicago Central Communities Study photograph collection, ICHi-176172.

(fig. 7.1). It was a highly inefficient and land-intensive system. Efforts had been under way since the early 1950s to consolidate rail lines and shift passenger traffic to a terminal west of the Loop, a move that would potentially open up hundreds of acres of land directly south of down-town for new development. Mayor Daley had appointed a Rail Terminal Authority in 1955 mainly for the purpose of setting such a process in motion.[16] However, railroad consolidation was a two-edged sword. Under the best of circumstances, it would pave the way for new development that would anchor the southern end of the Loop, helping to preserve the compactness of the central business district that business leaders viewed as a key asset of the city's downtown. But should new development on the site fail to materialize, business leaders feared it could end up being used for public housing or some other purpose that threatened rather than complemented activities in the Loop. Few developments were more frightening to the downtown business community than the northward expansion of the South Side ghetto.

The CCAC's involvement in the rail terminal area dated back to the organization's founding days, when Holman Pettibone reported at the second meeting of the executive committee in April 1956 that Mayor Daley had asked him to participate on a committee "to consider a railroad terminal on the south side of the Central Area."[17] While that effort went nowhere, activity heated up the following year when the CCAC proposed the terminal area site as a possible location for a new University of Illinois campus in Chicago. The university had set up a temporary campus on Navy Pier in 1946 primarily to serve returning World War II veterans, but the board of trustees ultimately determined that a permanent Chicago facility was needed. Space would be a significant concern; the university wanted at least 140 acres.[18]

Although university officials initially favored a suburban site for the new campus, Mayor Daley and the CCAC pushed hard for a city location. After a February 1957 meeting with a member of the university's site selection committee the CCAC asked the Real Estate Research Corporation, a private consulting firm founded by Daley's housing and redevelopment coordinator James Downs, to examine the feasibility of a number of centrally located sites for the university, including the rail terminal area.[19] That May, Pettibone wrote a letter to university president David Henry making a case for "possible sites in or adjacent to the central business district of Chicago."[20] The letter identified three possible campus locations bordering the Loop, including the rail terminal area, and it was on the latter site that Pettibone focused most of his attention. As it happened, the university had already considered and rejected the other two sites, but it had not yet considered the terminal area. President Henry was open to the idea, particularly since efforts to secure a suburban location for the campus were faltering. In March 1958 the board of trustees hired the Real Estate Research Corporation to conduct its own study of possible sites, requesting an in-depth analysis of two sites in particular, one being the terminal area.[21]

Momentum for the terminal site was building. When the 1958 Development Plan was released that August, Mayor Daley strongly signaled his own preferences. The terminal area was identified as the planned location of the new campus, even if the university trustees had yet to commit. Whether the CCAC persuaded the city to endorse this location is unknown, although by this time it was clearly the organization's preferred option, a position that was undoubtedly communicated to the city's planning staff, if not Daley himself. Such questions aside, there was still one major hurdle that would have to be cleared. The city did not have site control. Far from it, the land was owned by multiple railroad companies, any one of which could kill the entire project if it refused to strike a deal for the sale of its property. In April 1959 Daley began a series of meetings with railroad officials to try to reach an agreement.[22] By this point, time was of the essence. The university insisted that a site be made available no later than July 1960 so that classes could begin at the new campus by the fall semester of 1963.[23] As negotiations with the railroads began, it became clear that there were two key obstacles. The railroads were asking for a much higher price for the land than the city was prepared to pay, and they were not enthusiastic about the city's terminal consolidation plan in the first place. After all, passenger rail was on the decline. Why should they agree to sign "expensive long-term leases for the use of a new terminal when they already had very inexpensive leases for the use of the old terminals," as one study put it?[24]

After several months of meetings, the chair of the Rail Terminal Authority complained of "great inertia" on the part of the railroads.[25] Seeing the handwriting on the wall, the university trustees voted to endorse Garfield Park—a city park on the West Side that Daley had identified as an acceptable alternative to the terminal area in the event the latter site could not be delivered in time—as its preferred location for the new campus.[26] Business leaders, including the CCAC, immediately mobilized against the Garfield Park location, fearful that a once-in-a-lifetime opportunity to anchor the Loop and wall it off from blighted areas farther south was about to slip through their hands. Garfield Park was several miles west of downtown; a campus there would provide no boost to downtown revitalization. For the next year, the CCAC devoted "constant attention" to the campus location issue.[27] Lobbying and the threat of lawsuits by the CCAC and fellow business leaders eventually eliminated the Garfield Park site, but the effort still ended in disappointment. With the railroads refusing to budge, the new campus was built not in the South Loop but in a mostly Italian American residential area farther west. Protests by neighborhood residents—the largest yet by any group in the path of the urban renewal wrecking ball—cost Daley politically. Equally problematic, efforts had been set in motion to open up railroad land south of the Loop for new development, but there was no longer a project for the area on the table.[28]

*   *   *

It would be one thing if the CCAC's failure in connection with the university campus location had been accompanied by visible accomplishments elsewhere, but for the most part it was not. In the several years since the publication of the 1958 Development Plan, the CCAC had gone from a seemingly powerful, up-and-coming organization poised to have a major impact on the city's downtown area to a group that increasingly appeared to have lost its way. Others with an interest in the city's downtown took notice. At a June 1961 meeting of MHPC's executive committee, the suggestion was raised that MHPC take a more active role in downtown redevelopment. While one committee member expressed concern that this might produce "jealousy" on the part of the CCAC, others argued that the latter organization's ongoing ability to play a leadership role was in question. The meeting minutes were blunt: "It was the general feeling that the Chicago Central Area Committee has fallen down because it did not have top flight planners, its members were overanxious not to irritate anyone and it had no program for implementing its plan."[29]

CCAC chairman Harold Moore seemed to confirm this gloomy outlook in a January 1961 communication to the board of directors. Wrote Moore, "At a recent Board meeting, one of the members of the Board commented upon the fact that he felt our group had not been really effective in bringing about the results which were considered important. I have been pondering that comment at great length, because I believe that, to a large degree, this is true." Perhaps, suggested Moore, the organization had "relied too heavily on the hope that the mere publishing of the names of the members of the Board would carry sufficient weight to bring about results." While the "lack of concrete accomplishment" was distressing, it was "unthinkable" that the CCAC should reduce its efforts. The central area had significant problems that required intervention and leadership. "It is only by keeping the spotlight right on the conditions which need strengthening or correcting and by working steadily to bring about the necessary action, either through our own efforts or though stimulating the efforts of others, that we shall ultimately accomplish worthwhile results."[30]

One possible way to produce more tangible results was to stop relying so much on the actions of other parties—which the CCAC could not easily control—and begin to sponsor its own projects. With the location of

the new University of Illinois campus southwest of downtown and the future of the rail terminal site unresolved, such an opportunity presented
itself. In 1962 the CCAC turned its attention to the area once again, this
time with a plan of its own. The plan—prepared for the CCAC by the
high-powered consulting and architectural team of Real Estate Research
Corporation, Barton-Aschman and Associates, and Skidmore, Owings
& Merrill—was presented to the CCAC board of directors at a December 1962 board meeting. Frederick "Ted" Aschman gave the presentation, titled "The Near South Side—A Chicago Opportunity." What was
proposed was the most ambitious plan yet to rearrange land use in the
central area or any other location in the city. If carried out as planned,
it would completely remake a roughly two-thousand-acre section of the
city's Near South Side extending from the Loop to Twenty-Fifth Street.
In place of the railroad lines, light manufacturing, and "low-grade housing" that presently occupied the area, the consultants imagined new
residential communities for up to 100,000 people "in probably six separate neighborhoods, with new elementary schools and one new high
school." Some space would also be reserved for light industry and use by
nearby universities. It would be the city's largest urban renewal project
ever, nearly the size of all previous renewal projects combined.[31] Some
displacement would be unavoidable—the area included approximately
8,000 residents. However, according to Aschman, "the suggested program would probably result in the removal of only 4,000 of these."[32]

During the next several months, Aschman had "tentative discussions"
with representatives from the Housing and Home Finance Agency, the
city's Department of Urban Renewal, and the Ford Foundation to gauge
interest in and possible support for an urban renewal project in the area
under consideration.[33] Ford was brought into the discussion because Aschman believed an extensive study of the area was needed before planning could proceed further. Ford, it was hoped, might be persuaded to finance the study. The foundation's president Henry Heald not only had
deep Chicago connections but, as president of IIT during the 1940s, had
helped set the city's urban redevelopment program in motion. He was
expected to be a sympathetic figure.[34]

Curiously, the CCAC deliberately chose not to reach out directly to
Mayor Daley during this time. Instead it was determined that Barton-
Aschman would prepare a presentation for Daley to be delivered at some
future date, and that this would be the first occasion the subject was
broached with the mayor.[35] The meeting with Daley—off the record to

ensure confidentiality—finally took place on December 12, 1963, almost exactly one year after the plan was originally presented to the CCAC board. In attendance, along with the mayor, were Aschman, Downs, and several CCAC board members.[36] At the meeting Daley gave his consent for the CCAC "to continue the work on a private basis and without publicity." He also promised to write a letter of support for the project, which he ultimately furnished. But that was the extent of the mayor's involvement. In the end, Daley never warmed to the initiative. He had been stung two years earlier by the angry protests over the University of Illinois West Side campus location, a response he had not seen coming. At this point he had little stomach for another massive clearance project that might well inspire similar demonstrations. But the CCAC had also handled its outreach to the mayor badly. As a partnership building exercise, the project was an unqualified failure. Rather than bring Daley in early in the planning process and try to achieve buy-in from the mayor, the CCAC arrogantly chose to present the plan to him as a fait accompli, long after the organization had finalized its own initial plans. Not surprisingly, Daley never took ownership of the project.

For the next several years the initiative limped along, with virtually no participation by the city. Aschman prepared a presentation for a meeting with the Ford Foundation and Commissioner William Slayton of the Urban Renewal Administration scheduled for June 1964, but for unknown reasons the meeting never took place.[37] CCAC board member David Kennedy finally spoke with Ford president Henry Heald about the project in the spring of 1965, and it was agreed that a meeting between foundation representatives and the CCAC "could now be arranged."[38] The meeting took place several months later, but Ford ultimately denied the request for funding.[39] Undaunted, the CCAC began working "with the city and the Railroad Terminal Commission in the development of a proposal which will soon be presented to the Urban Renewal Division of the Housing and Home Finance Agency."[40] That effort, however, also failed to bear fruit. As with the site selection process for the University of Illinois campus, intransigence on the part of the railroads continued to represent a key stumbling block. The last mention of the initiative in the CCAC's files, contained in the organization's planned 1967 program, provides a fitting epitaph for the project: "Even though the railroad terminal consolidation may be some time away and even though some of the problems at the moment seem to be insurmountable, the South Side Redevelopment Area is still one of our greatest assets. A study of this area at this time, with funds supplied by one or more foundations, could result in a plan to be used when consolidation does appear to be in sight."[41]

In the end, the project proved to be an all-around disappointment. It was the only major central area redevelopment project the CCAC had sponsored or been seriously involved with during this time, and three solid years of effort had failed to move the initiative beyond the preliminary planning stages. To be sure, the city's downtown was booming, and the CCAC could take some credit for that. The 1958 Development Plan it had played a role in preparing had helped set the downtown construction boom in motion, sorting out differences among the various downtown interests and signaling to developers the city's expectations about what form new development should take and where it should occur.[42] Beyond that, however, the CCAC played at best a supporting role in downtown redevelopment. It carried out or commissioned studies focusing on such activities as parking, public transit, traffic, and housing. It weighed in on public issues like zoning, lakefront development, and air rights. It worked actively to improve the appearance of the Loop, at one point initiating a Loop beautification program. These were the kinds of activities that consumed the bulk of committee staff time, and city officials most likely viewed these contributions favorably. But such efforts, as useful as they were, did not cause any real estate deals to be struck or any ground to be broken. What the CCAC most certainly was *not*—at least at this stage—was an organization actively partnering with the city around the redevelopment of the downtown area. The cranes and construction crews that peppered the Loop, making the city's downtown feel at times like one big construction site, were largely the result of the actions of others.

The Making of a Power Structure

As the CCAC struggled to advance its proposal for the redevelopment of the Near South Side, the city moved ahead with its own planning efforts. At Daley's request, the Department of Planning began preparations in the early 1960s for the production of a new comprehensive plan, the first citywide planning effort undertaken in nearly two decades.[43] In addition to the comprehensive plan itself there were to be sixteen development area plans, each focusing on a particular subarea of the city, including the central area. The CCAC was anxious to engage with the process. In the fall of 1963, organization leaders met with Daley's planning director Ira Bach, offering "to cooperate with the Planning Department in the further development of a comprehensive Central Area plan."[44] As a first step, the CCAC agreed to form a special committee on planning and research whose job it would be to review and possibly update the organization's planning principles for the central area, originally developed in connection with the 1958 Development Plan.

The committee finished its work during the summer of 1964 and presented its findings to the CCAC board at an August meeting.[45] Ted Aschman, whose consulting firm Barton-Aschman and Associates had been brought in to provide technical assistance, spoke for the committee. In his presentation Aschman reiterated the importance of the planning principles developed for the 1958 Development Plan. Both the accessibility and the compactness of the central business district should be preserved and strengthened, now as then. In addition, peripheral areas—areas bordering the Loop—presented new development opportunities that should be exploited. However, these areas, representing in some cases a blighting influence on downtown properties, required renewed attention. Large sections of the near-downtown area were "under-developed, obsolete, or blighted, and thus subject to imminent rebuilding." It was essential that these areas be redeveloped in ways that complemented and enhanced activities in the central business district. Housing was emphasized. Pointing to the South Side rail terminal area as one example, the report argued that "major opportunities exist for the development of new residential areas that could accommodate several hundred thousands of persons." For the most part, people living in these new communities should be "families whose livelihoods are dependent upon [downtown] activity and employment."[46]

This theme—that areas bordering the Loop should be redeveloped to house middle-class professionals—had been repeated for decades, with few results. That had to change. The central business district was booming, but all that was threatened if nearby areas did not supply downtown establishments with the kind of workforce and customer base they demanded. Enthused with Aschman's presentation, the CCAC board voted to approve the report "and its presentation to the Department of City Planning." At the CCAC's urging, Daley agreed to adopt the report as the city's own policy statement for the central area.[47] By June 1965 the Department of Planning was in the process of preparing final artwork and maps for the document, with an anticipated publication date of August 1. However, for unknown reasons planning commissioner John Duba got cold feet, and the publication and distribution of the report were postponed indefinitely.[48]

For the next several years, central area planning proceeded at a snail's pace, and the relationship between the CCAC and the city's planning department (renamed, in 1965, the Department of Development and Planning) grew into a sometimes heated rivalry over who would control the planning process for the area. The new Comprehensive Plan of Chicago was finally released in 1966, followed by fifteen of the sixteen subarea plans during the next two years. Only the central area plan remained unfinished. In May 1968 the city's new planning commissioner, Lewis Hill, gave a presentation on the central area plan to the CCAC membership, a high-profile event held at the Union League Club.[49] By this time the CCAC was becoming impatient, and Hill's talk did not inspire confidence. During the following months, the CCAC approached the commissioner on several occasions with offers to "either cooperate with the Department in the development of the Central Area Chapter or, if requested, . . . to prepare a Chapter for the Central Area." Hill was noncommittal, although after "frequent requests" the CCAC did eventually receive a set of galley proofs as the document was being finalized for publication in December 1968.[50] The proofs were disappointing, containing incorrect information and lacking policy statements on such important matters as zoning and lakefront development. Nevertheless, convinced that this was the best they were likely to get, the CCAC recommended that the city "complete and publish the report," pledging to cooperate with Hill and his staff "in making studies of specific problems not covered by the report."[51]

Despite the CCAC's endorsement of the plan, Commissioner Hill ultimately chose not to go forward with publication. Admitting that the plan was—as the CCAC had insisted—incomplete, Hill, with the help of federal urban development funds, commissioned a set of consultant studies to provide additional information needed to inform the planning process. The studies, carried out by the Real Estate Research Corporation and Barton-Aschman and Associates in 1969 and 1970, shed further light on the problems and opportunities presented by areas bordering the central business district. The research largely supported the CCAC's earlier recommendation that new housing for middle-class residents be emphasized in such areas, not surprising given the involvement of Barton-Aschman in the preparation of the CCAC's own planning principles for the central area. Yet the new studies also raised troublesome questions about the central area's current population. The report by the Real Estate Research Corporation was particularly blunt, observing at one point that the crime rate in the near-downtown area had increased in recent years, a finding accompanied by the observation that the minority population of central area neighborhoods was expanding. The ramifications were potentially serious. As the report cautioned, "If the Central Business District becomes surrounded by major housing areas occupied by low- and moderate-income households, this may discourage some large firms from continuing to locate their headquarters and offices there. Any significant discouragement of this type could cause a serious loss of at least potential future employment gains, and perhaps an absolute decline in Central Business District employment opportunities."[52]

The racial undertones were unmistakable, yet the city's consultants were giving voice to concerns that had been expressed in Loop boardrooms and city hall for several years by that point. It was 1970, four years after Martin Luther King Jr. had led open housing marches into all-white Chicago neighborhoods and just two years after King's assassination had sparked violent uprisings on the city's West Side, not far from downtown. Daley's attack on the slums had ended in failure, and the city's racial boundaries were in play. Due in part to the razing of South Side neighborhood shopping areas through the urban renewal program and in part to the growing numbers of African Americans residing in the central area, blacks were an increasingly visible presence downtown, raising concerns that whites might abandon the Loop.[53] Not only were there more black shoppers and entertainment seekers, but the types of establishments catering to them were in some cases unsettling to whites. As one observer recounted, "Mayor Daley was allegedly furious with the Plitt theatres for running continuous movies with such titles as 'The Black Six—See the Biggest and the Baddest Waste 150 Dudes,' and the seemingly endless stream of Kung Fu movies. The west side of State Street was also characterized as a 'strip of Super-Fly clothes shops.'"[54] The solution to this perceived problem, according to the city's consultants, lay in part in the proper rebuilding of the near-downtown area, so that "middle- and high-income units would predominate on all large-sized sites."[55] The consultants did not say as much but the implication was clear: such housing developments, unaffordable to most blacks, would reverse the demographic shift currently under way, resulting in a "gradual 'whitening' of the Loop," as one set of analysts put it.[56]

With the work of its consultants now complete, the Department of Development and Planning was anxious to move ahead with the planning process. As a first step, the department produced a summary and analysis of the Barton-Aschman and Real Estate Research Corporation studies, using information the consultants provided but drawing its own conclusions about what the data and other information implied. Once again, the CCAC found the department's efforts wanting. In a review of the city's report, CCAC staff complained that too much emphasis was placed on "social problems" and the "social ills" of central area neighborhoods, problems the city proposed to address in the new plan. The city, it seemed, held out hope for rehabilitating the area. Business leaders were chiefly interested in changing the area's demographics, not improving the quality of life for existing low-income residents. "Granted," the CCAC wrote, "there is a great need for good-quality residential neighborhoods in which low-income and moderate-income households can live, but these problems must be treated separately from the Development of a Physical Plan for the Central Area."[57]

By this time one of the city's own consultants, Real Estate Research Corporation chairman and CCAC board member James Downs, was also concerned that the city would fail to produce the type of central area plan that business leaders wanted. In January 1971, Downs penned a lengthy memorandum to the CCAC board that set in motion a chain of events that would both shape the course of central area planning for decades to come and realign the city's power structure. Downs proposed a radical step: that the CCAC "volunteer to assume the initiative from the City of Chicago" and undertake the preparation of a central area plan of its own "for adoption and publication by the City." The Department of Development and Planning, he argued, was simply not up to the task. In language that was at times brutally frank, Downs carefully spelled out his concerns. The downtown building boom notwithstanding, the Loop was in trouble, as evidenced by several key trends. The first was "the considerably increased needs for security forces" to protect downtown businesses, followed by a "perceptible increase in the proportion of blacks both during and after working hours." Here Downs was amplifying concerns his own consulting firm had raised in its report to the city. But there were other issues as well. Most important, the evening population of the Loop had been reduced to "minuscule numbers." Restaurants, entertainment spots, and cultural attractions were all experiencing a decline in patronage after hours, with the result that the city's downtown was "no longer the recreational and cultural center it once was." Not only that, but there were fewer establishments to draw people to the downtown area in the first place. As Downs observed, "small street level retail and service establishments" had undergone a marked reduction in recent years.[58]

Taken together, these developments indicated "simply a decline in the quality of life in the central area." In part the Loop was a victim of its own success. As Downs pointed out, the loss of storefront businesses—including retail, restaurants, and certain entertainment spots—was due largely to demolition associated with new building activity, most of which involved the construction of office towers. Such buildings, designed in many cases without ground-level commercial space, contributed little to downtown street life. As formerly diverse downtown streets gave way to an "unrelieved mass of utilitarian office buildings," fewer people frequented the downtown area after business hours simply because there were fewer commercial establishments catering to them. But there was no mistaking Downs's words: the problem was in part a racial one. Whites were avoiding the Loop, particularly during the evening hours, because they feared the presence of blacks. To supplement the CCAC's existing planning principles for the central area, Downs now suggested a new one: "social compatibility." While vague—perhaps intentionally—on how this principle should guide planning, Downs could not have been clearer about what it meant. Racial and ethnic change in the Loop and nearby areas was moving in an unhealthy direction, one incompatible with a solid, ongoing white presence downtown; whatever course the future of central area planning took, this situation had to be reversed.

Despite the price tag for the proposed plan—estimated at the time at $350,000—Downs's idea was received warmly by the CCAC board. Given his stature as a highly regarded real estate consultant with a long history of involvement in the city's redevelopment program, the positive response is perhaps not surprising. Equally important, however, his portrayal of the Loop's current troubles provided a rationale for a plan of action that many board members already endorsed: the rebuilding of the near-downtown area for middle- and upper-income housing. At an April meeting, members of the board voted unanimously to pursue the initiative, each member pledging to do his share to raise the needed funds.[59]

Two months later Downs was elected president of the board of directors, an indication of the high priority board members placed on the new planning effort.[60]

Of course there would be no CCAC sponsored plan unless the mayor gave his blessing to the idea, and this was by no means assured. For one thing, the city was nearing completion of its own central area plan, a plan that was now several years and several hundred thousand dollars in the making. Why abandon this effort in its final phase to turn over central area planning to a nongovernmental group? Daley would no doubt need convincing. That spring Downs and CCAC president Kenneth Zwiener were granted an audience with the mayor to make their case. Daley listened carefully while Downs laid out his proposal, eventually asking Planning Commissioner Hill to join the meeting. Hill indicated that his department's central area plan would be finished within sixty days. With the city's plan this close to completion, Daley was not prepared to make a decision. Instead he promised to furnish Downs with a copy of Hill's plan as soon as it was ready and to revisit the issue after the CCAC had had a chance to review the document.[61]

In truth, there was no way that Downs and the CCAC were going to be satisfied with any plan the city produced at this point. The organization had already committed to a $350,000 undertaking designed to produce the most bold, elaborate, attention-grabbing plan yet for the downtown area of any US city. Whatever Hill's staff produced, it would come nowhere near what the CCAC was prepared to do. Daley, perhaps recognizing this and no doubt influenced by the role his friend and former housing and redevelopment coordinator James Downs would play in the initiative, gave his go-ahead in the summer of 1971.[62] It was a dramatic turnaround for a mayor who little more than ten years earlier had complained to CCAC board member Hughston McBain about the organization's involvement in "projects and plans properly in the province of government." But much had changed since then. The rebuilding of the Loop was well under way, but little had been done to rehabilitate or redevelop many other portions of the central area. As Downs's own consulting work for the city had shown, these areas were on the decline, already posing a discernible threat to the central business district. With the urban renewal program now in its final days and federal resources dwindling, urban redevelopment would depend more than ever on private initiative and resources. Perhaps if downtown business leaders "owned" the

new central area plan, it would increase the chances that private investment would be forthcoming.

With Daley's approval in hand, the CCAC embarked on a two-year
planning effort that brought downtown business leaders and city officials
into increasingly close working relationships. That November, Skidmore,
Owings & Merrill was awarded the contract to produce the new plan,
and an eleven-member planning review committee was immediately
formed to work with the consultant and "guide the development of the
study."[63] The committee, chaired by Harold Jensen from Illinois Central
Industries, was composed of top executives from the city's leading corporate establishments, including First National Bank of Chicago, Peoples Gas, Illinois Bell, Commonwealth Edison, Continental Bank, Sears
Roebuck, Standard Oil, and Chicago Dock and Canal Trust.[64] Representing the city were Commissioner Hill and Deputy Planning Commissioner Martin Murphy. By all indications it was an active group, meeting
biweekly with Skidmore staff "to react and suggest changes in content
and approach."[65]

The plan itself was to be far reaching, covering a diverse range of
matters including traffic circulation, public transportation, pedestrian
passageways and malls, zoning incentives, the lakefront, the river system, parking, and the downtown business district. However, in keeping
with the views of Downs, Ted Aschman, and other corporate leaders,
the main focus was on the development of housing in areas bordering the
Loop. In an exercise to set the direction of the new plan, the nine corporate members of the planning review committee all selected this issue as their number-one priority.[66] As the CCAC explained in a communication to potential contributors, "Because of the great concern over
the growing imbalance in favor of the monolithic office and institutional
structure, to the detriment of other uses, primary emphasis is being
placed on the creation, at the boundaries of the Central Business District, of massive housing developments—'New Towns in Town.'" Planners, businessmen, and sociologists were all said to be convinced that the
Loop's existing cultural, entertainment, and shopping attractions would
remain viable "only with an infusion of moderate and middle-income
families at the immediate boundaries of downtown."[67]

The commitment of corporate resources to the new planning effort,
while substantial, was only the beginning. As it turned out, certain of
the city's business leaders were prepared to do much more than plan.

Even before Daley had given his approval to the initiative, Downs had begun talks with several other CCAC board members about resurrecting Aschman's proposal for the South Loop rail terminal area. It would be a drastically scaled-down version of what Aschman had originally proposed—three hundred acres with no displacement of residents, as opposed to the two thousand acres and relocation of four thousand residents in Aschman's original plan. Nonetheless, it would represent a significant start on the redevelopment of the Near South Side. Importantly, the project would not be carried out through the urban renewal program. Instead the city would partner with members of the private sector to finance and carry out the initiative. In early talks, the suggestion was that the city would use its bonding powers to purchase land from the railroads and lease it back to a limited-dividend corporation that the CCAC would create. The corporation would raise the necessary capital and redevelop the area as a middle-income housing development. As before, the railroads would have to be persuaded to sell the land to the city.[68]

The mayor was brought into the discussion in January 1972, several months after he had given the CCAC the green light to prepare a new central area plan. While noncommittal about the city's role, Daley was intrigued enough with the idea to keep the conversation going.[69] What was being proposed was in some ways remarkable, a significant departure from the kinds of public-private partnerships that had characterized the urban renewal period. The area in question was not a slum, but neither was it achieving land values anywhere near its potential. The urban renewal program had tried—and largely failed—to reconcile two objectives: the elimination of slums and the achievement of the highest and best use of land. Perhaps the latter goal could become the centerpiece of a new kind of public-private partnership in which the removal of slums and the provision of adequate housing for residents of blighted areas might or might not be central to the undertaking.

Such new ideas notwithstanding, the break with the past was by no means complete. As plans for what was now being called the South Loop New Town progressed, the legacy of the urban renewal period was very much in evidence. Ideas and practices from the slum clearance and redevelopment program were not simply cast aside; instead they were selectively repackaged to fit new circumstances. Gone was the focus on clearing slums and addressing housing conditions for low-income residents, but the notion of business-government cooperation in the redevelopment of land—an idea central to and originating with the urban renewal program—was still very much alive. Indeed, absent the experiences of the previous several decades, it is difficult to imagine an initiative such as this being proposed at all. As in the days when privatism dominated thinking about how the public and private sectors should properly engage one another in housing policy, business might have viewed city government more as an adversary than a potential partner—a regulatory force that acted principally to hold private initiative in check. Thanks largely to the city's urban renewal program, the real estate community and other business leaders had come to view city government in a much different way—as a force that created rather than curbed opportunities for profit.

But as these new redevelopment pioneers forged ahead with their plans, one can imagine how their thinking might have differed from that of their predecessors of the 1940s and 1950s, the latter group engaged as they were in a battle with the slums that they had every intention of winning. Years of experience now pointed to a different conclusion: that the slums were, for the most part, irredeemable. Efforts to create the good city would have to take the presence of poverty and blight as a point of departure, a reality the city's business leaders would have to work around, not fundamentally change. For the CCAC, this realization made the redevelopment and rehabilitation of the near downtown area all the more important. If slums could not be eliminated, they had to at least be kept at a safe distance from downtown. And those groups living in the near downtown area had to be "socially compatible" with the kinds of residents valued above all others. No small wonder that when details about the new initiative began leaking to the press in 1973, existing residents of central area neighborhoods—for the most part, low- and moderate-income—responded with alarm.

The View from the Neighborhoods

When the Chicago 21 plan was publicly unveiled by Mayor Daley in June 1973, most Chicagoans probably took little notice. By this time the rebuilding of the city's downtown had been under way for more than a decade. The Loop and its surroundings were already being dramatically transformed, and the new plan seemed to suggest more of the same. Even the proposed South Loop New Town, now expanded to a projected six hundred acres, would have likely raised few eyebrows among most

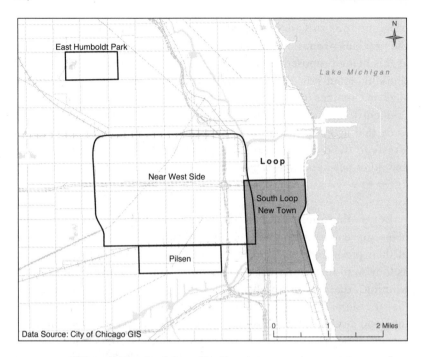

FIGURE 7.2. Chicago 21 Plan, South Loop New Town.

of the city's residents. However, residents of neighborhoods bordering
the downtown area viewed the new plan very differently. Chicago 21 singled out such neighborhoods as Pilsen, East Humboldt Park, the Near
West Side, and the Cabrini-Green public housing development north of
the Loop, arguing that all were "deficient in one or more of the elements
essential to a good community" (fig. 7.2). East Humboldt Park, for example, was characterized as "an older neighborhood which requires upgrading." Pilsen was said to be "an old community, currently in transition, which needs substantial conservation and rehabilitation to prevent
further physical deterioration."[70] The population of all four areas was
predominantly minority and low- to moderate-income. While the plan
contained no mention of slum clearance or displacement, the emphasis on the development of middle-income housing, especially in the proposed South Loop New Town, was unsettling to residents of these areas.
A decade earlier some eight thousand residents of the Harrison-Halsted
area southwest of the Loop had been removed, forcibly in many cases, to
make room for the new Chicago campus of the University of Illinois.[71]

For residents of Pilsen, East Humboldt Park, and the Near West Side in particular, the message of Chicago 21 seemed clear: Daley was now coming for them.

*   *   *

On March 18, 1974, CCAC executive director Jack Cornelius returned from vacation to find a letter from a group calling itself the Coalition of Central Area Communities (COCAC).[72] Cornelius, a former manager with Peoples Gas, had been in the position for less than a year. COCAC, the letter stated, represented communities "affected by the Chicago 21 Plan," including Pilsen, the Near West Side, East Humboldt Park, and Cabrini-Green. Key organizations from these four communities had come together to form the new coalition and had spent the previous several months developing a collective response to the Chicago 21 initiative. Coalition leaders were now prepared to take their concerns directly to the CCAC board of directors. A meeting with the board was requested "within the next three weeks."[73]

Cornelius immediately placed a call to Thomas Ayers, chairman of the CCAC board and president of Commonwealth Edison, the largest electric utility in Illinois. Several days went by without a reply from Ayers. Finally, more than a week later, Ayers responded: he would consider the request for a meeting but would make no commitment at this point. Cornelius relayed the disappointing news to a COCAC volunteer. The following day roughly fifty individuals from COCAC neighborhoods appeared at Ayers's office in the First National Bank building, demanding an audience with the business executive. A hastily prepared press release articulated the group's concerns. "We recognize," it said, "that the general thrust for the [Chicago 21] Plan came from a fear that the Loop area was being 'taken over' by the poor, the black, and the brown people" living in the near-downtown area. "Nothing in the Plan indicates that the rehabilitation of the communities will be for the present residents." Criticizing business leaders for preparing a plan "for 200,000 residents without consulting any of those residents," COCAC warned that residents of their communities "intend to stay where they are living now." If the Chicago 21 initiative was to go forward, these individuals would have to be acknowledged "as a legitimate and permanent element in the Central Area of this city."[74]

Ayers was away from his office when the group arrived, but when told of the day's events, he quickly agreed to a meeting with COCAC representatives. The meeting, which took place several days later on April 2, included ten members of COCAC, Ayers, Cornelius, and several other CCAC board members. After all had assembled, COCAC spokesperson Willie Baker, an organizer from the Near West Side, reiterated the group's request to meet with the full CCAC board. Ayers initially balked at the idea, offering to relay the organization's concerns to the board himself, but relented when group members became insistent. COCAC would be invited to attend the next board meeting as long as certain conditions were met: only ten COCAC members would be present, it would be a private meeting with no press, and COCAC would be given fifteen minutes for a presentation, to be delivered by a designated group representative. After conferring with fellow organization members, Baker agreed to the arrangement.[75]

Shortly before 3:00 p.m. six days later, COCAC leaders arrived at the offices of the Chicago Association of Commerce and Industry, where the April CCAC board meeting was scheduled to take place. With them were more than fifty individuals, all demanding entrance to the meeting. News releases had been sent to local media outlets, and calls had been made to alert reporters to the meeting. Cesar Olivo, a community organizer from Pilsen, assumed the role of spokesperson for COCAC. Reminded of the conditions for the meeting agreed to previously, Olivo responded that things would be done "the communities' way." Ayers, eager to avoid a confrontation with reporters present, agreed that all could enter the conference room, including members of the press. Olivo spoke first for COCAC, making several demands: that the CCAC expand its board of directors to include four members from each of the four COCAC communities, that COCAC be represented on the board of the corporation developing the proposed South Loop New Town, that the CCAC fund the preparation of a neighborhood plan for each of the four communities, and that communities have veto power over any project in their neighborhoods involving more than $100,000 in expenses. Other neighborhood representatives also spoke, and a "lengthy exchange" followed between coalition members and members of the board. Ayers concluded the meeting by indicating the board would make no commitments until members had had a chance "to digest and discuss" what had been presented.[76]

The CCAC's initial response was to try to avoid being drawn into a relationship with COCAC by arguing that it could not be put in the position of "working only with these groups."[77] However, recognizing their vulnerability to COCAC's claims of little or no neighborhood involvement in the Chicago 21 planning process thus far, members of the CCAC's planning review committee ultimately agreed to several follow-up sessions with a small group of COCAC representatives. Meetings held during the second part of April produced agreement on two matters: the CCAC would consider providing financial assistance for neighborhood planning efforts, and public meetings on the Chicago 21 plan would be held in each of the four COCAC community areas, to be attended by one or more CCAC representatives.[78] Meanwhile, the CCAC went to work on refurbishing its public image, hiring a public relations firm and drafting a new policy statement on community involvement in the Chicago 21 planning process, which read in part: "The Committee feels strongly that current residents should be encouraged to remain in their communities and that they should participate in the decision-making process affecting their neighborhoods." Chicago 21, it was emphasized, was not an urban renewal project involving "the bulldozer approach" to urban revitalization. Rather, it was intended "to strengthen the existing communities surrounding the city's downtown area."[79]

While pleased with the CCAC's willingness to participate in neighborhood public meetings and its openness to funding neighborhood plans, COCAC leaders found statements such as this less than reassuring, and for seemingly good reason. True, Chicago 21 was not urban renewal in the conventional sense; it had no provisions for slum clearance and forced removal of residents. Yet as we have seen, the initiative was born in part out of business leaders' concerns about the racial, ethnic, and class composition of central area communities. And if forced displacement—or its less politically charged cousin, gentrification—was not specifically advocated in the plan, neither was there any acknowledgment of the diversity of the central area population and the challenges that efforts to preserve that mix of groups would face as the area became home to growing numbers of middle- and upper-class residents. Nor was there any effort on the part of the CCAC—until neighborhood groups demanded it—to involve central area communities in the Chicago 21 planning process, despite the plan's specific recommendations for neighborhoods such as Pilsen, East Humboldt Park, the Near West Side, and Cabrini-Green. In short, regardless of what the organization now claimed, the CCAC had behaved as if decisions about the future of central area communities should be made by downtown business leaders, with a view toward maximizing real estate values and synergies with downtown rather than safeguarding the interests of the people currently living there.

For COCAC, the first order of business was to begin scheduling public meetings on the Chicago 21 plan in the four COCAC community areas, a plan of action that organizers believed—correctly, it turned out—would give them leverage in their negotiations with the CCAC. With some trepidation, the CCAC agreed to meetings in Pilsen and East Humboldt Park during the last week of May and the first week of June, respectively. Organizers diligently spread the word, turning out between 250 and 300 fearful and agitated residents for each session.[80] Representing the CCAC and the Chicago 21 initiative at these forums were several CCAC board members, several members of the planning review committee, and the lead planner from Skidmore, Owings & Merrill's project team. After opening comments describing the Chicago 21 planning process, members of the audience were invited to speak. As planning review committee chair Harold Jensen later described the experience, it was "baptism by fire" for the group of business leaders.[81] For more than two hours in each case, the group listened while neighborhood residents voiced their considerable displeasure with the CCAC and the Chicago 21 initiative as they understood it. The East Humboldt Park meeting went especially poorly from the CCAC's standpoint. Instead of beginning the meeting with an overview of Chicago 21 by the CCAC, an arrangement all had agreed to in advance, COCAC representatives insisted on presenting the information themselves. This resulted in what Cornelius described as "a garbled and inaccurate history of planning and highlights of Chicago 21" delivered by a set of presenters who were "very belligerent and demanding during their turn[s] at the microphone."[82] Receptive to the message, audience members responded predictably, with enthusiastic applause.

Noticeably absent from both of these meetings were any representatives from the city of Chicago. In late April, Cornelius wrote a letter to Planning Commissioner Hill, informing him of the small working sessions that the CCAC's planning review committee had been holding with several COCAC representatives. Would Hill or one of his staff be willing to participate? Given that the city played "the key role in the programming and decision-making processes," it would be appropriate, Cornelius told Hill, that there "be representation from at least your department as these talks proceed."[83] Hill never responded, nor did he or any of his staff attend any subsequent sessions or participate in public meetings of any kind.[84] Chicago 21 was officially the city's plan; Daley had been happy to claim it as his own when it was unveiled a year earlier. Now that controversy had erupted, however, he wanted no part of it. The mayor was discovering an additional advantage of his new partnership with the CCAC: where convenient, he could let the business community be the owners of the new plan. Facing an election the following year and lackluster support among black voters, Daley was particularly anxious to avoid any appearance of insensitivity to minority issues and concerns.[85] As far as the neighborhoods were concerned, it was the CCAC's plan, and neither Daley nor his staff did anything to disabuse them of that notion.

During the weeks when public meetings were taking place in Pilsen and East Humboldt Park, the private working sessions with representatives from COCAC member groups continued. It soon became clear that these groups, unlike many of the individual residents who attended the public meetings, were not opposed to the Chicago 21 initiative per se. Rather, they were upset because they had not been included in the planning process. While angry with the CCAC over this omission, they also viewed the situation as an opportunity to extract resources from the business community—in particular, funding for individual neighborhood plans, which they proposed be incorporated into the more comprehensive Chicago 21 plan. By this point the CCAC was anxious to put an end to the public meetings, which were drawing unwanted attention to the organization's failure to engage near-downtown residents in the Chicago 21 planning process. For Jensen and Cornelius, the two individuals increasingly becoming the face of the CCAC in its dealings with the central area communities, a relatively small sum of money for the preparation of neighborhood plans seemed like a reasonable price to pay to satisfy COCAC and make the controversy go away. Jensen promised COCAC that he would raise the issue at the June meeting of the CCAC board of directors, with a recommendation that the board "help finance this planning effort."[86] A process was mapped out: Skidmore, Owings & Merrill would work with neighborhood groups to prepare a template for the community plans, including estimates for staff time and total financial requirements. If the board agreed to the arrangement, the CCAC would make a financial commitment, but the cost would be shared with the neighborhood groups, which would need to raise funds in order to participate.

At the June meeting of the CCAC board, Jensen gave a presentation on the neighborhood meetings in Pilsen and East Humboldt Park, followed by a recommendation that the CCAC "be prepared to match dollars (up to $50,000) from community groups and other sources to pay for needed second-level planning in the neighborhoods."[87] It was a contentious meeting. While Jensen's proposal had some support, others were adamantly opposed to the idea, arguing that the preparation of detailed neighborhood plans lay outside the scope of the Chicago 21 initiative. There was also anger with the way the community meetings had gone. The city's business leaders were used to being treated with deference and respect. For some, it was unconscionable that the CCAC should allow itself to be singled out and demeaned in this fashion. Writing to Jensen and Cornelius after the East Humboldt Park meeting, one business leader present described the event as "demeaning not only to those present representing the Chicago Central Area Committee but to all of the Loop Business Establishment." As he argued, "The abusive, arrogant and completely inaccurate accusations made by hand picked and other neighborhood representatives and heartily applauded by the audience should not be tolerated" in public outreach sessions such as this.[88] Still, while board members deeply resented the situation in which they now found themselves, an outright rejection of Jensen's proposal would only bring more community meetings and more controversy. In the end, it was agreed that a final decision would be deferred until Skidmore had completed its work and the cost and scope of the community plans were better understood.

With forward movement on the possible funding of neighborhood plans, there was a noticeable thawing of relations between the CCAC's Cornelius and Jensen and the COCAC member groups with whom they were working. Cornelius recorded the following comments about a June meeting with a Pilsen neighborhood group: "A much better rapport and spirit of cooperation was exhibited during this meeting and progress was made towards finding a way to structure a joint effort." Likewise, notes from a meeting with an East Humboldt Park group several weeks later described the atmosphere as "cordial and friendly."[89] Yet collegiality had its limits. After the CCAC's June board meeting, Cornelius contacted COCAC's Willie Baker, requesting that a proposed public meeting on the Near West Side be postponed until Skidmore had completed its work and the CCAC board had decided what, if any, contribution the organization would make toward the financing of neighborhood plans. Baker initially agreed, telling Cornelius "that was fine with him." However, the following week Baker phoned with urgent news. "We are in trouble," he said. Several neighborhood groups insisted that the meeting be held as scheduled. A split was developing within COCAC between groups that had formed relationships with the CCAC and were actively seeking planning funds, and those excluded from such discussions who had nothing to gain by cooperating with the CCAC and wanted to keep the pressure on. When informed by Baker of the groups' insistence on holding the meeting, Cornelius refused to budge, telling Baker there was "no point in further public meetings" at this stage. Two days later, a group of Near West Side residents held a demonstration in the lobby of the First National Bank Building, where Thomas Ayers's office was located. Cornelius quickly caved, and a firm date of July 16 was set for the meeting.[90]

The Near West Side public meeting was another opportunity for COCAC to flex its muscles prior to the CCAC board's vote on the funding of neighborhood plans, and organizations from the Near West Side took full advantage. COCAC's Willie Baker, seemingly a clever tactician, met with Cornelius and several other CCAC representatives prior to the meeting and was "very helpful" in advising them about "the concerns of the various groups on the West Side."[91] At the meeting, however, Baker played to the crowd. In his opening comments he characterized the event as a "union of peoples from various backgrounds, races and ethnic groups, shouting their indignation over a plan for their neighborhoods which they had no voice in the making."[92] Warning audience members that "rich developers" were plotting to displace them, he insisted that the "poor and powerless" would not be moved. Later on Cornelius was asked to sign a statement promising that the Chicago 21 plan would not displace existing residents. When he refused, "a chorus of boos and obscenities" followed.[93] In a memorandum to Ayers, Cornelius summarized the proceedings: "The tenor of the meeting in general was the same as was expressed in the previous two public meetings—a misunderstanding and misinterpretation of the proposals in Chicago 21, distrust of the representatives of 'big business,' suspicion about motives and the fear that big business is out to rip off the poor and the powerless."[94]

Six days after the Near West Side meeting, Skidmore, Owings & Merrill came back with its cost estimates and template for neighborhood plans, information that Jensen would present to the CCAC board at its

August meeting. By this time Jensen had become a pivotal figure in the negotiations between the CCAC and COCAC member groups. Initially wary of COCAC, he seemed to experience an epiphany of sorts as the summer progressed. In late June he penned a letter to Ayers in which he excitedly described a new neighborhood planning initiative in New York City.[95] The initiative, known as "miniplans," involved plans "tailored to the needs of individual communities," produced through close consultation with local civic organizations. Implemented by New York City plan commissioner John E. Zuccotti, a strong proponent of neighborhood involvement in city planning, the miniplans were intended to complement the city's master plan by providing "more attention to local needs and desires."[96] Wrote Jensen: "There is a striking parallel between these events in the neighborhoods of New York and what we are about—or at least attempting—in our efforts with the central area communities here in Chicago." In a position that seemed to diverge sharply from the attitudes of Downs, Aschman, and other members of the CCAC, Jensen cautioned against too much gentrification in the Chicago 21 initiative. "I think it is important," he argued, "that [we] maintain a perspective that goes beyond the South Loop New Town. In my mind, it is just as important that we keep our 'existing customers' as it is that we find new ones!" With his newfound sensitivities to the concerns of neighborhood residents, Jensen increasingly became the link that would bridge the views of seemingly aloof corporate executives with those of hardened community organizers.

When the CCAC board met for its August meeting, Jensen—this time with Skidmore's cost estimates in hand—once again made his pitch for a contribution of up to $50,000 "to help pay for detailed planning in four neighborhoods" included in the Chicago 21 initiative.[97] Emphasizing that organizations would need to raise matching funds and that participation by the city was also expected, Jensen urged board members to vote in favor of the proposal. By this time most had resigned themselves to the need for some kind of CCAC support for neighborhood-level planning as the price for going forward. After "considerable discussion," a motion to approve the recommendation passed unanimously.

It had been a long, hot summer. Business leaders had received an education in community organizing and had been introduced to the community's perspective on downtown revitalization, a point of view most, until then, had had little understanding of or appreciation for. Under pressure from the neighborhoods they had been forced to make certain concessions. There would be neighborhood plans, financed in part by the CCAC, and those plans would become part of the Chicago 21 initiative, an outcome certain business leaders found distasteful. Still, COCAC was hardly in a position to gloat. In the bigger scheme of things what the CCAC actually gave up amounted to very little. A few neighborhood plans would not fundamentally alter the course of the Chicago 21 initiative, assuming business leaders did not waver in their commitment to seeing it through. They would, however, bring a halt to the contentious—and, for business leaders, politically embarrassing—public meetings that COCAC had insisted upon holding. With a process now in place to fund the community plans, the meetings came to an end, along with COCAC's major source of leverage with the business community. Increasingly the talk was of partnership and collaboration rather than confrontation. As one recipient of planning funds explained, "The Chicago 21 proposal—while in theory not displacing any existing neighborhoods—will bring significant changes. . . . We felt that the best guarantee to achieve the goals of both the plan and the people was to form an alliance with the proponents—to be heard and to help."[98] When in June 1975 Pilsen Neighbors—the first of what turned out to be only two COCAC member organizations to receive planning funds—signed the agreement with the CCAC to initiate its neighborhood planning process, there were smiles all around. And no one seemed to notice the irony when it was announced that the consultant the organization had hired to produce its neighborhood plan was Barton-Aschman and Associates.

*   *   *

As the Chicago 21 initiative moved ahead in the aftermath of the COCAC protests, the impact of the new program on the city's power structure was increasingly evident. The Daley administration's low profile during this period notwithstanding, the city was very much an equal partner with the CCAC in the initiative. It had taken years, but a firm and intimate alliance between the city's business leadership and the Daley administration—a new convergence of power—was finally emerging, built chiefly around plans to remake the near-downtown area in a way that best complemented the Loop's corporate, retail, and entertainment functions. While the new partnership—combining the regulatory and financial powers of government with private initiative and investment—bore the distinct imprint of the urban renewal period, missing from this new program was the objective of ridding the city of its slum districts, a goal central to the city's redevelopment and renewal program since it was launched in the late 1940s. With downtown business elites seizing the reins of central area planning and diminishing hopes for the elimination of slums, the redevelopment of land for its highest and best use became, increasingly, the singular focus of development policy. Working hand in hand with their partners in city government, business leaders took the remnants of the attack on the slums and shaped them into a downtown redevelopment program that sought an accommodation with the slums rather than their elimination.

Still, as the COCAC protests had shown, efforts to achieve the highest and best use of land would have to take into account the preferences of neighborhood residents in areas targeted for upgrading. Twenty years earlier the Chicago Land Clearance Commission had successfully cleared 100 acres of land to make way for the Lake Meadows housing development, mostly without incident. Opposition from the 4,633 families living there at the time was for the most part weak and fragmented.[99] A decade later, however, when Daley announced plans for the new University of Illinois campus in the Harrison-Halsted neighborhood southwest of downtown, the political costs proved to be substantially higher. Having observed other neighborhoods in the path of the wrecking ball and determined not to experience the same fate, residents organized and led marches on city hall. Shaken and embarrassed by the protests, Daley moved doggedly ahead. After that, however, he became far more cautious in his use of the city's urban renewal powers and more sensitive to the views of neighborhood residents. When organized opposition to the Chicago 21 plan surfaced, city officials took notice. Efforts to revitalize the Loop and its surroundings would not be derailed, but the concerns of central area residents would have to be addressed in some fashion.

As we have just seen, the principal way that protests by COCAC member groups were brought to an end was through the promise of planning funds for selected organizations and the incorporation of neighborhood plans into the Chicago 21 initiative. Over time, confrontation gave way to collaboration and partnership. In his observations of Atlanta's postwar neighborhood movement in *Regime Politics*, Clarence Stone was struck by a nearly identical phenomenon in that city: a tendency by neighborhood groups to pull back from confrontation and reach an accommodation with the city's political and economic elites. For Stone, this behavior was explained by the resources and opportunities available through participation in a powerful and productive enterprise. As in Chicago, that enterprise was the business-government partnership—the urban *regime*—forged around the redevelopment of the downtown area. Neighborhood organizations outside of and potentially disadvantaged by this power structure faced a choice: they could oppose the regime and seek alternative policies, a position facing long odds; or they could join forces with the new partnership, typically in exchange for some small benefit or opportunity that elites were willing to offer as the price for their cooperation. For at least some organizations, accommodation with the power structure was the rational decision. Challenges from the neighborhoods were deflected not through political domination and control but through small opportunities that made participation in the new enterprise the more attractive option.

Certainly the story of COCAC is in many ways consistent with Stone's view of urban power relations. For certain organizations the temptation to "go along to get along," as Stone puts it, was great. Still, a somewhat different interpretation gives neighborhood groups more agency than Stone seems to acknowledge. Viewed within a longer historical trajectory of neighborhood redevelopment and renewal, COCAC's opposition to the Chicago 21 plan reveals significant change in the attitudes and behavior of neighborhood actors. Not so many years earlier, plans for rearranging land use in the central area could proceed almost as if the preferences of people living there were irrelevant to the decision-making process. As the CCAC's Holman Pettibone coldly pronounced in 1957, "The central area is not a slum but it has some disgraceful areas. The only thing to do is to tear them down."[100] The idea that existing neighborhood residents should be consulted in such decisions most likely did not occur to him. With opposition to urban renewal still fragile and disjointed, efforts to achieve the highest and best use of land seemed to be limited chiefly by the resources available to support the redevelopment program.

By the 1970s, the leaders of the city's redevelopment program found their actions considerably more constrained. "Urban renewal" had become a politically poisonous term, particularly for African Americans, who had experienced the greatest displacement of any group. As key members of Daley's electoral coalition, blacks had to be treated with some sensitivity, as did other minority groups. Ted Aschman's plan to relocate four thousand central area residents in order to remake the Near South Side would not fly in this new political environment. With communities now hypersensitive to the issue of displacement, even a plan such as Chicago 21 that proposed no forced relocation of residents became a call to action for neighborhood groups. As junior partners and willing participants in the Chicago 21 initiative, members of COCAC would not profoundly influence the trajectory of the program. Any leverage they had vanished when the protests and public meetings came to an end. Yet their very presence was an indication of how much had changed. Efforts to refashion the near-downtown area into a collection of upscale residential communities would have to take existing residents of the area into account, and even gentrification would be watched carefully to determine its impact on the character of central area communities.

As plans moved ahead for Chicago 21's signature project, the South Loop New Town, this was the reality that business leaders were forced to confront. The low- and moderate-income African American and Latino residents of Pilsen, the Near West Side, and East Humboldt Park were not going anywhere, at least not anytime soon. If a viable new community for middle-class residents was to be built in the South Loop, the people choosing to live there would have to accept this fact. Above all, they would have to be convinced that the presence of low-income minorities in nearby communities did not threaten their safety, security, and sense of well-being. If the crime, gangs, and other problems of those areas did not spill over into the new community, if schools and other services could be provided at a quality matching that of well-to-do suburban communities, and if racial boundaries could be stabilized in some fashion, perhaps it could work.

CHAPTER EIGHT

Learning to Live with the Slums

In April 1993, word began to spread that Chicago mayor Richard M. Daley, eldest son of the former mayor and machine boss Richard J. Daley, was in the process of purchasing a townhouse in a new South Loop development called Central Station. Built during the early 1990s on a sixty-nine-acre site just south of downtown, Central Station was planned as a community of condominiums and luxury townhomes catering to downtown professionals. Daley's move was politically symbolic. It would mean leaving the white working-class community of Bridgeport, the South Side machine stronghold where he had lived virtually his entire life. During his father's tenure as mayor, Bridgeport had become a symbol of white resistance to racial succession. Many believed that had it not been for the elder Daley's presence, the neighborhood would have succumbed to white flight and racial transition, like so many other South Side communities. For many South Side whites, the younger Daley's presence in Bridgeport was ongoing reassurance that the mayor was, deep down, one of their own. Still, the city was changing, and for the most part it was near-downtown communities in places like the South Loop that were in the ascendance. This was the new Chicago, home to a rapidly expanding multicultural corporate workforce with expensive tastes and money to spend. To move from Bridgeport to the South Loop was to cross a yawning cultural divide. For Daley it meant, as one local newspaper put it, "leaving his tribe to live with the Yuppies."[1]

Mayor Daley's new home was located in an area that would undergo explosive redevelopment during the next two decades. Even as Daley prepared to sign the closing papers in the autumn of 1993, observers described his adopted neighborhood as "one of the hottest properties in recent memory in the city."[2] It was a remarkable transformation. Twenty years earlier, as the South Side ghetto continued to expand and the Loop became a destination for growing numbers of African American shoppers and entertainment seekers, civic leaders had viewed the Near South Side with trepidation. With the attack on the slums ending in failure, the possibility seemed genuine that this land would eventually house large concentrations of low-income blacks—an extension of the South Side Black Belt all the way to the Loop's southern boundary. Observers at the time warned ominously of a city on the brink of perilous decline. What they forecast was not a dual city—divided into sets of privileged and declining neighborhoods—but a mostly black, low-income metropolis surrounded by middle-class suburban enclaves. As one veteran of the city's urban renewal program warned in 1968, "As more white people flee to the suburbs and the non-white population multiplies, Chicago will become a prime case of apartheid by default. The whites will man the ramparts of their suburbs while the city becomes the citadel of the black and the poor. . . . If present trends continue, the central city could become a huge black poorhouse."[3]

What such doomsday forecasts failed to anticipate was both the attraction that near-downtown living would eventually hold for the legions of corporate office workers employed in the city's rapidly growing central business district, and the possibility that revitalized neighborhoods could coexist alongside areas of concentrated poverty. The error is not surprising. Leaders of the city's urban renewal program had watched in dismay as neighborhood conservation efforts during the 1950s and 1960s proved insufficient to prevent the slums from expanding into stable areas, triggering white flight to the suburbs. Slums were like a cancerous tumor, they believed. Left unattended, they would inevitably spread to uninfected portions of the city, creating new pockets of blight. As the urban renewal program came to an end with no resolution to the problem of blighted areas in sight, leaders of the program were understandably pessimistic about the prospects for neighborhood stability and revitalization. Given their experiences with the fight against slums, the idea of a dual city—where revitalized and impoverished neighborhoods would exist alongside one another in some kind of equilibrium—would have seemed foreign and unfathomable.

These individuals correctly perceived that neighborhood conservation was, in most cases, no match for an expanding slum. But developments like Central Station staked their territorial claims through a process vastly different from the conservation efforts undertaken by neighborhoods before them, also in the paths of potentially expanding slums. As a strategy for holding the line against encroaching blight, conservation had one key shortcoming: in many cases it worked against the grain of real estate markets. As real estate speculators fully understood, there was money to be made through property transactions whose end result was the penetration of slums into the city's conservation areas. Most important was the "blockbusting" of white neighborhoods on the edges of the ghetto. As racial transition appeared imminent, fearful whites could be persuaded to sell at a discount. Black renters and home buyers, desperate to escape the overcrowded Black Belt and with few alternative housing options, were easy targets—forced to pay a premium while speculators and unscrupulous landlords pocketed the difference. Where profits lay in the expansion of slums, neighborhood conservation faced a steep disadvantage.[4]

By contrast, new developments such as Central Station harnessed real estate markets instead of fighting them. By driving up the price of near-downtown land and signaling to the real estate community that the South Loop area was ripe for high-end residential development, Central Station and other nearby developments set the pattern for future land use. If conservation was a holding action, gentrification was an accelerant, driving middle- and high-income housing development south and west into areas formerly seen as threats to downtown.[5] Now it was the low-income and minority residents of these communities who were on the defensive. As gentrification replaced conservation as the principal mechanism for preserving a middle-class presence in the city, the expansion of slums into the city's most desirable locations—near downtown and along the lakefront—became less of a concern to civic and business leaders. While poverty and blight were by no means disappearing, they were in some cases shifting locations in accordance with the development community's perceptions of the highest and best use of land in a given area. Slums could be tolerated as long as they were well out of sight of downtown and did not interfere with the gentrification of nearby communities.

While Central Station rode the wave of the overheated real estate market for South Loop property, it did not set the redevelopment process in motion. Market mechanisms alone were insufficient for that purpose. Decades before ground was broken on Central Station, the city's business leaders, acting through the Chicago Central Area Committee, identified the Near South Side as a prime location for new middle-income housing that would provide patrons for downtown retail and cultural establishments and near-downtown living opportunities for office workers. As we saw in chapter 7, the building of new housing developments here was a key recommendation of the CCAC's Chicago 21 plan of 1973. This chapter examines how redevelopment was initiated, through a new middle-income housing development called Dearborn Park built on fifty-one acres of former railroad land just south of downtown. As we shall see, a small group of business leaders and urban renewal veterans came together to produce what one observer described as "a different kind of urban renewal project, one conceived and directed by corporate committee."[6] Through the mechanism of conversion, these actors took the public-private partnership of urban renewal as a point of departure, reworking key ideas to accomplish goals substantially different from those of the renewal period. Guided by their experiences with urban renewal but pursuing new and different objectives, the planners and developers of Dearborn Park sought to engage with the city's blighted areas in vastly different ways. Their actions were informed not by a new policy paradigm but by the conviction that the existing set of ideas for engaging with the slums had proved ineffective. Like housing reformers of the 1930s, disillusioned with privatism but lacking a coherent alternative approach, their efforts belonged to a broader search for new ideas about how urban regeneration might best be achieved.

"A Different Kind of Urban Renewal"

Dearborn Park began as a series of discussions among several leading members of the CCAC about redevelopment possibilities for the rail terminal area south of the Loop. Key participants in what became known informally as the South Loop Group included Thomas Ayers, president of Commonwealth Edison; Gordon Metcalf, chairman of the board and chief executive officer of Sears, Roebuck and Company; and Donald Graham, chairman of the board and chief executive officer of Continental Illinois National Bank, the Midwest's largest bank at the time. By the end of 1971 the group had expanded to include James Downs, Ferd Kramer, and Philip Klutznick, all veterans of the city's urban renewal program. Also joining the group were John Perkins, president of Continental Bank, and Warren Skoning, vice president for real estate at Sears.[7]

At Downs's urging, the group identified residential development as the preferred redevelopment option for the rail terminal area.[8] By this time the planning process for the CCAC's new Chicago 21 Plan was under way, led by the architectural firm of Skidmore, Owings & Merrill, and the activities of the South Loop Group dovetailed closely with this effort. Both Perkins and Skoning were members of the CCAC's planning review committee, created to assist Skidmore with the preparation of the Chicago 21 plan. A key component of the plan was the creation of what planners called the South Loop New Town—a residential area for up to 120,000 people to be built on a six-hundred-acre portion of the abandoned railyards and other underutilized land south of downtown. A natural division of labor emerged. The CCAC, with the assistance of Skidmore, would provide a conceptual plan for the South Loop residential area, while the South Loop Group would focus on the refinement and implementation of the plan. It was a tall order. Ownership of the railyards was divided among some thirteen different railroad companies, the group had no financing lined up, and the city had not committed itself to any specific role.[9]

These were formidable obstacles, but the group did at least have a reasonably coherent vision for what it wanted to accomplish and a rationale to support it. Apart from the boost to downtown that new middle-income neighborhoods were expected to provide, members of the group viewed the initiative as a pilot project for addressing the demographic changes the city was experiencing, especially the loss of white residents to the suburbs. During the 1960s the city's white population declined by some 570,000 residents while the number of African American residents increased by 300,000.[10] The vast majority of whites leaving the city were middle-income families, attracted to new suburban areas in part by what they perceived as superior housing options there. The South Loop New Town would target these individuals, providing the "ambiance of a suburban community" at a cost below that of comparable housing developments in the suburbs.[11] Like the model housing developments of the 1920s, it would be a demonstration project—one ideally imitated by others, stimulating the development of badly needed middle-income housing in the city. As one participant in the discussions recalled, "We want[ed] to show that this can work, it can pay for itself, so that it can be repeated elsewhere. So it isn't a charity operation."[12]

There were reasons for optimism. By the 1970s Chicago was in the throes of urban economic restructuring. On the positive side, the city

was emerging as a global corporate and financial center, home to dozens of Fortune 500 companies and the corporate services firms that ca-
tered to them. Much of this activity was concentrated in the central business district, fueling the growth of office building construction in the
Loop. Between 1962 and 1977, more than 32 million square feet of office space was built in the downtown area, bringing the total amount of
downtown office space to some 80 million square feet.[13] Accompanying the construction boom, not surprisingly, was a significant increase in
downtown employment. By 1972 the central business district employed
222,668 workers, 17 percent of all workers employed in the city.[14] It was
mainly these workers and their families, planners hoped, who would be
the residents of the new South Loop community. Their growing numbers
inspired hope that demand for housing in the new community would
be healthy.

Of course urban economic restructuring also had a significant down-
side. Most important was the loss of manufacturing jobs that came with
the closure and relocation of many of the city's industrial establishments,
beginning in the 1950s and 1960s and accelerating during the following
decades. Between 1972 and 1983 alone, Chicago lost 131,000 manufacturing jobs, a decline of 34 percent.[15] African Americans were particularly hard hit by deindustrialization. Most blue-collar blacks had limited formal education and were thus badly positioned for transition to
the well-paying knowledge-intensive jobs opening up in the expanding
service sector. As a consequence, deindustrialization produced a spike
in poverty and unemployment in black neighborhoods. Of Chicago's
seventy-seven community areas, only one had a poverty rate greater
than 40 percent in 1970. By 1980 the number had risen to nine community areas, all overwhelmingly black. In 1970 no community area had an
unemployment rate greater than 19 percent; by 1980 there were ten such
community areas, again largely black.[16] The deepening impoverishment
of the city's African American neighborhoods further eclipsed the vision of a slum-free city, an idea pursued by better-housing activists from
the beginning of the century through the urban renewal years. By the
1970s the failures of urban renewal, combined with escalating poverty
within black neighborhoods, produced widespread pessimism that such
areas could ever be rehabilitated. For the planners of Dearborn Park,
this meant persuading prospective residents to forgo the suburbs in order to choose a neighborhood minutes away from nearby public housing
projects and other economically distressed communities.

By early 1972, members of the South Loop Group were clear about their goal—the construction of a middle-class community in the South Loop area. What they were uncertain about was the formula through which this would be accomplished. Nothing like this had ever been attempted in Chicago. There was no blueprint to follow, although urban renewal provided a starting point. In particular, all agreed that the project would require a public-private partnership of some kind. Beyond that the details were murky. As Thomas Ayers stated at the time, "Absolutely essential to the success of the Plan is the marriage of private enterprise with the public sector. I am not sure of all of the dimensions of such a marriage, but it will involve public and private monies in a way that will make this project competitive with the suburban alternative." The project would, in Ayers's words, require "a wide variety of new concepts, new responsibilities."[17] The urban renewal formula would get them only so far. This was not a slum, and prospects for both a government-funded write-down of land costs and use of the city's eminent domain powers to acquire property—key mechanisms of urban renewal—seemed remote.

In the end it fell to Philip Klutznick to lay out proposed responsibilities for the public and private sector participants in the South Loop initiative. Klutznick was the developer of the planned community of Park Forest in the south Chicago suburbs, along with several suburban shopping centers. He and Ferd Kramer were the only members of the South Loop Group with actual development experience, giving their opinions and ideas added weight. Klutznick proposed that the new development be financed through a limited-dividend corporation whose profits would be capped at 6.5 percent. He envisioned between fifty and one hundred corporate subscribers contributing up to $350,000 each. The cap on earnings would hold costs down, making housing prices more affordable. In addition, it would help to avoid the impression that the business community was out to make a killing with the new development. The city's proposed role was twofold: it would purchase the land and provide necessary infrastructure and public services, including water, sewer, streets, schools, and park space. Once the city had title to the land it would lease it to the corporation, which would develop the new housing.[18]

Mayor Daley met with members of the group on multiple occasions during 1972 and seemed receptive to the plan, although he made no commitments, as was his style. Politically, the project posed some hazards for Daley. Not long before, he had endured criticism for urban renewal projects that displaced low- and moderate-income families to provide housing for the middle class. The South Loop development would not displace anyone, but it would represent another public-private partnership whose end result would be housing for middle-class residents, not poor people. And the business community's role made the mayor especially vulnerable to claims that big money was driving the decision-making process.[19]

With the apparent support of the mayor, the group moved ahead. The immediate challenge they faced was the issue of site control. For decades, proposals to do something with the South Loop railyards had been stymied by the railroad companies' unwillingness to part with their land holdings. By the 1970s, however, the railroads were finally ready to deal. With the rise in automobile use and the growth of trucking during the postwar era, both passenger and freight rail service had gone into steep declines. Between 1969 and 1972, all four passenger rail stations serving the South Loop were shuttered, and the remaining passenger service was taken over by Amtrak and moved to Union Station, west of the Loop.[20] Railroad companies, several of which were in bankruptcy proceedings by this time, began forming partnerships to consolidate land holdings so that property could be sold in parcels appropriately configured for redevelopment.[21]

In early 1972 John Perkins and Thomas Ayers began a series of discussions with several railroad companies owning South Loop property. At first the talks seemed promising. Perkins, reporting on discussions with a real estate executive from one company, described him as "under pressure to get something going" and "anxious to move ahead."[22] Several months later Ayers reported that the trustees of the Penn Central Railroad, currently in bankruptcy, were "enthusiastic about the [South Loop] project," having directed the company's financial adviser "to proceed with negotiations as soon as we are ready to do so."[23] When it came to negotiating a price, however, the discussions floundered. Construction of middle-income housing was possible only to the extent that the land could be purchased at a discount, well below ten dollars per square foot. The railroads wanted considerably more than that—as much as fifty dollars per square foot.[24] This was out of the question. As one city planner maintained, even ten dollars per foot "was not a price that would see Dearborn Park built. It would have had a completely different future."[25]

Meanwhile, unbeknownst to Ayers, Perkins, and their colleagues, Daley began his own discussions with the railroads. By this time the mayor seemed to be growing skittish about Klutznick's proposal, particularly the suggestion that the city be the landowner for the new development. In an April 1973 meeting with Perkins, Daley proposed an alternative idea that had evolved out of his meetings with the railroad companies: perhaps the railroads might undertake the development themselves, minimizing the city's role and solving the problem of land costs.[26] This, however, was not what the members of the South Loop Group wanted to hear. The family-friendly middle-income community they had in mind would need to be carefully planned. If development decisions were turned over to the railroads, there was no telling what might be built there. Even if the city insisted on residential development, there was no way to ensure that the group's vision of a suburb in the city would be achieved.

Despite the mayor's new line of thinking, members of the South Loop Group continued to hold out hope that a deal with the railroads could be struck. Several months before his meeting with Daley, Perkins had learned that Chicago Bears owner George Halas had begun negotiations through a third party to acquire a fifty-one-acre parcel of South Loop property jointly owned by three railroads. Halas wanted to use the property, just south of the recently closed Dearborn Station, to build a new football stadium that would replace the antiquated Soldier Field currently used by the Bears. However, Halas did not want to build the stadium himself; he wanted the city to build it and lease it to the Bears organization. Recognizing that Halas's plans might well come to nothing, two of the railroads involved in the deal contacted Perkins. Should the negotiations between Halas and the city break down, they asked, would the South Loop Group be interested in the property?[27]

That summer, it was learned that Halas had obtained an option on the site for $7.3 million—only $3.25 per square foot, an astonishingly low price. But there was still no commitment from the city to build the new stadium. Both Downs and Klutznick pushed back hard against the proposal, arguing that a sports stadium would be incompatible with the kind of neighborhood they hoped to create in the South Loop.[28] In the end, Daley refused to support the idea. Halas, finally conceding defeat, instructed his attorney in May 1975 to transfer the option on the property to the limited-dividend corporation that Klutznick and his colleagues had by this time established to finance the South Loop development.[29] The Bears owner did not attempt to renegotiate the price, a windfall for the South Loop Group. With land costs this low, a range of housing types would be possible, including low-density townhomes that families would find attractive. At fifty-one acres, the site was a small piece of the six hundred acres members of the South Loop Group had imagined they would develop. But it would at least allow for the construction of a proto-type neighborhood that would hopefully kick start a more extensive re-development process.

By now considerable progress had also been made on the plan for fi-nancing the new development. In 1973 Ayers and several other members of the South Loop Group began a series of informal conversations with other members of the business community to gauge interest in the pur-chase of stock that Klutznick's proposed limited-dividend corporation would issue to raise the cash necessary to finance the project. The dis-cussions were sufficiently encouraging that a decision was reached to move ahead with the plan. The new corporation, called Chicago 21 Cor-poration after the CCAC's downtown plan, was established in January 1974. At the first board meeting held on January 17, Ayers was elected chairman of the board, Perkins was elected president, while Klutznick was named chair of the executive committee.[30]

The effort to solicit stock subscriptions for the new corporation be-gan in earnest during the months before the articles of incorporation were filed with the Illinois secretary of state. Klutznick's proposed cap of $350,000 per investor—intended to prevent any one company from exercising undue influence—was raised to $1 million, and by May 1974 seven companies had pledged the maximum. Smaller commitments from an additional eleven companies brought the total to $9.4 million in pledges.[31] For investors, purchase of Chicago 21 stock was by no means a moneymaking proposition. A prospectus given to all companies express-ing interest warned that the corporation's principal purpose was "not to maximize a financial return to its stockholders, but rather to see to the successful redevelopment of the South Loop area." This would in-volve "a high degree of risk, and the Corporation's stock might there-fore become worthless."[32] In speaking with potential investors Ayers was equally blunt. "We always stressed that their corporate contribution might never be returned," he later said. "And, boy, we made a point of that."[33] Still, by the end of 1974, Chicago 21 had commitments of just over $13 million in stock purchases, less than hoped but still sufficient to move ahead with the first phase of development.[34] With few ideas of their own about how the city's downtown might be protected from encroach-ing blight, companies signed on to the experiment, hopeful that even if the monetary rewards were negligible or nonexistent, the new development would at least mark a turning point of some kind.

By summer 1975 the leaders of the Chicago 21 Corporation had made significant headway on the portions of the South Loop initiative deemed private-sector obligations. The limited-dividend corporation had been established, an initial round of financing had been secured, and the corporation controlled the option on the former Halas property (although the hope was still that the city would eventually purchase the land). The Daley administration, however, was dragging its feet on the proposed public-sector obligations. There was still no commitment to city ownership of the property, nor had the administration officially agreed to provide infrastructure and other services. A year later the city was still noncommittal. Convinced by this time that the city's proposed role would need to be modified, Ayers and several other members of the corporation met with Daley, offering to purchase the land outright rather than lease it from the city. In return, the city would furnish infrastructure and public services. This arrangement, it was felt, would make the project more palatable to the mayor since the corporation "would be asking the City only for those expenditures normally provided by government."[35] The hunch was correct; Daley was agreeable to the proposal. Six months later he died suddenly of a massive heart attack, but by that time the formula for the new development was largely in place. In July 1977 ground was broken for the first housing units in Dearborn Park.

A New Community—But for Whom?

Studies of Dearborn Park have typically used materialist arguments to explain the business community's decision to undertake the new development. Concerned, as one study suggested, about "their own brick-and-mortar holdings in the Loop," business leaders developed the project to create an environment in the South Loop area that would both complement and provide a stimulus to their downtown revitalization efforts.[36] There is no question that material interests played a key role in the development of Dearborn Park. For example, Continental Bank, one of eight companies that made the maximum $1 million contribution and provider of the corporation's first construction loan, had extensive property holdings in the Loop, a key motivating factor. As one Continental executive recalled,

The Loop was going solid black. And the black thing came in from the homes, and it all started to go north, and the black shopping centers in the black communities kind of closed down, and people started shopping on State Street. . . . The concern I had was that Continental had a lot of property. . . . We not only owned the bank, but we owned the building across the street, 170-something Jackson Blvd. We owned 310 S. LaSalle, we owned the parking lot there, and we had ideas about other buildings. Subsequently, we ended up owning all kinds of things.[37]

For this and other likeminded individuals, Dearborn Park was chiefly a means of protecting the Loop's southern flank and reestablishing a solid white presence in the central business district—both seen as important steps in the preservation of downtown real estate values. Material concerns explain this outlook, yet materialist arguments can take us only so far in understanding the motivations and behavior of the project's sponsors. Certain participants in the initiative had broader visions for what Dearborn Park might accomplish, their views shaped not simply by interests but also by ideas about how to best address pressing urban problems. Nowhere is this more apparent than in discussions about the demographics of the new community.

Although Dearborn Park was envisioned as a mostly white middle-income community, planners also stressed that the development would be integrated and accommodate a range of income groups, including low- and moderate-income families and individuals. In a 1972 letter to Daley following up on one of the early meetings of the South Loop Group with the mayor, Continental Bank's Donald Graham wrote, "We have in mind a community that would include completely integrated opportunities in the housing field, both economically and racially, from the subsidized level to the semi-luxury level."[38] Klutznick in particular pushed hard for economic as well as racial diversity. Dearborn Park would "house families from the full economic spectrum," he insisted, "with a great majority of the housing being within the range of the city's solid middle class of policemen and firemen and schoolteachers and Loop office workers."[39] These were people with annual incomes between $12,000 and $18,000, individuals and families for whom attractive housing options in the central city were becoming increasingly scarce. Roughly 70 percent of residents would fall into this category, with another 18 percent upper-income and 12 percent lower-income. With respect to racial diversity, planners maintained that Dearborn Park would have a demographic composition similar to "the racial and ethnic make-up of the metropolitan area."[40]

In part the emphasis on diversity was politically motivated. Business leaders knew that in the wake of urban renewal and the controversies spawned by city-supported redevelopment efforts catering to the middle class, an all-white development for downtown professionals would be po-litically untenable. Yet there was more to it than simple political expe-diency. Several members of the South Loop Group—particularly Ayers, Klutznick, and Kramer—had become deeply involved in efforts to ad-dress racial progress in the city. Years earlier Ayers had served as medi-ator of the open housing summit at which Daley, Martin Luther King Jr. and the Chicago Real Estate Board reached a tentative agreement on open occupancy. Following that effort he helped found the Leadership Council for Metropolitan Open Communities, a group that pushed for the enforcement of open housing laws in Chicago. Ayers was also closely involved with Chicago United, an interracial group of business and civic leaders that focused on race relations in the city.[41]

Kramer and Klutznick were also at the forefront of antidiscrimina-tion efforts in Chicago, chiefly in the housing field. Kramer in particular was convinced that segregation was destroying the city. With an expand-ing black population, he argued, there could be no stable equilibrium between the city's black and white neighborhoods. As long as whites re-mained fearful of black neighbors and the practice of blockbusting re-mained lucrative for realtors, the result would be a steady exodus of the city's white population to the suburbs and an expansion of all-black neighborhoods in the central city. The only way to halt this process was to convince middle-income whites that they had nothing to fear from integrated neighborhoods and housing developments.[42] Kramer's Prai-rie Shores urban renewal project was intended in part to serve this pur-pose—to demonstrate to whites that integrated housing could work. As Kramer later recalled, "We felt that it was not only important to rebuild the area physically to make it attractive with large open areas, landscap-ing that was finer than that of luxury buildings, convenient shopping and recreational facilities, but it was also important to break the pattern of racial segregation in the city, and to try to achieve an ideal racial bal-ance."[43] When it opened in 1958, Prairie Shores was 77 percent white and 23 percent black.[44]

For Kramer, Ayers, and Klutznick in particular, Dearborn Park was not simply an effort to revitalize the city's downtown. It was that, to be sure. But it was also a demonstration project for interracial living, a beacon for a postracial urban society that would hopefully change rigid patterns of thinking about race and housing and inspire others in the development community to undertake similar projects. The Chicago these business leaders envisioned was not a dual city but a city of neighborhoods where families of different races and income groups would live alongside one another in at least relative harmony. This vision of Chicago's future won the group some support within the black community, despite the project's obvious downtown focus. As one black leader explained in his endorsement of the project, "We will see whites, blacks, poor, middle income, senior citizens, young adults, children, owners and renters all living in one community together—living together not as fearful and resentful adversaries but as peaceful and productive neighbors. . . . I see [whites] being less resistant to integration if it is proven that blacks and whites can live peacefully and productively together."[45]

But if the planners of Dearborn Park were in agreement that racial diversity would be a feature of the new development, they were less certain about the mechanisms through which the desired racial balance could be created and sustained. The common wisdom at the time was that integrated housing developments could work as long as whites were solidly in the majority of residents. If the proportion of black residents reached a certain tipping point, whites would flee.[46] At Prairie Shores, Kramer initially used an informal quota system to maintain a ratio of roughly 75 percent white and 25 percent black tenants.[47] With the passage of the Fair Housing Act of 1968, however, quotas became illegal. Kramer, a member of the President's Committee on Equal Opportunity in Housing, provided testimony on the proposed bill to the Senate Banking and Currency Committee, urging that the bill be modified to allow for the continued use of quotas to "foster integration." As he argued, "If the bill is enacted, it might well be that a real estate owner or agent who wants to promote integration will be in violation under the Act if, after he has rented or sold to a number of Negroes, he turns down a Negro family in an effort to maintain a racial balance, and to avert complete inundation which would result in another 100% ghetto."[48] In the case of Prairie Shores, the forecast was at least partially accurate. Following passage of the new legislation, Prairie Shores remained a middle-income development but soon lost the vast majority of its white tenants.

Achieving an acceptable racial balance at Dearborn Park in the era of fair housing laws became a topic of heated discussion among the leaders of the Chicago 21 Corporation. It was clear that persuading middle-income whites to live in the South Loop would be no simple matter. In 1974 the corporation commissioned a survey of 1,200 city and suburban residents to determine perceptions of the proposed South Loop community and gauge interest in living there. Roughly 30 percent of black respondents were favorably disposed to living in such a neighborhood, compared with 10 percent of whites. Only 7 percent of suburban residents expressed interest in living in the South Loop; most expected the development would be predominantly black and low income. When asked to agree or disagree with the statement "There will be racial stability," only 38 percent of suburban residents and 28 percent of central city whites responded affirmatively. Safety, schools, and racial stability were all identified as concerns among the majority of white respondents.[49]

The seeming wariness toward the new development on the part of whites raised concerns that the project could become mostly African American. This possibility was compounded by the emphasis on housing affordability. Planners knew they would have to offer bargains to attract residents—especially whites—to the new untested community. But the low prices would make the community affordable to many middle-income blacks. And if the corporation followed through with its commitment to some low-income housing, even poor black families could afford Dearborn Park. A study the corporation commissioned in 1976 to provide guidance on the question of racial balance concluded that a demographic mix of higher than 20 percent black would be unsustainable. "Without control," the consultants warned, "there has been a total failure to achieve interracial communities."[50] Arrangements should be made "to maintain Black occupancy levels at 18 percent or less" and to market rental units to "young, high-income blacks."[51] How either of these two goals could be achieved without violating fair housing laws was unspecified.

Despite the Fair Housing Act, the use of racial quotas was a subject of discussion among leaders of the Chicago 21 Corporation. Given his experience with Prairie Shores, Kramer in particular pushed hard for some kind of quota system.[52] Others, however, were more cautious. It was a highly sensitive topic; one person involved in the discussions urged that "if at all possible this be a subject discussed privately only."[53] In 1977 the corporation's executive committee approved an affirmative action policy statement that explicitly rejected quotas, promising "equal opportunity for housing, furnishing of goods and services and employment to all individuals regardless of race, color, religion, sex, or national origin."[54] Yet there is some evidence that the process for the sale and rental of housing units was not entirely color-blind. In one instance, an employee of Kramer's real estate firm Draper and Kramer—which handled sales and rentals for Dearborn Park—worried about setting up an advance marketing program because "to have minority people wait that long only to find out they are not going to get an apartment will create a tremendous amount of hostility."[55] In response, the corporation's chief executive suggested a meeting to "discuss our strategy to screen residents in a social as well as economic manner."[56] In 1980 Kramer reported to the executive committee that a mother and daughter whose application had been rejected had complained to the Department of Housing and Urban Development (HUD), "alleging that they were victims of racial discrimination." After reviewing the case, HUD officials "advised that a cash settlement should be offered."[57]

Whether through racial quotas or otherwise, Dearborn Park did achieve racial diversity. By 1996, seventeen years after the first family moved in, the development was roughly 58 percent white, 30 percent black, and 12 percent Asian or Hispanic.[58] The percentage of black residents was largely unchanged from 1980, the first year of operations. Economic diversity, by contrast, proved to be far more elusive. Early promises that Dearborn Park would be a community of modest-income schoolteachers and bus drivers fell by the wayside, as did the commitment to low-income housing. Income projections for typical Dearborn Park residents ratcheted steadily upward—from the $12,000 to $18,000 range in 1974, to between $21,000 and $25,000 in 1977, to between $35,000 and $45,000 in 1981, just over one year after the development opened its doors.[59] As one person involved with the project observed, "The people who moved in were young business types, what we would classify today as Yuppies. They had the money."[60] Low-income housing was limited to one building in which subsidized units for elderly residents were available. Anything beyond this was seen as potentially threatening to the primary goal of attracting middle-income residents.

In the end Dearborn Park fell victim to the same kinds of forces that plagued the model housing developments of the 1920s—costs could not be lowered sufficiently to make the development affordable to the economic groups it was intended to serve. It was not for lack of trying. Leaders of the Chicago 21 Corporation took various steps to try to achieve housing affordability. First were the corporate contributions. Stockholders in Chicago 21 were restricted to a 6.5 percent cap on earnings, an amount substantially lower than the 15 or 20 percent returns investors at the time were earning on comparable development projects.[61] As it turned out, investors actually lost money; for each $100 share they got $41 back.[62] Steps were also taken to reduce mortgage costs for homebuyers. In 1979 as the development was preparing to open, Kramer worked with five Chicago banks to arrange a mortgage pool of $23 million for thirty-year fixed-rate mortgages at 10 percent interest, at least two points below the going rate. By 1981, when rates on conventional mortgages had climbed to 16.5 percent, buyers at Dearborn Park were paying 6.5 points below that.[63] Banks also worked with Chicago 21 to arrange generous construction financing. In 1978 the corporation secured a construction loan of $45 million from Continental Bank and First Federal Savings for the first phase of development. Interest was capped at 10 percent, a major windfall. By the time the loan matured in 1981, the prime rate had risen to 18.9 percent.[64]

Despite all this, development costs remained a significant concern. Skyrocketing interest rates meant that when a new construction loan was needed in 1981, the corporation had to pay close to 20 percent interest, nearly double what had been paid on the previous loan.[65] In addition, the pool of money assembled through stock subscriptions proved to be substantially less than the $30 million leaders of Chicago 21 had set as their original goal. An initial round of stock offerings generated $13.9 million in subscriptions; a subsequent round brought the total to $21 million, still well below the target. And contrary to plans, $7.3 million of this amount had to be spent on land costs when the city balked at purchasing the fifty-one-acre site and leasing it to the corporation.[66] Since there was less cash to work with than expected, the original plan to offer a mix of rentals and condominiums had to be scrapped. Concerned that rental units might not lease quickly enough to meet loan payments, leaders of the corporation decided that rentals would be limited to the building for low-income seniors.[67] Everything else would be for sale. This, of course, made Dearborn Park unaffordable to anyone—low- or middle-income— who could not scrape together the required down payment.

One way to address the affordability dilemma would have been to seek government housing subsidies of some kind, through such initiatives as HUD's Section 8 new construction and housing certificate programs. Both programs, however, would have opened the door to low-income renters at Dearborn Park, and Kramer in particular was dead set against renting to any low-income persons other than seniors.[68] Kramer's position on housing subsidies was no doubt influenced by his observations of the South Commons urban renewal project, a development that Draper and Kramer had bid on back in 1965. As noted in chapter 6, Kramer's firm lost the bid to a developer who proposed a large percentage of Section 221(d)(3) moderate-income housing. In a statement to the commissioners of the Department of Urban Renewal, Kramer had cautioned against housing subsidies, arguing that they would threaten the project's racial balance—particularly since there was already a substantial concentration of low-income housing in the area. His predictions were on the mark; South Commons soon became nearly all black, with most of its units subsidized by HUD.[69] In Kramer's mind, housing subsidies could lead to a similar fate for Dearborn Park. Surveys had already shown that middle-income whites were skeptical of living in the South Loop. The presence of low-income minorities in the new development would not help matters.

It is possible that Kramer's instincts were right, although South Commons and the South Loop were two very different places. One was located in the heart of the South Side Black Belt, the other adjacent to downtown and a large contingent of middle-class office workers who might be enticed by the proximity to work and other downtown attractions. In any case, the failure to achieve an economic balance at Dearborn Park was a disappointment. This was a community of professionals— lawyers, physicians, accountants, architects, and educators.[70] Racial diversity only partially masked the economic segregation that marked the new development—a pattern that was increasingly observable elsewhere in the city and that Dearborn Park mirrored rather than disrupted. As one black leader said of the new community, "It continues the patterns that are existing, and that is you cordon off poor and low-income people into sections for themselves. It's just a form of apartheid."[71]

Fortress Loop

From the beginning, it was clear to the planners of Dearborn Park that the surroundings of the new community would present certain challenges for marketing the development to middle-class residents. Grant Park and the downtown lakefront were only several blocks east of Dearborn Park, but getting there required navigating a corridor of underutilized warehouse buildings and low-income housing, mainly single-room occupancy residential buildings. To the south, along State Street, was the heaviest concentration of public housing anywhere in the United States. Just seven blocks south of the first phase of Dearborn Park were the Raymond Hilliard Homes, a 342-unit CHA high-rise project. Another five blocks south, also on State Street, were the Dearborn Homes, followed by Stateway Gardens and the Robert Taylor Homes. The three CHA projects combined represented a total of 6,793 public housing units, mostly in high-rise structures.[72] To the north of Dearborn Park was the Loop, just a few short blocks away. But in between were more empty and half-empty loft buildings, remnants of the city's former printing district, which was just beginning to experience gentrification and the conversion of lofts to residential and commercial space. During non-business hours the streets were largely deserted.

Even before a site for the new South Loop development had been identified, members of the South Loop Group determined that given the surroundings, significant steps would have to be taken to reassure residents and prospective residents that safeguards were in place to minimize threats to personal safety and property. The Chicago 21 Corporation's 1974 survey of city and suburban residents identified fear for personal safety as the biggest concern about living in the South Loop. Only 15 percent of suburban respondents and 18 percent of city respondents expressed the belief that the crime rate would be low.[73] Planners perceived nearby low-income neighborhoods as a key threat. As one individual involved in discussions about security for the new development observed, "What evidence we do have tells us that crime against persons is partly a function of proximity to concentrated areas of low income, high unemployment, unstable families, etc."[74] An early suggestion was to "incorporate some sort of wall around the development with around-the-clock security at the entrances."[75] Use of a private security service was discussed. Ferd Kramer had been impressed with the work of the Michael Reese security force at Prairie Shores, which he said gave "this renewed neighborhood a small town sense of security." As Kramer observed at the time, the officers were "courteous, tough, and efficient, and if there are any strangers lurking in the neighborhood, they are questioned immediately and if they have no business being there, they are escorted out of the neighborhood."[76]

Security planning for Dearborn Park began in earnest with the commissioning of an environmental security report in 1976.[77] As the consultant began his study, planning for the new development was in the early stages; neither zoning decisions nor architectural drawings had been finalized. This made it possible to incorporate the consultant's recommendations into the design of the project. A collaborative working relationship developed between the security consultant and the land planners, architects, and developer, resulting in a plan for Dearborn Park "whose design largely reflects the input of the security consultant."[78]

The basic philosophy of the security consultant—a view embraced by the leaders of the Chicago 21 Corporation—was that Dearborn Park faced substantial external threats, particularly from nearby low-income neighborhoods. These threats could be mitigated, however, through judicious planning and design. The most important objective was to discourage access to the development by outsiders. This was accomplished in several ways, most importantly by the design and layout of streets and residential buildings. The first phase of Dearborn Park was a six-square-block area bordered by Polk Street to the north, State Street to the east, Roosevelt Road to the south, and Clark Street to the west (fig. 8.1). State Street and Roosevelt Road were both major arterial streets used by residents of the mostly black, low-income South and West Sides to travel to and from the downtown area. At the suggestion of the security consultant, who recommended "the limitation of access points into the development from the major surrounding thoroughfares," phase 1 of Dearborn Park was planned with only one entry for automobiles.[79] Cars could not enter the development from the north, south, or west side. Only to the east, at the intersection of State and Ninth Streets, was there automobile access. Streets within the development—with the exception of Ninth Street—ended in cul-de-sacs. Even pedestrian access was carefully controlled; entryways were limited to a sidewalk at Polk Street and gated entrances along State Street to enable residents to more easily walk to and from their downtown workplaces to the north.

Security was also a key consideration in the design and placement of residential buildings at Dearborn Park. All residential structures in the development's first phase faced inward onto interior streets, parking lots, or courtyards.[80] Fencing was placed along State Street, viewed by planners as a boundary that required extra protection. Residential buildings on State Street were high-rise and mid-rise structures, creating a virtual wall along much of the street. Along Clark Street, another major north-south arterial, a nine-foot concrete wall screened low-rise buildings from

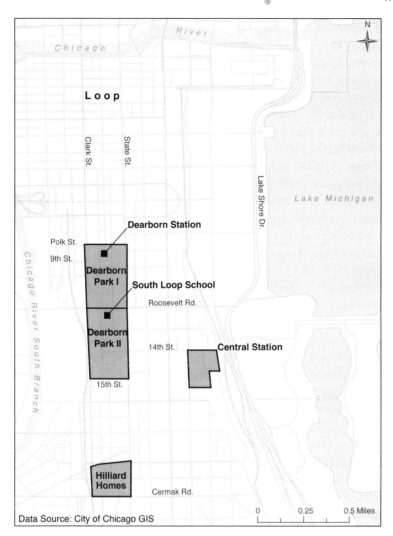

FIGURE 8.1. Dearborn Park and nearby developments.

view. In other locations landscaping was used to make the neighborhood less visible from the outside and discourage entry by nonresidents.

In addition to the design of streets and buildings, several other steps were taken to control access to the neighborhood by outsiders. A key area of concern was the location of bus stops or commercial establishments near entrances to the community, which might "encourage non-resident use and [provide] reason for community entry."[81] The security consultant recommended that bus stops be located "to prevent easy entry to the community," ideally some distance away from the neighborhood perimeter.[82] Bus lines along Roosevelt Road and State Street were especially worrisome to planners because the intersection of the two streets at the eastern border of Dearborn Park was a major transfer point for bus passengers, many of whom were low-income minority residents from the South and West Sides. By one account, early suggestions included rerouting certain buses and making others express buses so that transfers would be minimized.[83] Neither of these steps was ultimately taken, not least because of the fierce public backlash they would have undoubtedly provoked.

Along with transit stops, large commercial establishments such as supermarkets were seen as a negative. Like public transit, they would bring outsiders to the neighborhood. The consultant recommended that nearby shopping facilities "be limited in type and size to those used as a neighborhood convenience, i.e., small grocery, drug store, etc., to reduce attraction of non-resident users."[84] For years the only store serving Dearborn Park was a White Hen Pantry at the corner of Ninth Street and Plymouth Court.

Finally, the presence in Dearborn Park of certain outdoor recreational facilities also became a topic of concern in security planning discussions. Leaders of the Chicago 21 Corporation were convinced that such amenities would be needed to make the development competitive with suburban communities.[85] The Chicago Park District agreed to develop and maintain four public parks in Dearborn Park, two in the northern half of the development and two in the southern half—the area south of Roosevelt Road developed as phase 2 of Dearborn Park (fig. 8.1). There were tennis courts, jogging paths, softball diamonds, and ample green space—features that helped sell the community to prospective homebuyers. The concern, however, was that these same features might make the parks an attraction for nonresidents, and because they were operated by the Chicago Park District their use could not be legally restricted to residents only. But if outsiders could not be banned altogether, their presence could at least be minimized. The security consultant recommended that "public open spaces and recreational elements" be designed "to strongly discourage use by non-residents." Two principal suggestions were made. First, parks and recreational facilities "should be sized and located to reduce or eliminate visibility and accessibility from off-site." Second, amenities such as basketball courts, "which naturally attract large numbers of out-of-area teenagers," were to be avoided.[86] These recommendations were followed. Dearborn Park had no basketball courts, and its parks were accessible—and for the most part visible— only from within the community.

Some have argued that without enhanced security measures, Dearborn Park would have most likely failed. As one planner maintained, "When the development began, if it had not been enclosed, you wouldn't have been able to market it." The fortresslike effect created by the design and layout of streets and buildings was "a big marketing plus."[87] Yet these design features also exposed the Chicago 21 Corporation to criticism. A Harvard University professor of urban planning and design who had seen some of the early renderings was struck by the defensive approach taken by the planners. "It was abundantly clear in the first designs that I saw that there was a kind of paranoia . . . to secure this project from surrounding communities."[88] A common complaint was that Dearborn Park "treats the street as a boundary line instead of a room, an approach which is antithetical to urban living. The eyes are on the courtyards, not on the street."[89] The *Chicago Tribune* offered a similar appraisal, arguing that Dearborn Park

> deliberately keeps the pressure-cooked city at bay. It is turned in on itself, behind brick walls, railings, gates and discreet dead ends. Its patios and sheltered courtyards, swimming pools and secluded doorways are genial and open to the skies—but closed in at ground level. All that, of course, may be standard procedure in today's security-driven America. But it hardly is the open hand and the diverse way of life that cities supposedly promote.[90]

From a new urbanist standpoint, the design of Dearborn Park may have been lacking in certain respects. But given the cast of characters who pioneered the new development, it is not very surprising that the design took the form it did. The security concerns held by Ferd Kramer and Philip Klutznick in particular—both key figures in the planning effort— were shaped in no small part by their involvement with the city's urban renewal program. For years both had harbored hopes of a city free of slums in which blighted neighborhoods no longer posed a threat to stable areas of the city. Indeed both had been convinced that the elimination of slums was needed to secure the city's survival. Now, however, with the problem of slums as pressing as ever and leaders of the city's renewal program effectively conceding defeat, new ideas about how to maintain the city's viability were needed. For Klutznick and Kramer, developments like Dearborn Park were one possible response—a means of holding on to middle-class residents even as nearby slums continued to fester. For such experiments to work, however, certain protections were needed. In the eyes of many middle-class residents, the city was a dangerous place—the South Loop especially so. Such fears were best addressed by acknowledging them forthrightly and planning accordingly, erecting defenses that would keep the chaos and disorder lurking nearby at a safe distance.

Both Klutznick and Kramer, as well as others involved in the planning of Dearborn Park, hoped for a different future for the city. Instead of privileged, mostly white neighborhoods walling themselves off from less fortunate (and less white) communities, they imagined existing spatial divides along racial and class lines melting away over time. With its racial—if not economic—diversity, Dearborn Park was seen as an important start in such a direction, an effort to transcend the present pattern of neighborhood segregation along racial lines. But if a postracial Chicago were even achievable, it was certainly some distance off. For now, planners would have to be content with a less perfect vision of diversity—partially welcoming, partially repelling. And the real lesson of Dearborn Park—that privileged residential enclaves could exist alongside areas of blight and economic distress—would not be lost on those members of the real estate community for whom profits, not racial progress and other social objectives, were the principal motivation. Watching with great interest from the sidelines, such individuals developed ideas of their own about how the Dearborn Park experience might inform future development opportunities, in the South Loop and elsewhere in the city.

School Wars

When, in July 1977, ground was broken for the first housing units in Dearborn Park, the new community—constructed as it was on former railyards—did not fall within the boundaries of any existing school district. There was no question that public education, along with security, would play an important role in determining the fate of the new development. Given the emphasis on attracting middle-income families with school-age children—and persuading families to choose Dearborn Park over suburban communities with high-quality public schools—the presumption was that public education programs would have to compare favorably to the offerings of well-to-do suburbs. It would be a tall order. The Chicago Public School system had a well-deserved reputation for mismanagement and poor service delivery. The 1974 survey of metro-area residents commissioned by Chicago 21 found that only 31 percent of suburban residents and 43 percent of city residents believed that the schools serving Dearborn Park would be excellent.[91] Considerable work would have to be done to counter negative expectations and to convince parents that as residents they would benefit from first-rate educational opportunities available to their children. As one person familiar with Chicago 21's educational planning efforts recounted, "It seems that what was going to be offered was an enhanced program, something better than what was going to be offered in adjacent communities. I was told by [Dearborn Park officials] that only by offering such a program could they hope to attract the market they wanted."[92]

Early on, leaders of Chicago 21 established an education committee to initiate planning for its public education program, including the construction of a new public school that would serve Dearborn Park families. At the recommendation of Skidmore, Owings & Merrill, leaders of Chicago 21 concluded that restoring the abandoned century-old Dearborn Station at the northern boundary of Dearborn Park was the most desirable option for new school facilities serving the South Loop (fig. 8.1). The landmark building would be "completely renovated and redesigned as a combined K–8 school and community center," with classrooms on the first two floors and community meeting areas, a community library, and activities for seniors on the third floor.[93] Not only was the space attractive, but Chicago 21 already had site control—the building was included in the fifty-one acres purchased from the railroads. In December 1978 the plan received a boost when the Chicago City Council authorized the Public Building Commission to purchase the portion of Dearborn Station to be used as the new school.[94] However, the momentum was short lived. At an April 1979 meeting of the Chicago 21 board, the Dearborn Park project manager reported that bids for the station renovation work were up to $2 million over budget "and that the whole matter was being reexamined by the school system and the Public Building Commission."[95] That fall, after meeting with the mayor and city planning commissioner, Thomas Ayers concluded that the project would have to be abandoned.[96]

For the next several years there was little movement on the school situation. When the Dearborn Station renovation plan was discarded, the Chicago School Board purchased five townhomes from the Chicago 21 Corporation to be used as temporary classroom facilities until a new school was constructed. However, at this point Dearborn Park had very few school-aged children; as of January 1982 the development had only twenty-three children of elementary school age. The superintendent of schools wanted at least twice that many before activating the classrooms.[97] For several years, despite continuous pressure from Dearborn Park residents and leaders of the Chicago 21 Corporation, the superintendent refused to budge. Finally a compromise was reached. In May 1984 the board of education committed to "the establishment of a kindergarten, first and second grade facility in the Dearborn Park townhomes" owned by the board. Additional grades would be added on a yearly basis until a permanent K–8 facility was constructed. The program would begin operations that fall.[98]

The opening of the new school was cause for celebration in Dearborn Park, but it drew sharp criticism from parents of school-aged children in the Raymond Hilliard Homes public housing project several blocks south (see fig. 8.1). Under the board of education's plan, the school did not serve Hilliard Homes residents, although its northern boundary extended several miles to include children from downtown residential highrises in the north Loop.[99] Hilliard Homes, opened in 1966, was the last high-rise public housing project constructed by the CHA. By this time the shortcomings of earlier high-rise developments were becoming apparent, and the design and management of Hilliard Homes incorporated some of these lessons. Tenants were carefully screened, there was some racial diversity, and efforts were made to include a balance of working and nonworking families. Such steps earned the development a reputation as the most successful of the CHA's high-rise projects. By the 1980s, however, the CHA seemed to lose interest in the project. Maintenance deteriorated, the screening of tenants stopped, and the project became crime-ridden. In 1988 an eight-year-old boy was found hanged to death in a stairwell, his hands and feet bound. The crime was never solved.[100]

For years parents of school-aged children at Hilliard Homes had been asking the Chicago School Board to build a new elementary school that would serve their neighborhood. At the time, children from the CHA project in grades three through eight attended an elementary school in nearby Chinatown. To get there they had to navigate a busy intersection at Cermak Road and walk below an expressway through a dark block-long tunnel littered with garbage.[101] Children in kindergarten, first, and second grades attended school in a complex of mobile classrooms directly across the street from Hilliard Homes. The eighteen-year-old mobile units, designed as temporary structures, were infested with rats and cockroaches and leaked during rainfalls. After touring the facility in 1984, school superintendent Ruth Love called it "the worst school" she had ever seen.[102]

When the Dearborn Park townhomes school began operations in 1984, Hilliard parents asked that their children be bused to the new facility until a school serving Hilliard Homes and the surrounding area was constructed. The school board denied the request, noting that children living in the CHA development were outside of the school boundaries. The board did, however, agree to replace the deteriorating mobile units with a new building—a $1.2 million prefabricated structure made of corrugated metal that opened in January 1986. The building itself was an improvement, but parents complained that the facility was overcrowded and badly equipped. It was also surrounded on three sides by an auto salvage yard. Said one parent, "This is what they tell us. 'Your kids are junk. Your kids have to go to school in a junkyard.'"[103]

Meanwhile, with the termination of plans for a permanent South Loop school in Dearborn Station, the school board had given its go-ahead to the construction of a new school building within the Dearborn Park development. The 1.5-acre site just south of Roosevelt Road was purchased by the school board in spring 1986 for just over $600,000— at $10 per square foot, a handy profit for the Chicago 21 Corporation (see fig. 8.1).[104] When ground was broken for the building that July, the school's attendance boundaries had not yet been established. Hilliard Homes parents were cautiously optimistic. "I just want to make sure that our kids are given a chance to apply, just like the yuppies' kids," said one resident.[105] However, residents of Dearborn Park were opposed to an attendance area that included Hilliard Homes, fearing it would result in the influx of large numbers of low-income, mostly black, children into the new school. A flyer created by Friends of Dearborn Park School urged residents to contact the school superintendent. "The people from the Hilliard Homes housing project are pressuring the Board to be allowed to send large numbers of housing project children to our school. For many reasons we are against this."[106]

Leaders of the Chicago 21 Corporation were also concerned about the attendance boundary, especially the effects it might have on the marketing of Dearborn Park to middle-income families. Ferd Kramer took a particular interest in the issue, insisting to school board president George Munoz that Dearborn Park would be "seriously damaged" by the inclusion of Hilliard Homes in the attendance area.[107] Kramer had been through this before. At Prairie Shores a new elementary school was built "virtually on the project site." However, it was opened up "to public housing children outside of the area" and became nearly all black, like other nearby schools.[108] As a result, the married couples at Prairie Shores—both African American and white—generally moved away when their children reached school age. As Kramer said at the time, "The discriminating type of Negro and white tenant we have at Prairie Shores will not send their children to segregated schools. Therefore, at that stage of their lives they move to the periphery of the city or the suburbs where the schools are more to their liking."[109] With the construction of the South Loop School to serve the middle-class residents of Dearborn Park, Kramer thought this issue had been addressed. Now the whole plan was threatening to unravel.

In February 1987 the new school superintendent Manford Byrd proposed a compromise plan. Children from Hilliard Homes in kindergarten and grades one and two would continue to attend the new branch school adjacent to the CHA project, while those in grades three through eight would have the option of attending the South Loop School in Dearborn Park.[110] The compromise pleased no one. Hilliard Homes parents wanted all their elementary school–aged children to have access to the South Loop School, while Dearborn Park residents worried that the enrollment of any children from the CHA project would cause middle-class parents to abandon the school. Kramer was distraught, convinced that the plan would "undoubtedly inundate the school with the children from the public housing projects." The end result would most likely be "the residents of Dearborn Park either moving out or sending their children to private schools."[111] Desperate to make his case with the city's political leadership, he asked a fellow Chicago 21 board member and friend of current mayor Harold Washington to raise the issue with the mayor. Washington, however, was unlikely to be swayed. The city's first African

American mayor, Washington had been elected by a coalition of African Americans, Latinos, and white liberals. A key source of the mayor's political strength were the leaders of the city's neighborhood movement, vocal critics of what many viewed as an elite power structure dominated by downtown business leaders. Few issues lent themselves as well to the perceived downtown-versus-the-neighborhoods divide as the conflict over the South Loop School attendance plan. Washington had little to gain politically by siding with business leaders in the dispute.[112]

The contradictions of the Chicago 21 leadership's education plan were on full display. Their suburb in the city could be successful, they believed, only if it were served by a top-notch public school, but any such school could not be genuinely public if nearby children were excluded simply because they happened to live in public housing. As the controversy dragged on during the spring of 1987, media coverage intensified, including articles in *Newsweek* magazine and the *New York Times*.[113] Word began to seep out that the school would be exceptionally well equipped, featuring a dance room with wall-to-wall mirrors and changing rooms, a music room with several pianos, an arts room with a pottery kiln, a science lab, a computer room, and a small theater with a stage and twelve rows of seats.[114] Residents of Dearborn Park were portrayed in the media as "elite young professionals" determined to exclude outsiders from the privileged educational opportunities their children were about to enjoy.[115] It was a public relations failure of mammoth proportions. Still, Dearborn Park residents were unapologetic, at times seemingly incapable of comprehending any point of view other than their own. One resident later explained, "The programs that [Dearborn Park parents] wanted and tried to create there were not the programs that the Hilliard people needed for their children. They needed the remedial programs, not the enrichment programs."[116]

That May the board of education approved Superintendent Byrd's proposal with minor changes.[117] Three years later, however, Byrd's successor Ted Kimbrough pushed through a new attendance plan that required children in kindergarten and first grade from both Hilliard Homes and Dearborn Park to attend the branch school across the street from the CHA project. Starting in second grade, children from both neighborhoods would attend the South Loop School. Criticizing Byrd's plan as "reminiscent of the Jim Crow South," Kimbrough insisted that barring children living in Hilliard Homes from the vastly superior South Loop School until third grade—while Dearborn Park children faced no such restrictions—was discriminatory.[118] Not surprisingly, no Dearborn Park parents chose to bus their children to the branch school. These children attended private schools or magnet schools, the latter being superior public schools that accepted enrollments on a citywide basis through a lottery system.[119] Meanwhile as the percentage of students at the South Loop School who were minority and low-income steadily increased, Dearborn Park parents sought other options for these children as well. When the South Loop School initially opened in 1988, it had a racial and ethnic mix of roughly one-third white, one-third black, and one-third Latino and Asian. By 1993, out of a total enrollment of 568 children, only 31 were white. Two years later the number of Dearborn Park children attending the South Loop School was down to 7.[120] As one resident said disappointedly, "The neighborhood has abandoned the school. The community has more or less washed its hands of it."[121]

With private schools becoming, increasingly, the default option for Dearborn Park parents, the economic diversity that planners had envisioned for the development became even more elusive. Escalating construction costs and insufficiently deep corporate subsidies had already driven housing prices beyond the reach of many middle-income families. Now parents would have to factor the cost of private school tuition into their budgets as well. For the planners of Dearborn Park the outcome was deeply disappointing. Initially convinced that city officials would sympathize with their efforts to bring back the middle class and ultimately see things their way, they were instead handed a difficult lesson in city politics. And the end result—one of the unintended consequences of the effort to create a public school for South Loop residents—was to further reinforce the divide between neighborhoods of privilege such as Dearborn Park and those of economic distress and hardship.

The Dual City

In the twenty-some years since the final units of Dearborn Park were completed, residential development in the South Loop has exceeded all expectations. An area long written off as a crime-infested "wasteland"—a place middle-class residents did not venture—has become Chicago's most active location for residential construction.[122] Between 2000 and 2006 alone, the number of South Loop housing units nearly doubled from 7,700 to approximately 14,000.[123] As one real estate agent observed,

TABLE 8.1. **Characteristics of South Loop and Near South Side, 1990–2010**

Year	Area population	Percent black	Percent white non-Hispanic	Percent Hispanic	% population below poverty level	% population with BA degree or higher
1990	23,207	36.6	25.9	15.6	27.6	15.3
2000	32,343	36.6	24.5	15.6	25.1	26.7
2010	63,242	16.2	40.4	17.1	18.5	53.2

Source: US Census Bureau, 1990, 2000, and 2010 Decennial Census. Area boundaries are Jackson Boulevard to the north, Lake Shore Drive to the east, the Stevenson Expressway to the south, and the Dan Ryan Expressway to the west.

Dearborn Park "used to be at the edge of the world. Now it's in the middle of things."[124] By all indications, the vision of the Chicago Central Area Committee—whose Chicago 21 Plan proposed a "miniature supercity" of 120,000 residents in the South Loop area—is well on its way to being realized. The area's population was a mere 23,207 residents in 1990. By 2010 it had risen to 63,242, fueled by proximity to downtown and the area's rehabilitated image as a hip, upscale neighborhood with multitudinous entertainment options and other amenities. As table 8.1 indicates, the new residents are increasingly white and middle class.

The redevelopment and revitalization of the South Loop has been accompanied by extensive gentrification elsewhere in the city during the past several decades, especially areas close to downtown and along the lakefront north of the central business district.[125] Portions of both Pilsen and the Near West Side—neighborhoods targeted for rehabilitation in the Chicago 21 plan—either have already gentrified or are experiencing significant gentrification pressures.[126] Near Northwest Side neighborhoods such as Wicker Park and Logan Square along the Chicago Transit Authority's elevated Blue Line have also experienced substantial upgrading. Other areas have not fared as well. Accompanying the gentrification boom has been an even larger increase in the number of community areas of very low socioeconomic status, which grew from twenty-nine in 1970 to forty-five in 2010, all majority African American or Latino neighborhoods on the city's South and West Sides. Meanwhile, as high-poverty and high-income neighborhoods have expanded, middle-income neighborhoods have decreased, falling from thirty community areas in 1970 to just nine in 2010. By 2010 only 10 percent of the city's population lived in middle-socioeconomic status neighborhoods, down from 35 percent in 1970.[127] As University of Illinois at Chicago planners John Betancur and Janet Smith conclude, the data reveal "a city that is becoming more polarized, diverging further into gentrified and ghettoized neighborhoods with few places in between."[128]

As in other cities, gentrification in Chicago has been politically controversial, producing a housing affordability crisis that has hit middle-income residents particularly hard. Under pressure from constituents, the city council approved an ordinance in 2007 requiring developers of residential projects for which zoning changes or other special city approval is necessary to make 10 percent of housing units affordable to families earning below the metropolitan area's median income of $75,000.[129] However, the new rule contained a major loophole; developers could bypass the restriction by paying $100,000 per unit into a city fund used to subsidize affordable housing. Most chose this option. By 2015 the ordinance had resulted in the creation of just 189 affordable units in market-rate developments, while generating $53 million from in-lieu fees.[130] The new revenue source, while welcome, did little to promote neighborhood income diversity. As one housing advocate complained, "Almost none of the money has been used to build affordable housing in the neighborhoods where new development is happening, where the most affordable housing is being lost. It doesn't create balanced development. It further divides the city."[131]

The city's approach to gentrification can be viewed as part of a broader shift toward neoliberal urban policies aggressively pursued by Mayor Richard M. Daley and his successor Rahm Emanuel. As it is elsewhere, neoliberalism in Chicago is distinguished above all by the reorientation of city government around entrepreneurial functions and activities, particularly those aimed at fostering a healthy business climate.[132] Gentrification is a key component of the neoliberal toolkit because it creates the kinds of neighborhoods desirable to the young, well-educated professionals that many businesses seek to recruit. Moreover, by boosting property values and tax liabilities, gentrification produces a revenue source that can be tapped for public improvements that further enhance the attractiveness of the city's most desirable areas.

While neoliberal policies and ideas have been praised by some for fueling Chicago's downtown renaissance and further solidifying the city's global status, others have cited growing disparities among neighborhoods, racial and ethnic groups, and economic classes as evidence that neoliberalization is leaving certain populations behind.[133] According to a 2014 Brookings Institution study, Chicago is the eighth most unequal city in the country. Income for the top 5 percent of employed city residents is more than ten times that of the bottom 20 percent.[134] Previous administrations, especially that of Mayor Harold Washington during the 1980s, responded to rising inequality with policies and programs designed to improve prospects for the city's most vulnerable residents, taking the view that market failures necessitated aggressive policy intervention.[135] Such thinking, however, runs counter to the neoliberal, market-driven philosophy embraced by many of the city's contemporary civic and political leaders.

In certain respects Chicago's dual city of today looks very different from the one set in motion by the Central Area Committee and the development of Dearborn Park. Unlike before, neighborhoods today are generally upgraded not through the building of entire communities in fortresslike fashion but on a parcel-by-parcel basis—through loft conversions, rehabilitation of single-family homes and apartment buildings, teardowns, and the like. For an individual neighborhood the cumulative effect is a significant transformation in its character, property tax base, and attractiveness to middle- and upper-income professionals, a process that takes years—and in some cases decades—to complete. While the case of Dearborn Park does not fit this pattern, the project was a key stepping-stone in the genesis of today's dual city. Through Dearborn Park and other developments of its time, the city transitioned from the urban renewal period—when stable middle-class neighborhoods were perceived as under attack by expanding slums—to the mindset of today, where economically distressed areas are viewed as much less of a threat. The process of working through Dearborn Park—its struggles over public education, its ambivalent stance toward urbanism, its successes and failures with racial and income diversity—helped pave the way for those who came afterward. Over time, through the ideas and efforts of those who followed in Dearborn Park's footsteps, the city learned to live with the slums. The notion of a dual city became, for all practical purposes, the conventional wisdom—the de facto policy paradigm for engaging with areas of blight and economic distress.

What might the planners of Dearborn Park say about the city that Chicago has become? Some would surely offer no apologies, pointing to the revitalization of near-downtown areas as vindication of their arguments long ago that a solid middle-class presence in the city's central area was both possible and necessary for the revival of the city's downtown. For others, however, especially those who envisioned Dearborn Park and future South Loop neighborhoods as model communities that would demonstrate how people of different races and income groups could share the same streets and neighborhoods, praise might be more qualified. The real lesson of Dearborn Park and the gentrification it helped inspire was not that racial and economic segregation could be transcended but that such divisions could be accommodated within a broader vision of urban transformation. Dearborn Park was not the inspiration for the dual city of today, but neither was it inconsistent with such an outcome. It played a role in stemming white flight and bringing middle-class residents back to the city, but not in the way that certain of its planners imagined and hoped it would.

Conclusion

I began this book with a simple argument—that efforts to confront problems of slums and blight in twentieth-century Chicago cannot be properly understood without reference to the ideas held by those actors most influential in determining the city's policy approaches. As we have seen, various groups mobilized around programs and policies to contain, manage, and reverse the spread of slums. Oftentimes material interests in one form or another were at stake. However, neither material interest nor historical context can fully explain the strategies these actors endorsed and pursued. Rather, actors were guided in part by ideas, including policy paradigms, that made certain policy directions more appealing than others. As this book has shown, there were three paradigms that shaped decision making across discrete periods in twentieth-century Chicago—privatism, the public-private partnership of urban renewal, and the dual city. As paradigms changed, the strategies endorsed by influential groups shifted as well. A key consequence of these ideational shifts is that by the end of the twentieth century, the city's civic and political leaders had all but abandoned the goal of eliminating slums, an objective that had been central to the city's policy efforts from the dawn of the century through the 1960s.

Given the influential role of policy paradigms in shaping perceptions and behavior and the dramatic change in policy approaches that occurred as paradigm shifts took place, an important objective of this book has been to identify the key mechanisms through which paradigm change was effected. In chapter 1, I developed a model of paradigm change that included a set of factors, both endogenous and exogenous to the policy process, through which change was hypothesized to occur. How well does this model explain the outcomes described in this book? To answer this question, I begin with a brief review of the model's key features. As chapter 1 illustrates, the model has two parts, one focused on the paradigm's stability and propensity for change, the other on the mechanisms through which change takes place. With respect to the former, paradigms may in some cases represent stable sets of ideas that are largely unchallenged, meaning that exogenous factors such as economic crises or other disruptions must be invoked to explain how change occurs. In other cases, however, paradigms may be prone to change—due to poor fit with institutional arrangements, inconsistency of paradigmatic goals and ideas, or feedback effects that mobilize groups around alternative policy ideas. Any of these endogenous factors may play a role—either in conjunction with or in the absence of exogenous disruptions—in creating opportunities for new policy paradigms to displace existing ones.

Should a policy paradigm prove to be vulnerable to rival sets of ideas, change may take one of several forms. It may be "punctuated," meaning that new ideas largely displace older ones in relatively rapid fashion. Alternatively, change may occur more gradually and involve a more partial reconstruction of existing ideational arrangements. In the latter case, two mechanisms—layering and conversion—may be particularly significant. Both are important in determining whether a new policy paradigm represents a more or less stable set of ideational arrangements. If the replacement paradigm is constructed by retaining portions of an existing one and layering new policy ideas onto older ones, the likelihood increases that some incongruency will surface among paradigm goals and ideas. Older ideas may fail to align with newer ones in ways that produce coherent opportunities for calculated policy intervention. By contrast, new paradigms developed through conversion—the reorientation of existing ideas around goals that better meet the needs of powerful societal groups—may lead to more stable ideational outcomes, especially when groups are well positioned to help institutionalize the ideas they champion.

The history of paradigm change in Chicago detailed in this book reveals considerable instability in the conventional wisdom for addressing problems of slums and blight. For much of the twentieth century two key endogenous factors—weak alignment between paradigm and institutional arrangements, and incongruency among paradigm goals and ideas—repeatedly frustrated the efforts of actors drawing on the conventional wisdom at the time to inform the strategies they pursued. In early twentieth-century Chicago it was the former of these two factors that was most in evidence. With privatism dominating thinking about how slum housing should be rehabilitated, Progressive Era housing reformers championed restrictive housing regulations to force building owners to better construct and maintain their properties, betting that slums could be eliminated through more stringent government oversight of housing conditions. New ordinances were passed by city council, but the city's machine-style institutional arrangements made their enforcement highly irregular, particularly in the city's working-class immigrant wards—the very places most likely to exhibit slum conditions. Later on, when reformers turned to model housing developments as a vehicle for providing improved housing opportunities for the laboring classes, institutional arrangements once again posed an obstacle. In this case, however, it was the absence of collective bargaining and minimum-wage laws, which together made it all but impossible for those at the bottom end of the wage scale to pay rents sufficiently high to cover the costs of even the most inexpensively built standard housing.

By the 1940s, privatist thinking about slum rehabilitation had largely given way to the new paradigm of public-private partnerships. But the change in the conventional wisdom did not take place through a rapid, wholesale rejection of older ideas and their replacement with completely different ones. Instead actors reconstructed ideational arrangements in piecemeal fashion, discarding certain ideas, retaining others, and adding new ones. Most important, the goal of eliminating slums—an objective long viewed as essential in preserving the city's long-term viability—was carried forward from the privatist period. However, layered on top of this goal was a new one—achieving the highest and best use of land—that largely replaced privatism's other key objective of providing safe and sanitary housing for residents of the city's slum districts. As argued in chapter 6, this layering process produced the unintended effect of extending and reproducing slums rather than eliminating such conditions, frustrating the city's urban renewal pioneers and leading to a search for new ideas about how to best engage with the city's blighted areas.

Both of these endogenous factors—poor fit between paradigm and institutional arrangements in the former case and the clash of paradigm goals in the latter—worked against the stability of existing policy paradigms, creating openings for new ideas to surface and win support. Yet endogenous factors alone are insufficient to explain the paradigm shifts that ultimately took place. In both cases, economic disruptions also played a role. In the case of privatism, New Deal housing initiatives prompted by the collapse of housing markets during the early years of the Great Depression upended the conventional wisdom for rehabilitating slums, ushering in a decades-long period of experimentation in housing reform that culminated in new state and federal urban-renewal legislation. In the case of urban renewal, the onset of urban economic restructuring during the 1960s seemed to seal the fate of inner-city minorities, whose disappointing experiences with renewal programs were now accompanied by deindustrialization and the rise of extreme poverty and concentrated disadvantage in the city's most economically distressed areas. In short, policy paradigms that were in both cases unstable and vulnerable to challenge were thrown further into crisis by changing economic conditions that put paradigm goals even more out of reach.

To a great extent, the experiences of these two policy paradigms stand in stark contrast to Chicago's most recent paradigm for engaging with areas of poverty and economic distress—what I call the dual city. In contrast to the instability of earlier policy paradigms and their failure to deliver on paradigm goals, the dual city has featured considerably greater resilience. Initiated largely through the Chicago 21 planning process and further institutionalized through the development of Dearborn Park and gentrification of other areas, the dual city—defined here as a development agenda featuring both gentrification and tacit acceptance of entrenched high-poverty neighborhoods—has long represented the conventional wisdom among those whose views matter the most. What explains the resiliency of the dual city paradigm? An important consideration is the process through which this paradigm was constructed, involving a partial reworking and reorientation of existing paradigm goals around new objectives championed in particular by an increasingly mobilized and cohesive downtown business community. Spurred into action by the city's urban renewal program, the city's business leadership used that program's pioneering concept—the public-private partnership—to shift development policy in a direction that had little to do with ending slums. Through the mechanism of conversion, paradigm goals were brought into sync with the objectives of the city's most powerful actors, an alignment of ideas and political influence that would prove to have tremendous staying power.

For broad stretches of the twentieth century, the three policy paradigms on which this book focuses informed thinking and behavior regarding problems of slums and blight in Chicago, guiding actions in ways that generally conformed with the conventional wisdom at the time. Yet as this book has shown, there were also transitional periods—decades long in at least one case when no coherent set of ideas was in place to guide behavior. During these "unsettled times," ideas proliferated about how to best ensure the city's viability in the face of vexing problems with chronic economic distress.[1] With paradigmatic assumptions increasingly relaxed, political behavior grew more eccentric. Well-worn policy approaches gave way to policy experimentation that took place largely on a trial-and-error basis. Actors, uncertain about where their interests lay or how best to realize them, sought guidance in the form of policy ideas, endorsing those approaches they viewed as most consistent with the agendas they championed. Over time, as new approaches won converts among those actors influential enough to make a difference, new policy paradigms were born and gradually institutionalized.

To be sure, economic interests were at the forefront of policy experimentation during these transitional periods. Yet precisely because of the uncertainty that existed, the way forward was often far from clear, and actors with similar material interests at times interpreted crisis conditions in vastly different ways. In the case of Dearborn Park, for example, certain business leaders appeared to view the new development as little more than an effort to kick-start a gentrification process that would initiate the long-desired influx of middle-class residents into areas surrounding the city's downtown. Others, however, feared that racial transition and the steady decline of the city's middle-income white population would overwhelm any effort to revitalize the city's downtown. For developers such as Philip Klutznick and Ferd Kramer, Dearborn Park, by including a mix of races and economic groups, would demonstrate to Chicagoans that integrated neighborhoods could be successful. If the experiment were brought to scale through the efforts of additional housing developers, the problem of white flight might be brought under control. In sum, for one set of business leaders the key problem was the threat posed to downtown by encroaching blight; for another, racial transition and white flight—problems affecting the city as a whole—represented a parallel and equally troublesome threat that Dearborn Park might address. A materialist approach would predict widespread agreement among business leaders about the goals and objectives of Dearborn Park. That views varied as widely as they did strongly suggests that ideas about the development and the purposes it should serve, not interests alone, guided behavior in nontrivial ways.

Returning once again to my original question of how well the model introduced in chapter I serves as an explanatory device for the paradigm shifts described in this book, it would appear that the model effectively captures the broad changes in thinking and behavior that the narrative details. Policy paradigms in twentieth-century Chicago were well entrenched for substantial periods of time, facilitating certain kinds of policy initiatives while largely ruling out others. At key junctures, however, endogenous factors with destabilizing effects combined with external economic shocks to tip the balance in favor of change. Mechanisms through which change took place—both layering and conversion—helped determine whether new paradigms were themselves more or less stable sets of ideational arrangements.

If the model is persuasive in the Chicago case, can it be applied elsewhere to explain the influence of policy paradigms in other twentieth-century American cities also wrestling with problems of slums and economic distress? The answer, of course, depends on the extent to which the Chicago experience was in some way unique, limiting our ability to extend the lessons of this study to a broader set of cases. In fact the experiences of other cities closely track those of Chicago in key respects. The three paradigms on which this book focuses were in evidence in one form or another in all major American cities during the twentieth century, each one dominant at roughly the same time its counterpart in Chicago served as the conventional wisdom. All large cities experienced the transition from privatism to the public-private partnership of urban renewal, and all underwent this transition through a layering of newer ideas onto older ones, a process that—as in Chicago—entangled programs in contradictions that proved impossible to unravel. In cities across the country, downtown business leaders mobilized during the 1960s and 1970s, reworking policy ideas generated through now-discredited urban renewal programs and applying them more directly to the rebuilding of downtown and the revalorization of select neighborhoods. In city after city, the dual city paradigm emerged as the conventional wisdom for engaging with chronically distressed areas—places that by this time seemed largely impervious to policy intervention.[2]

Not all cities experienced these transitions in precisely the same ways, but the key features of the story are similar from place to place. Over time, areas of economic distress went from places to be rehabilitated to places to be managed and policed. They would exist alongside—and in a perpetual state of tension with—those areas of the city where investment flowed and people of means chose to live and spend their money.

For many cities, Chicago included, it was an arrangement that enabled city boosters to speak convincingly about urban renaissance and "come-back cities" even as poverty and hopelessness in the most economically distressed neighborhoods grew further entrenched.

Reproducing the Dual City

This book argues that the dual city paradigm came into being through a confluence of factors. Most important, the internal contradictions of urban renewal combined with deindustrialization and urban economic restructuring to create widespread pessimism about the prospects for rehabilitating slum and blighted areas. Loss of faith in the existing set of ideas for engaging with the city's slum districts created openings for new ideas to circulate and potentially win support. Dominating this contest was a powerful new coalition led by the Chicago Central Area Committee, which, through the Chicago 21 planning process, first articulated the essential features of the dual city. Downtown Chicago would be revitalized through the rebuilding and upgrading of central area neighborhoods, creating corridors of privilege largely impenetrable by the forces of blight steadily eroding neighborhood well-being in areas farther south and west of downtown. If slums could not be rehabilitated, the city would have to learn how to live with them.

These developments, more than any others, explain how the idea of a dual city emerged and gained influence, especially among the city's civic and political leaders. But the factors responsible for bringing a new policy paradigm into being are not necessarily the same as those responsible for reproducing that set of ideas over time. For all its faults, the dual city paradigm has shown remarkable resilience and longevity, considerably more than that of its two predecessors in twentieth-century Chicago, privatism and the public-private partnership of urban renewal. To understand why the dual city remains the conventional wisdom of today, nearly a half-century after it was first articulated by the city's business leadership, and why indeed these ideas seem more entrenched and widely accepted than ever, we must look carefully at the processes through which the dual city has become institutionalized.

A good place to begin is with the economy, and here we continue to see factors at work today that were important in the emergence of this set of ideas. As many observers have documented, globalization and the hypermobility of capital have exacerbated the bifurcated wage structure that began to emerge in major American cities, Chicago included, during the 1970s. The manufacturing jobs that disappeared in rapid fashion during the 1970s and 1980s—jobs that had for decades provided family-supporting wages for workers with limited formal education—have not come back. Instead the city's economy is dominated increasingly by various service-sector occupations whose wages fall for the most part at either the high or the low end of the pay scale.[3] These macroeconomic developments have played a major role in the reproduction of Chicago's dual city, especially when accompanied by neoliberal policy ideas about the sanctity of market mechanisms and the futility of efforts that work against the grain of structural economic change.

For many of the city's African American residents in particular, the effects of urban economic restructuring are compounded by those of segregation and racial discrimination. Chicago remains one of the most racially segregated cities in the country, ranking third among major US metropolitan areas in a 2015 Brookings Institution study.[4] As sociologists Douglas Massey and Nancy Denton have demonstrated, segregation dramatically increases the effects of economic disruptions on a given social group by concentrating those effects in certain neighborhoods, creating "a set of mutually reinforcing and self-feeding spirals of decline."[5] As economic restructuring undercut the earning power of African Americans during the 1970s and 1980s, high levels of segregation in Chicago and other cities led to dramatic income declines and widespread joblessness across entire neighborhoods. Instead of jobs and careers in the mainstream economy, gangs, drug use, and imprisonment became the norm. The presumption today is widespread that these poor, overwhelmingly black neighborhoods are largely dysfunctional, semipermanent, and in need of heavy policing and social control.[6] While liberals and conservatives argue about the extent to which residents of such areas are themselves implicated in these circumstances, most are in agreement that the prospects for change are daunting.

While economic change, poverty, and segregation have played ongoing roles in the production and reproduction of the dual city, other factors are more recent. The coalition that first envisioned and articulated the notion of a dual city as part of the Chicago 21 planning process is long defunct. Chicago, like most other contemporary cities, no longer has a cohesive group of civic and economic elites working actively to plan and bring about the physical transformation of the city, as in the case of Chicago 21 and Dearborn Park. More than any other group, the Chicago Central Area Committee was instrumental in bringing the dual city of today into being. But neither this organization nor any comparable group is responsible for sustaining this set of ideas and practices over time. Instead today's dual city is perpetuated in large part through real estate markets and the individual actions of developers, landlords, tenants, and property owners, all seeking to position themselves favorably in the markets in which they compete. In a process that is largely self-reinforcing, faith in the investment potential of certain areas stimulates neighborhood upgrading, even as areas nearby continue to decline. The dual city is institutionalized as the perception grows that such an arrangement is workable—that property can hold and gain value even when surrounded by areas of acute economic distress. The farther gentrification extends its reach into once struggling neighborhoods, the stronger the perception becomes that a dual city is indeed a functional model for the social and spatial organization and reorganization of the city. And the further that areas of concentrated disadvantage sink into decline, the more it appears that there is no realistic alternative.

While the workings of real estate markets are a key dynamic in the reproduction of today's dual city, markets are always structured by rules and incentives put in place by government, measures influenced by the neoliberal orientation of public policy in contemporary Chicago.[7] Neoliberalism, like the dual city, is a policy paradigm, and the ideas that each of these paradigms represents are mutually reinforcing. To a great extent, the notion of a dual city makes neoliberal policies and ideas more palatable. If entrenched high-poverty neighborhoods are a condition that cities can learn to manage—and, perhaps more important, one that resists treatment—then why not focus on making cities more entrepreneurial? Perhaps there will at least be some benefits that trickle down to less fortunate residents. By the same token, neoliberal ideas serve to further institutionalize the dual city by encouraging policy approaches that deepen and extend divisions among neighborhoods, racial and ethnic groups, and social classes. The logic of capitalism and the workings of market mechanisms, including real estate markets, tilt in the direction of greater inequality. To the extent that neoliberal ideas encourage public officials to harness and unleash market forces while doing little to mitigate their deleterious effects, social and spatial divisions will no doubt continue to deepen. Neoliberalism is not structurally ordained, but like the dual city, it is becoming more and more the conventional wisdom for urban governance. Departures are increasingly a matter of degree rather than kind.[8]

Continuity and Change

Chicago is becoming a city of the very rich and the very poor with fewer and fewer people in between. We're becoming a city with glittering buildings surrounded by crumbling neighborhoods. A city with the finest restaurants, surrounded by communities full of people who can't afford a decent meal. A city with some job growth in a small area downtown, surrounded by a vast area where unemployment rates are 25 to 30 percent. A city with fancy shopping areas surrounded by other areas with boarded-up business districts.[9]

The above words were spoken by Jesus "Chuy" Garcia in a speech to the City Club during Chicago's 2015 mayoral race. Garcia, a little-known former alderman, state senator, and Cook County commissioner, was attempting to unseat incumbent mayor Rahm Emanuel, in office since 2011. Taking a page from New York City mayor Bill de Blasio's "tale of two cities" playbook, which helped power his progressive-leaning mayoral campaign to victory in 2013, Garcia sought to move the dual city paradigm from conventional wisdom to object of contestation.

Emanuel seemed to be vulnerable to this kind of attack. Four years earlier he had been a late entry into the 2011 mayoral contest, a race that suddenly appeared to be wide open after Mayor Daley's surprise announcement in September 2010 that he would not seek a seventh term. A native Chicagoan, Emanuel had served in Congress representing Illinois's Fifth District before joining the Obama administration in 2009 as the president's chief of staff. With his White House connections and the help of his brother Ari, a Hollywood talent agent, Emanuel quickly opened up a wide funding advantage over his five competitors. David Geffen, Steven Spielberg, and Steve Jobs were all major donors. Donald Trump contributed $50,000.[10] In the end, Emanuel coasted to victory with 55 percent of the vote, winning forty of the city's fifty wards. With endorsements from President Obama and former President Bill Clinton, he carried all but one of the city's majority African American precincts, soundly beating the three black candidates in the race.[11]

Emanuel quickly gained a reputation as a hard-driving mayor who would not shy away from tackling urgent problems. However, due in part to these same qualities, the new mayor's first term was plagued by con-troversy. Emanuel inherited a set of daunting fiscal problems that threat-ened the city's credit rating, including a budget deficit of $600 million, $20 billion in unfunded pension liabilities, and a $1 billion deficit in the public school system's operating budget.[12] The new mayor responded to these fiscal challenges with a set of deeply unpopular austerity measures, including the closure of forty-nine public schools located predominantly in African American and Latino neighborhoods, a move that set off widespread protests on the city's South and West Sides.[13] Emanuel was also criticized for failing to do more to address the epidemic of gun vio-lence in the city; homicides in 2012 rose to 506, an increase of 16 percent over the previous year.[14] These developments, along with the mayor's popularity with business leaders and white professionals, helped feed a growing narrative—especially among minority groups and progres-sive whites—that Emanuel's chief priority was to ensure that the pros-perity of downtown and gentrifying neighborhoods continued under his watch. As one resident of the city's Logan Square neighborhood com-plained, "He's always coming here to ride his bike and look like he's part of everyday people, but he's not. He's for the money."[15]

As the February 2015 mayoral election approached, Emanuel seemed far from invincible. Sixty percent of African American residents sur-veyed in an August 2014 *Chicago Tribune* poll expressed disapproval with the mayor's job performance.[16] While Emanuel ultimately fin-ished first among the five candidates in the race, he was forced into a runoff contest with his closest competitor, Chuy Garcia, when he failed to win an outright majority of the votes. Garcia continued to hammer away at his "two Chicagos" message. "People are feeling the effects of inequality in this city, and they don't like it," he told one interviewer. "Rahm has run this city for the benefit of the select few, the high rollers, hedge fund managers, big developers."[17] Garcia promised to end school closures, hire a thousand new police officers, and protect pension and health care benefits for public employees. Emanuel was dismissive. With a campaign war chest of $30 million (compared with Garcia's $5.2 mil-lion), the mayor saturated local television and radio stations with attack ads, portraying Garcia as naive and fiscally irresponsible.[18] Some warned that a Garcia victory could trigger a Detroit-style fiscal collapse.[19] When the votes were tallied, Emanuel won decisively, beating his rival by more than ten percentage points. As expected, Garcia handily won the city's Latino wards. However, both majority African American and majority white precincts went strongly for Emanuel, the former by fifteen points and the latter by thirty points.[20] As one analyst concluded, Garcia's "tale of two cities" message was "a theme that never caught on."[21]

The outcome of Chicago's 2015 mayoral contest reveals just how entrenched the dual city policy paradigm has become, not simply within policy circles but among neighborhood residents across the city, both rich and poor. Emanuel's strong showing in the city's African American wards and the tepid response from many blacks to Garcia's "two Chicagos" campaign is powerful evidence of the extent to which the dual city has become accepted and internalized even by those groups most disadvantaged by this set of practices and beliefs. Still, for all its seeming stability the dual city paradigm represents a precarious set of ideational arrangements, its legitimacy resting on a series of dubious claims—that the city displays no favoritism toward certain neighborhoods over others in development decisions; that all neighborhoods receive the same quality of public services; that laws are enforced equally in all parts of the city, for all racial and ethnic groups; that any disadvantages experienced by growing up in certain neighborhoods can be overcome through hard work and perseverance; and that racial discrimination in employment and housing markets has been largely eliminated through civil rights laws and diminishing racial prejudices. The key contradiction of the dual city may be its requirement for political support from large numbers of urban voters whose own experiences seem to be at odds with such claims.

There is resistance, and it can be observed in social movements like Black Lives Matter and the Right to the City. If real change does come to Chicago and other cities, it will likely be the consequence of organizing efforts that mobilize enough people on the losing end of the urban renaissance to have an impact on elections and policymaking processes. But should change happen, it may also come because someone advances a set of radically different policy ideas sufficiently persuasive to cause widespread defection from the conventional wisdom of today in favor of something different. If this book illustrates anything, it is that change involves more than seizing the reins of power and elevating certain interests over others. As Chuy Garcia discovered, it is more than simple rejection of the status quo. Rather, real change involves articulating a vision and presenting a set of policy solutions that penetrate conventional thinking to the core, turning the spotlight on ideas long taken for granted and opening them up to careful scrutiny and comparison with meaningful alternatives. When such ideas are proposed and attract sufficient interest and support, particularly among those with enough power and resources to have an impact, policy can move in radically different directions.

History shows that opportunities for consequential change are rare, and that when change does occur it is not always for the better. At present, interests, ideas, and institutions are substantially aligned around the dual city—in Chicago and elsewhere. The resilience of this paradigm into the future may depend on the extent to which it continues to deliver benefits to the powerful and the privileged, the degree to which its contradictions can be successfully managed, and the presence or absence of alternative policy ideas that those disadvantaged by the dual city might rally around.

Epilogue

It's 7:45 on a sunny April morning and I'm standing in front of a Chicago-bound train at the Milwaukee Intermodal Station, waiting to load my bicycle onto the luggage car. My destination: Chicago's South Loop and Near South Side. I want to see firsthand how Dearborn Park seems to have fared, forty years almost to the month after ground was broken for the development. I also want to tour the surrounding area, the remainder of the several hundred acres of once-abandoned rail-yards, warehouse buildings, and blighted housing that stood between the Loop and the South Side Black Belt. From there I'll head south to Prairie Shores, South Commons, and Lake Meadows, where urban renewal got its start in the 1950s. The bike seems like the most efficient touring option.

At 9:25 a.m. the train pulls into Union Station, just west of the Loop. I collect my bike and haul it upstairs to the Jackson Street entrance. In heavy traffic, I ride down Jackson to Clark Street and turn right. Several minutes later I pull up in front of the old Dearborn Station. I park my bike and go inside. The station has gone through several incarnations since plans to locate the new South Loop School there were scrapped in the 1970s. A proposed Rouse-style festival marketplace never got off the ground. During the 1990s, tenants included a mix of eating establishments, small businesses, and music and ballet schools. The restaurants and coffee shops have since closed, along with many of the other establishments, and the anchor tenant now—perhaps fittingly given the experience of the South Loop School—is the private South Loop Montessori School, established in 2012. Tuition for elementary students is $13,860 per year.[1]

Back outside, I hop back on my bike and cycle into Dearborn Park.

The streets are largely empty at this hour on a weekday morning, save for a few dog walkers. More signs of life are visible in the park located at the development's southern end. There several moms are chatting while their toddlers dig in the sandbox. Another dog walker passes by. Nearly everyone I see is white.[2] By all appearances Dearborn Park seems to have fared well after all these years. Trees that were newly planted in the late 1970s are now mature, forming an inviting canopy over narrow interior streets. Building exteriors are seemingly well maintained, while plants, shrubbery, and lawns are carefully clipped. Maintenance workers are applying a fresh coat of paint to a fence bordering State Street as I ride past.

Yet as I cycle up and down the tree-lined streets, what stands out the most is not the appearance of Dearborn Park itself but rather what surrounds it. To the south, east, and west of the development are towering new residential buildings—some condo, some rental—catering to downtown professionals. One Thousand South Clark, a twenty-seven-story structure looking down on Dearborn Park from the west, boasts a ten-thousand-square-foot fitness facility, a sixty-foot indoor/outdoor swimming pool, and a one-sixth-mile rooftop running track. Monthly rentals for two-bedroom apartments start at $3,000. Three-floor townhomes, with terraces and 2,600 square feet of living space, rent for $6,800 per month. Residential buildings like this one extend for blocks in all three directions. I try to imagine what it was like when the first residents moved into Dearborn Park thirty-eight years ago—when none of this was here. Back then the fortresslike design that developers insisted on was understandable, perhaps even serving a purpose. Now it seems oddly superfluous, as if the yuppies living in Dearborn Park perceive some sinister element among their even wealthier yuppie neighbors living across the street.

To get the flavor of things I head east along Roosevelt Road toward Central Station, where former Mayor Richard M. Daley took up residence in the early 1990s. Daley no longer lives here, but his presence—along with the construction of Dearborn Park—is credited with helping to ignite the South Loop residential boom.[3] I pause momentarily at the corner of Roosevelt Road and Indiana Avenue. The view is dramatic. From the gentle slope I have just climbed I look down on Grant Park and Millennium Park to the north, framed by the spectacular downtown skyline. To the east is Lake Michigan and the museum campus. Behind me are two massive high-rise residential buildings, twin peaks towering over Grant Park's southern boundary. Central Station is a mix of high-rises and three-story brick townhomes, but cycling through the area it is the high-rises that command attention, and there are many of them—imposing structures of thirty stories or more in some cases. A residential building under construction at 1200 South Indiana will have seventy-six stories. The highest and best use of land in this portion of the South Loop seemingly knows few bounds, and for those who can afford it, this is high-density living at its finest, with breathtaking views and many of downtown Chicago's most popular attractions within easy walking distance.

It's almost noon. After a quick stop for lunch I head south along State Street. Below Sixteenth Street the new development begins to thin out considerably, as does the pedestrian traffic. At Cullerton Avenue, the northeast tower of Hilliard Homes suddenly emerges on my right—a reminder that despite the gentrification taking place, there is still a low-income presence here. Like the rest of the South Loop, Hilliard Homes has gone through a metamorphosis during the past two decades. The buildings, purchased from the CHA by a private developer in 1999, underwent an extensive $100 million renovation during the early 2000s, and the development is now operated as a partnership between the new owner and the CHA. Roughly half of Hilliard Homes' 654 units are reserved for public housing residents, the other half for moderate-income renters. All applicants are carefully screened, including criminal background checks.[4] I cycle around the perimeter of the development. Despite the unorthodox shape of the buildings—two round towers, two crescent-shaped structures—the development still has the feel of public housing, with its concrete exterior walls and fenced verandas. Still, residents have praised the renovations and the new management's close screening of tenants. With housing options for low- and moderate-income residents in the South Loop increasingly scarce, Hilliard Homes fills an important void. I wonder how long it will last.

Back on State Street I continue south, toward the once-massive corridor of high-rise public housing that lined the western side of the street for several unbroken miles. By this time I have nearly reached the southernmost boundary of the South Loop redevelopment area mapped out by the CCAC in its 1973 Chicago 21 Plan. Redevelopment has, for the most part, not yet penetrated this area. Weak demand for real estate is evident in numerous vacant lots lining the street. At Thirty-Fifth Street, ten blocks south of the CCAC's proposed redevelopment zone, I arrive at the northern end of the former Stateway Gardens CHA public housing development, part of Chicago's Bronzeville neighborhood. The distinctive high-rise towers have long since been demolished; in their place is a series of low-rise apartment buildings between three and five stories tall. Looking across Thirty-Fifth Street, I spot the familiar green and white logo of Starbucks. The new development, called Park Boulevard, will eventually include 1,316 housing units—a mixture of apartments, condominiums, townhouses, and single-family homes. Like Hilliard Homes, the project represents a partnership between the CHA and private developers. Roughly one-third of the housing units are public housing, one-third are subsidized affordable units, and one-third are market-rate units.[5] The buildings are an attractive mix of styles; none would seem out of place in the gentrifying South Loop. I ride down a side street and pause for a moment in a small, well-maintained park encircled by apartment buildings. Nothing here suggests the presence of danger of any kind. I imagine standing in this same spot twenty years earlier looking up at one of the massive high-rise public housing structures that once towered over the neighborhood. The difference is hard to fathom. Surely this represents an improvement.

Yet as I take in the surroundings, I cannot help but wonder what has become of those individuals who failed to pass the background checks, drug tests, and other intrusive screenings required of those seeking residence in attractive mixed-income developments such as this. A few moments later, heading east on Thirty-Seventh Street, I find a clue. As I cycle beneath the L tracks east of State Street, the surroundings change dramatically. Blight is everywhere. I pass by a low-rise wood-frame apartment building badly in need of paint and repairs. Several units are boarded up. Others look like they may be vacant. Nearby two-story single family homes or duplexes are in similar condition, some evidently unoccupied. Front yards are lined by rusting chain-link fences. There are numerous vacant lots, littered with trash. It is hard to imagine, but years earlier when Stateway Gardens was still here, these homes might have been considered a step above the notorious public housing project nearby. I look down the street. At the end of the block is a young man engaged in conversation with the driver of a car idling in the middle of the intersection. I wonder if a business transaction is taking place. Caution gets the best of me, and I decide it is time to turn around.

Neighborhoods like this one are ubiquitous on the city's South and West Sides, and they present vexing concerns. As everyone knows, Chicago's most pressing social problems—including homicides, gangs, drug trafficking, arrests, joblessness, substandard housing, and poor educational attainment—are disproportionately concentrated in places like these. Yet as urgent as these problems are and as badly as these neighborhoods cry out for rehabilitation, revitalization efforts today do not consume public officials in the way they did decades earlier, when the elimination of slums and blight rose to the top of the city's policy agenda. Policy today reflects a different orientation—a kind of thin-lipped pragmatism that finds success in incremental improvements that fall some distance short of the steps needed to create functional neighborhoods in the multitude of locations where dysfunction presently reigns. Public housing is in the midst of transformation, public education has been reformed, new antipoverty initiatives are regularly introduced, but the sense of urgency of the sort displayed years ago by leaders of the city's urban renewal program—and, before that, Progressive Era housing reformers—is not there. Only rarely do city officials today claim as their objective the wholesale transformation of the city's economically distressed communities, and even more infrequently do officials behave as if this is their objective. Instead, both public officials and civic leaders seem resigned to making the best of what all agree is an unfortunate situation—one deserving of attention but ultimately resistant to change.

If the behavior of the city's civic and political leaders suggests something less than alarm over the existence of vast areas of poverty and blight, the actions of the middle-class residents of Chicago's gentrifying areas—many of whom live in close proximity to impoverished communities—suggest a similar sort of accommodation. Occupants of the South Loop's new condominiums and apartment buildings are no doubt aware that areas of blight and concentrated poverty are not far away, but if this is a cause for concern it is not being reflected in real estate prices. These families and individuals have chosen to live there knowing full well that nearby economically distressed areas are unlikely to be transformed anytime soon. Their commitment to the area is not contingent on any ongoing effort to eradicate slum conditions on the city's South and West Sides and faith that such efforts will ultimately prevail. Instead, like the city's civic and political leaders, these residents seem to have largely come to terms with the status quo. Any concerns they may have for their personal safety and property are eased somewhat by sophisticated security systems, a visible police presence in the area, and, in the most exclusive buildings, twenty-four-hour doormen.[6]

Back on State Street, I head north toward the Loop, three miles away. A short detour to the east takes me past Lake Meadows and Prairie Shores. I pull over to the side of King Drive, get off my bike, and gaze up at the Corbusian steel and glass towers, artifacts of an earlier paradigm for engaging with the city's slum districts. Decades ago, this was to be the start of an all-out effort to rid the city of its slum and blighted areas—an effort that would not end until the last blighted building in the last blighted neighborhood was replaced. How far we have come from this kind of thinking. Certainly urban renewal was not the answer; there can be no argument there. Yet perhaps there is something to be learned from the insistence of leaders of the city's renewal program that few urban problems were more urgent than the plight of slum dwellers. As Ferd Kramer, speaking to a group of Baltimore business leaders in 1952, implored, "We all recognize that slums are the spawning ground not only of disease and delinquency, but also of insecurity and frustration. They are the most strident examples of Democracy's failure, and they are here, spreading for miles, to be seen, photographed, and used against us by our enemies."[7] Cold War undertones aside, how many of today's political leaders would speak with such passion about the economically distressed communities of the present? How many would insist that the days of tolerating such conditions must end—that complacency must give way to a renewed commitment to create healthy, livable neighborhoods in all areas of the city?

I look at my watch. It's almost 4:00 p.m. My train leaves in an hour. Ahead of me the downtown skyline beckons, several miles north. Somewhere out there, high up in one of those South Loop high-rises I rode past earlier, somebody is fixing his gaze in this direction. From the living-room window of his luxury condominium he looks out on this part of the city every day, but it is as foreign to him as another country. The city he knows is elsewhere—in the South Loop, Millennium Park, downtown, and neighborhoods of a certain kind. The problems of the South Side are not his problems, and he does not think of them as he looks beyond Prairie Shores and Lake Meadows, beyond Hyde Park farther south. For him Chicago is a place of opportunity and excitement—a place to make money, to build a career, to enjoy life to the fullest. I get back on my bike and start pedaling.

Notes

Chapter One

1. Max Weber, Hans Gerth, and C. Wright Mills, *From Max Weber: Essays in Sociology* (New York: Oxford University Press, 1946), 280.

2. Chicago Police Department, Clearmap Crime Summary, accessed January 1, 2019, gis.chicagopolice.org/clearmap_crime_sums/startpage.htm#.

3. John J. Betancur and Janet L. Smith, *Claiming Neighborhood: New Ways of Understanding Urban Change* (Urbana: University of Illinois Press, 2016), 43; Nathalie P. Voorhees Center for Neighborhood and Community Improvement, *The Socioeconomic Change of Chicago's Community Areas (1970–2010)* (Chicago, 2014).

4. Robert J. Sampson, *Great American City: Chicago and the Enduring Neighborhood Effect* (Chicago: University of Chicago Press, 2012), 104–5.

5. Louise Drusilla Walker, "The Chicago Association of Commerce: Its History and Policies" (PhD diss., University of Chicago, 1941), 179; Report of the Committee on Housing Conditions, April 12, 1909, City Club Papers, Chicago History Museum Research Center (hereafter City Club Papers), box 10, folder 1.

6. Chicago Committee for Housing Action, "A Housing and Redevelopment Program for Chicago," 1947, 1.

7. Metropolitan Housing Council, "Reclaiming Chicago's Blighted Areas" (Chicago: Metropolitan Housing Council, 1946), Metropolitan Planning Council Records, University of Illinois at Chicago, Special Collections and University Archives (hereafter MPC Records), box 23, folder 279; Ferd Kramer, speech to South Side Renting Men's Association, March 14, 1945, Ferdinand Kramer Papers, University of Chicago, Special Collections Research Center (hereafter Kramer Papers), box 4, folder 3.

8. Jane Jacobs, *The Death and Life of Great American Cities* (New York: Random House, 1961).

9. Peter A. Hall, "Policy Paradigms, Social Learning, and the State: The Case of Economic Policymaking in Britain," *Comparative Politics* 25 (1993): 275–96.

10. John L. Campbell, "Institutional Analysis and the Role of Ideas in Political Economy," *Theory and Society* 27 (1998): 384.

11. Campbell, "Institutional Analysis and the Role of Ideas in Political Economy," 389.

12. Rawi Abdelal, Mark Blyth, and Craig Parsons, "Introduction: Constructing the International Economy," in Rawi Abdelal, Mark Blyth, and Craig Parsons, eds., *Constructing the International Economy* (Ithaca, NY: Cornell University Press, 2010), 3.

13. Mark Blyth, "Structures Do Not Come with an Instruction Sheet: Interests, Ideas, and Progress in Political Science," *Perspectives on Politics* 1 (2003): 695–706; Andreas Gofas and Colin Hay, "Varieties of Ideational Explanation," in Andreas Gofas and Colin Hay, eds., *The Role of Ideas in Political Analysis: A Portrait of Contemporary Debates* (London: Routledge, 2010), 13–55; Colin Hay, "Ideas and the Construction of Interests," in Daniel Béland and Robert Henry Cox, eds., *Ideas and Politics in Social Science Research* (New York: Oxford University Press, 2011), 65–82.

14. Judith Goldstein and Robert O. Keohane, "Ideas and Foreign Policy: An Analytical Framework," in Judith Goldstein and Robert O. Keohane, eds., *Ideas and Foreign Policy: Beliefs, Institutions, and Political Change* (Ithaca, NY: Cornell University Press, 1993), 4; Mark Blyth, *Great Transformations: Economic Ideas and Institutional Change in the Twentieth Century* (Cambridge: Cambridge University Press), 39–40.

15. Hay, "Ideas and the Construction of Interests," 72–73.

16. Blyth, *Great Transformations*; Mark Blyth, "Powering, Puzzling, or Persuading? The Mechanisms of Building Institutional Orders," *International Studies Quarterly* 51 (2007): 761–77; Hay, "Ideas and the Construction of Interests," 70–71.

17. There are several perspectives in the ideational literature on why knowledge of an actor's material interests may be insufficient to explain behavior. Blyth argues that periods of economic crisis create uncertainty among actors about how to proceed. At such times "actors are unsure as to what their interests actually are, let alone how to realize them." Ideas become necessary to interpret the crisis to actors and to provide possible solutions. "They diagnose 'what has gone wrong' and 'what is to be done.'" See Blyth, *Great Transformations*, 9–10. Others argue that uncertainty in choice situations is not limited to times of crisis but is instead far more pervasive. As Judith Goldstein maintains, "Political choice invariably occurs in conditions of uncertainty: entrepreneurs rarely know which policy idea will maximize their interests." See Judith Goldstein, *Ideas, Interests, and American Trade Policy* (Ithaca, NY: Cornell University Press, 1993), 3. In this view, the implication is that uncertainty is the rule rather than the ex-

ception, meaning that ideas must matter most if not all the time. Finally, some scholars argue there may in some instances be multiple outcomes that could be considered optimal for a given actor or set of actors. In such cases, choices cannot be explained by reference to interests alone. See Goldstein and Keohane, "Ideas and Foreign Policy," 17–20; and G. John Ikenberry, "Creating Yesterday's New World Order: Keynesian 'New Thinking' and the Anglo-American Postwar Settlement," in Judith Goldstein and Robert O. Keohane, eds., *Ideas and Foreign Policy: Beliefs, Institutions, and Political Change* (Ithaca, NY: Cornell University Press, 1993), 57–86.

18. Alexander Wendt, *Social Theory of International Politics* (Cambridge: Cambridge University Press, 1999), chap. 3.

19. Elisabeth Anderson, "Experts, Ideas, and Policy Change: The Russell Sage Foundation and Small Loan Reform," *Theory and Society* 37 (2008): 278. Sheri Berman makes a similar argument: "Ideational analysts argue that interests are neither given, nor can they be inferred from the (economic) environment; instead, they evolve out of the ideas and beliefs held by actors themselves." See Sheri Berman, *The Social Democratic Moment: Ideas and Politics in the Making of Interwar Europe* (Cambridge, MA: Harvard University Press, 1998), 30.

20. Abdelal, Blyth, and Parsons, "Introduction: Constructing the International Economy," 9.

21. Blyth, "Structures Do Not Come with an Instruction Sheet," 698.

22. John L. Campbell, "Ideas, Politics, and Public Policy," *Annual Review of Sociology* 28 (2002): 29.

23. Craig Parsons, "Showing Ideas as Causes: The Origins of the European Union," *International Organization* 56 (2002): 52.

24. Clarence N. Stone, *Regime Politics: Governing Atlanta, 1946–1988* (Lawrence: University Press of Kansas, 1989). For a more recent presentation of Stone's view of the role of ideas in urban political development, see Clarence N. Stone, "Reflections in Regime Politics: From Governing Coalition to Urban Political Order," *Urban Affairs Review* 51 (2015): 101–37.

25. Campbell, "Institutional Analysis and the Role of Ideas in Political Economy," 385.

26. Vivien A. Schmidt, "Ideas and Discourse in Transformational Political Economic Change in Europe," in Grace Skogstad, ed., *Policy Paradigms, Transnationalism, and Domestic Politics* (Toronto: University of Toronto Press, 2011), 46.

27. Campbell, "Institutional Analysis and the Role of Ideas in Political Economy," 386; Grace Skogstad and Vivien A. Schmidt, "Introduction: Policy Paradigms, Transnationalism, and Domestic Politics," in Skogstad, ed., *Policy Paradigms, Transnationalism, and Domestic Politics*, 7; Berman, *Social Democratic Moment*, 21.

28. Campbell, "Ideas, Politics, and Public Policy," 28.

29. Jal Mehta, "The Varied Roles of Ideas in Politics: From 'Whether' to 'How,'" in Béland and Cox, eds., *Ideas and Politics in Social Science Research*, 44.

30. Marcus Carson, Tom R. Burns, and Dolores Calvo, eds., *Paradigms in Public Policy: Theory and Practice of Paradigm Shifts in the EU* (Frankfurt am Main: Peter Lang, 2010), 17.

31. David Harvey, *A Brief History of Neoliberalism* (Oxford: Oxford University Press, 2005); Manfred B. Steger and Ravi K. Roy, *Neoliberalism: A Very Short Introduction* (Oxford: Oxford University Press, 2010); Bob Jessop, "Liberalism, Neoliberalism, and Urban Governance: A State-Theoretical Perspective," *Antipode* 34 (2002): 452–72; Jamie Peck and Adam Tickell, "Neoliberalizing Space," *Antipode* 34 (2002): 380–404.

32. Timothy P. R. Weaver, *Blazing the Neoliberal Trail: Urban Political Development in the United States and the United Kingdom* (Philadelphia: University of Pennsylvania Press, 2016). For more on neoliberalism and urban development see Jason Hackworth, *The Neoliberal City: Governance, Ideology, and Development in American Urbanism* (Ithaca, NY: Cornell University Press, 2007).

33. Peter A. Hall, "Policy Paradigms, Social Learning, and the State: The Case of Economic Policymaking in Britain," *Comparative Politics* 25 (1993): 275–96.

34. Hall, "Policy Paradigms, Social Learning, and the State," 279.

35. Hall, "Policy Paradigms, Social Learning, and the State."

36. Alan M. Jacobs, "How Do Ideas Matter? Mental Models and Attention in German Pension Politics," *Comparative Political Studies* 42 (2009): 252–79.

37. Jacobs, "How Do Ideas Matter?," 259–60.

38. Path dependence is a concept used in historical institutionalist scholarship to explain how institutions develop over time. The argument is that institutions and institutional arrangements frequently exhibit stability over extended periods. At key junctures, however, choice points surface at which consequential change is possible. Once a new institutional "path" is selected, positive feedback mechanisms tend to reinforce this trajectory until the next choice point appears. See Paul Pierson, *Politics in Time: History, Institutions, and Social Analysis* (Princeton, NJ: Princeton University Press, 2004); and James Mahoney, "Path Dependence in Historical Sociology," *Theory and Society* 29 (2000): 507–48.

39. Sheri Berman, "Ideas, Norms, and Culture in Political Analysis," *Comparative Politics* 33 (2001): 239.

40. Kathryn Sikkink, *Ideas and Institutions: Developmentalism in Brazil and Argentina* (Ithaca, NY: Cornell University Press, 1991): 2.

41. Goldstein and Keohane, *Ideas and Foreign Policy*, 21.

42. William H. Riker, "Implications from the Disequilibrium of Majority

Rule for the Study of Institutions," *American Political Science Review* 74 (1980): 432–46.

43. Goldstein and Keohane, *Ideas and Foreign Policy*, 21.

44. Daniel Béland and Robert Henry Cox, "Introduction: Ideas and Politics," in Béland and Cox, eds., *Ideas and Politics in Social Science Research*, 13.

45. Parsons, "Showing Ideas as Causes."

46. Weaver, *Blazing the Neoliberal Trail.*

47. Goldstein, *Ideas, Interests, and American Trade Policy*, 12; Hall, "Policy Paradigms, Social Learning, and the State"; Sheri Berman, "Ideational Theorizing in the Social Sciences since 'Policy Paradigms, Social Learning, and the State,'" *Governance* 26 (2013) 217–37; Campbell, "Ideas, Politics, and Public Policy."

48. Hall, "Policy Paradigms, Social Learning, and the State," 278. See also Thomas S. Kuhn, *The Structure of Scientific Revolutions*, 2nd ed. (Chicago: University of Chicago Press, 1970).

49. Frank R. Baumgartner and Bryan D. Jones, *Agendas and Instability in American Politics* (Chicago: University of Chicago Press, 1993).

50. Robert C. Lieberman, "Ideas, Institutions, and Political Order: Explaining Political Change," *American Political Science Review* 96 (2002): 697–712; Karen Orren and Stephen Skowronek, "Beyond the Iconography of Order: Notes for a 'New Institutionalism,'" in Lawrence C. Dodd and Calvin Jillson, eds., *The Dynamics of American Politics: Approaches and Interpretations* (Boulder, CO: Westview, 1994), 311–30.

51. Lieberman, "Ideas, Institutions, and Political Order," 701.

52. Skogstad and Schmidt, "Introduction: Policy Paradigms, Transnationalism, and Domestic Politics," 10.

53. Kuhn, *Structure of Scientific Revolutions*, 84–85.

54. Kuhn, *Structure of Scientific Revolutions*, 166.

55. Kathleen R. McNamara, *The Currency of Ideas: Monetary Politics in the European Union* (Ithaca, NY: Cornell University Press, 1998); Goldstein, *Ideas, Interests, and American Trade Policy*, 13–14; Berman, "Ideas, Norms, and Culture in Political Analysis," 234; Blyth, *Great Transformations*, 4–7.

56. Campbell, "Ideas, Politics, and Public Policy," 23.

57. Berman, "Ideas, Norms, and Culture in Political Analysis," 234.

58. Stephen Skowronek, *Building a New American State: The Expansion of National Administrative Capacities, 1877–1920* (Cambridge: Cambridge University Press, 1982); Theda Skocpol, *Protecting Soldiers and Mothers: The Political Origins of Social Policy in the United States* (Cambridge, MA: Harvard University Press, 1992).

59. See especially Margaret Weir and Theda Skocpol, "State Structures and the Possibilities for 'Keynesian' Responses to the Great Depression in Sweden, Britain, and the United States," in Peter B. Evans, Dietrich Rueschemeyer, and

Theda Skocpol, eds., *Bringing the State Back In* (Cambridge: Cambridge University Press, 1985), 107–63.

60. Schmidt, "Ideas and Discourse in Transformational Political Economic Change in Europe," 42. See also Skogstad and Schmidt, "Introduction: Policy Paradigms, Transnationalism, and Domestic Politics," 9–10.

61. Skocpol, *Protecting Soldiers and Mothers*, 59. On the feedback effects of public policies see also E. E. Schattschneider, *Politics, Pressures, and the Tariff* (New York: Prentice-Hall, 1935), 288; Paul Pierson, "When Effect Becomes Cause: Policy Feedback and Political Change," *World Politics* 45 (1993): 595–628; Jacob S. Hacker, *The Divided Welfare State: The Battle over Public and Private Social Benefits in the United States* (Cambridge: Cambridge University Press, 2002); and Evelyne Huber and John D. Stephens, *Development and Crisis of the Welfare State: Parties and Policies in Global Markets* (Chicago: University of Chicago Press, 2001).

62. There is an extensive literature on institutional path dependence in historical institutionalist scholarship. For important works see Pierson, *Politics in Time*; Paul Pierson, "Increasing Returns, Path Dependence, and the Study of Politics," *American Political Science Review* 94 (2000): 251–67; Paul Pierson, "Not Just What, but *When*: Timing and Sequence in Political Processes," *Studies in American Political Development* 14 (2000): 72–92; James Mahoney, *The Legacies of Liberalism: Path Dependence and Political Regimes in Central America* (Baltimore: Johns Hopkins University Press, 2001); Mahoney, "Path Dependence in Historical Sociology"; Jack A. Goldstone, "Initial Conditions, General Laws, Path Dependence, and Explanation in Historical Sociology," *American Journal of Sociology* 104 (1998): 829–45.

63. Kathleen Thelen, *How Institutions Evolve: The Political Economy of Skills in Germany, Britain, the United States, and Japan* (Cambridge: Cambridge University Press, 2004). See also James Mahoney and Kathleen Thelen, "A Theory of Gradual Institutional Change," in James Mahoney and Kathleen Thelen, eds., *Explaining Institutional Change: Ambiguity, Agency, and Power* (Cambridge: Cambridge University Press, 2010), 1–37; Kathleen Thelen, "How Institutions Evolve: Insights from Comparative Historical Analysis," in James Mahoney and Dietrich Reuschemeyer, eds., *Comparative Historical Analysis in the Social Sciences* (Cambridge: Cambridge University Press, 2003), 208–40; Kathleen Thelen, "Historical Institutionalism in Comparative Politics," *Annual Review of Political Science* 2 (1999): 369–404; Wolfgang Streek and Kathleen Thelen, *Beyond Continuity: Institutional Change in Advanced Political Economies* (Oxford: Oxford University Press, 2005).

64. Thelen, *How Institutions Evolve*, 35.

65. Mahoney and Thelen, "Theory of Gradual Institutional Change," 16. See also Jack Lucas, "Urban Governance and the American Political Development Approach," *Urban Affairs Review* 53 (2017): 338–61.

66. Mahoney and Thelen, "Theory of Gradual Institutional Change," 18.

67. For an example of the application of the concepts of layering and conversion to explain ideational change, see Daniel Béland, "Ideas and Institutional Change in Social Security: Conversion, Layering, and Policy Drift," *Social Science Quarterly* 88 (2007): 20–38.

68. Skogstad and Schmidt, "Introduction: Policy Paradigms, Transnationalism, and Domestic Politics," 10.

69. Karen Orren and Stephen Skowronek, "Institutions and Intercurrence: Theory Building in the Fullness of Time," in Ian Shapiro and Russell Hardin, eds., *Political Order: Nomos XXXVIII* (New York: New York University Press, 1996), 111–46. See also Karen Orren and Stephen Skowronek, *The Search for American Political Development* (Cambridge: Cambridge University Press, 2004); Karen Orren and Stephen Skowronek, "The Study of American Political Development," in Ira Katznelson and Helen V. Milner, eds., *Political Science: The State of the Discipline* (New York: W. W. Norton, 2002), 722–54; Orren and Skowronek, "Beyond the Iconography of Order." For an insightful application of the APD approach to the study of urban governance, see Lucas, "Urban Governance and the American Political Development Approach."

70. Lieberman, "Ideas, Institutions, and Political Order," 702.

71. Thelen, "How Institutions Evolve," 228–30.

72. Robert H. Salisbury, "Urban Politics: The New Convergence of Power," *Journal of Politics* 26 (1964): 775–97. See also Arnold R. Hirsch, *Making the Second Ghetto: Race and Housing in Chicago, 1940–1960* (Chicago: University of Chicago Press, 1983); Gregory D. Squires, ed., *Unequal Partnerships: The Political Economy of Urban Redevelopment in Postwar America* (New Brunswick, NJ: Rutgers University Press, 1989); Chester W. Hartman, *Yerba Buena: Land Grab and Community Resistance in San Francisco* (San Francisco: Glide Publications, 1974); Stone, *Regime Politics*; Roy Lubove, *Twentieth-Century Pittsburgh: Government, Business, and Environmental Change* (New York: John Wiley & Sons, 1969); Jon C. Teaford, *The Rough Road to Renaissance: Urban Revitalization in America, 1940–1985* (Baltimore: Johns Hopkins University Press, 1990); Barbara Ferman, *Challenging the Growth Machine: Neighborhood Politics in Chicago and Pittsburgh* (Lawrence: University Press of Kansas, 1996); Clarence N. Stone and Heywood T. Sanders, eds., *The Politics of Urban Development* (Lawrence: University Press of Kansas, 1987); Susan S. Fainstein, Norman I. Fainstein, Richard Child Hill, Dennis Judd, and Michael Peter Smith, eds., *Restructuring the City: The Political Economy of Urban Redevelopment* (New York: Longman, 1983); Thomas H. O'Connor, *Building a New Boston: Politics and Urban Renewal, 1950–1970* (Boston: Northeastern University Press, 1993).

73. Richard Child Hill, "Crisis in the Motor City: The Politics of Economic Development in Detroit," in Fainstein et al, eds., *Restructuring the City*, 80–125.

74. Mike Davis, *City of Quartz: Excavating the Future in Los Angeles* (London: Verso, 1990).

75. William Julius Wilson, *The Truly Disadvantaged: The Inner City, the Underclass, and Public Policy* (Chicago: University of Chicago Press, 1987); William Julius Wilson, *When Work Disappears: The World of the New Urban Poor* (New York: Vintage Books, 1996); Thomas J. Sugrue, *The Origins of the Urban Crisis: Race and Inequality in Postwar Detroit* (Princeton, NJ: Princeton University Press, 1996); Thomas J. Sugrue, "The Structures of Urban Poverty: The Reorganization of Space and Work in Three Periods of American History," in Michael B. Katz, ed., *The "Underclass" Debate: Views from History* (Princeton, NJ: Princeton University Press, 1993), 85–117; John D. Kasarda, "Urban Change and Minority Opportunities," in Paul E. Peterson, ed., *The New Urban Reality* (Washington, DC: Brookings Institution, 1985); John D. Kasarda, "Urban Transition and the Underclass," *Annals of the American Academy of Political and Social Science* 501 (1989): 26–47.

76. John Hull Mollenkopf and Manuel Castells, *Dual City: Restructuring New York* (New York: Russell Sage Foundation, 1991).

77. Sam Bass Warner Jr., *The Private City: Philadelphia in Three Periods of Growth* (Philadelphia: University of Pennsylvania Press, 1968).

78. My thanks to Timothy Weaver for this suggestion. See Rogers M. Smith, "Which Comes First, the Ideas or the Institutions?" in Ian Shapiro, Stephen Skowronek, and Daniel Galvin, eds., *Rethinking Political Institutions: The Art of the State* (New York: New York University Press, 2006), 111. On the combined importance of ideas, interests, and institutions in political development, see also Lieberman, "Ideas, Institutions, and Political Order"; Orren and Skowronek, *Search for American Political Development*; and Timothy P. R. Weaver, "By Design or by Default: Varieties of Neoliberal Urban Development," *Urban Affairs Review* 54 (2016): 238.

Chapter Two

1. Hugh Heclo, *Modern Social Politics in Britain and Sweden: From Relief to Income Maintenance* (New Haven, CT: Yale University Press, 1974), 312.

2. "To Discuss the Housing Problem," *Chicago Tribune*, January 25, 1897, 4.

3. Thomas Lee Philpott, *The Slum and the Ghetto: Immigrants, Blacks, and Reformers in Chicago, 1880–1930* (Belmont, CA: Wadsworth, 1991), 93–94.

4. Philpott, *The Slum and the Ghetto*, 31.

5. Warner, *Private City*.

6. Donald L. Miller, *City of the Century: The Epic of Chicago and the Making of America* (New York: Simon & Schuster, 1996), 488.

7. Miller, *City of the Century*; Finis Farr, *Chicago: A Personal History of*

America's Most American City (New Rochelle, NY: Arlington House, 1973); Bessie Louise Pierce, *A History of Chicago*, vol. 3, *The Rise of a Modern City* (New York: Alfred A. Knopf, 1957).

8. Miller, *City of the Century.*

9. Charles Edward Merriam, *Chicago: A More Intimate View of Urban Politics* (New York: Macmillan, 1929), 100; Harold F. Gosnell, *Machine Politics: Chicago Model* (Chicago: University of Chicago Press, 1937); Dick Simpson, *Rogues, Rebels, and Rubber Stamps: The Politics of the Chicago City Council from 1863 to the Present* (Boulder, CO: Westview, 2001).

10. Sidney I. Roberts, "The Municipal Voters' League and Chicago's Boodlers," *Journal of the Illinois State Historical Society* 53 (1960): 117–48.

11. Roberts, "Municipal Voters' League and Chicago's Boodlers," 120–28; William T. Stead, *If Christ Came to Chicago!* (Chicago: Laird & Lee, 1894), 177–86; Simpson, *Rogues, Rebels, and Rubber Stamps*, 62.

12. See, for example, "A Boodle Ordinance," *Chicago Tribune*, October 10, 1888, 4; "One Way of Regulating Boodle Aldermen," *Chicago Tribune*, August 16, 1891, 12; "Boodlers Must Go," *Chicago Tribune*, March 18, 1892, 1; and "Distribution of the Bribe Money," *Chicago Tribune*, March 26, 1892, 2.

13. Miller, *City of the Century.*

14. Miller, *City of the Century*, 434; Loomis Mayfield, "The Reorganization of Urban Politics: The Chicago Growth Machine after World War II" (PhD diss., University of Pittsburgh, 1996).

15. Farr, *Chicago*, 200–201.

16. Maureen A. Flanagan, *Charter Reform in Chicago* (Carbondale: Southern Illinois University Press, 1987), 37.

17. Lincoln Steffens, *The Shame of the Cities* (New York: Hill and Wang, 1962), 167.

18. Roberts, "Municipal Voters' League," 143.

19. Michael Patrick McCarthy, "Businessmen and Professionals in Municipal Reform: The Chicago Experience, 1887–1920" (PhD diss., Northwestern University, 1971), 32.

20. McCarthy, "Businessmen and Professionals in Municipal Reform," 33.

21. Philpott, *The Slum and the Ghetto*, 85.

22. Jane Addams, *Twenty Years at Hull House* (New York: Macmillan, 1912), 316.

23. Jane Addams, "Why the Ward Boss Rules," in Christopher Lynch, ed., *The Social Thought of Jane Addams* (Indianapolis: Bobbs-Merrill, 1965), 124–33. Addams observed that the alderman "bails out his constituents when they are arrested, or says a good word to the police justice when they appear before him for trial; uses his 'pull' with the magistrate when they are likely to be fined for a civil misdemeanor, or sees what he can do to 'fix up matters' with the State's attorney when the charge is really a serious one" (124).

24. "Studying Social Problems," *Chicago Tribune*, July 16, 1899, 44.

25. Cyrus McCormick was the inventor of the mechanical reaper and founder of the McCormick Harvesting Machine Company, which, along with several other companies, became International Harvester in 1902. His daughter Anita McCormick Blaine was a wealthy philanthropist who used the family fortune to support progressive causes, including housing reform. See Gilbert A. Harrison, *A Timeless Affair: The Life of Anita McCormick Blaine* (Chicago: University of Chicago Press, 1979).

26. Robert Hunter, *Tenement Conditions in Chicago* (Chicago: City Homes Association, 1901).

27. Hunter, *Tenement Conditions in Chicago*, 92.

28. "Report on Tenements," *Chicago Tribune*, June 3, 1901, 12; see also "Tenement Conditions in Chicago: Report of Investigation by the City Homes Association," *Chicago Tribune*, June 2, 1901, 37.

29. Hunter, *Tenement Conditions in Chicago*, 15–16.

30. "Law to Protect the Tenant," *Chicago Daily News*, December 18, 1902, 19; "Council Passes Tenement Rule," *Chicago Tribune*, December 18, 1902.

31. Hunter, *Tenement Conditions in Chicago*, 19.

32. "For Better Tenement Houses," *Chicago Tribune*, December 19, 1902.

33. Philpott, *The Slum and the Ghetto*, 102–3; Edith Abbott, *The Tenements of Chicago, 1908–1935* (Chicago: University of Chicago Press, 1936), 59–61.

34. Abbott, *Tenements of Chicago*, 62.

35. Philpott, *The Slum and the Ghetto*, 104.

36. Henry E. Cordell to George H. Holt, April 12, 1910, City Club Papers, box 11, folder 6; Philpott, *The Slum and the Ghetto*, 104–5.

37. "Asks Hull House to Bring Proof," *Chicago Tribune*, April 15, 1903, 16; "Filth in 19th Ward," *Chicago Daily News*, April 17, 1903, 16.

38. "Asks Hull House to Bring Proof"; see also "The Slums Landlord," *Chicago Tribune*, April 24, 1903, 12; and Abbott, *Tenements of Chicago*, 63–64.

39. "The Tender Heart of the Alderman," *Chicago Tribune*, January 8, 1903, 6.

40. "Slums Landlord."

41. Louise Drusilla Walker, "The Chicago Association of Commerce: Its History and Policies" (PhD diss., University of Chicago, 1941), 179; Report of the Committee on Housing Conditions, April 12, 1909, City Club Papers, box 10, folder 1. The City Club Committee on Housing Conditions began meeting in October 1908. The Association of Commerce housing improvement committee formed in 1911. The two groups worked closely with one another.

42. Carl Smith, *Urban Disorder and the Shape of Belief: The Great Chicago Fire, the Haymarket Bomb, and the Model Town of Pullman* (Chicago: University of Chicago Press, 1995). See also Richard Schneirov, *Labor and Urban Politics: Class Conflict and the Origins of Modern Liberalism in Chicago, 1864–97* (Urbana: University of Illinois Press, 1998).

43. Philpott, *The Slum and the Ghetto*, 231.

44. "Studying Social Problems," *Chicago Tribune*, July 16, 1899, 44.

45. Philpott, *The Slum and the Ghetto*, 231.

46. "Attack the Slums," *Chicago Tribune*, July 7, 1913, 6.

47. Carl Smith, *The Plan of Chicago: Daniel Burnham and the Remaking of the American City* (Chicago: University of Chicago Press, 2006).

48. The omission was deliberate. Planners at the time believed that private housing fell outside the scope of city planning; city plans should concern themselves principally with public infrastructure, not private property. See Philpott, *The Slum and the Ghetto*, 108.

49. McCarthy, "Businessmen and Professionals in Municipal Reform," 138.

50. "More Inspectors Needed," *Chicago Tribune*, December 15, 1911, 12.

51. "'Model Houses' for City's Poor," *Chicago Tribune*, June 29, 1911, 14.

52. Philpott, *The Slum and the Ghetto*, 107; minutes, Committee on Housing Conditions, October 30, 1911, City Club Papers, box 13, folder 3; Report of the Committee on Housing Conditions of the City Club of Chicago, April 16, 1912, City Club Papers, box 13, folder 3. Philpott reports that Ball also used his connections in the settlement house community to enlist settlement workers as "unofficial inspectors and research associates" whose efforts complemented the activities of the Sanitary Bureau's official inspectors. Ball further developed close ties with the Chicago School of Civics and Philanthropy, whose faculty members and graduate students surveyed seventeen tenement areas between 1908 and 1917, providing Ball with useful information with which to assess the performance of the tenement house ordinance of 1902 and to develop support for housing reform.

53. Report of the Committee on Housing Conditions, April 12, 1909, City Club Papers, box 10, folder 1; Philpott, *The Slum and the Ghetto*, 107.

54. Philpott, *The Slum and the Ghetto*, 106.

55. Philpott, *The Slum and the Ghetto*, 107.

56. Minutes, Committee on Housing Conditions, January 21, 1909, City Club Papers, box 10, folder 4. The City Club Committee on Housing Conditions took a strong interest in the proposal for a tenement house department, bringing Ball in for a December 1908 meeting to present on the pros and cons of creating such a department. While committee members ultimately chose not to pursue the initiative at that time, they found considerable merit in the idea, concluding that such a department would be necessary for adequate enforcement of housing laws.

57. Philpott, *The Slum and the Ghetto*, 110. Philpott quotes Ball's new chief assistant: "I got that appointment from Mayor Thompson in recognition of the work I did in the 50th precinct of the 33rd Ward."

58. Draft memorandum re Committee on Housing Conditions Activities, 1915, City Club Papers, box 17, folder 3.

59. "Hope Springs in Vain in Breast of Flat Seeker," *Chicago Tribune*, April 9, 1919, 10.

60. Abbott, *Tenements of Chicago*, 66.

61. "Chicago Short 50,000 Houses; U.S., 1,000,000," *Chicago Tribune*, May 22, 1919, 13. According to the *Tribune*, the housing shortage was "probably as great as the city has ever known." See "Wiping Out the Slums," *Chicago Tribune*, April 19, 1919, 8.

62. "May Take City Decade to Catch Up on Housing," *Chicago Tribune*, December 28, 1919.

63. "May Take City Decade to Catch Up on Housing," *Chicago Tribune*.

64. Philpott, *The Slum and the Ghetto*, 117.

65. See Alzada P. Comstock, "Chicago Housing Conditions, VI: The Problem of the Negro," *American Journal of Sociology* 18 (1912): 241–42. The study, done by a graduate student under the supervision of Hull House resident and University of Chicago professor Sophia Breckinridge, was one of the first to document housing conditions for African Americans. Philpott notes that the study was significant as well because it identified a "color line" outside which it was nearly impossible for African Americans to find housing. Two separate markets thus existed for housing: one for blacks and another for whites. See Philpott, *The Slum and the Ghetto*, 157–60.

66. Philpott, *The Slum and the Ghetto*, 163–71. See also Chicago Commission on Race Relations, *The Negro in Chicago: A Study of Race Relations and a Race Riot* (Chicago, 1922); and Allan H. Spear, *Black Chicago: The Making of a Negro Ghetto, 1890–1920* (Chicago: University of Chicago Press, 1967), 209–12.

67. Philpott, *The Slum and the Ghetto*, 169. See also Chicago Commission on Race Relations, *Negro in Chicago*; William M. Tuttle Jr., *Race Riot: Chicago in the Red Summer of 1919* (Urbana: University of Illinois Press, 1996); and Spear, *Black Chicago*, 212–13.

68. Carl Sandburg, *The Chicago Race Riots, July, 1919* (New York: Harcourt, Brace and Howe, 1919); Chicago Commission on Race Relations, *Negro in Chicago*; Tuttle, *Race Riot*.

69. Chicago Commission on Race Relations, *Negro in Chicago*. See also Philpott, *The Slum and the Ghetto*, 226.

70. Both before and after the race riots, black and white civic groups—including the Chicago Urban League, the Chicago Real Estate Board, and the Association of Commerce—developed plans for building programs in the Black Belt. While black leaders were hesitant to be identified with building efforts premised on the principle of segregation, several prominent blacks stated publicly that many African Americans would be content to remain within the Black Belt if they had access to adequate housing. No serious discussion of integrated housing developments took place. See Philpott, *The Slum and the Ghetto*, chap. 9.

71. Philpott, *The Slum and the Ghetto*, 94.

72. "Enforcement of Housing Laws," *Chicago Tribune*, January 23, 1902, 12.

73. "New Tenement Idea Hit," *Chicago Tribune*, October 8, 1906, 6.

74. Philpott, *The Slum and the Ghetto*, 91. See also Abbott, *Tenements of Chicago*, 481–83.

75. Leila Houghteling, *The Income and Standard of Living of Unskilled Laborers in Chicago* (Chicago: University of Chicago Press, 1927).

76. Elizabeth A. Hughes, "Living Conditions for Small-Wage Earners in Chicago" (City of Chicago, Department of Public Welfare, 1925).

77. Abbott, *Tenements of Chicago*, 483.

78. Vivien Hart, *Bound by Our Constitution: Women, Workers, and the Minimum Wage* (Princeton, NJ: Princeton University Press, 1994); Laura Murphy, "An 'Indestructible Right': John Ryan and the Catholic Origins of the U.S. Living Wage Movement, 1906–1938," *Labor: Studies in Working Class History of the Americas* 6 (2009): 57–86.

79. Hart, *Bound by Our Constitution*.

80. Murphy, "'Indestructible Right,'" 78. The movement for a minimum wage had a strong Chicago connection. Florence Kelley, a nationally prominent social reformer and early Hull House resident, was general secretary of the National Consumers' League, the most active national group on minimum-wage legislation in the US. See Hart, *Bound by Our Constitution*, chapter 4; and Kathryn Kish Sklar, *Florence Kelley and the Nation's Work: The Rise of Women's Political Culture, 1830–1900* (New Haven, CT: Yale University Press, 1995).

81. "Women Demand Wages Be Fixed," *Chicago Tribune*, September 29, 1912, 1.

82. "Asks State Law for Living Wage," *Chicago Tribune*, January 28, 1913, 2.

83. "Call Rosenwald in Vice Quiz," *Chicago Daily News*, March 2, 1913, 3; "Big Store Heads Tell of Wages at 'Slavery' Inquiry," *Chicago Tribune*, March 8, 1913, 1.

84. "State Commission Studies Stores and Wage System," *Chicago Tribune*, March 9, 1913, 1; "Girls May Win Voluntary Raise," *Chicago Tribune*, April 1, 1913, 4; "Promise to Obey Law for a Minimum Wage," *Chicago Daily News*, March 10, 1913, 1. Some employers were more skeptical of the proposal. See "William C. Thorne is Girl Inquiry Witness," *Chicago Daily News*, March 10, 1913.

85. "Rosenwald Calls Vice Commission 'Sensation Maker,'" *Chicago Tribune*, June 7, 1913, 1. See also "Rosenwald Assails O'Hara Vice Probers," *Chicago Daily News*, June 6, 1913, 1.

86. "Bill to Provide Minimum Wages," *Chicago Tribune*, May 21, 1913, 4; "Wage Bill in Big Clash," *Chicago Daily News*, May 21, 1913, 2.

87. Hart, *Bound by Our Constitution*, 101.

88. Hart, *Bound by Our Constitution*, 101.

89. "Legislators Hear Pitiful Tales of Traffic in Girls," *Chicago Tribune*, March 1, 1913, 1; "Vice Profits 1,700 Men," *Chicago Daily News*, March 1, 1913, 3; "Girls Weep on Stand at the Vice Inquiry," *Chicago Daily News*, March 15, 1913.

90. "Minimum Wage a Blow to Women, Siegel's Opinion," *Chicago Tribune*, March 13, 1913, 1; "Social Workers on the Relation of Woman's Wage to White Slavery," *Chicago Tribune*, June 22, 1913, H4; "Raps Social Barriers," *Chicago Daily News*, March 13, 1913, 3.

91. "$1,000,000 Plan to Yield Homes to 250 Workers," *Chicago Tribune*, June 22, 1919, A6.

92. "$1,000,000 Plan to Yield Homes to 250 Workers." See also Philpott, *The Slum and the Ghetto*, 233.

93. Quoted in Philpott, *The Slum and the Ghetto*, 235.

94. "Model Homes to Solve Race Problem, Plan," *Chicago Tribune*, October 26, 1919, A11.

95. "Housing Project Passes Reef of Increased Cost," *Chicago Tribune*, August 27, 1920.

96. Philpott, *The Slum and the Ghetto*, 241.

97. "The Housing Bill," *Chicago Tribune*, May 20, 1927, 10.

98. "The Housing Bill," 10.

99. "Mayor's Commission Meets to Organize Fight against Slums," *Chicago Tribune*, August 4, 1926, 31.

100. Philpott, *The Slum and the Ghetto*, 254.

101. Morris Robert Werner, *Julius Rosenwald: The Life of a Practical Humanitarian* (New York: Harper & Brothers, 1939), 275; "Rosenwald Plans Model Flats for Colored Chicagoans," *Chicago Tribune*, July 8, 1928, B1.

102. "Field Plans Great Housing Project Here," *Chicago Tribune*, November 19, 1927, 1; "Field Announces Big Housing Plan," *Chicago Daily News*, November 19, 1927, 5; Philpott, *The Slum and the Ghetto*, 261.

103. Philpott, *The Slum and the Ghetto*, 263.

104. "Rosenwald Plans Model Flats"; "Permit Obtained for Rosenwald Building Project," *Chicago Tribune*, January 16, 1929, 16; "Council Action on Field Home Project Asked," *Chicago Tribune*, January 6, 1928, 31.

105. "Permit Obtained for Rosenwald Building Project."

106. "Council Action on Field Home Project Asked."

107. "Public Service Building Corporation Plan Lauded by Field Flats' Manager," *Chicago Tribune*, March 26, 1939, A1.

108. "Garden Flats Flourish in Drab Locality," *Chicago Tribune*, September 29, 1929, B7.

109. Werner, *Julius Rosenwald*, 276.

110. Werner, *Julius Rosenwald*, 278.

111. Stephen D. Becker, *Marshall Field III: A Biography* (New York: Simon and Schuster, 1964), 114.

112. Philpott, *The Slum and the Ghetto*, 263.

113. Becker, *Marshall Field III*, 114; Philpott, *The Slum and the Ghetto*, 263.

114. "The Kessinger Rent Bill," *Chicago Tribune*, March 17, 1921, 8.

115. "Illinois Senate Votes Chicago Housing Quiz," *Chicago Tribune*, February 25, 1921, 3; "Tenants Unite for War on Rent Hogs," *Chicago Daily News*, August 25, 1920, 3; "Ask Senate Rent Probe," *Chicago Daily News*, August 26, 1920, 1; "City Is Ready with Laws for Rent Hogs," *Chicago Daily News*, August 30, 1920, 3; "'Rent Plot' Charged by Tenants' Leader," *Chicago Daily News*, February 23, 1921, 3; "Rent Hits Colored Folk, Says Anderson," *Chicago Daily News*, February 28, 1921, 5.

116. "Housing 'Plots' May Be Sifted by Legislature," *Chicago Tribune*, February 17, 1921, 8. See also "Chicago Housing Quiz Is Voted by Senate," *Chicago Daily News*, February 24, 1921, 1; "Plan Building Boom to Bring Rents Down," *Chicago Daily News*, February 14, 1921, 1.

117. "In the Housing Problem," *Chicago Tribune*, February 19, 1921, 6.

118. "Council Aims Two Blows at Rent Gougers," *Chicago Tribune*, March 12, 1921, 1.

119. "Drive for Rent Act Today," *Chicago Tribune*, March 16, 1921, 1; "Labor Unions Asked to Aid Tenants' War," *Chicago Daily News*, March 7, 1921, 3; "Doubt if Laws Will Solve Rent Problems," *Chicago Daily News*, March 11, 1921, 4; "Rent Bill Is Hot Topic," *Chicago Daily News*, March 12, 1921, 1; "Landlords in Rent Army," *Chicago Daily News*, March 14, 1921, 1.

120. The senate vote was twenty-two in favor and seventeen opposed. Four additional votes in favor were needed for the bill to advance. See "Bill to Appoint a Body to Halt Landlords Lost," *Chicago Tribune*, May 19, 1921, 1.

121. "Bill to Appoint a Body to Halt Landlords Lost," 1.

122. "Brand Rent Bill Knell of New Building," *Chicago Tribune*, March 23, 1921, 1.

123. "Kessinger Rent Bill"; "No Patent Relief for High Rents," *Chicago Tribune*, March 10, 1921, 8.

124. "No Patent Relief for High Rents."

125. "In the Housing Problem."

126. "Brand Rent Bill Knell of New Building"; "Protect the Tenants," *Chicago Tribune*, March 24, 1921, 8.

127. "Drive for Rent Act Today."

128. Abbott, *Tenements of Chicago*, 479.

Chapter Three

1. Harold Ickes, speech at ceremonies initiating Williamsburg PWA slum clearance project, New York, NY, January 3, 1936, Harold L. Ickes Papers,

1815–1969, Library of Congress, Washington, DC (hereafter Ickes Papers), box 413.

2. A third piece of housing legislation was also passed during this legislative session. As discussed later in this chapter, S. 549 provided state grants of up to $6.5 million mainly to house veterans or "disaster victims." See Edward J. Fruchtman, Illinois Housing Legislation 1947 (Chicago: Chicago Housing Authority, 1947). Since this statute played only a minor role in defining the new formula for urban redevelopment that would be used to redevelop Chicago's blighted areas, I do not mention it in the body of the text until the concluding sections of the chapter.

3. Hirsch, *Making the Second Ghetto*, 100.

4. Goldstein, *Ideas, Interests, and American Trade Policy*, 2.

5. Blyth, *Great Transformations*, 10.

6. Berman, "Ideas, Norms, and Culture in Political Analysis," 237; Goldstein, *Ideas, Interests, and American Trade Policy*, 13; Mehta, "Varied Roles of Ideas in Politics," 31; Campbell, "Institutional Analysis and the Role of Ideas in Political Economy;" John W. Kingdon, *Agendas, Alternatives, and Public Policies* (New York: Harper Collins, 1984).

7. Blyth, *Great Transformations*, 8–10; Berman, "Ideas, Norms, and Culture in Political Analysis," 236; Goldstein, *Ideas, Interests, and American Trade Policy*, 3.

8. Mehta, "Varied Roles of Ideas in Politics," 31.

9. Hall, "Policy Paradigms, Social Learning, and the State," 280.

10. Heclo, *Modern Social Politics in Britain and Sweden*, 305–6.

11. McNamara, *Currency of Ideas*, 58; Berman, "Ideas, Norms, and Culture in Political Analysis," 235; Goldstein, *Ideas, Interests, and American Trade Policy*, 11; Campbell, "Ideas, Politics, and Public Policy," 29; Campbell, "Institutional Analysis and the Role of Ideas in Political Economy," 380; Blyth, *Great Transformations*, 8–11.

12. Campbell, "Institutional Analysis and the Role of Ideas in Political Economy," 387.

13. Hall, "Policy Paradigms, Social Learning, and the State," 280.

14. Hall, "Policy Paradigms, Social Learning, and the State," 280.

15. "U.S. to Rebuild Chicago 'Slum' for $12,500,000," *Chicago Tribune*, September 26, 1934, 1; "PWA Head Finds Housing Plans Lure Chiselers," *Chicago Tribune*, September 28, 1934, 30; "PWA Head Asks Owners Accept Housing Plans," *Chicago Tribune*, September 29, 1934, 25; "Start Action for 37-Block Housing Plan," *Chicago Daily News*, September 25, 1934, 1.

16. "Housing Project for West Side Halted by Ickes," *Chicago Tribune*, April 12, 1935, 3; "Orders West-Side Housing Plan Cut; Hits 'Chiselers,'" *Chicago Daily News*, April 11, 1935, 1.

17. Devereux Bowly Jr., *The Poorhouse: Subsidized Housing in Chicago*, 2nd ed. (Carbondale: Southern Illinois University Press, 2012), 19–23.

18. Harold L. Ickes, *Back to Work: The Story of PWA* (New York: Macmillan, 1935); see also Harold L. Ickes, "The Place of Housing in National Rehabilitation," *Journal of Land and Public Utility Economics* 11 (1935): 109–16.

19. Timothy L. McDonnell, *The Wagner Housing Act: A Case Study of the Legislative Process* (Chicago: Loyola University Press, 1957), 49.

20. Gail Radford, *Modern Housing for America: Policy Struggles in the New Deal Era* (Chicago: University of Chicago Press, 1996), 184; see also Alexander von Hoffman, "The End of the Dream: The Political Struggle of America's Public Housers," *Journal of Planning History* 4 (2005): 222–53; D. Bradford Hunt, "Was the 1937 Housing Act a Pyrrhic Victory?," *Journal of Planning History* 4 (2005): 195–221; and J. Joseph Huthmacher, *Senator Robert F. Wagner and the Rise of Urban Liberalism* (New York: Atheneum, 1968), 206–16.

21. Edith Elmer Wood, *The Housing of the Unskilled Wage Earner* (New York: Macmillan, 1919).

22. Edith Elmer Wood, *Recent Trends in American Housing* (New York: Macmillan, 1931), 1.

23. Wood, *Recent Trends in American Housing*, 9. D. Bradford Hunt suggests that Wood's argument was the likely source of Franklin Roosevelt's claim in his second inaugural address that one-third of the nation was "ill housed." See D. Bradford Hunt, *Blueprint for Disaster: The Unraveling of Chicago Public Housing* (Chicago: University of Chicago Press, 2009), 19.

24. Berman, "Ideas, Norms, and Culture in Political Analysis," 234.

25. Radford, *Modern Housing for America*, 88.

26. Quoted in Radford, *Modern Housing for America*, 88.

27. Hall, "Policy Paradigms, Social Learning, and the State."

28. Barbara Deckard Sinclair, "Party Realignment and the Transformation of the Political Agenda: The House of Representatives, 1925–1938," *American Political Science Review* 71 (1977): 940–53; Kristi Andersen, *The Creation of a Democratic Majority, 1928–1936* (Chicago: University of Chicago Press, 1979); John H. Mollenkopf, *The Contested City* (Princeton, NJ: Princeton University Press, 1983), 56–60.

29. Sinclair, "Party Realignment and the Transformation of the Political Agenda."

30. McDonnell, *Wagner Housing Act*, 54–55; von Hoffman, "End of the Dream," 226–27.

31. McDonnell, *Wagner Housing Act*, 29; von Hoffman, "End of the Dream," 230.

32. McDonnell, *Wagner Housing Act*, 30.

33. Gail Radford argues that Ickes's decision to continue the Hoover administration's approach of subsidizing private housing developers rather than embarking immediately on a program of housing construction was due in part to the PWA's limited capacity during its initial months. With little staff or admin-

istrative support structures, the PWA "could not have handled a housing program that required more than responding to applications." See Radford, *Modern Housing for America*, 94–95.

34. Radford, *Modern Housing for America*, 92.

35. "Chicago Seeks $100,000,000 of U.S. for Housing," *Chicago Tribune*, October 12, 1933, 7.

36. McDonnell, *Wagner Housing Act*, 34–35.

37. Radford, *Modern Housing for America*, 96.

38. Radford, *Modern Housing for America*, 99.

39. "Ickes Housing Plan Is Assailed by Fish," *New York Times*, November 13, 1933, 6.

40. Ickes, *Back to Work*, 233. See also Harold Ickes, speech to the National Public Housing Conference, Washington, DC, January 19, 1935, Ickes Papers, box 413.

41. "Denies Slum Loans Offer Competition," *New York Times*, September 4, 1933, 5.

42. "Big Slum Program Indicated by Ickes," *New York Times*, January 20, 1935, 24; Radford, *Modern Housing for America*, 95. As Ickes himself put it, "Our private initiative, as sometimes happens when the goal is a social good instead of a private profit, was unable or unwilling to undertake much that was worthwhile. With the failure of private enterprise to provide low-rent housing, even with substantial Government aid, the Housing Division decided it would have to do its own constructing and operating." Ickes, speech to the National Public Housing Conference.

43. Hall, "Policy Paradigms, Social Learning, and the State," 280.

44. Radford, *Modern Housing for America*, 106. As Ickes envisioned it, "In some cities the management and operation of these housing developments will appear to the hungry self-seeker as manna from the heavens. Undoubtedly, in the wrong hands, such a project could be made to yield power and graft. But so long as these projects remains under Federal control, there will be 'nothing doing' for the seekers after graft or special privilege." Harold Ickes, address at the ceremonies inaugurating demolition of slum areas, Atlanta, GA, September 29, 1934, Ickes Papers, box 412.

45. "Federal Housing Planned by Ickes," *New York Times*, October 11, 1933, 25.

46. Ickes, "Place of Housing in National Rehabilitation."

47. Quoted in von Hoffman, "End of the Dream," 244.

48. Statement of M. D. Carrel, meeting of September 10, 1935, MPC Records, box 199, folder 1852.

49. Ickes, "Place of Housing in National Rehabilitation," 113.

50. "Big Slum Program Indicated by Ickes," *New York Times*, January 20, 1935, 24; "Ickes Says Housing Is a Federal Job," *New York Times*, June 21, 1936,

N1; "Denies Slum Loans Offer Competition," *New York Times*, September 4, 1933, 5.

51. "Ickes Says Housing Is a Federal Job." See also Harold Ickes, speech to the National Association of Real Estate Boards, Pittsburgh, PA, October 22, 1937, Ickes Papers, box 414.

52. See Catherine Bauer, *Modern Housing* (Boston: Houghton Mifflin, 1934). For sources on Bauer and her involvement with the RPAA see H. Peter Oberlander and Eva Newbrun, *Houser: The Life and Work of Catherine Bauer* (Vancouver: University of British Columbia Press, 1999); Radford, *Modern Housing for America*; Elizabeth Ann Milnarik, "The Federally Funded American Dream: Public Housing as an Engine for Social Improvement, 1933–1937" (PhD diss., University of Virginia, 2009).

53. Henry Wright, "New Homes for a New Deal, II: Abolishing Slums Forever," *New Republic* 78 (February 21, 1934): 44.

54. Albert Mayer, "New Homes for a New Deal, I: Slum Clearance—But How?," *New Republic* 78 (February 14, 1934): 9.

55. Catherine Bauer, "'Slum Clearance' or 'Housing,'" *Nation* 137 (December 27, 1933): 731.

56. Bauer, "'Slum Clearance' or 'Housing,'" 731. See also Albert Mayer, Henry Wright, and Lewis Mumford, "New Homes for a New Deal, IV: A Concrete Program," *New Republic* 78 (March 7, 1934): 91–94.

57. Radford, *Modern Housing for America*, 103.

58. D. Bradford Hunt characterizes the 1937 Housing Act as a compromise between progressive housing reformers, closely allied with Senator Wagner, and the modern housing planners aligned with the RPAA. According to Hunt, Bauer's role in drafting the Wagner bill was instrumental in realizing certain RPAA priorities, including the ability under certain conditions to construct public housing on vacant land without engaging in slum clearance. See Hunt, *Blueprint for Disaster*, chap. 1.

59. Radford, *Modern Housing for America*, 178.

60. "Ickes Says Housing Is a Federal Job," *New York Times*, June 21, 1936, N1; "Facing the Problem of Slums," *New York Times*, March 1, 1936, SM7; "Ickes Says Slum War Will Aid All Realty; Convention Urges Easing of FHA Loans," *New York Times*, October 23, 1937, 34. See also Ickes, "Place of Housing in National Rehabilitation."

61. "Col. Horatio B. Hackett Defends Chicago Housing Program," *Chicago Tribune*, May 6, 1934, B12.

62. "New Deal Housing Too Costly for the Poor," *Chicago Tribune*, April 23, 1939, G3.

63. "Federal Project Fails to Benefit Ill Housed Third," *Chicago Tribune*, April 29, 1938, 8.

64. On Washington, DC, see, for example, "Capital Housing Venture Classic

Federal Fiasco," *Chicago Tribune*, April 26, 1938, 4; on Milwaukee, see "Housing Unit's Tenants Drawn from Top Half," *Chicago Tribune*, April 28, 1938, 6.

65. The *Chicago Tribune* published a thirteen-part series of highly critical articles on public housing in April and May 1938. The stories, written by reporter Joseph Ator, focused in particular on the failure of federal public housing projects to provide shelter for the bottom third of income earners. A concluding editorial criticized the "extravagance" of the federal housing program, arguing that "more strict enforcement of fire and sanitary ordinances would accomplish a great deal." See "The Housing Failure; Its Lessons," *Chicago Tribune*, May 26, 1938, 16.

66. Radford, *Modern Housing for America*, 102.

67. Radford, *Modern Housing for America*, 103.

68. See "New Deal Housing Too Costly for the Poor," *Chicago Tribune*, April 23, 1939, G3.

69. "Public Housing Bill Assailed by Senators," *Chicago Tribune*, June 15, 1938, 5.

70. "Estimate Load Put on Citizens by U.S. Housing," *Chicago Tribune*, November 22, 1937, 12.

71. Radford, *Modern Housing for America*, 178.

72. Radford, *Modern Housing for America*, 189.

73. "Builders Act to End Slums," *Chicago Tribune*, December 14, 1938, 1. Oscar W. Rosenthal, a developer and head of the Illinois State Housing Board, was named director of the Chicago Building Congress. Arthur Kruggel, president of the Chicago Real Estate Board, was named vice president of the organization. Paul Angell, vice president of the Chicago Real Estate Board, was appointed secretary.

74. "Chicago Points New Way to Slum Clearance," *Chicago Tribune*, August 14, 1938, G4.

75. "Chicago Slum Removal Plan Is Explained," *Chicago Tribune*, May 7, 1939, B9.

76. "Scope of New Slum Clearing Plan Outlined," *Chicago Tribune*, September 28, 1938, 25. See also "Builders Act to End Slums," *Chicago Tribune*, December 14, 1938, 1; and "National Group Supports Plan to Clear Slums," *Chicago Tribune*, May 7, 1939, B9. The public service building corporation proposal was developed by a small group of real estate entrepreneurs that included developer and past president of the Chicago Real Estate Board J. Soule Warterfield, current president of the Chicago Real Estate Board Arthur Kruggel, NAREB's Herbert U. Nelson, and vice president of the Chicago Real Estate Board Paul Angell. See "Chicago Points New Way to Slum Clearance."

77. "Civic Leaders Favor Plan to Reclaim Slums," *Chicago Tribune*, August 16, 1938, 19; "Asks Rebuilding of Old Housing in Slum Fight," *Chicago Tribune*, October 30, 1938, C14; "Chicago A. of C. Supports Slum Clearance Plan,"

Chicago Tribune, May 13, 1939, 25; "Mayer Urges Quick Passage of Slum Bills," *Chicago Tribune*, June 7, 1939, 31.

78. "Scope of New Slum Clearing Plan Outlined."

79. "Scope of New Slum Clearing Plan Outlined." See also "Building Leaders and Federal Housing Authorities Debate Ways to Stimulate Construction," *Chicago Tribune*, November 6, 1938, C14; "Angell Named to Realty Body Housing Group," *Chicago Tribune*, December 25, 1938, 8; "National Group Supports Plan to Clear Slums," *Chicago Tribune*, May 7, 1939, B9.

80. "Rebuilding the Cities," *Chicago Tribune*, May 4, 1939, 16.

81. "Chicago Points New Way to Slum Clearance."

82. "State Housing Chief Supports Slum Program," *Chicago Tribune*, June 11, 1939, C9.

83. "Two Amendments May Kill Land Grab Measure," *Chicago Defender*, April 26, 1941, 13. The *Chicago Defender*, the principal newspaper serving the city's African American community, repeatedly expressed concerns that the public service building corporation plan would displace blacks. See, for example, "Housing Program May Move Race from Southside," *Chicago Defender*, April 15, 1939, 14; "A Program of Action: On Chicago's Acute Housing Problem—How We Can Work Our Way Out," *Chicago Defender*, May 13, 1939, 13; "We Condemn Building Corporation Bill," *Chicago Defender*, May 20, 1939, 14.

84. "Two Amendments May Kill Land Grab Measure."

85. "U.S. Announces Second Housing Project Here," *Chicago Tribune*, October 26, 1934, 31. The *Tribune* reported that the development would be "devoted entirely to apartments for upward of 1,400 colored families." See also "Chicago Gets $7,000,000 Housing Plan," *Chicago Daily News*, October 25, 1934, 1.

86. "Report of the Committee on Public Housing of the Metropolitan Housing Council" (Chicago: Metropolitan Housing Council, 1937), MPC Records, box 187, folder 1738. See also "U.S. Halts All Work on Chicago House Projects," *Chicago Tribune*, July 19, 1935, 8.

87. "Second PWA Housing Unit Here is Killed," *Chicago Tribune*, March 26, 1936, 27.

88. "Report of the Committee on Public Housing of the Metropolitan Housing Council."

89. The Jane Addams Homes PWA project was located in an area that included African Americans, and thirty black families were admitted to the 1,027-unit development. As Hunt observes, these families were offered apartments "in a far corner of the project, close to a neighboring black community." See Hunt, *Blueprint for Disaster*, 55.

90. "Slum Clearance Bill Introduced in Legislature," *Chicago Daily News*, March 29, 1939, 33; "Slum Clearing Act Introduced in Legislature," *Chicago Tribune*, March 30, 1939, 33.

91. "House Pushes Slum Bills to Second Reading," *Chicago Tribune*, June 28,

1939, 25. See also "Aldermen Hit Housing Bill as Home Rule Peril," *Chicago Daily News*, May 4, 1939, 8.

92. "Land Grab Is Checked thru Council Edict," *Chicago Defender*, June 17, 1939, 23; "Council Group Pushes Plan for Slum Clearance," *Chicago Daily News*, June 7, 1939, 9.

93. "Senate Passes Slum Clearing Enabling Bills," *Chicago Tribune*, June 23, 1939, 5.

94. "Senate Passes Slum Clearing Enabling Bills."

95. "Fight for Slum Clearance Will be Continued," *Chicago Tribune*, July 2, 1939, A7.

96. "Slum Clearing Bill Is Given Final Touches," *Chicago Tribune*, February 9, 1941, D5. There was also some media pressure for government action on the housing problem. See, for example, "Chicago Talks about Its Slums, but Never Acts," *Chicago Daily News*, December 23, 1940, 1; "Slum Problem Is with Us to Stay—Unless," *Chicago Daily News*, December 24, 1940, 5.

97. Chicago Building Congress, "The Illinois Neighborhood Redevelopment Corporation Law" (Chicago, 1941), MPC Records, box 587, folder 5028.

98. "Gov. Green Signs Land Grab Bill," *Chicago Defender*, July 19, 1941, 13.

99. "Three Chicago Areas are Designated as Blight Spots," *Chicago Tribune*, July 18, 1941, 11.

100. "Study Blighted Districts That May Be Rebuilt," *Chicago Tribune*, October 4, 1941, 23.

101. "Redevelopment Ordinance Bill Is Passed by State," *Chicago Tribune*, November 15, 1941, 10.

102. "Seek Priority Ratings on City Slum Projects," *Chicago Tribune*, November 13, 1941, 33.

103. In December 1943 a circuit court judge ruled that the 1941 redevelopment legislation was unconstitutional, arguing that private development projects to be carried out by the proposed neighborhood redevelopment corporations did not meet the threshold for public use required for the provision of eminent domain powers. This decision was reversed by the Illinois Supreme Court in January 1945 following an appeal by the city of Chicago. See "Test of Illinois Slum Clearing Law Is Begun," *Chicago Tribune*, December 9, 1943, 30; "Private Slum Clearing Held Vital to City," *Chicago Tribune*, December 15, 1943, 29; "Court to Study Slum Clearing Act's Validity," *Chicago Tribune*, December 16, 1943, 38; "Private Slum Clearing Law Ruled Invalid," *Chicago Tribune*, December 28, 1943, 21; "Uphold Slum Project Act, Court Is Asked," *Chicago Tribune*, April 19, 1944, 27; "Cite Slum Act Ruling as Basic Law Argument," *Chicago Tribune*, January 18, 1945.

104. Quoted in Mark I. Gelfand, *A Nation of Cities: The Federal Government and Urban America, 1933–1965* (New York: Oxford University Press, 1975), 125.

105. Metropolitan Housing Council, "Reclaiming Chicago's Blighted Areas" (Chicago: Metropolitan Housing Council, 1946), 5, MPC Records, box 23, folder 279.

106. See Guy Greer and Alvin Hansen, "Urban Redevelopment and Housing: A Program for Post-War," National Planning Association, Planning Pamphlet 10, Urban Redevelopment and Housing, December 1941. For a detailed account of both the NAREB and Hansen and Greer proposals, see Gelfand, *Nation of Cities*, chap. 4.

107. Gelfand, *Nation of Cities*, 116.

108. Arthur W. Binns, "Housing and Blighted Areas," *National Real Estate Journal* 42, no. 1 (1941): 16.

109. Gelfand, *Nation of Cities*, 127.

110. "Private Funds Held Vital in Slum Clearing," *Chicago Tribune*, December 19, 1940, 31; "We Condemn Building Corporation Bill," *Chicago Defender*, May 20, 1939, 14.

111. Metropolitan Housing Council, "Interim Report on Post War Planning and Housing" (Chicago: Metropolitan Housing Council, 1944), 2, MPC Records, box 22, folder Planning 1942–44.

112. Metropolitan Housing Council, "Summary of Work of Committee on Post War Planning," MPC Records, box 22, folder Planning 1942–44.

113. Metropolitan Housing Council, "Interim Report on Post War Planning and Housing."

114. Metropolitan Housing Council, Minutes of a Special Meeting of the Executive Committee, March 26, 1945, MPC Records, box 19, folder 149. See also "City-State Pact to Speed War on Blighted Areas," *Chicago Tribune*, February 5, 1945, 11; and "Slum Program Called Too Good to Let Pass By," *Chicago Tribune*, April 2, 1945, 11.

115. Roger Biles, *Big City Boss in Depression and War: Mayor Edward J. Kelly of Chicago* (DeKalb: Northern Illinois University Press, 1984), 120.

116. "Green and Kelly Meet Today on City Problems," *Chicago Tribune*, January 30, 1945, 4.

117. Biles, *Big City Boss in Depression and War*, 131.

118. "Green and Kelly May Confer on Problems Here," *Chicago Tribune*, January 25, 1945, 25; "Green and Kelly Meet Today on City Problems," *Chicago Tribune*, January 30, 1945, 4; "Kelly Confers with Gov. Green on State Issues," *Chicago Tribune*, January 31, 1945, 9; "Kelly, Green Pledge Aid to Constitution Change," *Chicago Daily News*, January 30, 1945, 1; Biles, *Big City Boss in Depression and War*, 131–32.

119. Metropolitan Housing Council, Minutes of a Special Meeting of the Executive Committee, March 26, 1945; P. P. Pullen to Kenneth Rice, April 28, 1945, Holman Pettibone Papers, Chicago History Museum (hereafter Pettibone Papers), box 2, folder 3, Chicago History Museum.

120. Metropolitan Housing Council, Minutes of a Special Meeting of the Executive Committee, March 26, 1945.

121. Martin Meyerson and Edward C. Banfield, *Politics, Planning, and the Public Interest: The Case of Public Housing in Chicago* (New York: Free Press, 1955), 83.

122. "Key Housing Bill Passes Senate, 48–0," *Chicago Daily News*, April 4, 1945, 7.

123. After a heated debate, the city council passed an ordinance approving Kelly's plan to award state redevelopment funds to the CHA. However, the new ordinance included an amendment requiring city council approval for all projects proposed by the CHA under the new legislation. See "Council Votes CHA 5 Million, but Keeps Reins," *Chicago Tribune*, November 9, 1945, 2; "Kelly Meets Reversal in Council," *Chicago Daily News*, October 25, 1945, 3; "Council Acts in Housing Shortage," *Chicago Daily News*, November 8, 1945, 16; "Get Together on Chicago Housing," *Chicago Daily News*, November 8, 1945, 14.

124. "Aldermen Fight Plan for CHA to Spend Millions," *Chicago Tribune*, October 26, 1945, 34; "Green Opposes Kelly on Slum Housing Issue," *Chicago Tribune*, November 7, 1945, 21.

125. "State Protests Use of Funds on Public Housing," *Chicago Tribune*, November 1, 1945, 11.

126. "After 2½ Years CHA Has No Public Housing Underway on 3 Sites," *Southeast Economist*, August 9, 1948, 1.

127. Metropolitan Housing Council, "Reclaiming Chicago's Blighted Areas," 5.

128. Metropolitan Housing Council, Memorandum for Discussion with Urban Redevelopment Committee, Pettibone Papers, box 2, folder 5.

129. Metropolitan Housing Council, Memorandum for Discussion with Urban Redevelopment Committee, Pettibone Papers, box 2, folder 5, 5.

130. Metropolitan Housing Council, "Reclaiming Chicago's Blighted Areas," 9.

131. Metropolitan Housing Council, Memorandum for Discussion with Urban Redevelopment Committee, 4, 7.

132. On the magnitude of Chicago's postwar housing shortage, see "Housing Bonds Sound Venture, Mayor Asserts," *Chicago Tribune*, September 26, 1947, 25; and "Civic Leaders Endorse Bonds to Clear Slums," *Chicago Tribune*, October 28, 1947, 4.

133. Ferd Kramer, speech to American Society of Planning Officials, August 15, 1950, Kramer Papers, box 8, folder 8.

134. Campbell, "Institutional Analysis and the Role of Ideas in Political Economy," 387.

135. Henry A. Neil, "The Chicago Land Clearance Commission" (MA thesis,

University of Chicago, 1952); "Heald Proposes 4 Steps to End Chicago Slums," *Chicago Tribune*, October 18, 1946, 7.

136. Ferd Kramer, speech to the Citizens Planning and Housing Association, Baltimore, MD, May 6, 1948, Kramer Papers, box 4, folder 3.

137. Metropolitan Housing Council, "Reclaiming Chicago's Blighted Areas"; "Heald Proposes 4 Steps to End Chicago Slums"; Hirsch, *Making the Second Ghetto*, 104.

138. Skogstad and Schmidt, "Introduction: Policy Paradigms, Transnationalism, and Domestic Politics," 15.

139. Metropolitan Housing Council, "Reclaiming Chicago's Blighted Areas," 9. On the discourse of the urban crisis and its evolution since the postwar era, see Timothy Weaver, "Urban Crisis: The Genealogy of a Concept," *Urban Studies* 54 (2017): 2039–55.

140. Metropolitan Housing Council, "Reclaiming Chicago's Blighted Areas," 7.

141. Metropolitan Housing Council, Minutes of the Board of Governors Meeting, December 17, 1946, MPC Records, box 3, folder 37. See also Metropolitan Housing Council, Minutes of the Board of Governors, June 4, 1947, MPC Records, box 3, folder 38.

142. Metropolitan Planning Council, Minutes of the Board of Governors, June 4, 1947. Not all MHPC board members were in favor of using a local housing authority for both public housing construction and assembly of land for private redevelopment. See Milton Mumford to Hughston McBain, May 16, 1947, Pettibone Papers, box 3, folder May 1947.

143. Mumford to McBain, May 16, 1947; see also Holman Pettibone to Hughston McBain, July 11, 1946, Pettibone Papers, box 2, folder 1946.

144. Biles, *Big City Boss in Depression and War*, 145; Peter Joseph O'Malley, "Mayor Martin H. Kennelly of Chicago: A Political Biography" (PhD diss., University of Illinois at Chicago, 1980), 33.

145. Biles, *Big City Boss in Depression and War*, 147.

146. Biles, *Big City Boss in Depression and War*, 146; O'Malley, "Mayor Martin H. Kennelly of Chicago," 36.

147. Biles, *Big City Boss in Depression and War*, 148.

148. Roger Biles, *Richard J. Daley: Politics, Race, and the Governing of Chicago* (DeKalb: Northern Illinois University Press, 1995), 29.

149. O'Malley, "Mayor Martin H. Kennelly of Chicago," 58–60.

150. Neil, "Chicago Land Clearance Commission," 26.

151. Hirsch, *Making the Second Ghetto*, 107–8.

152. Hirsch, *Making the Second Ghetto*, 105–6. See also Pettibone to McBain, July 11, 1946.

153. Kramer, speech to the Citizens Planning and Housing Association, 4.

154. Hirsch, *Making the Second Ghetto*, 107–12.

155. Fruchtman, Illinois Housing Legislation 1947.

156. H. D. Pettibone, memorandum, May 6, 1947, Pettibone Papers, box 3, folder May 1947; "Housing Bill, 38 Others Signed by Gov. Green," *Chicago Tribune*, July 3, 1947, 2.

157. "Housing Bonds Sound Venture, Mayor Asserts," *Chicago Tribune*, September 26, 1947, 25; "Ask 39 Million City Bonds," *Chicago Tribune*, September 30, 1947, 1.

158. Kramer, speech to the Citizens Planning and Housing Association, 6.

159. Metropolitan Housing Council, memorandum on Metropolitan Housing Council's role in the history of redevelopment, 1947, MPC Records, box 200, folder 1854.

160. Kramer, speech to the Citizens Planning and Housing Association, 7–8.

161. "Business Group Board Backs 2 Housing Issues," *Chicago Tribune*, October 12, 1947, WC; "13 Groups Back Slum Clearing Bond Program," *Chicago Tribune*, October 15, 1947, 41; "Planning Group Backs Proposed Housing Bonds," *Chicago Tribune*, October 24, 1947, 37; "Civic Leaders Endorse Bonds to Clear Slums," *Chicago Tribune*, October 28, 1947, 4.

162. "The Housing Bonds," *Chicago Tribune*, October 30, 1947, 16.

163. Heclo, *Modern Social Politics in Britain and Sweden*, 305.

164. "Slum Clearance," *Chicago Tribune*, November 6, 1947, 18.

Chapter Four

1. "22 Year Plan: A New Face for Chicago," *Chicago Tribune*, August 23, 1958, 1. See also "City's $1.5-Billion Plan," *Chicago Sun-Times*, August 23, 1958, 1; "A New Master Plan: Heart of City to be Remade, Revitalized," *Chicago Sun-Times*, August 22, 1958, 1.

2. The plan identified the boundaries of the central area as extending north to North Avenue, east to Lake Michigan, south to Twenty-Fifth Street, and west to Ashland Avenue.

3. James L. Greer, "The Politics of Decline and Growth: Planning, Economic Transformation, and the Structuring of Urban Futures in American Cities" (PhD diss., University of Chicago, 1983), 135.

4. Joel Rast, *Remaking Chicago: The Political Origins of Urban Industrial Change* (DeKalb: Northern Illinois University Press, 1999).

5. The population of Chicago's central area was 146,837 in 1990. It had grown to 215,894 by 2010. US Census Bureau, 1990 and 2010 Decennial Census, summary tape file 1.

6. See, for example, Skocpol, *Protecting Soldiers and Mothers*, 57–60; Pierson, "When Effect Becomes Cause"; Wier and Skocpol, "State Structures and

the Possibilities for 'Keynesian' Responses to the Great Depression"; Margaret Weir, "When Does Politics Create Policy? The Organizational Politics of Change," in Ian Shapiro, Stephen Skowronek, and Daniel Galvin, eds., *Rethinking Political Institutions: The Art of the State* (New York: New York University Press, 2006), 171–86.

7. Salisbury, "Urban Politics." See also Stone, *Regime Politics*; and John H. Mollenkopf, *The Contested City* (Princeton, NJ: Princeton University Press, 1983).

8. Richard Child Hill, "Crisis in the Motor City"; Rast, *Remaking Chicago*; Roy Lubove, *Twentieth-Century Pittsburgh*; Marc V. Levine, "Downtown Redevelopment as an Urban Growth Strategy: A Critical Appraisal of the Baltimore Renaissance," *Journal of Urban Affairs* 9 (1987): 103–23; O'Connor, *Building a New Boston*.

9. Stone, *Regime Politics*; Squires, *Unequal Partnerships*; Levine, "Downtown Redevelopment as an Urban Growth Strategy"; Ferman, *Challenging the Growth Machine*; Richard E. DeLeon, *Left Coast City: Progressive Politics in San Francisco, 1975–1991* (Lawrence: University Press of Kansas, 1992); Stephen L. Elkin, "State and Market in City Politics: Or the 'Real' Dallas," in Stone and Sanders, *Politics of Urban Development*, 25–51.

10. See, for example, Greer, "Politics of Decline and Growth"; Richard White, *"It's Your Misfortune and None of My Own": A History of the American West* (Norman: University of Oklahoma Press, 1991); O'Connor, *Building a New Boston*.

11. See Dennis Keating, Norman Krumholz, and John Metzger, "Cleveland: Post-populist Public-Private Partnerships," in Squires, *Unequal Partnerships*, 121–41; Nancy Kleniewski, "Neighborhood Decline and Downtown Renewal: The Politics of Redevelopment in Philadelphia, 1952–1962" (PhD diss., Temple University, 1982); Robert W. Wells, *This Is Milwaukee* (Garden City, NY: Doubleday, 1970).

12. The emphasis on eliminating slums altogether was connected to the belief that slums were like a cancerous tumor (a commonly used analogy at the time) that would threaten the health of stable areas of the city unless they were completely eradicated. See, for example, Chicago Plan Commission, *Master Plan of Residential Land Use of Chicago* (Chicago: Chicago Plan Commission, 1943), 81.

13. Hirsch, *Making the Second Ghetto*, 17.

14. Chicago Plan Commission, *Master Plan of Residential Land Use of Chicago*, 74–91.

15. Teaford, *Rough Road to Renaissance*, 19.

16. Biles, *Big City Boss in Depression and War*.

17. Metropolitan Housing Council, draft report, "Reclaiming the Blighted Areas of Chicago: The Program of the Metropolitan Housing Council," 1946, MPC Records (pre-recataloging), box 3, folder 37.

18. "Rebuilding of Slums Termed Important for Loop Business," *Chicago Tribune*, January 31, 1947, 27.

19. Civic Federation, 57th Annual Report (Chicago, 1950); "Clark Opposes Tax Exemption in Housing Plan," *Chicago Tribune*, April 20, 1945, 14; "Slum Program's Danger Is Cited by Civic Group," *Chicago Tribune*, May 11, 1945, 26.

20. See Chicago Association of Commerce, Annual Reports, 1945 and 1947.

21. Hirsch, *Making the Second Ghetto*.

22. Hirsch, *Making the Second Ghetto*. Chapter 4 of *Making the Second Ghetto* describes some of the same developments examined in this chapter. However, Hirsch's interpretation of these events differs from mine in two key respects. First, Hirsch downplays fragmentation within the downtown business community during the early postwar years, suggesting that MHPC and its partners represented "large Loop interests" (101). Second, Hirsch does not distinguish between redevelopment approaches pursued by neighborhood planning organizations and those initiated by downtown interests. I argue that the orientation of neighborhood planning groups differed from and at times conflicted with redevelopment approaches pursued by downtown actors.

23. Alexander von Hoffman, "A Study in Contradictions: The Origins and Legacy of the Housing Act of 1949," *Housing Policy Debate* 11 (2000): 299–326; Mollenkopf, *Contested City*, 78; Gelfand, *Nation of Cities*, 151–56.

24. Roger Biles, *The Fate of Cities: Urban America and the Federal Government, 1945–2000* (Lawrence: University Press of Kansas, 2011), 31.

25. Minutes of the Meeting of the Redevelopment Committee, August 9, 1950, MPC Records, box 530a, folder 4.

26. Minutes of the Meeting of the Redevelopment Committee, August 9, 1950, MPC Records, box 530a, folder 4, 21.

27. Minutes of the Meeting of the Redevelopment Committee, August 9, 1950, MPC Records, box 530a, folder 4, 30.

28. "Sign Housing Contract; Act to Get U.S. Aid," *Chicago Tribune*, July 2, 1949, 12.

29. "City's Housing Aids to Open Negotiations Today for U.S. Funds," *Chicago Tribune*, July 21, 1949, 3; "Chicago Paves Way for Early Housing Grant," *Chicago Tribune*, July 22, 1949, 3.

30. "U.S. Grants City 14.4 Millions to Clear Slums," *Chicago Tribune*, February 25, 1950, 7.

31. "City Is Granted $1,754,750 by U.S. for Land Fund," *Chicago Tribune*, June 6, 1952, B16; "U.S. Grants 3½ Millions for Michael Reese Project," *Chicago Tribune*, September 25, 1954, 13; "Sign Contracts for U.S. Slum Tract Grants," *Chicago Tribune*, December 16, 1954, C15.

32. The Chicago Plan Commission was an advisory body dependent upon city council for its budget and for approval of its plans. Business leaders com-

plained that that the commission's subservient relationship to city council made it a "creature of the aldermen," compromising the professionalism of the agency. See Ferd Kramer, draft letter to Alderman John Duffy re Plan Commission appropriation, December 9, 1948, MPC Records (pre-recataloging), box 22, folder 3; and Metropolitan Housing Council, minutes of a Special Meeting of the Executive Committee, July 13, 1944, MPC Records (pre-recataloging), box 3, folder 34. With a limited budget, the commission was forced to spend much of its time responding to service requests from individual aldermen, limiting its ability to carry out constructive planning. See William M. Spencer, letter to Mayor Martin Kennelly re Plan Commission budget, November 27, 1953, MPC Records (pre-recataloging), box 57, folder 1168. For additional sources on the weakness of the Chicago Plan Commission, see Edward C. Banfield, *Political Influence: A New Theory of Urban Politics* (New York: Free Press, 1951), 301; and Joel Rast, "Regime Building, Institution Building: Urban Renewal Policy in Chicago, 1946–1962," *Journal of Urban Affairs* 31 (2009): 173–94.

33. Holman Pettibone, "Outline of a Long Range Program for the Redevelopment of Blighted Areas in the City of Chicago," July 22, 1947, Pettibone Papers, box 3, folder July 1947.

34. Miles Colean, A Proposal to Construct Two Redevelopment Projects in Chicago, 1947, Pettibone Papers, box 3, folder July 1947.

35. Colean, Proposal to Construct Two Redevelopment Projects in Chicago.

36. The Housing Act of 1949 included a requirement that redevelopment be "predominantly residential," but the provision was loosely defined, and there was no requirement that new private housing developments contain units affordable to current residents of blighted areas.

37. Metropolitan Housing Council, Medical Center Area Redevelopment Plan, 1945, MPC Records (pre-recataloging), accession no. 75–104, box 14, folder 7.

38. Metropolitan Housing Council, draft press release re study by Redevelopment Committee, 1947, MPC Records (pre-recataloging), accession no. 75–104, box 20, folder 12.

39. Hirsch, *Making the Second Ghetto*, 106.

40. Colean, Proposal to Construct Two Redevelopment Projects in Chicago, 8.

41. Colean, Proposal to Construct Two Redevelopment Projects in Chicago, 19.

42. Illinois Institute of Technology, Michael Reese Hospital, South Side Planning Board, Metropolitan Housing Council, Pace Associates, and Chicago Housing Authority, "An Opportunity for Private and Public Investment in Rebuilding Chicago" (Chicago, 1947).

43. Hirsch, *Making the Second Ghetto*.

44. Illinois Institute of Technology et al., "An Opportunity," 18.

45. Hirsch, *Making the Second Ghetto*.

46. Neil, "Chicago Land Clearance Commission."

47. Neil, "Chicago Land Clearance Commission."

48. South Side Planning Board, Annual Report, 1952. For a more extensive discussion of the role of the South Side Planning Board's role in urban renewal on Chicago's South Side, see Michael Carriere, "Chicago, the South Side Planning Board, and the Search for (Further) Order: Toward an Intellectual Lineage of Urban Renewal in Postwar America," *Journal of Urban History* 39 (2012): 411–32.

49. Colean, Proposal to Construct Two Redevelopment Projects in Chicago, 7. It was Pettibone and Mumford who directed Colean to expand his analysis to include an area on the Near South Side. See Milton Mumford, letter to Miles L. Colean re work assignments, May 22, 1947, Pettibone Papers, box 3, folder May 1947. The area selected for study was a small 25-acre parcel located three miles south of the Loop immediately east of the IIT campus. The selection of a site this far removed from downtown violated preferences on the part of certain leaders of the redevelopment program that redevelopment efforts concentrate first on areas adjoining the central business district. However, to assuage concerns within the black community that redevelopment planning ignored the housing needs of the city's African American population, it was eventually agreed that a Near South Side project be planned "either first or contemporaneously with another project for white persons." See Holman Pettibone, memorandum re conversation with Mayor Kennelly, May 6, 1947, Pettibone Papers, box 3, folder May 1947.

50. Colean, Proposal to Construct Two Redevelopment Projects in Chicago, 29.

51. Illinois Institute of Technology et al., "Opportunity."

52. "Homes Project Held a Leader for Many More," *Chicago Tribune*, July 23, 1948, 12. By the time ground was broken for the new development in 1952, the project had been expanded from 60 acres to 101 acres.

53. Department of City Planning, "Locational Patterns of Major Manufacturing Industries in the City of Chicago" (Chicago, 1960); Real Estate Research Corporation, "Industrial Functions in the Chicago Central Communities" (Chicago, 1970).

54. South Side Planning Board, *An Opportunity to Rebuild Chicago through Industrial Development on the Central South Side* (Chicago, 1953).

55. Raymond J. Spaeth and Reginald R. Isaacs, undated draft memorandum re South Side Planning Board industrial study, MPC Records (pre-recataloging), accession no. 75-104, box 26, folder 8.

56. South Side Planning Board, *Opportunity*, 1.

57. South Side Planning Board, *Opportunity*, 25.

58. South Side Planning Board, *Opportunity*, 14.

59. Greer, "Politics of Decline and Growth"; Real Estate Research Corporation, "Industrial Functions."

60. Greer, "Politics of Decline and Growth"; Rast, *Remaking Chicago*.

61. South Side Planning Board, Statement of Position on the Central Area Plan, October 15, 1958, American Society of Planning Officials Records, University of Illinois at Chicago, Special Collections (hereafter ASPO Records), box 3, folder 27.

62. South Side Planning Board, minutes of council meeting, Dec. 17, 1958, ASPO Records, box 3, folder 27.

63. John Black, memorandum to Morris Hirsch re technical planning study, 1955, ASPO Records, box 3, folder 28.

64. South Side Planning Board, minutes of the executive committee, March 7, 1956, ASPO Records, box 3, folder 27; "Offers New S. Side Rebuilding Plan," *Chicago Daily News*, November 26, 1957.

65. Philip M. Klutznick, letter to Holman Pettibone and Milton Mumford re meeting with Land Clearance Commission and Chicago Plan Commission, July 6, 1949, Pettibone Papers, box 5, folder June–August 1949.

66. Holman Pettibone, memorandum to file re meeting with officers of Northwestern Mutual Life Insurance Co., November 29, 1949, Pettibone Papers, box 5, folder October 27–December 1949.

67. "West Side Unit Seeks to Build Planning Group," *Chicago Tribune*, October 17, 1948, W7.

68. Like those on the Near South Side, Near West Side planners viewed the mixing of industrial, commercial, and residential land uses and absence of space for industrial expansion as the key problems for West Side industry. See Near West Side Planning Board, press release, April 2, 1951, Pettibone Papers, box 6, folder January–June 1951.

69. Near West Side Planning Board, proceedings of the public meeting, June 15, 1949, ASPO Records, box 1, folder 3.

70. Near West Side Planning Board, proceedings of the public meeting, June 15, 1949,4.

71. Near West Side Planning Board, proceedings of the public meeting, June 15, 1949,

72. The area, immediately west of the Loop, was bounded by Harrison Street, Halsted Street, Roosevelt Road, and Ashland Avenue.

73. Roy Christianson, letter to Frank C. Rathje re planning inspection program, January 19, 1950, Pettibone Papers, box 5, folder January–February 1950.

74. L. D. McKendry, memorandum re meeting with representatives of the Near West Side Planning Board, December 5, 1950, Pettibone Papers, box 6, folder December 1950.

75. "Citizens Seek to Redevelop N.W. Side Area," *Chicago Tribune*, August 25, 1945, NW1.

76. Walter J. La Buy, letter to Holman Pettibone re Near Northwest Side Redevelopment Council, May 9, 1947, Pettibone Papers, box 3, folder May 1947.

77. "Citizens Seek to Redevelop N.W. Side Area."

78. Philip M. Klutznick, Memorandum of Discussions Relative to Redevelopment Project on the Near Northwest Side of Chicago, July 14, 1950, Pettibone Papers, box 6, folder June–October 15, 1950.

79. Klutznick, Memorandum of Discussions. See also Philip M. Klutznick, letter to Oran Mensik re Northwest Side redevelopment project, February 12, 1953, Pettibone Papers, box 8, folder January–February 1953.

80. "Land Clearance Unit to Survey Near N.W. Area," *Chicago Tribune*, October 22, 1950, NW4.

81. L. D. McKendry, memorandum re meeting with Judge La Buy, 1950, Pettibone Papers, box 6, folder December 1950.

82. "Savings-Loan Funds to Back New Housing," *Chicago Tribune*, August 8, 1953, 6.

83. Klutznick, letter to Oran Mensik.

84. "2 Civic Groups Plan Fight on Slums, Blight," *Chicago Tribune*, February 7, 1954, NW1.

85. "2 Civic Groups Plan Fight on Slums, Blight." See also Metropolitan Housing and Planning Council, minutes of the meeting of the Redevelopment Committee, November 5, 1953, MPC Records (pre-recataloging), box 24, folder 280.

86. Metropolitan Housing and Planning Council, minutes of the meeting of the Redevelopment Committee.

87. Chicago Plan Commission, "A Plan for the Central Area of Chicago" (Chicago, 1952).

88. Milton C. Mumford, letter to Holman Pettibone re proposed Committee for a New Chicago, May 12, 1952, Pettibone Papers, box 7, folder January–May 1952; see also "Plan Chairman Presses Drive to Build City," *Chicago Tribune*, February 5, 1952, 12.

89. Earl Kribben, minutes of the third meeting of General Wood's Group, November 30, 1953, Pettibone Papers, box 7, folder January–May 1952.

90. Kribben, minutes of the third meeting of General Wood's Group.

91. Mumford, letter to Holman Pettibone re proposed Committee for a New Chicago.

92. Leverett Lyon, memorandum to Holman Pettibone re Committee for a New Chicago, May 15, 1952, Pettibone Papers, box 7, folder January–May 1952.

93. Lyon, memorandum to Holman Pettibone re Committee for a New Chicago.

94. "Proposed Civic Center Hailed by Chicagoans," *Chicago Tribune*, March 18, 1954, 5; "Civic Center Plans Backed by Architects," *Chicago Tribune*, March 19, 1954, 16.

95. "Civic Center Plans Backed by Architects."

96. Percy Wood, "$288,100,000 Ft. Dearborn Project Approved in Revised Form," *Chicago Tribune*, July 22, 1955, 2.

97. Wood, "$288,100,000 Ft. Dearborn Project Approved in Revised Form." The Fort Dearborn project sponsors included Mark Brown, retired president, Harris Trust and Savings Bank; Willis Gale, chairman, Commonwealth Edison Company; Arthur Leonard, president, City National Bank and Trust Company; Hughston McBain, chairman, Marshall Field; Holman Pettibone, chairman, Chicago Title and Trust Company; Gilbert Scribner, Winston & Company; and Lawrence Stern, chairman, American National Bank and Trust Company.

98. Banfield, *Political Influence*.

99. Banfield, *Political Influence*. See also "North Siders Opposed Plan for Projects," *Chicago Tribune*, February 23, 1957, 9.

100. Banfield, *Political Influence*, 130.

101. Banfield, *Political Influence*, 144.

102. Banfield, *Political Influence*, 141–42.

103. "Build in Loop Drive Opened by New Group," *Chicago Tribune*, January 18, 1957.

104. Banfield, *Political Influence*.

105. "Leaders of Chicago Plan for Greater Central Area," *Chicago Tribune*, September 8, 1957, 5.

106. Banfield, *Political Influence*.

107. "Leaders of Chicago Plan for Greater Central Area"; Chicago Central Area Committee, draft brochure, 1956, Pettibone Papers, box 11, folder August–December 1956.

108. The original members of the executive committee of the Chicago Central Area Committee were Joseph Block, president, Inland Steel Company; Fairfax Cone, president, Foote, Cone & Belding; Otto Eitel, president, Bismarck Hotel Company; Newton Farr, partner, Farr, Chinnock & Sampson; Wayne Johnston, president, Illinois Central System; William Kahler, president, Illinois Bell Telephone Company; Homer Livingston, president, First National Bank; Hughston McBain, chairman, Marshall Field; Charles Murphy, partner, Naess & Murphy; William Patterson, president, United Airlines; John Pirie Jr., president, Carson, Pirie, Scott & Co.; and Kenneth Zwiener, president, Harris Trust & Savings Bank. See Chicago Central Area Committee, draft brochure.

109. Chicago Central Area Committee, draft brochure, , 7.

110. Banfield, *Political Influence*; "Group Pushes Building Boom in Loop Area," *Chicago Tribune*, December 26, 1961, 13.

111. O'Malley, "Mayor Martin H. Kennelly of Chicago."

112. See Biles, *Richard J. Daley*; and Milton Rakove, *Don't Make No Waves, Don't Back No Losers: An Insider's Analysis of the Daley Machine* (Bloomington: Indiana University Press, 1975). Daley's principal source of leverage in deal-

ings with city council was the control he exercised as party boss over the city's vast army of patronage workers. Loyal aldermen were rewarded generously with patronage positions, while disloyal aldermen saw the patronage positions at their disposal cut.

113. Biles, *Richard J. Daley*; Ferman, *Challenging the Growth Machine*; Rast, *Remaking Chicago*.

114. Banfield, *Political Influence*, 154.

115. Banfield, *Political Influence*, 155–56.

116. Department of City Planning, *Development Plan for the Central Area of Chicago* (Chicago, 1958), 24.

117. Department of City Planning, *Development Plan for the Central Area*, 8.

118. Department of City Planning, *Development Plan for the Central Area*, 26. Housing and other redevelopment efforts would be carried out "using all of the known urban renewal techniques, by public and private organizations, and developers under provisions of federal, state, and local urban renewal and housing legislation" (24).

119. Also included in the 1958 Development Plan were proposals for new government buildings as anchors for the North and South Loop, a new University of Illinois campus immediately south of downtown, the elimination of near-downtown railyards, and transportation improvements to improve access to the central business district.

Chapter Five

1. Metropolitan Housing and Planning Council, minutes of the meeting of the Board of Governors, February 8, 1950, MPC Records (pre-recataloging), box 3, folder 40.

2. John McKinlay to Martin Kennelly, January 26, 1950, Pettibone Papers, box 5, folder January–February 1950.

3. Metropolitan Housing and Planning Council, minutes of the meeting of the Board of Governors, February 8, 1950; "Near West Side Area Organizes to Fight Blight," *Chicago Tribune*, September 28, 1950, A3.

4. As one early planning document for redevelopment of the downtown area stated, the program was "not intended primarily to house present residents within the redevelopment, although portions of an area should be available to some of the present occupants." See "First Draft—4/14/47," Pettibone Papers, box 2, folder January–April 1947.

5. "Near West Side Area Organizes to Fight Blight."

6. Roy T. Christiansen to Frank C. Rathje, January 19, 1950, Pettibone Papers, box 5, folder January–February 1950.

7. Metropolitan Housing and Planning Council, Minutes of the Meeting of the Board of Governors, February 8, 1950.

8. Metropolitan Housing and Planning Council, article 3—Work Program (draft report, undated), MPC Records (pre-recataloging), supplement 3, box 24, folder 4.

9. See, for example, Salisbury, "Urban Politics: The New Convergence of Power"; Stone, *Regime Politics*; Squires, *Unequal Partnerships*; Fainstein et al., *Restructuring the City*; Stone and Sanders, eds., *Politics of Urban Development*.

10. Stone, *Regime Politics*, 3.

11. Amy Bridges, *Morning Glories: Municipal Reform in the Southwest* (Princeton, NJ: Princeton University Press, 1997), 14.

12. Skocpol, *Protecting Soldiers and Mothers*, 54.

13. Teaford, *Rough Road to Renaissance*, 54–66.

14. Lorin Peterson, *The Day of the Mugwump* (New York: Random House, 1961).

15. Robert H. Salisbury, "The Dynamics of Reform: Charter Politics in St. Louis," *Midwest Journal of Political Science* 5 (1961): 260–75; Howard N. Mantel, "Reorganization of the New York City Government," *Public Administration* 48 (1970): 191–212; Barry Gottehrer, "Urban Conditions: New York City," *Annals of the American Academy of Political and Social Science* 371 (1967): 141–58; O'Connor, *Building a New Boston*.

16. State Study Commission for New York City, "Report of the Temporary State Commission to Study the Organizational Structure of the Government of the City of New York" (New York: State Study Commission for New York City, 1953), 28.

17. Joseph Richard Fink, "Reform in Philadelphia: 1946–1951" (PhD diss., Rutgers University, 1971); Joseph D. Crumlish, *A City Finds Itself: The Philadelphia Home Rule Charter Movement* (Detroit: Wayne State University Press, 1959), 95.

18. Salisbury, "Dynamics of Reform," 268.

19. O'Connor, *Building a New Boston*, 51.

20. Skowronek, *Building a New American State*. Skowronek examines how US governing institutions were reworked during the early twentieth century to create a modern bureaucratic state. As he observes, industrialization placed new demands on government which could be met only imperfectly through the weak and decentralized governing institutions of the late nineteenth century. The nation's growing social and economic complexity produced a need for centralized administrative capacity and a strong federal bureaucracy. However, institutions did not evolve organically in response to new governing demands, as much of the existing scholarship on this period seemed to suggest. State building involved more than simply making the established state more efficient; it required build-

ing an altogether different kind of state. This meant confronting and ultimately dismantling an established structure of power supported by entrenched interests.

21. Metropolitan Housing and Planning Council, "Modernizing the City's Organization for Renewal" (draft 3), 1956, MPC Records (pre-recataloging), box 4, folder 46.

22. Joseph Pois to Alderman Becker, March 18, 1953, Robert E. Merriam Papers, University of Chicago, Regenstein Library, Special Collections Research Center (hereafter Merriam Papers), box 23, folder 1.

23. Hunt, *Blueprint for Disaster*, 82.

24. Neil, "Chicago Land Clearance Commission," 24. Officials of the Land Clearance Commission also complained about lack of cooperation from the Plan Commission, whose "lag in master planning" undermined the ability of the Land Clearance Commission to meet the requirements of the Housing Act of 1949. See Metropolitan Housing and Planning Council, minutes of the meeting of the Redevelopment Committee, October 11, 1950, MPC Records (pre-recataloging), supplement 3, box 15, folder 6.

25. Metropolitan Housing and Planning Council, *Conservation* (Chicago: Metropolitan Housing and Planning Council, 1953), 1:33; Neil, "Chicago Land Clearance Commission," 47.

26. Chicago Plan Commission, *Master Plan of Residential Land Use of Chicago* (Chicago: Chicago Plan Commission, 1943), 93.

27. Hirsch, *Making the Second Ghetto*, 149; Hunt, *Blueprint for Disaster*, 79.

28. "Slums' Growth Branded City's Major Problem," *Chicago Tribune*, December 6, 1952, 7.

29. "Asks More Effort to Stop Older Neighborhood Decay," *Chicago Tribune*, June 25, 1952, B6.

30. The other agency was the Neighborhood Redevelopment Commission, whose creation also required state legislation, in this case an amendment of the Neighborhood Redevelopment Corporation Act of 1941. As reported in chapter 3, the 1941 legislation authorized eminent domain powers for developers undertaking projects in blighted areas, with the condition that they secure at least 60 percent of the property in the project area by private contract. This provision proved to be unworkable. The act was amended in 1953 to permit condemnation if at least 60 percent of property owners gave their consent to the project, an easier threshold to meet. The Neighborhood Redevelopment Commission was created to oversee such projects, and was principally the doing of the University of Chicago, which viewed the new legislation as a potentially valuable tool for conservation efforts in the Hyde Park area. See Hirsch, *Making the Second Ghetto*, 151–52.

31. Peter H. Rossi and Robert A. Dentler, *The Politics of Urban Renewal: The Chicago Findings* (New York: Free Press of Glencoe, 1961), 77–79; Hirsch, *Making the Second Ghetto*, 149–50. MHPC's interest in conservation may have

been driven in part by the organization's close connections with the University of Chicago and Hyde Park–Kenwood community areas where the university was located. As Rossi and Dentler (77–78) note, more than one third of MHPC's board members in 1952 either lived in Hyde Park or Kenwood or were University of Chicago graduates. MHPC's conservation study included an in-depth case study of Hyde Park-Kenwood, along with nearby Woodlawn, and the city's first conservation project was focused on this area.

32. "Bill for Seizing Slums by Cities Sent to Senate," *Chicago Tribune*, May 15, 1953, 2; "Map War on Slums in Chicago," *Chicago Daily News*, May 13, 1953, 16; Hirsch, *Making the Second Ghetto*, 150.

33. "Bold Measures Needed to Halt Slums," *Chicago Tribune*, May 28, 1953, 10; "Illinois Senate Passes Bill to Prevent Slums," *Chicago Tribune*, June 9, 1953, 19; "House Passes Bills to Block Slum Growth," *Chicago Tribune*, June 27, 1953, 9; "Here Are the Issues in Public Housing Bill," *Chicago Daily News*, May 6, 1953, 24; "Anti-slum Bill Goes to Stratton," *Chicago Daily News*, June 26, 1953, 1.

34. Arnold Hirsch argues that Chicago's new conservation program "served as a model" for the federal Housing Act of 1954. See Hirsch, *Making the Second Ghetto*, 136. While Hirsch provides no evidence that framers of the federal legislation looked specifically to Chicago for inspiration, the new legislation did emphasize conservation along with more traditional slum clearance. See Gelfand, *Nation of Cities*, 171–75; and Ashley A. Foard and Hilbert Fefferman, "Federal Urban Renewal Legislation," in James Q. Wilson, ed., *Urban Renewal: The Record and the Controversy* (Cambridge, MA: MIT Press, 1966), 96–97.

35. "City Conservation Board a Record of Failures," *Chicago Daily News*, May 23, 1959, 8.

36. Metropolitan Housing and Planning Council, "The Unification of Urban Renewal Agencies in Chicago," May 4, 1959, MPC Records (pre-recataloging), supplement 3, box 29, folder 17.

37. Chicago City Council, Summary of the Proceedings of the Meeting of the Housing Committee's Subcommittee on the Public Administration Service Report (Chicago, 1953); Chicago Home Rule Commission, *Modernizing a City Government* (Chicago: University of Chicago Press, 1954); Banfield, *Political Influence*.

38. When the Chicago Plan Commission presented its Preliminary Comprehensive City Plan to city council in 1946, an MHPC board member present observed that "the City Council showed great apathy asking few questions except a half-hearted one as to letting the railroads work out a transportation plan without any insider on the committee." See Metropolitan Housing and Planning Council, minutes of the meeting of the Board of Governors, July 2, 1946, MPC Records (pre-recataloging), box 3, folder 37.

39. Martin Meyerson and Edward C. Banfield, *Politics, Planning, and the*

Public Interest: The Case of Public Housing in Chicago (New York: Free Press of Glencoe, 1955), 66.

40. Chicago Home Rule Commission, *Report and Recommendations: A Report to Mayor Richard J. Daley and the Chicago City Council* (Chicago: University of Illinois at Chicago, 1972), 118.

41. Quoted in Simpson, *Rogues, Rebels, and Rubber Stamps*, 107. Statements such as this by Kennelly were a convenient rationale for the mayor's reluctance to try to impose his will on city council. In reality Kennelly was in no position to dominate city council given his lack of influence within the Democratic Party organization.

42. "1,800 Flats will be Built on South Side," *Chicago Tribune*, July 22, 1948, B6; "1,400 Homes Assured for Blight Area," *Chicago Tribune*, July 27, 1949, 1; "Study Insurance Co. Slum Cleanup Offer," *Chicago Daily News*, July 22, 1948, 16.

43. Hunt, *Blueprint for Disaster*, 124.

44. "Mammoth Slum Building Plan Given Council," *Chicago Tribune*, July 13, 1950, 12.

45. "1,400 Homes Assured for Blight Area"; "Cottage Grove Closing Plan Stirs Protests," *Chicago Tribune*, August 25, 1950, 21; "South Side Leaders Hit Plan to Close Cottage Grove Av.," *Chicago Daily News*, August 25, 1950, 8.

46. Neil, "Chicago Land Clearance Commission," 67–68.

47. "Suit Ties Up Housing Project," *Chicago Defender*, January 21, 1950, 11.

48. "Seek to Halt New York Life Homes in Chicago," *Chicago Defender*, January 27, 1951, 4. In February 1950, Chicago received a $14.4 million grant from the US Housing and Home Finance Agency to be used in part for the Lake Meadows project. The grant was funded by the Housing Act of 1949. See "U.S. Grants City 14.4 Millions to Clear Slums," *Chicago Tribune*, February 25, 1950, 7.

49. Hirsch, *Making the Second Ghetto*, 130–31.

50. "Plan to Cut Off Cottage Grove Is Condemned," *Chicago Tribune*, September 3, 1950, S5; Neil, "Chicago Land Clearance Commission," 68–69.

51. Metropolitan Housing and Planning Council, minutes of the meeting of the Executive Committee, July 6, 1949, MPC Records (pre-recataloging), box 10, folder 104. A subcommittee of the Plan Commission conducted a study of traffic requirements in the project area and recommended that Cottage Grove remain open. The Plan Commission voted 30–7 to reject the recommendation of its own subcommittee. See "Closing of Cottage Grove Av. to Be Fought Out in Council," *Chicago Tribune*, October 4, 1950, A1.

52. Neil, "Chicago Land Clearance Commission," 52–53.

53. "Start Clearing of Housing Site Early in April," *Chicago Tribune*, March 28, 1950, 2.

54. Ferd Kramer, Speech to the American Society of Planning Officials, National Planning Conference, August 15, 1960, Kramer Papers, box 8, folder 8.

55. Otto Nelson to Martin Kennelly, May 12, 1950, Pettibone Papers, box 6, folder June-October 1950.

56. "Cottage Grove Plans Backed by Kennelly," *Chicago Tribune*, November 17, 1950, 1; "Kennelly Urges O.K. on Housing," *Chicago Daily News*, November 16, 1950, 24.

57. "Cottage Grove Slum Project OK'd by Council," *Chicago Tribune*, December 14, 1950, 4; "O.K. Housing Project for South Side," *Chicago Daily News*, December 13, 1950, 14.

58. "U.S. Approves Slum Project, Says N.Y. Life," *Chicago Tribune*, April 2, 1951, 17.

59. Public Administration Service, *Government Organization for Redevelopment and Housing in the City of Chicago: A Report to the Committee on Housing of the City Council* (Chicago, 1952), 21.

60. Public Administration Service, *Government Organization for Redevelopment and Housing in the City of Chicago*, 20. There is also evidence the committee on relocation was not very active. According to an aide to Alderman Robert Merriam, when asked how many times representatives from the CHA had met with the committee, the CHA official in charge of the agency's relocation program responded: "What is the committee on relocation?" See Norman Elkin to Robert Merriam, February 11, 1953, Merriam Papers, box 23, folder 8.

61. Public Administration Service, *Government Organization for Redevelopment and Housing*, 3.

62. Hunt, *Blueprint for Disaster*, 123.

63. Quoted in Meyerson and Banfield, *Politics, Planning, and the Public Interest*, 156–57.

64. Hunt, *Blueprint for Disaster*, 84–91; "Kennelly Calls for Showdown in Housing Issue," *Chicago Tribune*, August 10, 1948, 3.

65. Meyerson and Banfield, *Politics, Planning, and the Public Interest*, 219.

66. "Mayor OK's 9 Relocation House Sites," *Chicago Tribune*, August 12, 1948, 1.

67. Meyerson and Banfield, *Politics, Planning, and the Public Interest*, 130.

68. Hunt, *Blueprint for Disaster*, 90.

69. Meyerson and Banfield, *Politics, Planning, and the Public Interest*, 199–200.

70. Citizens Committee to Fight Slums, "Housing Action Report of 1954" (Chicago, 1954), 23, Merriam Papers, box 22, folder 12.

71. Public Administration Service, *Government Organization for Redevelopment and Housing*, 10.

72. The agencies that would be subsumed into the new department included the Chicago Land Clearance Commission, the Chicago Housing Authority, the Office of the Housing and Redevelopment Coordinator, the Chicago Dwellings

Association, and the Bureau of Housing Inspection of the Chicago Department of Buildings.

73. Norman Elkin to Benjamin Becker, March 10, 1953, Merriam Papers, box 23, folder 1. See also "Council Unit Raps Housing Muddle," *Chicago Daily News*, May 27, 1953, 6.

74. Memorandum on Public Administration Survey on Housing Agencies, May 20, 1952, Merriam Papers, box 23, folder 1.

75. Joseph Pois to Subcommittee of the City Council Housing Committee, March 18, 1953, Merriam Papers, box 23, folder 1.

76. Metropolitan Housing and Planning Council, minutes of the meeting of the Legislative Committee, November 26, 1952, MPC Records (pre-recataloging), box 18, folder 203.

77. A similar conclusion was reached by the Citizens Committee to Fight Slums, a group spearheaded by MHPC in 1953 following a ten-part *Chicago Daily News* series on tenement fires. See Amanda I. Seligman, *Block by Block: Neighborhoods and Public Policy on Chicago's West Side* (Chicago: University of Chicago Press, 2005), 48. A 1954 report by the committee concluded that "as an ultimate objective a single, powerful overall City agency is undoubtedly desirable. As of early 1954 such unification is premature, in the Committee's judgment. When and if the structure of Chicago's government is modernized and simplified, the time for this major overhaul of housing administration will have arrived." See Citizens Committee to Fight Slums, "Housing Action Report of 1954," 23.

78. "Council of 15, More Pay Asked by Civic Group," *Chicago Tribune*, May 1, 1953, B5; "Bill Revamping Council Ready for Legislators," *Chicago Tribune*, May 13, 1953, 2; "Rival Plan Irritates Kennelly," *Chicago Daily News*, May 1, 1953, 12.

79. "Aldermen Scoff at Plan to Cut Their Numbers," *Chicago Tribune*, May 8, 1953, B13; "Aldermen Vote 8–5 against Changing City Government," *Chicago Daily News*, May 29, 1953, 4: "Aldermen Reject Cut in Members," *Chicago Daily News*, June 11, 1953, 13.

80. Metropolitan Housing and Planning Council, minutes of the meeting of the Board of Governors, June 5, 1953, MPC Records (pre-recataloging), box 4, folder 43; minutes of the meeting of the Legislative Committee, November 26, 1952, MPC Records (pre-recataloging), box 18, folder 203; minutes of the meeting of the Board of Governors, May 9, 1952, MPC Records (pre-recataloging), box 4, folder 42. MHPC President Ferd Kramer became an active member of Citizens of Greater Chicago in 1952, when the organization's charter reform campaign was in the planning stages.

81. The bill was opposed by the city council committee on judiciary and state legislation and by Democratic members of the senate municipalities committee. See "Chicago Home Rule Plan Hits Snag in Senate," *Chicago Tribune*, May 28,

1953, 6; and "Aldermen Vote against Change in City Charter," *Chicago Tribune*, May 30, 1953, A8.

82. "Illinois Senate Kills Chicago Charter Bill," *Chicago Tribune*, June 24, 1953, 18; "Council Revamp Killed," *Chicago Daily News*, June 23, 1953, 3.

83. "Mayor, Reform Group in Tiff over Charter," *Chicago Tribune*, May 8, 1953, B13; "Mayor Hints Dislike for Revamp Plan," *Chicago Daily News*, June 8, 1953, 5. The commission's title was somewhat misleading. While a key purpose of the group was to examine possibilities for expanded home rule powers for Chicago, the commission devoted considerable attention to modernizing and re-organizing Chicago's government, which was considered to be a necessary pre-cursor to home rule. See General Wood's Group, minutes of the Third Meeting, November 30, 1953, Pettibone Papers, box 7, folder January-May 1952.

84. Chicago Home Rule Commission, *Modernizing a City Government*; "Tells Steps for City's Home Rule," *Chicago Daily News*, November 17, 1954, 36.

85. The two initiatives were not entirely independent. The technical advisory committee of the Chicago Home Rule Commission included two individuals who helped draft the Citizens of Greater Chicago charter reform bill.

86. "How Not to Draft a City Budget," *Chicago Tribune*, November 15, 1954, 24; "35 Man City Council Is Endorsed by Club," *Chicago Tribune*, January 14, 1955, 5; "Council Unit Backs 'Executive' Budget," *Chicago Daily News*, January 17, 1955, 6.

87. O'Malley, "Mayor Martin H. Kennelly of Chicago," 267–68.

88. Len O'Connor, *Clout: Mayor Daley and His City* (Chicago: Henry Regnery, 1975), 84–85.

89. Biles, *Richard J. Daley*, 55–62; Rakove, *Don't Make No Waves, Don't Back No Losers*, chap. 4.

90. "Daley Vows Greater City," *Chicago Tribune*, April 21, 1955, 1. In his fifteen-minute speech Daley made direct references to the Home Rule Commis-sion and its findings, stating that he hoped city council would act positively on the commission's recommendations "to relieve the council of administrative and technical duties . . . and permit the aldermen to devote most of their time to legislation."

91. "Vote to Give Daley Control of City Budget," *Chicago Tribune*, April 21, 1955, A8. According to political scientist and former Chicago alderman Dick Simpson, the transfer of budget-making powers from city council to the mayor's office "had the profound effect of changing Chicago government from a strong council–weak mayor form of government to a strong mayor–weak council gov-ernment in practice." See Simpson, *Rogues, Rebels, and Rubber Stamps*, 123.

92. "Modernizing the City Government," *Chicago Tribune*, June 22, 1955, 22; "Rule over Driveway Permits Surrendered by City Council," *Chicago Tri-bune*, March 29, 1956, 1. As head of the Democratic Party organization, Daley did not support reforms—such as reducing the size of city council or creating

at-large council seats—that would have undermined the power of the machine.
See "Smaller City Council Plan Hit by Daley," *Chicago Tribune*, February 17,
1960, 12.

93. Metropolitan Housing and Planning Council, minutes of a special meeting of the Executive Committee, July 13, 1944, MPC Records (pre-recataloging),
box 3, folder 34. See also Ferd Kramer to John Duffy, December 9, 1948, MPC
Records (pre-recataloging), box 22, folder 3.

94. Metropolitan Housing and Planning Council, Article III—Work Program, 1950, MPC Records (pre-recataloging), supplement 3, box 24, folder 4.
When the Plan Commission voted in 1950 to reclassify a portion of the Near
West Side from a "blighted" area to a "rehabilitation" area, MHPC attributed
the decision to the Plan Commission's lack of independence from city council.
According to an MHPC planning document, "The [Plan] Commission brushed
planning principles aside in a flagrant submission to the pressure of two public officials who were definitely 'off the reservation' in presuming to determine
planning decisions." The "two public officials" were the ward alderman and the
city building commissioner. See Metropolitan Housing and Planning Council, Article II—Organization—How the Official Planning Agency Works, 1950,
MPC Records, box 22, folder 3.

95. In a November 1953 letter to Mayor Kennelly, Plan Commission Chairman William Spencer complained that the commission had "not received an increase in its appropriation for many years." According to Spencer, the commission's appropriation in 1953 was nearly the same as it was in 1942, despite the
agency's increased costs and workload. See William Spencer to Martin Kennelly, November 27, 1953, MPC Records (pre-recataloging), box 57, folder 1166.

96. James Downs to Richard J. Daley, February 28, 1956, MPC Records (pre-
recataloging), box 19, folder 4.

97. Metropolitan Housing and Planning Council, minutes of the meeting of
the Board of Governors, April 6, 1956, MPC Records (pre-recataloging), box 4,
folder 46.

98. Paul M. Green, "Mayor Richard J. Daley and the Politics of Good Government," in Paul M. Green and Melvin G. Holli, eds., *The Mayors: The Chicago Political Tradition* (Carbondale: Southern Illinois University Press, 2005),
144–59. See especially 154–55.

99. Department of City Planning, *Development Plan for the Central Area of
Chicago* (Chicago, 1958).

100. Metropolitan Housing and Planning Council, minutes of the meeting of the Legislative Committee, November 26, 1952, MPC Records (pre-
recataloging), box 18, folder 203; Joseph Pois to subcommittee of the city council housing committee, March 18, 1953, Merriam Papers, box 23, folder 1.

101. Metropolitan Housing and Planning Council, "Facts on the Metropoli-

tan Housing and Planning Council of Chicago: A Citizen Crusade to Rebuild the City," undated, 25, MPC Records (pre recataloging), box 10, folder 108.

102. Metropolitan Housing and Planning Council, draft press release re administrative reorganization, May 6, 1957, MPC Records (pre-recataloging), box 19, folder 2.

103. Metropolitan Housing and Planning Council, minutes of the meeting of the Committee on Organization and Administration, March 20, 1958, MPC Records (pre-recataloging), box 1, folder 4; minutes of the meeting of the Committee on Administrative Organization, November 8, 1960, MPC Records (pre-recataloging), box 1, folder 2.

104. Metropolitan Housing and Planning Council, minutes of the meeting of the Committee on Legislation, November 12, 1958, MPC Records (pre-recataloging), box 1, folder 2.

105. Metropolitan Housing and Planning Council, "Modernizing the City's Organization for Renewal," draft 3, 1956, MPC Records (pre-recataloging), box 4, folder 46. The six agencies recommended for consolidation were the Chicago Land Clearance Commission, the Chicago Housing Authority, the Chicago Dwellings Association, the Community Conservation Board, the Neighborhood Redevelopment Commission, and the Office of the Housing and Redevelopment Coordinator.

106. Minutes of the meeting of the Committee on Legislation, November 12, 1958.

107. Draft press release re administrative reorganization, May 6, 1957.

108. MHPC initially presented Mayor Daley with two proposed bills, one that would allow the unification of all urban renewal agencies and another that permitted unification of all agencies except housing authorities, which would have to be kept separate. The latter alternative was consistent with MHPC's preferences. Oddly, however, Daley chose the former option, undoubtedly aware that any such proposal would face a hostile reception in the General Assembly, particularly among downstate legislators. See minutes of the meeting of the Committee on Legislation, November 12, 1958. Daley's choice appears to raise questions about his commitment to administrative reorganization at this time.

109. Holman Pettibone to Richard J. Daley, January 30, 1957, Pettibone Papers, box 11, folder January 1957. Pettibone's letter to Daley included two attachments—a 1952 letter from Pettibone to Mayor Kennelly and a 1956 letter from Pettibone to MHPC director George Dovenmuehle—in which Pettibone describes in detail his ideas about administrative reorganization in urban renewal policy. See Holman Pettibone to Martin Kennelly, September 18, 1952, Pettibone Papers, box 8, folder September 1952; and Holman Pettibone to George H. Dovenmuehle, December 17, 1956, MPC Records (pre-recataloging), box 19, folder 2.

110. As Banfield argues, the preferred residents for the near-downtown area "were not the low-income whites and Negroes who lived closest to the Loop (the number of those had in fact increased) but people with purchasing power to support the great stores, banks, and entertainment places that were the heart of Chicago." Banfield, *Political Influence*, 126. The Central Area Committee proposed "use of the city's slum clearance powers" to provide sites for extensive middle-class residential development in the near-downtown area. See "Urges Action on Loop Plan, CTA Subsidy," *Chicago Tribune*, January 22, 1960, C9.

111. Metropolitan Housing and Planning Council, "Modernizing the City's Organization for Renewal," draft 3.

112. Metropolitan Housing and Planning Council, "Modernizing the City's Organization for Renewal," draft 3.

113. Minutes of the meeting of the Committee on Administrative Organization, November 8, 1960; minutes of the meeting of the Committee on Legislation, November 12, 1958; Metropolitan Housing and Planning Council, "The Unification of Urban Renewal Agencies in Chicago," May 4, 1959, MPC Records (pre-recataloging), supplement 3, box 29, folder 17. The reasons for Daley's lack of support for the bill are unclear. However, by agreeing to sponsor the legislation, knowing it would likely go down to defeat, Daley minimized the potential for damage to his relationships with both MHPC and the Central Area Committee.

114. Minutes of the meeting of the Committee on Administrative Organization, November 8, 1960.

115. Minutes of the meeting of the Committee on Administrative Organization, November 8, 1960.

116. Metropolitan Housing and Planning Council, minutes of the meeting of the Committee on Administrative Organization, November 18, 1960, MPC Records (pre-recataloging), box 1, folder 3. Doyle's opposition to MHPC's proposal may have also been softened by reports that he was considered to be a leading candidate to head the new department. See "City's Urban Renewal Unit to Be Big Spender," *Chicago Tribune*, September 10, 1961, H47.

117. Chicago Association of Commerce and Industry, minutes of the meeting of the Community Development Division, March 13, 1961, Pettibone Papers, box 13, folder March-May 1961.

118. Holman Pettibone, notes of meeting with John C. Melaniphy and William R. Dillon, April 20, 1961, Pettibone Papers, box 13, folder March-May 1961.

119. Holman Pettibone, outline of a proposed consolidation of administrative organization and procedure, April 10, 1961, Pettibone Papers, box 13, folder March-May 1961.

120. "Urge Merger of Two Urban Renewal Units," *Chicago Tribune*, May 26, 1961, C7.

121. "City Council Unit Endorses Merged Renewal Agency," *Chicago Tribune*, May 19, 1961, A4.

122. "Community Development Program Makes Big Strides under Agency Merger," *Chicago Tribune*, April 7, 1963, I25.

123. Bridges, *Morning Glories*; Skocpol, *Protecting Soldiers and Mothers*. Skocpol's emphasis is not so much on the winners and losers in contests over institutional change as on the extent to which existing institutional arrangements provide advantages for certain groups seeking to influence public policy and disadvantages for others.

124. O'Connor, *Clout*, 132–39; Rakove, *Don't Make No Waves, Don't Back No Losers*, 76–89; Adam Cohen and Elizabeth Taylor, *American Pharaoh: Mayor Richard J. Daley—His Battle for Chicago and the Nation* (Boston: Little, Brown, 2000), chap. 6; Ferman, *Challenging the Growth Machine*, 58–61; Gregory D. Squires, Larry Bennett, Kathleen McCourt, and Philip Nyden, *Chicago: Race, Class, and the Response to Urban Decline* (Philadelphia: Temple University Press, 1987), 158–63.

Chapter Six

1. Ferd Kramer, speech to conference of Baltimore business leaders, April 18, 1952, Kramer Papers, box 4, folder 4.

2. "Building Boom Revives Downtown Area of Chicago," *Chicago Tribune*, December 24, 1961, 6.

3. "Building Boom Revives Downtown Area of Chicago."

4. Chicago Central Area Committee, draft brochure, 1956, Pettibone Papers, box 11, folder August-December 1956.

5. "Leaders of Chicago Plan for Greater Central Area," *Chicago Tribune*, September 8, 1957, 5.

6. Chicago Land Clearance Commission, "Location of Commission's 26 Redevelopment Projects, Comprising 895 Acres," July 1961. The two residential projects were the 33.8-acre Carl Sandburg Village on the Near North Side and the 17.7-acre Noble Square development on the Near Northwest Side. The other central area projects included two industrial projects, a shopping center, and portions of the new University of Illinois at Chicago campus.

7. Chicago Plan Commission, *Master Plan of Residential Land Use of Chicago*, 81.

8. Chicago Committee for Housing Action, "Housing and Redevelopment Program for Chicago," July 11, 1947.

9. Daley's housing and redevelopment coordinator James Downs was one of the more outspoken members of Daley's cabinet on the danger posed by slums

to stable areas of the city. In a May 1953 speech to the Chicago Association of Commerce, Downs warned, "We have reached the point where we will soon be faced with a completely decaying city if we do not take definite steps to prevent the exploitation of property at the periphery of the present slums. If we are to keep Chicago great . . . we must do something to prevent the complete deterioration of neighborhoods." See "Public Support Urged to Fight Growing Slums," *Chicago Tribune*, May 27, 1953, B8.

10. "Chicago Slum Removal Plan Is Explained," *Chicago Tribune*, May 7, 1939, B9.

11. Carl W. Condit, *Chicago, 1930–70: Building, Planning, and Urban Technology* (Chicago: University of Chicago Press, 1974), 84–100.

12. Condit, *Chicago, 1930–70*, 100.

13. Condit, *Chicago, 1930–70*, 100–114. See also Rachel Weber, *From Boom to Bubble: How Finance Built the New Chicago* (Chicago: University of Chicago Press, 2015), 99–100.

14. Condit, *Chicago, 1930–70*, 94.

15. D. Bradford Hunt and Jon B. DeVries, *Planning Chicago* (Chicago: American Planning Association, 2013), 28–29.

16. O'Connor, *Clout*, 135–39.

17. "The Chicago Coalition Is Still Holding Together," *Fortune*, September 11, 1978.

18. "Chicago Coalition Is Still Holding Together."

19. See, for example, Barbara Ferman, "Chicago: Power, Race, and Reform," in H.V. Savitch and John Clayton Thomas, eds., *Big City Politics in Transition* (London: Sage, 1991), 50; and Cohen and Taylor, *American Pharaoh*, 294–95.

20. Chicago Central Area Committee, news release on bond issue, June 7, 1966, Chicago Central Area Committee Papers (hereafter CCAC Papers), box 8.

21. Quoted in Hunt, *Blueprint for Disaster*, 142.

22. Metropolitan Housing and Planning Council, minutes of the Board of Governors meeting, December 5, 1958, MPC Records, box 4, folder 28.

23. Metropolitan Housing and Planning Council, minutes of the Board of Governors, April 6, 1956, MPC Records, box 3, folder 24.

24. Hunt, *Blueprint for Disaster*, 138.

25. "Daley Hits Critics of Slum Program," *Chicago Tribune*, March 8, 1966, 8; "Daley Defends the Role of Public Housing Projects," *Chicago Sun-Times*, March 8, 1966, 19.

26. Hirsch, *Making the Second Ghetto*, 243.

27. Hirsch, *Making the Second Ghetto*, 17; Janet L. Abu-Lughod, *New York, Chicago, Los Angeles: America's Global Cities* (Minneapolis: University of Minnesota Press, 1999), 230.

28. Cohen and Taylor, *American Pharaoh*, 339, 429.

29. "Lake Meadows Development a Show Piece," *Chicago Tribune*, May 13, 1957, 3.

30. "Vast Project Changes Face of South Side," *Chicago Tribune*, June 4, 1959, S6.

31. "Projects to Double Tax Yield," *Chicago Tribune*, May 3, 1962, S10.

32. "Lake Meadows Final Building Ready July 1," *Chicago Tribune*, May 22, 1960, D49.

33. "Kennedy Visit to Integrated Area Is Added," *Chicago Tribune*, October 1, 1960, 6. Lake Meadows was innovative in part because it was deliberately marketed as an integrated project. The first buildings rented were nearly all black, but later buildings achieved white populations as high as 75 percent. By 1967 the racial breakdown for the entire development was roughly 75 percent black and 25 percent white. See "Racial Integration Is Underway in High Rise Housing Complexes," *Chicago Tribune*, April 6, 1967, H2.

34. "Vast Project Changes Face of South Side."

35. "1st Hospital Apartment Opens Here Today," *Chicago Sun-Times*, June 4, 1958, 20; "Prairie Shores Skyscrapers to Go in Service," *Chicago Tribune*, June 2, 1958, A1; "Begin 3rd Prairie Shores Project Far Ahead of Schedule," *Chicago Tribune*, November 15, 1959, 20. Like Lake Meadows, Prairie Shores was an integrated project, but it was mostly white. By 1967 the development's African American population was roughly 25 percent, compared with a black population in Lake Meadows of about 75 percent. See "Racial Integration Is Underway in High Rise Housing Complexes."

36. "Vast Project Changes Face of South Side."

37. "Chicago Spirit Meets a Challenge; Lifts Near South Side Out of Slums," *Chicago Tribune*, November 9, 1958, 12.

38. "Projects to Double Tax Yield."

39. "Housing Hearing in Chicago," *Chicago Defender*, March 11, 1959, 11; "Urban Renewal on the Midway," *Chicago Defender*, August 17, 1960, 10. As Arnold Hirsch has argued, it was not so much that the University of Chicago had a strong interest in preserving Hyde Park as an interracial community. It was more that the area had a growing black population, making the creation of an all-white enclave in Hyde Park all but impossible to achieve by the mid-1950s. The compromise was to remove the area's most deteriorated dwellings and replace them with middle- and upper-income housing. This would allow blacks living in standard housing to remain, while ensuring that most residents of redeveloped areas would be white. Urban renewal thus reversed the growing influx of black residents into Hyde Park. See Hirsch, *Making the Second Ghetto*, chap. 5; and Rossi and Dentler, *Politics of Urban Renewal*.

40. "Sandburg Village Spurs Area's Renewal," *Chicago Tribune*, May 5, 1963, N25.

41. "Daley Calls for 6 Billion to End Slums," *Chicago Tribune*, February 1, 1959, 1; "Daley Asks U.S. Help to Rebuild Chicago," *Chicago Sun-Times*, February 1, 1959, 3.

42. "Daley Pledges End of Slums in 5 or 6 Years," *Chicago Tribune*, March 22, 1962, 4; "Daley, Aides Set Goal: End Chicago's Slums," *Chicago Tribune*, April 1, 1962, 1.

43. "City Finance Group OK's Vote on Bonds," *Chicago Tribune*, April 29, 1966. See also "Council Unit Approves Big Bond Issue," *Chicago Sun-Times*, April 29, 1966, 32; "Out of Step on Bond Issue," *Chicago Sun-Times*, April 29, 1966, 47; "2 Aldermen Delay Council in Bond Vote," *Chicago Sun-Times*, April 30, 1966, 3.

44. Chicago City Missionary Society, "A Proposal for Moderate-Income Housing Development in the Hyde Park–Kenwood Urban Renewal Area," (Chicago, 1964), MPC Records, box 527, folder 4452.

45. Jack Meltzer, *Selected Aspects of Urban Renewal in Chicago: An Annotated Statistical Summary* (Chicago: Center for Urban Studies, University of Chicago, 1965), 49.

46. "Lake Meadows Development a Show Piece."

47. "Urban Renewal: Running Hard, Sitting Still," *Architectural Forum*, April 1962, 101; John J. Egan to Morris Hirsh, May 7, 1964, MPC Records, box 13, folder 2.

48. Hirsch, *Making the Second Ghetto*, chap. 4.

49. Ferd Kramer, speech to the American Society of Planning Officials, National Planning Conference, August 15, 1950, Kramer Papers, box 8, folder 8.

50. Chicago City Missionary Society, "Proposal for Moderate-Income Housing Development," 10; "Meadows Cuts Area Population in Half," *Chicago Defender*, November 13, 1962, 1.

51. Meltzer, *Selected Aspects of Urban Renewal in Chicago*.

52. Muriel Beadle, *The Hyde Park-Kenwood Urban Renewal Years: A History to Date* (Chicago: n.p., 1964), 9.

53. Chicago City Missionary Society, "Proposal for Moderate-Income Housing Development," 5.

54. Committee on Urban Progress, Subcommittee on Urban Renewal, Draft report, 1965, 8. MPC Records, box 540, folder 4569.

55. Robert C. Weaver, *The Urban Complex: Human Values in Urban Life* (Garden City, NY: Doubleday, 1964), 113.

56. R. Allen Hays, *The Federal Government and Urban Housing: Ideology and Change in Public Policy*, 2nd ed. (Albany: State University of New York Press, 1995), 102.

57. A. M. Prothro and Morton W. Schomer, "The Section 221(d)(3) Below Market Interest Rate Program for Low and Moderate Income Families," *New York Law Forum* 11, no. 16 (1965), 16–29. For additional sources on the Sec-

tion 221(d)(3) program see Henry J. Aaron, *Shelter and Subsidies: Who Benefits from Federal Housing Policies?* (Washington, DC: Brookings Institution, 1972), 128–33; and Alex F. Schwartz, *Housing Policy in the United States*, 2nd ed. (New York: Routledge, 2010), 157–58.

58. Chicago City Missionary Society, "Proposal for Moderate-Income Housing Development," 4. How well the Section 221(d)(3) program genuinely addressed the gap between public housing and affordable, market-rate housing was a matter of debate. Housing and Home Finance Agency Director Robert C. Weaver testified in 1965 that the program mainly served the upper tier of the moderate-income housing market and "did not take it all the way down." According to Weaver, "It serves a little bit of the layer between public housing and private but you have a whole lot left in there and this whole lot is getting larger as the interest rate goes up." Quoted in Aaron, *Shelter and Subsidies*, 129–31n4.

59. "New South Side Project May Decide Area's Future," *Chicago Tribune*, December 27, 1964, 7.

60. "Lively Bidding Shapes Up for 30 Slum Acres," *Chicago Tribune*, June 1, 1964, B6.

61. "New South Side Project May Decide Area's Future," *Chicago Tribune*, December 27, 1964, 7.

62. City of Chicago, Department of Urban Renewal, "Instructions to Prospective Redevelopers, Redevelopment Projects 6B, 6C, and 6D" (Chicago, 1964), MPC Records, box 523, folder 4406.

63. "Experts Split on South Side Renewal Plan," *Chicago Tribune*, January 25, 1965, B8; "S. Side Housing Project May Shape City's Future," *Chicago Sun-Times*, December 28, 1964, 30.

64. Statement of Ferd Kramer to commissioners, Department of Urban Renewal, December 10, 1964, MPC Records, box 525, folder 4420.

65. The competing bid was submitted by the Central South Development Company, headed by developer James P. McHugh. The proposed development included townhouses, low- and high-rise apartment buildings, playgrounds, a school, a community building, and a shopping center. It contained 1,619 residential units when fully built out. The first buildings rented were about 70 percent white and 30 percent black; within eight years, however, the development was 90 percent black. See Gerald D. Suttles, *The Man-Made City: The Land-Use Confidence Game in Chicago* (Chicago: University of Chicago Press, 1990), 160–68.

66. "Experts Split on South Side Renewal Plan." See also "City Weighs 4 Bids on 30.6-Acre South Side Tract," *Chicago Tribune*, August 13, 1964, N4; "Plan to Renew South Central Area Is Lauded," *Chicago Tribune*, November 13, 1964, 7; "City to Select Firm to Buy Renewal Site," *Chicago Tribune*, January 10, 1965, S1; "Renewal Unit OK's Sale of S. Side Tract," *Chicago Tribune*, January 22, 1965, A10.

67. "S. Commons Project Will Begin Today," *Chicago Tribune*, December 15, 1966, D14.

68. This perspective was held by Monsignor John Egan, who, along with Kramer, read a statement at the December 10, 1964, meeting of the urban renewal commissioners. Argued Egan: "The Kennedy administration developed the 221(d)(3) concept with just such projects as the present one in mind. The system has worked; it can work. And what is more important, it has the advantage that it guarantees against the mysterious transmutation of moderate income design into upper-income reality. . . . I am seriously afraid that if you depart from your criteria in this instance, you will be feeding the flames of dissatisfaction with the urban renewal program." See statement of Msgr. John J. Egan to commissioners, Department of Urban Renewal, December 10, 1964, MPC Records, box 523, folder 4410.

69. Fred P. Bosselman, memo to the Legislative Committee, Metropolitan Housing and Planning Council, January 1964, MPC Records, box 18, folder 206. Jane Jacobs's devastating and influential critique of urban renewal policy was published in 1961. See Jacobs, *Death and Life of Great American Cities*.

70. Metropolitan Housing and Planning Council, minutes of the meeting of the Committee on Urban Renewal, January 27, 1964, MPC Records, box 519, folder 4368.

71. "Home Was Where the Bulldozer Is," *Chicago Tribune*, April 18, 1971, H46.

72. Bosselman, memo to the Legislative Committee.

73. "Daley, Aides Set Goal: End Chicago's Slums."

74. "Urge 'No' Vote on 5 of 6 Bond Issues April 10," *Chicago Tribune*, March 23, 1962, 19; "The Bond Issue for Slum Clearance," *Chicago Tribune*, March 29, 1962, 14; "The Bond Issues," *Chicago Tribune*, April 8, 1962, 20; "Only Renewal Bonds Backed by Civic Group," *Chicago Sun-Times*, March 23, 1962, 3; "Tax Growth Seen in Renewal Area," *Chicago Sun-Times*, March 26, 1962, 24; Meltzer, *Selected Aspects of Urban Renewal in Chicago*, 58.

75. "Beaten Daley Won't Give Up on Bond Aims," *Chicago Tribune*, April 12, 1962, 3; "Bonds Out; Rumsfeld Wins," *Chicago Sun-Times*, April 11, 1962, 3; "66,000,000 in Six Bond Issues Defeated," *Chicago Sun-Times*, April 11, 1962, 3.

76. "All City Bond Issues Lose; Conti Wins," *Chicago Tribune*, April 11, 1962, 1. See also "Resentment Beat Bonds—Daley," *Chicago Sun-Times*, April 12, 1962, 3.

77. Metropolitan Housing and Planning Council, minutes of the meeting of the Board of Governors, September 21, 1962, MPC Records, box 5, folder 53.

78. John G. Duba, speech to the National Association of Housing and Redevelopment Officials, Denver, October 2, 1963. Reprinted in Meltzer, *Selected Aspects of Urban Renewal in Chicago*, 59–61.

79. Committee on Urban Progress, notes on COUP staff interviews, March 4, 1964, MPC Records (pre-recataloging), box 13, folder 6.

80. Committee on Urban Progress, "Urban Renewal Subcommittee Report," July 1964, MPC Records (pre-recataloging), box 13, folder 1.

81. Meltzer, *Selected Aspects of Urban Renewal in Chicago*, 64.

82. Dorothy Rubel to Thomas Nicholson, Ferd Kramer, and John W. Baird, January 21, 1964, MPC Records, box 41, folder 4574.

83. Committee on Urban Progress, Subcommittee on Urban Renewal, meeting agenda, July 21, 1964, MPC Records (pre-recataloging), box 13, folder 1.

84. Committee on Urban Progress, "A Precondition for Urban Renewal," draft statement, March 13, 1964, MPC Records (pre-recataloging), box 13, folder 1.

85. John J. Egan to Morris Hirsh, May 7, 1964.

86. Metropolitan Housing and Planning Council, minutes of the meeting of the Urban Renewal Committee, April 22, 1964, MPC Records, box 541, folder 4575.

87. Metropolitan Housing and Planning Council, minutes of the meeting of the Urban Renewal Committee, May 29, 1964, MPC Records, box 541, folder 4575.

88. Dorothy Rubel to George Dovenmuehle, July 30, 1964, MPC Records, box 541, folder 4575.

89. Meltzer, *Selected Aspects of Urban Renewal in Chicago*.

90. "Renewal Controversy Continues; Hailed by Some, Hated by Others," *Chicago Tribune*, March 27, 1966, T3.

91. Cohen and Taylor, *American Pharaoh*, 375.

92. "The Bond Victory," *Chicago Tribune*, June 16, 1966, 18.

93. "Tell City's Renewal Plan," *Chicago Tribune*, August 12, 1966, 1; "Daley's 'Rebuilding of City' Starts: $105-Million Renewal Project Set," *Chicago Sun-Times*, August 12, 1966, 2.

94. Cohen and Taylor, *American Pharaoh*, 329–31, 347–48; "Dr. King Will Occupy Chicago Slum Flat in New Rights Drive," *Chicago Defender*, January 8, 1966, 1.

95. Cohen and Taylor, *American Pharaoh*, 356. For a book-length treatment of the Chicago Freedom Movement see James R. Ralph Jr., *Northern Protest: Martin Luther King, Jr., Chicago, and the Civil Rights Movement* (Cambridge, MA: Harvard University Press, 1993).

96. "Dr. King Will Occupy Chicago Slum Flat in New Rights Drive."

97. "King's Wife with Him in Slum," *Chicago Defender*, January 27, 1966, 1.

98. "King Group's Novel Plan to Repair Slum," *Chicago Defender*, February 24, 1966, 1; "King Joins Tenants in Building Takeover," *Chicago Sun-Times*, February 24, 1966, 38; "Dr. King and the Slums," *Chicago Sun-Times*, February 25, 1966, 37; "King's Slum Project Snagged by Legality," *Chicago Sun-Times*, February 25, 1966, 40. See also Cohen and Taylor, *American Pharaoh*, 365–66;

and Beryl Satter, *Family Properties: Race, Real Estate, and the Exploitation of Black Urban America* (New York: Metropolitan Books, 2009), 184–85.

99. Cohen and Taylor, *American Pharaoh*, 362.

100. Quoted in Satter, *Family Properties*, 186. See also "Daley Asks King to Negro Policy Meeting," *Chicago Sun-Times*, March 15, 1966, 4.

101. "City to Begin Slum Search," *Chicago Tribune*, March 2, 1966, 1; "Bond Issue Votes for Public Works Hinted by Daley," *Chicago Sun-Times*, March 2, 1966, 3.

102. Cohen and Taylor, *American Pharaoh*, 369–72.

103. Satter, *Family Properties*, 186–87.

104. Satter, *Family Properties*, 187.

105. Cohen and Taylor, *American Pharaoh*, 366.

106. Satter, *Family Properties*, 191.

107. Cohen and Taylor, *American Pharaoh*, 382–83.

108. "A Digest of What Dr. King's Demanding," *Chicago Defender*, July 11, 1966, 1.

109. Quoted in Satter, *Family Properties*, 191.

110. "Daley Calls Parley of Clergy on Slums," *Chicago Tribune*, March 15, 1966, 1.

111. Metropolitan Housing and Planning Council, Policy Statement of the Metropolitan Housing and Planning Council concerning Open Occupancy, second draft, March 17, 1964, MPC Records, box 5, folder 37.

112. "Daley, King, Aides Meet on Rights," *Chicago Tribune*, July 12, 1966, 1.

113. "Daley, King, Aides Meet on Rights." See also "Mayor, Dr. King Fail to Agree," *Chicago Sun-Times*, July 12, 1966, 1.

114. "Daley, King, Aides Meet on Rights"; "Mayor, Dr. King Fail to Agree."

115. Cohen and Taylor, *American Pharaoh*, 392–96.

116. Cohen and Taylor, *American Pharaoh*, 395–96.

117. Cohen and Taylor, *American Pharaoh*, 396.

118. Cohen and Taylor, *American Pharaoh*, 397–99. Cohen and Taylor argue persuasively that King himself favored participation in the summit because he was losing faith in the Chicago campaign. Anxious by this time to claim "any kind of victory, even a negotiated one," King believed that the summit represented an opportunity for closure of some kind. Younger, "more militant" movement leaders wanted to continue the marches into white neighborhoods, arguing that direct negotiation with Daley would be unproductive.

119. Cohen and Taylor, *American Pharaoh*, 402–7. Note that by this time the Chicago Freedom Movement was directly targeting aspects of the city's existing programs to end slums—in particular the location of public housing units and the rehousing of persons displaced by urban renewal projects—that affected the ability of these programs to perform as intended.

120. Agreement of the Subcommittee to the Conference on Fair Housing

Convened by the Chicago Conference on Religion and Race, August 26, 1966, accessed June 2, 2017, cfm10.middlebury.edu/node/18.

121. "Keane Statement on Housing Irks King," *Chicago Tribune*, November 27, 1966, D33.

122. "Keane Statement on Housing Irks King."

123. Biles, *Fate of Cities*, 177–79.

124. Quoted in Cohen and Taylor, *American Pharaoh*, 525.

Chapter Seven

1. "Power Elite Drafts City Master Plan," *Chicago Tribune*, May 21, 1973, 1.

2. Quoted in Brian Berry, Irving Cutler, Edwin Draine, Y. Kiang, Thomas Tocalis, and Pierre de Vise, *Chicago: Transformation of an Urban System* (Cambridge, MA: Ballinger, 1976), 75.

3. "Power Elite Drafts City Master Plan."

4. Stone, *Regime Politics*.

5. See, for example, Stone and Sanders, eds., *Politics of Urban Development*; Ferman, *Challenging the Growth Machine*; Squires, ed., *Unequal Partnerships*; Stephen L. Elkin, *City and Regime in the American Republic* (Chicago: University of Chicago Press, 1987).

6. Salisbury, "Urban Politics."

7. "22 Year Plan: A New Face for Chicago," *Chicago Tribune*, August 23, 1958, 1; "Civic Leaders Hail Plan to Rebuild Loop," *Chicago Tribune*, August 24, 1958, 3; "City's $1.5-Billion Plan," *Chicago Sun-Times*, August 23, 1958, 1; "A New Master Plan: Heart of City to Be Remade, Revitalized," *Chicago Sun-Times*, August 22, 1958, 1.

8. See Banfield, *Political Influence*, 155. According to Banfield, "Holman Pettibone and the Central Area Committee denied that they had a part in preparing the Plan."

9. "Group Pushes Building Boom in Loop Area," *Chicago Tribune*, December 26, 1961, 13.

10. CCAC, minutes of the meeting of the Executive Committee, October 2, 1957, CCAC Papers, box 8.

11. CCAC, minutes of the meeting of the Executive Committee, December 19, 1957, CCAC Papers, box 8.

12. Hughston McBain to CCAC Board of Directors, February 18, 1959, CCAC Papers, box 8.

13. CCAC, minutes of the meeting of the Board of Directors, September 16, 1959, CCAC Papers, box 8.

14. CCAC, minutes of the meeting of the Board of Directors, September 16, 1959.

15. CCAC, minutes of the meeting of the Board of Directors, September 16, 1959.

16. Joint Action Committee of Civic Organizations, Chronology of Events, undated, MPC Records, box 521, folder 4391.

17. CCAC, minutes of the meeting of the Executive Committee, April 16, 1956, CCAC Papers, box 8.

18. George Rosen, *Decision-Making Chicago-Style: The Genesis of a University of Illinois Campus* (Urbana: University of Illinois Press, 1980), 34.

19. Rosen, *Decision-Making Chicago-Style*, 48–49.

20. Quoted in Heywood T. Sanders, *Convention Center Follies: Politics, Power, and Public Investment in American Cities* (Philadelphia: University of Pennsylvania Press, 2014), 246.

21. Rosen, *Decision-Making Chicago-Style*, 49–53.

22. Joint Action Committee of Civic Organizations, Chronology of Events.

23. Rosen, *Decision-Making Chicago-Style*, 65.

24. Rosen, *Decision-Making Chicago-Style*, 69.

25. Joint Action Committee of Civic Organizations, Chronology of Events.

26. Rosen, *Decision-Making Chicago-Style*, 66. Certain West Garfield Park residents were supportive of the university's proposed location in Garfield Park, partly because they thought it might help stabilize racial boundaries between their community and the increasingly black East Garfield Park neighborhood. See Seligman, *Block by Block*, chap. 4.

27. Randall H. Cooper, "A Report on Chicago Central Area Committee Activities in 1960," January 18, 1961, CCAC Papers, box 8.

28. The protests over the site selected for the University of Illinois campus were especially troublesome for Daley because the protesters were mostly working-class Italian American women—key members of Daley's electoral coalition. The demonstrators led marches on city hall and held sit-ins at Daley's office, drawing wide media attention. The conflict was said to have made Daley more cautious in taking on projects that had the potential to generate major protests. See Hunt and DeVries, *Planning Chicago*, 38; Cohen and Taylor, *American Pharaoh*, 224–33; and Rosen, *Decision-Making Chicago-Style*, 114–21.

29. MHPC, minutes of the meeting of the Executive Committee, June 16, 1961, MPC Records, box 19, folder 155.

30. Harold A. Moore, statement to the Board of Directors, Chicago Central Area Committee, January 18, 1961, CCAC Papers, box 8.

31. CCAC, minutes of the meeting of the Board of Directors, September 18, 1963, CCAC Papers, box 8.

32. CCAC, minutes of the meeting of the Board of Directors, December 19, 1962, CCAC Papers, box 8. The proposed project consisted of the area "bounded by Jackson Boulevard on the north, 25th Street on the south, the Dan Ryan Expressway on the west, and the lake on the east." Joining Aschman at the board

meeting were James Downs from the Real Estate Research Corporation and William E. Hartman from Skidmore, Owings & Merrill.

33. CCAC, minutes of the meeting of the Board of Directors, June 19, 1963, CCAC Papers, box 8.

34. CCAC, minutes of the meeting of the Board of Directors, December 19, 1962, CCAC Papers, box 8.

35. CCAC, minutes of the meeting of the Board of Directors, March 20, 1963, and June 19, 1963, CCAC Papers, box 8.

36. CCAC, minutes of the meeting of the Board of Directors, November 20, 1963, and December 18, 1963, CCAC Papers, box 8.

37. CCAC, minutes of the meeting of the Board of Directors, May 20, 1964, CCAC Papers, box 8.

38. CCAC, minutes of the meeting of the Board of Directors, June 16, 1965, CCAC Papers, box 8.

39. CCAC, Summary of 1965 Activities, December 10, 1965, CCAC Papers, box 8.

40. CCAC, Summary of 1965 Activities, December 10, 1965.

41. CCAC, 1967 Program, undated, CCAC Papers, box 8.

42. Banfield, *Political Influence*, chap. 5; Sanders, *Convention Center Follies*, chap. 6.

43. Hunt and DeVries, *Planning Chicago*, 41–42.

44. CCAC, minutes of the meeting of the Board of Directors, November 20, 1963.

45. CCAC, minutes of the meeting of the Board of Directors, August 20, 1964, CCAC Papers, box 8.

46. CCAC, "Restatement of Planning Principles," August 1964, CCAC Papers, box 8.

47. CCAC, minutes of the meeting of the Board of Directors, August 20, 1964, and December 10, 1965, CCAC Papers, box 8.

48. CCAC, minutes of the meeting of the Board of Directors, June 16, 1965, and December 10, 1965.

49. CCAC, Memorandum of Joint Meeting of the Board of Directors and Contributor Members, May 16, 1968, CCAC Papers, box 8.

50. CCAC, minutes of the meeting of the Board of Directors, December 19, 1968, CCAC Papers, box 8.

51. CCAC, minutes of the meeting of the Board of Directors, January 30, 1969, CCAC Papers, box 8.

52. Quoted in Greer, "The Politics of Decline and Growth," 136.

53. "Power Elite Drafts City Master Plan."

54. Quoted in Greer, "Politics of Decline and Growth," 140.

55. Greer, "Politics of Decline and Growth," 136–37.

56. Berry et al., *Chicago*, 77.

57. CCAC, "Review of Status Report and Summary, Central Communities Study," July 1970, CCAC Papers, box 8.

58. James Downs to CCAC Board of Directors, January 6, 1971, CCAC Papers, box 8.

59. CCAC, minutes of the meeting of the Board of Directors, April 12, 1971, CCAC Papers, box 8.

60. CCAC, minutes of the meeting of the Board of Directors, June 14, 1971, CCAC Papers, box 8.

61. CCAC, minutes of the meeting of the Board of Directors, June 14, 1971.

62. CCAC, minutes of the meeting of the Board of Directors, September 13, 1971, CCAC Papers, box 8.

63. CCAC, "Proposal for Financing a Central Communities Plan for the City of Chicago," August 8, 1972, CCAC Papers, box 8.

64. Corporate members of the planning review committee were A. Robert Abboud, First National Bank of Chicago; Willard J. Ball, Peoples Gas; Edward F. Bell, Illinois Bell; John Eilering, Commonwealth Edison; John H. Perkins, Continental Bank; Warren G. Skoning, Sears Roebuck and Company; W. E. McGinnity, Standard Oil; and Al Svoboda, Chicago Dock and Canal Trust.

65. CCAC, "Proposal for Financing a Central Communities Plan," 5.

66. CCAC, "Proposal for Financing a Central Communities Plan," 5.

67. CCAC, "Proposal for Financing a Central Communities Plan," 5–6.

68. Lois Wille, *At Home in the Loop: How Clout and Community Built Chicago's Dearborn Park* (Carbondale: Southern Illinois University Press, 1997), 12–18.

69. Wille, *At Home in the Loop*, 15–18.

70. Chicago Central Area Committee, *Chicago 21: A Plan for the Central Area Communities* (Chicago, 1973), 20.

71. Rosen, *Decision-Making Chicago-Style*, 128.

72. Cornelius kept a detailed log of telephone calls, meetings, and other communications with COCAC during the spring and summer of 1974. The description of events in this section is based in part on Cornelius's log.

73. Members of COCAC to Ayers, March 11, 1974, CCAC Papers, box 17.

74. COCAC press release, March 28, 1974; Cornelius log of communications with COCAC, March 18–28, 1974, CCAC Papers, box 17.

75. Cornelius log, March 29–April 4, CCAC Papers, box 17.

76. Cornelius log, April 8; COCAC, "Statement of Demands," April 8, 1974, both in CCAC Papers, box 17.

77. CCAC, minutes of the meeting of the Planning Review Committee and the Coalition of Central Area Communities, April 18, 1974, CCAC Papers, box 17.

78. Cornelius log, April 24, 1974, CCAC Papers, box 17.

79. CCAC, "Chicago Central Area Committee Policy regarding Chicago 21 Proposals and Community Participation," May 14, 1974, CCAC Papers, box 17.

80. For a detailed report on both meetings see Jack Cornelius to Thomas Ayers, May 24, 1974, and June 7, 1974, both in CCAC Papers, box 17.

81. Harold Jensen to Willie Baker, July 18, 1974, CCAC Papers, box 17.

82. Jack Cornelius to Thomas Ayers, June 7, 1974, CCAC Papers, box 17.

83. Jack Cornelius to Lewis Hill, April 23, 1974, CCAC Papers, box 17.

84. Hill sent one representative from the Department of Development and Planning to observe each of COCAC's public meetings on the Chicago 21 plan. However, these individuals did not participate in the meetings.

85. Wille, *At Home in the Loop*, 57.

86. Cornelius log, June 4–6, 1974, CCAC Papers, box 17.

87. CCAC, minutes of the joint meeting of the Board of Directors and the Chicago Central Area Research and Study Committee, June 10, 1974, CCAC Papers, box 17.

88. Charles Willson to Harold Jensen and Jack Cornelius, June 7, 1974, CCAC Papers, box 17.

89. Cornelius log, June 4, 1974, and June 24, 1974, CCAC Papers, box 17.

90. Cornelius log, June 11–21, 1974, CCAC Papers, box 17.

91. Cornelius log, July 9, 1974, CCAC Papers, box 17.

92. "Near West Side Group Boos Chicago 21 Plan," *Northwest Herald*, July 24, 1974, 1.

93. "Near West Side Group Boos Chicago 21 Plan."

94. Jack Cornelius to Thomas Ayers, July 17, 1974, CCAC Papers, box 17.

95. Harold Jensen to Thomas Ayers, June 27, 1974, CCAC Papers, box 17.

96. "Planning Unit Introduces Neighborhood 'Miniplans,'" *New York Times*, June 26, 1974, 1.

97. CCAC, minutes of the joint meeting of the Board of Directors and the Chicago Central Area Research and Study Committee, August 12, 1974, CCAC Papers, box 17.

98. "Pilsen Signs First Neighborhood Planning Pact," *Chicago Central Area Committee News*, June 1975, 1.

99. "Meadows Cuts Area Population in Half," *Chicago Defender*, November 13, 1962, 1.

100. "Leaders of Chicago Plan for Greater Central Area," *Chicago Tribune*, September 8, 1957, 5.

Chapter Eight

1. "Bridgeport Bomb: Daleys House Hunting," *Chicago Tribune*, April 1, 1993, D1.

2. "Bridgeport Bomb: Daleys House Hunting."

3. Philip M. Klutznik, "Can We Solve Chicago's Housing Problems?" May 21,

1968, Kramer Papers, box 4, folder 2. On the discourse of urban decline more generally during this period, see Robert A. Beauregard, *Voices of Decline: The Postwar Fate of U.S. Cities* (Oxford: Blackwell, 1993). As Beauregard demonstrates, following the racial disturbances of the 1960s the issue of race increasingly dominated representations of the urban crisis.

4. Hirsch, *Making the Second Ghetto*, 29–33; Seligman, *Block by Block*, chap. 6.

5. Some might argue that the development of Central Station was not gentrification because it did not cause the displacement of residents. However, the concept of gentrification has evolved over time, with some arguing that gentrification is simply "the transformation of neighborhoods from low value to high value" regardless of whether displacement occurs. See Alan Ehrenhalt, "What Exactly, Is Gentrification," *Governing*, February 2015. I use this more expansive definition of gentrification.

6. Wille, *At Home in the Loop*, 14. Wille's book offers an exceptionally thorough, if somewhat uncritical, treatment of the development of Dearborn Park. Many of the sources she used for the book are contained in the Ferdinand Kramer Papers collection at the University of Chicago Special Collections Research Center. I draw extensively on those sources—and to a lesser extent Wille's book—in my own discussion of Dearborn Park.

7. Donald Graham to Thomas Ayers et al., January 20, 1972, Kramer Papers, box 17, folder 9. See also Wille, *At Home in the Loop*, chaps. 1–2.

8. Philip Klutznick to file, December 1, 1971, Kramer Papers, box 17, folder 9.

9. Wille, *At Home in the Loop*, 26–29.

10. Wille, *At Home in the Loop*, 4.

11. Ayers, Thomas (1995, November 10), interview by L. Wille [tape recording], in *At Home in the Loop* book project, Kramer Papers, box 29, folder 1.

12. Elkin, Norman (1995, January 18), interview by L. Wille [tape recording], *At Home in the Loop* book project, Kramer Papers, box 29, folder 2.

13. Greer, "Politics of Decline and Growth," 105.

14. Squires et al., *Chicago*, 34–35.

15. Rast, *Remaking Chicago*, 88. As I argue in *Remaking Chicago*, the loss of manufacturing jobs cannot be explained through global market pressures alone. Public policy decisions including planning and zoning contributed to the loss of manufacturing establishments in certain parts of the city—especially where land-use conflicts arose between manufacturers and developers of new housing and retail space. However, the bulk of the manufacturing jobs lost during this period can be attributed to structural economic change.

16. William Julius Wilson, *The Truly Disadvantaged: The Inner City, the Underclass, and Public Policy* (Chicago: University of Chicago Press, 1987), 49–55.

17. Thomas Ayers, speech to Bright New City, April 15, 1974, Kramer Papers, box 22, folder 4.

18. Philip Klutznick, "A South Loop Scenario," September 6, 1972, Kramer Papers, box 22, folder 4.

19. Donald Graham to Richard J. Daley, February 17, 1972, Kramer Papers, box 17, folder 9; meeting minutes of South Loop Group, October 9, 1972, Kramer Papers, box 17, folder 9; Philip Klutznick to Thomas Ayers et al., October 27, 1972, Kramer Papers, box 22, folder 4.

20. Perry R. Duis and Glen E. Holt, "The South Loop Legacy," *Chicago Magazine*, September 1978, 238–40; Department of Development and Planning, "South Loop New Town: Guidelines for Development" (City of Chicago, 1975), 7–8; William Hartmann to Ferd Kramer, September 12, 1973, Kramer Papers, box 17, folder 7.

21. "Rail Owners Receptive to 'New Town' Plan," *Chicago Tribune*, January 14, 1973, 1.

22. John Perkins to Thomas Ayers et al., July 18, 1972, Kramer Papers, box 17, folder 7.

23. Thomas Ayers to James Downs et al., September 11, 1972, Kramer Papers, box 17, folder 7.

24. Ayers, interview by Wille.

25. Harder, Dennis (1995, January 24), interview by L. Wille [tape recording], *At Home in the Loop* book project, Kramer Papers, box 29, folder 2.

26. John Perkins to Charles Willson, April 17, 1973, Kramer Papers, box 22, folder 4. Daley's concerns about city ownership of the land were twofold. First, as landowner the city would have to acknowledge a significant role in subsidizing the project, exposing Daley to criticism by neighborhood groups. Second, if the project failed, the city would have no revenue stream with which to repay the bonds used to finance the land purchase. See John Perkins to Thomas Ayers et al., November 21, 1974, Kramer Papers, box 23, folder 1.

27. John Perkins to D. Graham et al., January 23, 1973, Kramer Papers, box 17, folder 4.

28. Wille, *At Home in the Loop*, 27–28.

29. Wille, *At Home in the Loop*, 58; Chicago 21 Corporation, meeting of the Board of Directors, March 25, 1975, Kramer Papers, box 17, folder 3.

30. Chicago 21 Corporation, minutes of the meeting of the Board of Directors, January 17, 1974, Kramer Papers, box 17, folder 4.

31. Commitments to Subscribe to Chicago 21 Corporation Stock, May 3, 1974, Kramer Papers, box 22, folder 4.

32. Chicago 21 Corporation, Private Offering of Securities, February 18, 1974, Kramer Papers, box 17, folder 4.

33. Quoted in Wille, *At Home in the Loop*, 40.

34. Chicago 21 Corporation, meeting of the Board of Directors, December 16, 1974, Kramer Papers, box 17, folder 3.

35. Robert Merriam to Thomas Ayers et al., June 2, 1976, Kramer Papers, box 23, folder 2.

36. David Emmons, *Dearborn Park / South Loop New Town: A Project in the Chicago 21 Plan* (Chicago: Citizens Information Service of Illinois, 1977), 16.

37. Perkins, John (1994, November 4), interview by L. Wille [tape recording], *At Home in the Loop* book project, Kramer Papers, box 29, folder 1.

38. Donald Graham to Richard J. Daley, February 17, 1972, Kramer Papers, box 17, folder 9.

39. Nory Miller, "South Loop New Town: Can It Make It?" *Inland Architect*, October 1974, 8.

40. Daniel J. Edelman, "Questions and Answers about the South Loop New Town" (Chicago, 1974), 3, Kramer Papers, box 28, folder 1; Philip Klutznick to Thomas Ayers et al., September 19, 1973, Kramer Papers, box 17, folder 7.

41. Ayers, interview by Wille.

42. Ferd Kramer, speech at Greater Pittsburgh Conference on Equal Opportunity in Housing, Pittsburgh, PA, November 30, 1965, Kramer Papers, box 5, folder 1.

43. Ferd Kramer, speech to Know Your Chicago, November 6, 1968, Kramer Papers, box 4, folder 7.

44. Ferd Kramer, speech to Urban Renewal Seminar, Mortgage Bankers Association of America and ACTION, St. Louis, MO, February 21, 1962, Kramer Papers, box 4, folder 6.

45. Leon D. Finney Jr., statement to the Chicago Plan Commission, June 23, 1977, Kramer Papers, box 20, folder 4.

46. Chicago Economic Development Corporation, *Dearborn Park Residential Market Study* (Chicago, 1976), 18–19, Kramer Papers, box 20, folder 3.

47. Kramer, speech to Know Your Chicago.

48. Ferd Kramer, testimony before the Housing and Urban Affairs Subcommittee of the Senate Banking and Currency Committee on Senate Bill 1358, August 23, 1967, Kramer Papers, box 4, folder 7.

49. Chicago 21 Corporation, Consumer Survey, October 1974, Kramer Papers, box 23, folder 1; Norman Elkin to Philip Klutznick, November 11, 1974, Kramer Papers, box 23, folder 1; Dearborn Park Corporation, press release, May 2, 1977, Kramer Papers, box 19, folder 12.

50. Chicago Economic Development Corporation, *Dearborn Park Residential Market Study*, 18.

51. Chicago Economic Development Corporation, *Dearborn Park Residential Market Study*, 49.

52. Bufalini, Carl (1995, May 8), interview by L. Wille [tape recording], *At Home in the Loop* book project, Kramer Papers, box 29, folder 2. As Bufalini recalled, "A major contribution that Ferd made was on the issue of racial balance. Nobody wanted to touch it, but Ferd, bless his heart, ran right into it and

said, 'Look, folks, let's be realistic . . . If you want to keep a balanced community you've got to set quotas.'"

53. Robert E. Merriam to Philip Klutznick and Thomas Klutznick, January 30, 1976, Kramer Papers, box 23, folder 2.

54. Dearborn Park Corporation, ninutes of the Executive Committee, June 1, 1977, Kramer Papers, box 18, folder 2.

55. Frank H. Livingston to Chicago 21 file, November 28, 1977, Kramer Papers, box 28, folder 3.

56. Livingston to Chicago 21 file, November 28, 1977.

57. Dearborn Park Corporation, minutes of the Executive Committee, June 13, 1980, Kramer Papers, box 18, folder 2.

58. Wille, *At Home in the Loop*, 173.

59. Edelman, "Questions and Answers about the South Loop New Town," 3; Robert Cassidy, "The Dearborn Park Railroad Job," *Chicago Reader*, December 16, 1977, 32; "Dearborn Park: Satisfaction Blossoms behind Grim Façade," *Crain's Chicago Business*, May 11, 1981, 25.

60. Kantoff, Sheldon (1995, April 27), interview by L. Wille [tape recording], *At Home in the Loop* book project, Kramer Papers, box 29, folder 2.

61. Wille, *At Home in the Loop*, 92.

62. Wille, *At Home in the Loop,*, 170.

63. Wille, *At Home in the Loop,*, 104–5.

64. Wille, *At Home in the Loop,*, 92.

65. Wille, *At Home in the Loop,*, 128.

66. Chicago 21 Corporation, meeting of the Board of Directors, December 16, 1974, Kramer Papers, box 17, folder 3; Chicago 21 Corporation, Shareholders meeting, December 16, 1976, Kramer Papers, box 17, folder 3; Wille, *At Home in the Loop*, 136–37.

67. Wille, *At Home in the Loop*, 88.

68. Wille, *At Home in the Loop,*, 63.

69. Suttles, *Man-Made City*, 166.

70. Thomas G. Ayers et al. to Stanton Cook, February 14, 1984, Kramer Papers, box 28, folder 5.

71. Compton, James (1995, January 20), interview by L. Wille [tape recording], *At Home in the Loop* book project, Kramer Papers, box 28, folder 9.

72. Hunt, *Blueprint for Disaster*, 2.

73. Chicago 21 Corporation, Consumer Survey.

74. Metropolitan Housing and Planning Council, Position Paper on Chicago 21 Plan, 1974, 4, Kramer Papers, box 23, folder 1.

75. A. L. Alcorn to file, August 22, 1972, Kramer Papers, box 17, folder 4.

76. Kramer, speech at Greater Pittsburgh Conference on Equal Opportunity in Housing.

77. Chicago 21 Corporation, minutes of the Executive Committee, March 1,

1976, Kramer Papers, box 17, folder 3; Chicago 21 Corporation, shareholders meeting, March 31, 1976, Kramer Papers, box 28, folder 2.

78. Chicago 21 Corporation, Developer Response to Environmental Security Report for South Loop New Town, 1977, 3, Kramer Papers, box 19, folder 3.

79. Dearborn Park Corporation, Application for a Planned Unit Development, June 23, 1977, 7, Kramer Papers, box 20, folder 4.

80. In phase 2 of Dearborn Park, a row of single-family homes on State Street south of Roosevelt Road faced outward toward the street. According to Wille, "The security of Dearborn Park was now so well established that a developer felt confident enough to turn the houses outward rather than inward." Wille, *At Home in the Loop*, 168.

81. Chicago 21 Corporation, Developer Response to Environmental Security Report, 49.

82. Chicago 21 Corporation, Developer Response to Environmental Security Report, 10.

83. Emmons, *Dearborn Park / South Loop New Town*, 3–4.

84. Chicago 21 Corporation, Developer Response to Environmental Security Report, 49.

85. Anthony Kramer to Ferd Kramer, August 15, 1972, Kramer Papers, box 17, folder 4.

86. Chicago 21 Corporation, Developer Response to Environmental Security Report, 25.

87. Barbara Lynne (1994, November 7), interview by L. Wille [tape recording], *At Home in the Loop* book project, Kramer Papers, box 28, folder 9.

88. Cassidy, "Dearborn Park Railroad Job," 33.

89. Nory Miller, "Dearborn Park: What's in a Name—and What Isn't," *Inland Architect*, June 1977, 15–16.

90. Quoted in Wille, *At Home in the Loop*, 176.

91. Chicago 21 Corporation, Consumer Survey.

92. Cassidy, "Dearborn Park Railroad Job," 33.

93. Dearborn Park Corporation, minutes of the shareholders meeting, March 28, 1977, Kramer Papers, box 18, folder 4; Donald Erickson to shareholders, Chicago 21 Corporation, October 1, 1976, Kramer Papers, box 23, folder 2; Emmons, *Dearborn Park / South Loop New Town*, 4.

94. Wille, *At Home in the Loop*, 97.

95. Dearborn Park Corporation, minutes of the Executive Committee, April 19, 1979, Kramer Papers, box 18, folder 2.

96. Wille, *At Home in the Loop*, 105.

97. Dearborn Park Corporation, minutes of the Executive Committee, December 8, 1981, Kramer Papers, box 18, folder 3.

98. Ruth Love to Ferd Kramer, May 18, 1984, Kramer Papers, box 20,

folder 10; Judith Hoch to *Crain's Chicago Business*, June 20, 1984, Kramer Papers, box 20, folder 10.

99. Wille, *At Home in the Loop*, 144.

100. Maya Dukmasova, "The Goldberg Variation: High-Rise Public Housing That Works," *Chicago Reader*, October 5, 2016.

101. "Enrollment Dilemma for Loop School," *Chicago Tribune*, December 4, 1987, A1.

102. "Anger Greets South Loop School Plan," *Chicago Tribune*, February 19, 1987, A1; "2 Schools Find 12 Blocks Make a Difference," *Chicago Tribune*, June 21, 1984, B1. The mobile classrooms were examples of Chicago's infamous "Willis Wagons," trailers placed in poor black neighborhoods during the 1960s by then school superintendent Benjamin Willis to avoid busing children from overcrowded inner-city schools to less crowded schools in white neighborhoods. See John Hall Fish, *Black Power / White Control: The Struggle of the Woodlawn Organization in Chicago* (Princeton, NJ: Princeton University Press, 1973), 55–56.

103. "Conflicts Remain in South Loop School Deal," *Chicago Tribune*, May 29, 1987, A4; "Urban Class Problem Stirs Chicago Debate," *New York Times*, March 25, 1987; "2 Schools Find 12 Blocks Make a Difference."

104. Harry Strasburg to Dearborn Park Corporation, March 27, 1986, Kramer Papers, box 21, folder 1.

105. "Work Starts on S. Loop School; Upscale Tilt Hit," *Chicago Sun-Times*, July 31, 1986.

106. Judith Hoch to Dearborn Park residents and stakeholders, August 1986, Kramer Papers, box 21, folder 1.

107. Ferd Kramer to George Munoz, September 8, 1986, Kramer Papers, box 20, folder 10.

108. Ferd Kramer, speech to ACTION, San Francisco, CA, April 6, 1964, Kramer Papers, box 5, folder 1.

109. Kramer, speech at Greater Pittsburgh Conference on Equal Opportunity in Housing.

110. "Anger Greets South Loop School Plan." Byrd's decision had to take into account the 1980 settlement of a US Department of Justice suit against the Chicago Board of Education, which mandated that the student body of any new school had to be at least 30 percent white and 30 percent minority within three years of opening. See Judy Hoch et al. to James Compton et al., August 1990, Kramer Papers, box 21, folder 1.

111. Ferd Kramer to James Brice, May 4, 1987, Kramer Papers, box 21, folder 1; Wille, *At Home in the Loop*, 149.

112. On Harold Washington's political base and the connection of the Washington administration to the city's neighborhood movement, see Pierre Clavel

and Wim Wiewel, eds., *Harold Washington and the Neighborhoods* (New Brunswick, NJ: Rutgers University Press, 1991); Gary Rivlin, *Fire on the Prairie: Chicago's Harold Washington and the Politics of Race* (New York: Henry Holt, 1992); and Ferman, *Challenging the Growth Machine*.

113. "Urban Class Problem Stirs Chicago Debate"; "War between the Classes," *Newsweek*, May 1, 1989, 64; "A City's Unwelcome Lesson about Schools and Class," *New York Times*, April 2, 1989.

114. "At Last, School's In for S. Loop Pupils, Parents," *Chicago Sun-Times*, February 16, 1988; "School's In for New South Loop," *Chicago Tribune*, February 16, 1988, B5.

115. Wille, *At Home in the Loop*, 146.

116. Lynne, interview by Wille.

117. "South Loop School Agreement Reached," *Chicago Tribune*, May 28, 1987, A1.

118. Wille, *At Home in the Loop*, 152.

119. Wille, *At Home in the Loop*, 147.

120. Wille, *At Home in the Loop*, 152–53.

121. R. Bruce Dold, "Shutdown and the Neighborhood School," *Notre Dame Magazine*, Spring 1991, 25.

122. "There Are No Small Plans in South Loop," *Chicago Tribune*, February 26, 1990, C1.

123. "South Loop on the Rise: Proposed Residential Towers Would Reshape City's Skyline," *Chicago Tribune*, October 4, 2015, 1; "Looking South; Construction in the South Loop (s Booming, but Buyers Are Taking their Time," *Chicago Tribune*, July 9, 2006, 16.1.

124. "How Far Can the Near South Go? Area Looks Golden—If the Market Cooperates," *Chicago Tribune*, October 20, 2002, 16.1.

125. Voorhees Center for Neighborhood and Community Improvement, *The Socioeconomic Change of Chicago's Community Areas*; Betancur and Smith, *Claiming Neighborhood*, 39–43. See also Mary Patillo, *Black on the Block: The Politics of Race and Class in the City* (Chicago: University of Chicago Press, 2007), for discussion of "black gentrification" in the North Kenwood–Oakland neighborhood on the Near South Side.

126. Carolina Sternberg and Matthew Anderson, "Contestation and the Local Trajectories of Neoliberal Urban Governance in Chicago's Bronzeville and Pilsen," *Urban Studies* 51 (2014): 3198–3214; John J. Betancur, "The Politics of Gentrification: The Case of West Town in Chicago," *Urban Affairs Review* 37 (2002): 780–814.

127. Voorhees Center for Neighborhood and Community Improvement, *Socioeconomic Change of Chicago's Community Areas*, 9–10.

128. Betancur and Smith, *Claiming Neighborhood*, 43.

129. "Mayor's Affordable-Housing Plan Passes; Critics Say Measure is Still a Good Start," *Chicago Tribune*, May 15, 2007, 2C1.

130. "Tougher Housing Rules Get Panel OK: Chicago's Revised Affordable-Units Ordinance Would Hike Opt-Out Fees," *Chicago Tribune*, January 15, 2015, 1.

131. "Affordable Housing Allies Say Proposal Falls Short," *Chicago Tribune*, December 11, 2014, 2.3. In March 2015 the city council approved an amendment to the ordinance that places restrictions on the ability of developers to pay fees in lieu of providing affordable housing units. Under the revised ordinance, developers must create at least 25 percent of the required affordable units, either within the building itself or at another location no more than two miles away. See "Aldermen Pass Stricter Housing Law: Developers Catch Break with Later Phase-In of Rules," *Chicago Tribune*, March 19, 2015, 3.

132. Euan Hague, Michael J. Lorr, and Carolina Sternberg, "Chicago: Neoliberal City," in Larry Bennett, Roberta Garner, and Euan Hague, eds., *Neoliberal Chicago* (Champaign: University of Illinois Press, 2016), 5; Larry Bennett, "Contemporary Chicago Politics: Myth, Reality, and Neoliberalism," in Bennett, Garner, and Hague, eds., *Neoliberal Chicago*, 82.

133. For a more sympathetic view of neoliberal policies under Mayor Richard M. Daley, see Costas Spirou and Dennis R. Judd, *Building the City of Spectacle: Mayor Richard M. Daley and the Remaking of Chicago* (Ithaca, NY: Cornell University Press, 2016). For more critical perspectives see Bennett, Garner, and Hague, *Neoliberal Chicago*; David Wilson and Carolina Sternberg, "Changing Realities: The New Racialized Redevelopment Rhetoric in Chicago," *Urban Geography* 33 (2012): 979–99; and Sternberg and Anderson, "Contestation and the Local Trajectories of Neoliberal Urban Governance in Chicago's Bronzeville and Pilsen."

134. Alan Berube, "All Cities Are Not Created Unequal," February 20, 2014, www.brookings.edu/research/all-cities-are-not-created-unequal/.

135. Clavel and Wiewel, *Harold Washington and the Neighborhoods*; Rast, *Remaking Chicago*; Ferman, *Challenging the Growth Machine*.

Conclusion

1. On "unsettled times" see Ann Swidler, "Culture in Action: Symbols and Strategies," *American Sociological Review* 51 (1986): 273–86; and William Sewell Jr., "A Theory of Structure: Duality, Agency, and Transformation," *American Journal of Sociology* 98 (1992): 1–29.

2. John H. Mollenkopf, *The Contested City* (Princeton, NJ: Princeton University Press, 1983); Christopher Klemek, *The Transatlantic Collapse of Urban*

Renewal: Postwar Urbanism from New York to Berlin (Chicago: University of Chicago Press, 2011); Teaford, *Rough Road to Renaissance*; Samuel Zipp, *Manhattan Projects: The Rise and Fall of Urban Renewal in Cold War New York* (Oxford: Oxford University Press, 2010); Hartman, *Yerba Buena*; Lubove, *Twentieth-Century Pittsburgh*.

3. John P. Koval, "An Overview and Point of View," in John P. Koval, Larry Bennett, Michael I. J. Bennett, Fassil Demissie, Roberta Garner, and Kiljoong Kim, eds., *The New Chicago: A Social and Cultural Analysis* (Philadelphia: Temple University Press, 2006), 9. See also Hague, Lorr, and Sternberg, "Chicago: Neoliberal City," 9.

4. William H. Frey, "Census Shows Modest Declines in Black-White Segregation," December 8, 2015, www.brookings.edu/blog/the-avenue/2015/12/08/census-shows-modest-declines-in-black-white-segregation/.

5. Douglas S. Massey and Nancy A. Denton, *American Apartheid: Segregation and the Making of the Underclass* (Cambridge, MA: Harvard University Press, 1993), 2.

6. On policing and mass incarceration, see Michelle Alexander, *The New Jim Crow: Mass Incarceration in the Age of Colorblindness* (New York: New Press, 2010).

7. Bennett, Garner, and Hague, *Neoliberal Chicago*.

8. Hackworth, *Neoliberal City*; Neil Brenner and Nik Theodore, "Cities and the Geographies of 'Actually Existing Neoliberalism,'" *Antipode* 34 (2002): 349–79; Weaver, *Blazing the Neoliberal Trail*.

9. "Chuy Garcia Goes on Attack, Says Rahm's Policies Fail Poor, Middle Class," *Chicago Sun-Times*, March 30, 2015.

10. Kari Lydersen, *Mayor 1%: Rahm Emanuel and the Rise of Chicago's 99%* (Chicago: Haymarket Books, 2013), 75–76.

11. Lydersen, *Mayor 1%*, 81.

12. "Emanuel Triumphs in Chicago Mayoral Race," *New York Times*, February 22, 2011; "Can Jesus Save Chicago?" *Economist*, March 26, 2015, www.economist.com/united-states/2015/03/26/can-jesus-save-chicago.

13. "Protests Fail to Deter Chicago from Shutting 49 Schools," *New York Times*, May 22, 2013.

14. "In a Soaring Homicide Rate, a Divide in Chicago," *New York Times*, January 2, 2013.

15. Mark Guarino, "In Chicago, Emanuel's Record Put to a Vote," *Al Jazeera English*, February 23, 2015, america.aljazeera.com/articles/2015/2/23/in-chicago-emanuels-record-put-to-a-vote.html.

16. "Re-election Bid Offers Test of Mayor's Appeal to 'Two Chicagos,'" *New York Times*, February 17, 2015.

17. "Mayoral Candidate Jesus 'Chuy' Garcia Takes 'Tale of Two Cities'

Message to Chicago in Race against Rahm Emanuel," *New York Daily News*, March 4, 2015.

18. Daniel Denvir, "What Rahm Emanuel's Win Means for the Left," April 8, 2015.,https://www.citylab.com/equity/2015/04/what-rahm-emanuels-win-means-for-the-left/389991/.

19. "Can Jesus Save Chicago?"

20. Illinois Campaign for Political Reform, "2015 Chicago Mayoral Runoff Election Analysis," April 15, 2015, www.ilcampaign.org/wp-content/uploads/2015/04/2015-Chicago-Mayoral-Runoff-Election-Analysis-ICPR_Kennedy.pdf.

21. Carol Felsenthal, "How Jesus 'Chuy' Garcia Lost the Election," *Chicago Magazine*, April 8, 2015, www.chicagomag.com/Chicago-Magazine/Felsenthal-Files/April-2015/Rahm-Garcia-Election/.

Epilogue

1. South Loop Montessori School, tuition and fees, accessed June 1, 2017, www.southloopmontessori.org/tuition-fees/.

2. Several weeks later I would cycle past this park once again, this time accompanied by DePaul University political scientist Larry Bennett. On a comfortably warm June morning, the park was considerably livelier and the patrons somewhat more diverse.

3. "The Near South a Revived Area Explodes with New Residential Development," *Chicago Tribune*, September 13, 1998, 1.

4. "Rehab in Store for CHA Landmark; $90 Million Project Planned for Hilliard Homes," *Chicago Tribune*, February 24, 2002, 16; "New Hilliard Homes Debut; $100 Million Rehab of Towers, Grounds 9 Years in the Making," *Chicago Tribune*, October 22, 2006, 4C; Maya Dukmasova, "The Goldberg Variation: High-Rise Public Housing That Works," *Chicago Reader*, October 5, 2016.

5. "$41 Million Rental Phase on Tap at Former Stateway Gardens," *Crain's Chicago Business*, May 16, 2012.

6. "Common Elements, Common Risks: Setting Up Lines of Defense Key to Condo Security," *Chicago Tribune*, May 29, 2011, 7.1.

7. Ferd Kramer, speech to conference of Baltimore business leaders, April 18, 1952, Kramer Papers, box 4, folder 4.

Index